THE

COOK BOOK

OF THE

UNITED STATES NAVY

NAVSANDA PUBLICATION NO. 7

1945 WORLD WAR II
CIVILIAN   REFERENCE   EDITION
UNABRIDGED CLASSIC WARTIME RECIPE MANUAL FOR LARGE-GROUP KITCHEN COOKERY,
SHIP GALLEYS, AND MESS HALL CAFETERIAS

U.S. DEPARTMENT OF THE NAVY

Doublebit Press

The

COOK BOOK

OF THE

United States Navy

BUREAU OF SUPPLIES AND ACCOUNTS

NAVSANDA PUBLICATION No. 7

[*REVISED 1945*]

UNITED STATES GOVERNMENT PRINTING OFFICE
WASHINGTON: 1945

TABLE OF CONTENTS

TABLE OF CONTENTS (Continued)

FOREWORD

Navy Department,
Bureau of Supplies and Accounts,
Washington, D. C., 1 July 1945.

The Cook Book of the United States Navy contains a summary of the principles of cookery, menu planning, and a comprehensive collection of recipes based on the newer knowledge of nutrition.

Many of the recipes were suggested and tested by commissary personnel of the Navy, and all the recipes have been developed and tested for practical use in the Navy.

Supplementary information which will be helpful to commissary personnel in preparing food of high standard is presented in tabular and other form.

In an attempt to assist with some of the feeding problems of the forces afloat and at advance bases, more recipes for dry provisions have been added in this edition.

W. J. CARTER,
Chief of the Bureau of Supplies and Accounts.

Food Preparation for the Mess

Food purchased by the Navy is high quality food. To maintain this high quality from the time it reaches the Navy stores until it is served to the mess, the food must have careful and intelligent handling in preparation and service.

Storage: Attention must be given to *proper storage* of the food when it is first received. The turnover of stored food should be carefully supervised so that the stores are moved in the same order as received. This has direct bearing on the condition of the food when issued for preparation.

Perishable foods should be put immediately under refrigeration and kept refrigerated until time for preparation.

Study the Menu and Recipes: The menu and recipes for the week should be carefully studied daily to determine the length of time necessary for preparation and cooking.

Preparation Period: The food should be prepared as near to the actual time for cooking as possible to prevent the loss of valuable vitamins and minerals.

The period of time elapsing between preparation and service to the mess should be as short as possible.

Have the Food Ready Just on Time: The actual cooking period should be completed just a few minutes prior to the serving period, making allowances for time necessary to carve meats or give the finishing touches to the cooked product.

Food that stands after cooking loses much of its fine flavor and nutritive value.

Standing at room temperature, several hours at a time, also exposes the food to spoilage bacteria. Therefore, it is important to serve cooked food hot and immediately after it has been cooked. Approximate cooking time is given in the recipes.

Overcooked Food Becomes Wasted Food: To retain full flavor, best texture, and highest nutritive value, food should never be overcooked. Cook it only to the proper degree of doneness.

Serve Hot Foods Hot and Cold Foods Cold: Hot foods allowed to cool and cold foods served warm are unappetizing and often become wasted food.

Watch Appearance and Consistency: Attention must be given to the appearance of the meal after it is prepared and to the manner of service of the food. This is especially helpful to morale. Make the food look attractive. Combine foods that are contrasting in texture and color. Avoid having foods all the same color and of similar texture in one meal.

Parsley for garnish, when available, or a dash of paprika for color, adds eye appeal and stimulates interest in the food.

Taste Each Dish Before Serving: Extra seasoning may be necessary before serving.

Place Food on Serving Tray Carefully: Food should be carefully portioned before service, then placed on the serving tray with care as the men pass by the service counter.

Keep Cooking Equipment Clean: It is important that cooking equipment be kept scrupulously clean. Be sure that thermostats and thermometers are carefully checked at periodic intervals.

Cook Vegetables in Small Quantities: To conserve the natural color, texture, flavor, and nutritive value of fresh vegetables, they must be cooked in relatively small quantities. As soon as they have cooked for the required length of time, they should be removed from the kettle and served immediately.

The cooking of vegetables should be a continuous process until everyone has been served.

Canned Vegetables: Since canned vegetables have been precooked they need only be heated to boiling temperature before serving. Excessive heating of canned foods at high temperatures will not only reduce the nutritive value but will also cause a decrease of palatability and appearance. It is preferable, therefore, to prepare the vegetables in small batches, rather than heat enough for the whole mess at one time and hold at a high temperature throughout the feeding period.

Prepare Just Enough Food to Be Consumed at Each Meal: The amount of food necessary for any given mess will vary in accordance with the care used in its preparation, the other foods on the menu, the likes and dislikes of the men to be fed, the care with which the food is served and the number of men present at each meal.

Absenteeism has a direct bearing on the amount of food necessary for the mess. Food should be prepared for the number of men who *will* be present at mess, not for the number assigned to the mess.

For these and other reasons, the amount of issue on a particular item may actually be less than the amount called for in the recipe.

Also, a large mess serving 1000 men will use less food than 10 messes each serving 100 men. To conserve food and avoid great amounts of leftovers, the following reductions are recommended:

For messes of 500 to 1000 men, reduce the amounts of ingredients in the recipe 5 per cent.

For messes of 1000 men or more, reduce the amounts of ingredients in the recipe 10 per cent.

The recipe for Knickerbocker Bean Soup, based on the requirements for 100 portions, is given as an example showing the quantities required for a mess of 1,000 men.

This calculation is made by multiplying each ingredient by 10 to obtain the amount required for 1000 portions on the 100 portion basis.

Since messes of 1000 or more men can effect savings of approximately 10 per cent, the quantity of ingredients required will be the amount calculated, less 10 per cent. For example, 7 pounds of beans, the quantity required in the Knickerbocker Bean Soup recipe for 100 portions, multiplied by 10 amounts to 70 pounds. This amount, 70 pounds, less 10 per cent, or 7 pounds of beans, is equal to 63 pounds, the quantity of beans required for a mess serving 1000 men.

Note how this recipe should appear when the amount of issue for 1000 men is inserted in the blank column reserved for this purpose.

KNICKERBOCKER BEAN SOUP

Yield: Approx. 6 gallons.

Portion: 1 cup (approx. 8 ounces).

INGREDIENTS	100 PORTIONS			1000 Portions
	WEIGHTS		AMOUNTS (approx.)	
	Pounds	Ounces		
Beans, white, dried	7	....	1 gallon	9 gallons
Water, cold	....	....	To cover	To cover
Water, boiling	....	....	4 gallons	36 gallons
Salt pork, cubed	....	12	1½ cups	3½ quarts
Carrots, chopped	....	4	¾ cup	6¾ cups
Onions, chopped	....	12	2½ cups	5½ quarts
Meat Stock (page 251).	....	....	2¾ gallons	24¼ gallons
Potatoes, diced	5	8	3½ quarts	8 gallons
Bacon fat or other fat.	....	4	½ cup	2¼ quarts
Tomatoes	6	6	1 No. 10 can (3¼ quarts).	9 No. 10 cans (7⅓ gallons)
Salt	....	2	¼ cup	2¼ cups
Pepper	....	¼	¾ tablespoon	6¾ tablespoons

Pick over, wash, and soak beans 2 to 3 hours. Do not drain.

Combine with boiling water, salt pork, carrots, and half the onions. Heat to boiling temperature. Cook about 3 hours or until beans are tender.

Add stock and potatoes. Cook about 30 minutes or until potatoes are tender.

Fry remaining onions in bacon fat about 3 minutes, or until lightly browned.

Add tomatoes, salt and pepper.

Combine all ingredients. Reheat.

3 ★

Sanitary Aspects of Food Preparation

The bacteria now recognized as being responsible, in most cases, for what is known as "Food Poisoning," are present even under sanitary conditions. They produce a poisonous substance (called toxin) in the food, which when eaten, causes serious illness.

These bacteria grow and multiply rapidly in warm temperatures, 65° F. to 115° F. during which time the toxin is produced. A growth period as short as 5 hours has been found long enough for the bacteria to produce sufficient toxin to cause illness. It is possible that under favorable conditions, enough toxin can be produced in even a shorter period of time to make the food dangerous. The interval between the preparation and serving of food should, therefore, be kept at a minimum.

Foods Most Susceptible

The foods which seem to be most susceptible to the development of bacterial food poisons are ham, chicken, turkey, chopped cooked meat and egg for sandwich fillings, cream fillings, custard filled puffs and eclairs, bread puddings, beef hash and tongue.

Dehydrated foods, during and following reconstitution, are also susceptible. Care should be taken not to allow the reconstituted products to remain at warm room temperatures more than 3 hours from the time water is added for reconstitution until time for serving them.

Quick-frozen foods which have been defrosted are highly perishable, and they should be used immediately after being defrosted.

Necessary Precautions

Cooked Ham and Other Meat: Cooked meats, when placed on a steam table, must be kept at a temperature of 130° F. or above.

Meat to be held after cooking should be placed in a refrigerator as soon as it is cool enough to handle. To insure that the meat is cooled rapidly, it should be placed in shallow pans and so arranged as to provide for adequate circulation of the cool air.

Bread Pudding and Cream Fillings: Bread puddings, custards, eclairs, pies and other desserts with cream fillings should be covered and placed in a refrigerator until serving time. In hot weather they should not be prepared at all.

Plan Meals To Avoid Having Left-overs: Meals should be so planned that left-over food is reduced to a minimum. However, if there are left-overs, they should be refrigerated as soon as possible.

Hot left-over food should be placed in the refrigerator as soon as it is cool enough to handle. Cold food should be placed in the refrigerator immediately following the service of food to the mess. All left-over food should remain in the refrigerator until time to prepare it for the meal. It should be used within 36 hours.

★4

Sandwich Fillings: Sandwich fillings made from ham, tongue, fried egg, egg salad, sausage and fish must be prepared quickly and just previous to making the sandwiches.

If the fillings need to be made 2 to 3 hours before using the sandwiches, place the filling in a refrigerator immediately after making it and keep refrigerated until time to make the sandwiches. Cover the sandwiches with wax paper instead of covering them with a damp cloth.

Keep Time Short Between Preparation and Serving: Cut the length of time between preparation and serving to the minimum. Food should always be served immediately after it has reached the right degree of doneness, if possible. If the food must be held, no more than 4 hours should elapse after removal of food from heat. The timing should begin at this point and not after the food has been sliced or otherwise prepared for service.

Cleanliness Is Imperative: All cooking and mess equipment must be kept scrupulously clean at all times. See that the dishwashing water is at a temperature of at least 120° F. to 140° F. and that the temperature of the rinse water is held at approximately 180° F. to 210° F.

Hands and clothing of all personnel handling food must be kept scrupulously clean at all times. Careful inspection is necessary to eliminate any men with infections. Personnel should be cautioned against sneezing or coughing in spaces where food is prepared and served.

Nutritional Value of Foods

The modern knowledge of nutrition indicates that foods serve specific functions in the body. Therefore, men need foods of different types in adequate quantities. All materials for building and maintaining strong, active bodies must be secured from the dairy products, eggs, fruits and vegetables, meats, and cereal products which are issued to the mess.

Abnormal supply conditions may make it necessary to substitute some foods for others. It is essential, therefore, to know which nutrients are required and which foods are richest in these nutrients.

The four cornerstones of the diet are proteins, vitamins, minerals, and energy-producing factors, all of which are essential to the maintenance of health.

PROTEINS

The substance in foods which are called proteins merit their name which means "to take first place." They furnish essential building and repairing material for muscles and tissues of the body and enter into many, if not all, of the body functions. They also furnish energy.

Protein from animal sources in general is superior to protein from vegetable sources. *Best sources:* Milk, eggs, meat, fish, and poultry. *Other sources:* Dried peas and beans, cereals, and vegetables.

VITAMINS

Vitamins are definite chemical substances present in food in minute quantities. They are necessary for growth and the maintenance of normal body functions. The effects of vitamins on health are spectacular. There are several known vitamins which must be adequately supplied in the diet. All are essential for good health, but each has certain special functions. A brief summary of the functions and sources of the better known vitamins is herewith presented.

Vitamin A

An adequate intake of vitamin A is necessary for normal resistance to infections and better vision in dim light. It may therefore be particularly important for all seamen standing night watches and for flyers. *Best sources:* Butter, liver, egg yolk, cheese, fish liver oils, yellow and green vegetables, and fruits.

Vitamin B_1

Vitamin B_1 (thiamin) affects morale and disposition, helps to prevent fatigue, maintains appetite, healthy nerves, and normal muscle action. This vitamin is destroyed by excessive heat. It is readily soluble in water and therefore is partially lost if cooking water is discarded.

Best sources: Liver and kidney, lean meat, especially pork, beans and peas, cereals with whole grain value, enriched flour, nuts, milk, and eggs.

Riboflavin

Riboflavin is essential to growth and normal nutrition for all ages. Deficiencies may result in digestive disturbances, nervous depression, general weakness, and poor conditions of the eyes and skin. Riboflavin is soluble in water and is destroyed by light. *Best sources:* Milk, lean meat, eggs, liver, green vegetables, peas, and beans.

Niacin

Niacin, a third water-soluble vitamin, prevents the deficiency disease called pellagra which is usually manifested by skin disorders, and in severe stages, mental disturbances. *Best sources:* Liver, lean pork, salmon, whole grain cereals and enriched flour, milk, and eggs.

Vitamin C

Vitamin C (ascorbic acid), "the sailor's vitamin" prevents scurvy, that scourge of long voyages in olden days which is now reduced because of better methods of food preservation such as canning and cold storage.

This vitamin is necessary to maintain the health of teeth and gums, to aid in resistance to infections, to prevent listlessness and fatigue and to maintain the strength of the bony structure and of the walls of the blood vessels. It is soluble in water and is partially destroyed by cooking, this loss being less in acid fruits and tomatoes. *Best sources:* Citrus fruits, raw vegetables, fresh fruits and fruit juices, tomatoes, raw or canned. *Other sources:* Green vegetables and potatoes, if not overcooked.

Vitamin D

Vitamin D is concerned with the efficient utilization of calcium and phosphorous in the normal development and growth of the bones and teeth. *Best sources:* Fish liver oils, egg yolk, liver, and irradiated food. Sunshine affects the skin in such a way as to produce vitamin D which is utilized in the same manner as vitamin D from food.

Although there may be requirements for other less well known vitamins, a well rounded diet that provides sufficient amounts of the vitamins listed above will in general supply these in adequate quantities.

MINERALS

Certain mineral elements are needed by the body for growth and maintenance of body structure and processes. Some of these are so widely distributed in foods that they are usually supplied in sufficient amounts in any diet. Calcium and iron, however, may be too low unless care is taken in food planning.

Calcium

Calcium, combined with phosphorous, furnishes the material from which bones and teeth are built, aids in the clotting of blood, and in regulating the action of nerves and muscles. Calcium is not quite as readily lost in cooking as are other minerals. *Best sources:* Milk, whole or skim (fresh, dehydrated), milk (evaporated), cheese. *Other sources:* Leafy vegetables, molasses, dried beans, or soy beans.

Iron

Iron is required for the formation of the coloring matter of the red blood cells. Unless sufficient amounts of this substance are present, the blood cannot efficiently carry oxygen to all parts of the body for the continuance of life. *Best sources:* Eggs, meat, molasses, green vegetables, dried fruits, dried beans, whole grain cereals, and enriched flour.

ENERGY-PRODUCING FOODS

Active men need large amounts of energy, 3,000 to 4,500 calories per day. In a well balanced diet it is estimated that approximately 10 to 15 per cent of the calories should be derived from protein; 55 to 70 percent from carbohydrate and 20 to 30 percent from fat. It is evident, therefore, that although protein is useful as an energy-producing food as well as for its muscle building function, the majority of the energy is supplied from carbohydrates such as starches and sugars and from fats. *Best sources:* Fats and oils; flour (bread, cakes, pastry), spaghetti, macaroni, rice and other cereals; sugar and sirups.

Suggestions for applying the principles of nutrition in a practical manner are presented in the following chapter on planning the menu.

The Menu

A menu is a food plan for a meal, a day, a week or longer.

A balanced menu is a menu which includes the foods required by the body for most efficient functioning.

Planning the menu, therefore, should be of primary importance to the commissary personnel, for upon it depends, to a great extent, the health and morale of the men in the general mess.

A Food Guide, specifying the basic foods required daily for a balanced menu, is included in this chapter. Study it carefully.

While the emphasis in menu planning is placed on the nutritive value of the food, attention must also be given to providing meals which are interesting, attractive, varied, and satisfying. This is helpful in maintaining good morale.

In addition to the main factors involved in planning the menu, many helpful suggestions are included throughout this book in conjunction with recipes and with other explanatory material.

PLANNING THE MENU

First, Know the Foods Essential for Good Nutrition: It is important that the Nutritional Value of Foods (page 6) and The Food Guide (page 11) be studied before starting to plan the balanced menu. Include these foods in each day's menu.

Check Your Menus: Be sure each food group in the Food Guide is represented in the menu. Emphasis is placed on the use of fruits and vegetables because of their valuable contribution of minerals and vitamins.

Become Acquainted With the Recipes in This Book: The numerous recipes developed and tested, particularly for Navy use, allow for a wide selection. The introduction to each section, and the notes and variations of the recipes contain helpful information for menu planning, food selection, and preparation.

Study the "Tables": They contain valuable information which pertains to food planning.

Plan the Menus a Week in Advance:
The Navy menu should be planned for an entire week sufficiently in advance to permit the ordering and receiving of required stores. This practice will allow time for figuring costs and for an orderly planning of the week's work, which are important factors in controlling the production of food necessary for a given mess.

Observe the Food "Likes and Dislikes" of the Men: Observe the food habits of the men, their likes and dislikes. This is helpful in planning and estimating the amount of food required for the number of rations to be prepared. Food left uneaten on the tray is wasted food.

Include Contrasting Foods in Each Menu: Foods contrasting in texture, color, and flavor tempt the appetite, give eye appeal, and increase the palatability of the meal.

Vary the Ways of Serving the Same Food: Avoid repetition. Become acquainted with the variations of the basic recipes. They offer a wide choice of ways to prepare a single food.

Consider the Climate: Whenever possible plan to serve cool, crisp, fresh foods and cool beverages in hot weather.

Use Fresh Foods in Season: Whenever practicable, this should be done. Fresh fruits and vegetables in season, can often be purchased at a lower cost than packaged products. By using them, it is possible to release processed products for ship and overseas use. Fresh foods purchased locally also help to relieve congestion in transportation.

Consider Cooking Equipment: Plan meals which can be prepared with the cooking equipment available. This insures better prepared meals and often prevents waste of food through improper cooking.

Use a Pattern for Planning the Day's Menu

Breakfast

Fruit: Fresh, frozen, evaporated, dehydrated, or canned fruits or fruit juices are used for appetizing as well as nutritional reasons. In one form or another, fruit is a welcome starter for the day, but need not be served for breakfast if it would be more useful in improving other meals.

Cereal: Cereal is a fuel food and has the advantage of being a carrier for milk. Serve hot or cold cereal depending on the supply, the climate, food habits of the men, or need for variety.

Main Dish: The main dish may be ham, bacon, eggs, sausage, creamed dried beef, fried mush, French toast, hot cakes, or other satisfying breakfast dishes. Do not have the same thing on the same day each week. If fried mush or French toast are on the menu, sirup, jam, or jelly should be served.

Bread: The bread should be varied as much as possible. Toast, rolls, cornbread, biscuits, coffee cake, doughnuts, and pan bread are some suggestions.

Jam or Jelly: Jam or jelly may be served in place of butter occasionally.

Beverage: The beverage may be either milk, coffee, tea, or cocoa.

Dinner

Soup: Soup may be served at either the noon or evening meal, whichever one needs the extra nourishment. When a vegetable soup is on the dinner menu, the salad may be omitted if desired. Soup is one means of getting men to eat vegetables.

Meat: Meat is always popular. The meat purchased by the Navy is of good quality. Many cuts are spoiled by poor cooking. Do not have meat cooked too long in advance of the service period. Study pages 110 to 120 for information on proper handling and cooking.

Gravy: Gravy or sauce is usually served with meat. Good gravy is smooth, well seasoned, and not greasy. Serve hot.

Vegetables: A leafy green or yellow vegetable besides potato is valuable because of flavor, appearance, and vitamin content. See pages 278 to 283 for pertinent information on vegetable preparation.

Relish: A relish may take the place of salad occasionally. Raw carrot strips, young onions, radishes, sliced raw turnips, chopped cabbage and green peppers, sliced cucumbers and onions, and pickled beets are suggestions.

Salads: Salads may be made from meat, greens, vegetables, or fruits. Serve as cold and crisp as possible.

Dessert: Dessert has a definite place in the menu because it gives a feeling of satisfaction. Many people crave sweets and are accustomed to having them at the end of the meal. Dessert adds calories and will round out a light meal. Serve lighter dessert with a heavy meal.

Beverage: This can be coffee, tea, cocoa, milk, or a fruit-ade.

Supper

Main Dish: Meat may or may not be used, according to supplies on hand. The supper meal is usually a lighter meal than dinner. This depends upon the activities of the crew. It should be heavy enough to keep the men from being hungry when they turn in at night. Combinations of meat and rice, macaroni and cheese, chili con carne, chop suey, creamed meat, thick chowders, baked beans, and similar dishes are excellent dishes to serve at the supper meal.

The supper meal is also a good time to utilize leftovers from dinner, if there are any. They must be attractive and appetizing on their reappearance and, if possible, completely changed. Combinations such as rice and stewed tomatoes, carrots and peas, cooked vegetables made into a salad, meat and potatoes for hash are a few examples of how leftover foods may be utilized.

Salad: A salad fits well into the supper meal. A fruit or vegetable or a chef's salad with mayonnaise or cream dressing, when served in addition to the main dish, is satisfying and helps to balance the meal nutritionally.

Dessert: If the supper meal is lighter than dinner, the dessert can be richer and one that yields more calories such as pastry or pudding.

Beverage: Beverage can be a choice of coffee, milk, cocoa, tea or fruit-ade. In warm weather or hot climates, a cool beverage such as iced tea or a cold fruit-ade is preferable.

The extent to which these patterns can be followed is affected by the variety of available supplies. These supplies are limited aboard ship by the amount of storage space and refrigeration.

A FOOD GUIDE FOR MENU PLANNING
Include One or More from Each of the Basic Foods Each Day

BASIC FOODS	RECOMMENDED DAILY (For 1 Man)	NUTRITION HIGHLIGHTS.
Milk and Milk Products: Fresh fluid, evaporated or powdered milk, and cheese.	1 pint (liquid) or equivalent.	Milk furnishes protein of good quality, high content of calcium, phosphorus, vitamins A, riboflavin and considerable B_1 (thiamin). Cheese: Five ounces of American cheddar cheese is about equal to 1 quart of milk in calcium, phosphorus, and protein content.
Eggs: Fresh, frozen, or powdered.	1 egg	Eggs are especially valuable for their complete proteins, iron, phosphorus, and vitamin A.
Butter	1 to 2 ounces..............	Butter is especially valuable for its vitamin A and fat content.
Meat, Fowl, Fish: Fresh, frozen, or canned..	1 or more servings of meat, fish, or fowl.	Meat furnishes complete proteins, phosphorus, iron, B_1 (thiamin), and riboflavin. Liver is especially high in vitamin A. Fish are important for protein and phosphorus. Salt water fish furnish iodine.
Legumes: Dried kidney, lima and Navy beans; dried peas; also peanut butter.	Once or twice a week.	Legumes are chiefly important as a source of energy, proteins, phosphorus, iron, thiamin. Because they are not a source of complete proteins, legumes should be used only as a supplement and not as a total substitution for the animal proteins.
Cereals and Bread: Cereals, whole grain or restored to whole grain value. Bread, enriched.	2 or more servings....	Cereals, with whole grain value, and bread, enriched, furnish energy, protein, bulk, iron, phosphorus and vitamins B_1, riboflavin and niacin.
Fruits: Fresh, frozen, canned, dried or dehydrated.	2 or more servings 1 fresh fruit when possible. Citrus fruit often.	Fruits supply vitamins, minerals and bulk. Citrus fruits are high in vitamin C. Yellow fruits supply generous amounts of vitamin A.
Vegetables: Fresh, frozen, canned, dried or dehydrated.	2 or more servings besides potato. 1 green or yellow vegetable each day and greens, cooked or in salads, often. Tomatoes often.	Vegetables furnish valuable vitamins, minerals and bulk. Some more than others. Green and yellow vegetables are valuable for vitamin A and iron. Use the outer dark green leaves of lettuce and cabbage in salads and soups. To save nutrients, use water in which vegetables are cooked for soups and gravies. Tomatoes, fresh or canned, are especially valuable for their vitamin C. Use them often, fresh or canned.

NOTE.—Other foods in form of desserts, sirups and sugar may be used to supplement the diet. Sugar supplies energy but makes no other dietary contributions.

SUBSTITUTE FOODS OF SAME NUTRITIVE VALUE

It may be necessary sometimes to substitute one food for another in a planned menu. Certain factors will require consideration:

1. Whether it is equivalent in nutritional value to the food originally planned, and if not, the adjustments necessary to make it so.

2. The acceptability of the substituted food in relation to the other foods on the menu.

A chart giving the nutritive values of the different classes of vegetables, and suggested substitutions, is listed in the section on vegetables (page 283).

SAMPLE MENUS

Bill of Fare for the General Mess

Each of these pattern menus is offered as a guide for planning the weekly Bill of Fare for the General Mess, aboard ship and ashore.

These are balanced menus, planned to meet the nutritional requirements of the moderately active Navy man needing approximately 3,000 to 4,500 calories daily.

The suggested food selections and combinations are based upon Navy food issues, ration allowances and recipes in this book.

When the fresh or other foods suggested in the menus are not available, they should be replaced by canned and dehydrated or other foods of approximately the same nutritional value.

SAMPLE MENU FOR SPRING

	BREAKFAST		DINNER		SUPPER	
MONDAY	Grapefruit Juice Cornflakes Grilled Sausages French Toast Maple Sirup Butter	Milk Coffee	Cream of Vegetable Soup Roast Beef Brown Gravy Buttered Potatoes Harvard Beets Carrot and Celery Salad Ice Cream Rolls Butter Coffee		Lamb Fricassee Mashed Potatoes Tossed Green Salad French Dressing Coconut Jelly Doughnuts Bread Butter	 Tea
TUESDAY	Stewed Rhubarb Hominy Grits Corned Beef Hash Poached Egg Danish Twists Butter	Milk Coffee	Chicken Broth Ham and Macaroni Salad Tomato Aspic Buttered Peas Lemon Meringue Pie Hot Biscuits Butter Coffee		Baked Pork Chops Hashed Browned Potatoes Glazed Carrots Cole Slaw Rice Custard Pudding Rolls Butter	 Milk

WEDNESDAY	Orange
	Shredded Wheat
	Griddle Cakes
	Maple Sirup
	Crisp Bacon
	Bread
	Butter
		Milk
		
		Coffee
			Creamed Chicken over
			    Biscuit
			Baked New Potato
			Savory Green Beans
			Crisp Celery
			Assorted Fruit Gelatin
			    Cubes
			Toast Butter Coffee
					Griddle-Broiled
					    Salisbury Steaks
					Potatoes Au Gratin
					Buttered Beets
					Lettuce Salad
					Ice Cream
					Bread
					Butter Fruit-ade	

THURSDAY	Stewed Prunes Oatmeal Grilled Sausages Scrambled Eggs Cinnamon Buns Jam	Milk Coffee	Cream of Green Pea Soup Roast Veal Natural Gravy Applesauce, canned Fried Hominy Buttered Spinach Cherry Roll Bread Butter Coffee		Creamed Chipped Beef on Toast Browned New Potatoes Mixed Vegetable Salad Boston Cream Pie Bread Butter	 Tea
FRIDAY	Half Grapefruit Cooked Whole Wheat Cereal Fried Cornmeal Mush Maple Sirup Crisp Bacon Bread Butter	 Milk Coffee	Tomato Juice Salmon Loaf Escalloped Potatoes Buttered Carrot Strips Waldorf Salad Angel Food Cake Bread Butter Coffee		Beef Stuffed Cabbage Rolls Franconia Potatoes Hearts of Lettuce Salad Thousand Island Dressing Pear Halves Coconut Butter Cookie Bread Butter Cocoa	
SATURDAY	Banana Dry Cereal Baked Beans Catsup Raisin Buns Butter	Milk Coffee	Spanish Beef Steaks Parsley Buttered Potatoes Fresh Asparagus Crisp Celery Green Onions Tapioca Cream Rolls Butter Lemonade		Knickerbocker Bean Soup Welsh Rarebit on Toast Pickled Beet and Onion Salad Mixed Fruit Cup Bread Butter Coffee	
SUNDAY	Sliced Pineapple Oatmeal Fried Egg Lyonnaise Potatoes Crisp Bacon Toast Butter	Milk Coffee	Beef Broth with Barley Sugar Baked Ham Sweet Potatoes Baked with Apples Buttered Corn Lettuce Salad French Dressing Strawberry Shortcake Rolls Butter Coffee		Cream of Tomato Soup Hot Potato Salad Buttered Green Beans Crisp Carrot Strips Orange Oatmeal Cookies Bread Butter Milk	

SAMPLE MENU FOR SUMMER

	BREAKFAST	DINNER	SUPPER
MONDAY	Fresh Peach Dry Cereal Milk Soft Cooked Egg Home Fried Potatoes Toast Butter Coffee	Green Split Pea Soup Roast Beef Natural Gravy Glazed Onions Corn on the Cob Perfection Salad Sliced Pineapple Bread Butter Coffee	Pigs in Blankets Hashed Browned Potatoes Sliced Tomato and Lettuce Salad French Dressing Berry Pie Bread Butter Coffee

TUESDAY	Chilled Cantaloupe
	Hot Wheat Cereal Milk
	Creamed Chipped Beef
	   on Cornbread
	Toast
	Jam Coffee
		Fricassee of Chicken
		Mashed Potatoes
		Buttered Asparagus
		Apple, Carrot and
		   Celery Salad
		Chilled Watermelon
		Hot Biscuits
		Butter Iced Tea
			Beef Loaf with
			   Barbecue Sauce
			Noodles with Buttered
			   Crumbs
			Cole Slaw Salad
			Strawberry Gelatin
			Bread
			Butter Lemonade

WEDNESDAY	Fresh Apricots
	Shredded Wheat Milk
	Navy Baked Beans with
	   Salt Pork
	Danish Twists
	Butter Coffee
		Roast Lamb Mint Sauce
		Escalloped New Potatoes
		French Fried Carrots
		Grapefruit and
		   Green Pepper Salad
		Vanilla Ice Cream
		Whole Wheat Bread
		Butter Coffee
			Cream of Chicken Soup
			Baked Luncheon Meat
			Sliced Cheese
			Cardinal Salad
			Chocolate Cake Square
			Rolls
			Butter Tea

THURSDAY	Chilled Half Grapefruit
	Hot Whole Wheat Cereal
	            Milk
	Grilled Canadian Bacon
	Hashed Browned Potatoes
	Bread
	Butter Coffee
		Vegetable Soup
		Cold Roast Beef
		Cold Potato Salad
		Spiced Beets
		Green Onions
		Spice Cake with
		   Marshmallow Frosting
		Hot Biscuits
		Butter Iced Tea
			Macaroni and Corn
			   Au Gratin
			Buttered String Beans
			Grilled Tomato
			Jellied Mixed Fruits
			Bread
			Butter Milk

FRIDAY	Fruit Cup
	Corn Flakes Milk
	Roast Beef Hash
	Catsup
	Cinnamon Buns
	Butter Coffee
		Broiled Halibut Steak—
		   Lemon Slice
		Potatoes Au Gratin
		Fresh Lima Beans
		Tossed Green Salad
		   French Dressing
		Peach Fudge Cookie
		Rolls Butter Coffee
			Omelet with Creole Sauce
			Browned Potatoes
			Buttered New Cabbage
			Pineapple Upsidedown
			   Cake
			Bread
			Butter Cocoa

SATURDAY	Fresh Berries Hot Wheat Cereal Milk French Toast Maple Sirup Grilled Sausages Bread Butter Coffee	Braised Liver Spanish Rice Buttered Fresh Peas Corn Relish Deep Dish Apple Pie Bread Butter Milk	Tomato Broth Salmon Salad French Fried Potatoes Crisp Carrot Sticks Brownies Rolls Butter Milk

SUNDAY	Chilled Fresh Plums
	Dry Cereal Milk
	Scrambled Eggs
	Crisp Bacon
	Sugar Doughnuts
	Toast
	Butter Coffee
		Griddle-Broiled Beef Steak
		Creamed New Potatoes
		Buttered String Beans
		Raw Vegetable Salad
		   French Dressing
		Fresh Peach Ice Cream
		Rolls
		Butter Iced Chocolate
			Cream of Green Pea Soup
			Assorted Sandwiches
			   (Sliced Egg, Lettuce
			   and Tomato, and Amer-
			   ican Cheese)
			Crisp Celery and Radishes
			Jelly Roll Milk

SAMPLE MENU FOR AUTUMN

	BREAKFAST	DINNER	SUPPER

MONDAY	Baked Apple
	Oatmeal Milk
	Griddle Cakes
	Maple Sirup
	Crisp Bacon
	Toast
	Butter Coffee
		Beef Broth with Barley
		Breaded Veal Cutlet
		Tomato Sauce
		Oven Browned Potatoes
		Mixed Cooked Vegetable
		  Salad
		Cranberry and Orange Pie
		Bread Butter Tea
			Pork Sausage Links and
			  Sauerkraut Pie
			Mashed Potatoes
			Waldorf Salad
			Soft Molasses Cookies
			Bread
			Butter Cocoa

TUESDAY	Orange Hot Wheat Cereal Milk Scrambled Eggs and Ham Coffee Cake Butter Coffee	Beef Stew with Vegetables Corn Fritters Lettuce Salad French Dressing Sliced Pickles Pineapple Ice Cream Bread Butter Tea	Noodle Soup Smothered Ham Slices Baked Potato Buttered Cauliflower Tomato Salad, Mayonnaise Apple Torte Bread Butter Coffee
WEDNESDAY	Banana Corn Flakes Milk Grilled Pork Sausages Lyonnaise Potatoes Toast Butter Coffee	Consomme Braised Veal Patties Mashed Potatoes Fried Eggplant Pickled Beet and Onion Salad Fruit Cup Rolls Butter Coffee	Broiled Beef Steak Browned Potatoes Mashed Hubbard Squash Dixie Relish Fresh Peach Cobbler Hot Biscuits Butter Coffee
THURSDAY	Chilled Melon Hot Whole Wheat Cereal Milk Roast Beef Hash Catsup Butterfly Buns Butter Coffee	Baked Canadian Bacon French Fried Potatoes Buttered Green Beans Orange Cole Slaw Pumpkin Pie Corn Bread Butter Fruit Punch	Tomato Rarebit on Toast O'Brien Potatoes Raw Vegetable Salad French Dressing Fruit and Rice Compote Toast Butter Tea
FRIDAY	Fresh Bartlett Pear Oatmeal Milk French Toast Maple Sirup Hashed Browned Potatoes Butter Coffee	Corn Chowder Oven Broiled Mackerel Spanish Sauce Mashed Potatoes Buttered Beets Crisp Celery Applesauce Cake Bread Butter Coffee	Spareribs with Barbecue Sauce Steamed Rice Buttered Broccoli Fresh Grapes Sugar Cookie Bread Butter Coffee

SATURDAY	Prunes
	Dry Cereal Milk
	Baked Beans
	Catsup
	Hot Biscuits
	Butter Coffee
		Roast Beef Natural Gravy
		Lyonnaise Potatoes
		Buttered Cabbage
		Carrot and Lettuce Salad
		French Dressing
		Banana Fritters with
		  Orange Sauce
		Whole Wheat Bread
		Butter Coffee
			Spaghetti Loaf
			Buttered Peas
			Fruit Salad Mayonnaise
			Gingerbread with
			  Frosting
			Bread
			Butter Milk

SUNDAY	Half Grapefruit
	Hot Wheat Cereal Milk
	Soft Cooked Eggs
	Grilled Bacon
	Toast
	Jam
	Butter Coffee
		Cream of Tomato Soup
		Baked Chicken and
		  Noodles
		Glazed Carrots
		Buttered Kale
		Cranberry Sauce
		Celery and Olives
		Maple Nut Ice Cream
		Rolls Butter Coffee
			Broiled Cheeseburgers
			  on Bun
			Potato Chips
			Escalloped Tomatoes
			Lettuce Salad French
			  Dressing
			Sliced Pineapple
			Ginger Cookies
			Bread Jam Coffee

SAMPLE MENU FOR WINTER

	BREAKFAST	DINNER	SUPPER
MONDAY	Prunes Oatmeal　　　　　Milk Grilled Sausages Home Fried Potatoes Whole Wheat Bread Butter　　　　　Coffee	Navy Bean Soup Fried Pork Chop　Gravy Hominy Spoonbread Buttered Green Peas Apple Cole Slaw Salad Lemon Cream Layer Cake Bread　Butter　Coffee	Meat Loaf Tomato Sauce Baked Potato Buttered Carrots Peach Half Sugar Cookies Bread　Butter　Cocoa
TUESDAY	Half Grapefruit Hominy Grits　　Milk Griddle Cakes Maple Sirup Crisp Bacon Toast Butter　　　　　Coffee	Tomato Broth Pot Roast of Beef Brown Gravy Mashed Potatoes Buttered Cabbage Crisp Celery Prune Whip Rolls　Butter　Coffee	Macaroni Au Gratin Stewed Tomatoes Mixed Vegetable Salad Devil's Food Cake with 　Coconut Frosting Bread Butter　　　　　Milk
WEDNESDAY	Chilled Figs Oatmeal　　　　　Milk Scrambled Eggs Hashed Browned Potatoes Cinnamon Buns Butter　　　　　Coffee	Cream of Celery Soup Veal Birds Franconia Potatoes Glazed Onions Lettuce Salad French Dressing Chocolate Ice Cream Bread　Butter　Coffee	Chop Suey over Cooked 　Noodles Pineapple Cole Slaw Apricot Cream Pie Whole Wheat Bread Butter　　　　　Coffee
THURSDAY	Canned Peaches Hot Wheat Cereal　Milk Grilled Bacon Soft Cooked Egg Coffee Cake Butter　　　　　Coffee	Consomme Baked Ham　　Mustard 　Sauce Baked Rice and Cheese Buttered Spinach Perfection Salad Mayonnaise Apple Crisp Cloverleaf Rolls Butter　　　　　Coffee	Grilled Frankfurters Relish Hot Potato Salad Banana Shortcake Buttered Toast Jam　　　　　Milk
FRIDAY	Orange Shredded Wheat　Milk French Toast Maple Sirup Cottage Fried Potatoes Bread Butter　　　　　Coffee	Cream of Corn Soup Fried Flounder Tartar Sauce Parslied Potatoes Buttered String Beans Waldorf Salad Cherry Pie Bread　Butter　Coffee	Chili Con Carne Steamed Rice Grapefruit and Celery 　Salad Butterscotch Pudding Bread Butter　　　　　Tea
SATURDAY	Apple Dry Cereal　　　Milk Baked Beans Raisin Buns Butter　　　　　Coffee	Vegetable Soup Swiss Steak French Fried Potatoes Stewed Tomatoes Lettuce Salad Jellied Mixed Fruits Whole Wheat Bread Butter　　　　　Coffee	Creamed Fish on Toast Succotash Sliced Pineapple Hot Gingerbread Bread Butter　　　　　Coffee
SUNDAY	Stewed Apricots Hot Wheat Cereal　Milk Fried Ham and Egg Butterfly Rolls Jam Butter　　　　　Coffee	Bouillon Roast Loin of Pork　Gravy Whipped Sweet Potatoes Buttered Asparagus Celery　　　　Applesauce Vanilla Ice Cream Rolls　Butter　Coffee	Noodles, Scalloped with 　Cheese, Tomatoes and 　Bacon Buttered Carrots Cranberry Orange Relish Hermits Bread Butter　　　　　Milk

General Information and Tables
Canned Foods

Commercially canned food is one of the most important types of preserved food used in Navy subsistence.

Carefully selected and prepared food is packed in containers and heated to definite processing temperatures for the proper length of time. These temperatures and processing times are selected to destroy or inhibit the subsequent growth of such bacteria as may be present on the food when it is packed. Therefore, properly canned food should keep as long as the seal of the container, or the container itself, is not broken.

If, however, the canned food should be stored at high temperatures, the bacteria which may not have been fully destroyed may become active and spoilage will result. As a precautionary measure, all canned food should be stored in a dry, cool place. High temperatures may also speed up corrosion of the cans and cause the deterioration of the flavor and texture of the contents.

Research studies show that the vitamin content of commercially canned foods is relatively high. Vitamin A and carotene (provitamin A), vitamin D, riboflavin and niacin appear to be very little affected by the canning process. In the case of water soluble nutrients, part of the vitamins and minerals are contained in the liquid surrounding the food in the can. Therefore, to obtain full nutritional benefit from canned foods, the liquids should be reserved for use in sauces, gravies and soups or should be concentrated by rapid boiling to ½ or ⅓ the original volume and served with the food.

Since canned foods have been fully cooked in the canning process, it is only necessary to heat them to boiling temperature just before serving. In this way, the vitamins are better retained, and the food is more attractive and palatable than if a long cooking period is used.

TABLE OF WEIGHTS AND AMOUNTS FOR No. 10 CANS

NUMBER OF No. 10 CANS	APPROX. WEIGHT		APPROXIMATE AMOUNTS			
	POUNDS	OUNCES	CUPS	PINTS	QUARTS	GALLONS
½	3	5	6½	3¼	1⅗	....
1	6	10	13	6½	3¼	....
4	26	8	52	26	13	3¼
8	53	....	104	52	26	6½
10	66	4	130	65	32½	8
12	79	8	156	78	39	9¾
16	106	....	208	104	52	13
20	132	8	260	130	65	16¼
24	159	....	312	156	78	19½
28	185	8	364	182	91	22¾
30	198	12	390	195	97½	24½

SUBSTITUTING ONE CAN SIZE FOR ANOTHER

1 No. 10 can equals 7 No. 1 tall cans.

1 No. 10 can equals 5 No. 2 cans.

1 No. 10 can equals 4 No. 2½ cans.

1 No. 10 can equals 3 No. 3 cylinders.

1 No. 10 can equals 2 No. 5 cans.

NUMBER OF CANS OF EVAPORATED MILK IN COMMON LIQUID MEASURES

Number of No. 1 Tall Cans	Approx. Weight		Approximate Amounts		
	Pounds	Ounces	Cups	Quarts	Gallons
½	....	7¼	⅚	....	....
1	....	14½	1⅔	....	....
4	3	10	6⅔	1⅔	....
8	7	4	13⅓	3⅓	....
10	9	1	16⅔	4⅙	1
12	10	14	20	5	1¼
16	14	8	26⅔	6⅔	1⅘
20	18	2	33⅓	8⅓	2
24	21	12	40	10	2½
28	25	6	46⅔	11⅔	2⅘
30	27	3	50	12½	3
1 No. 10 (Confectioners' Size)	8	....	15	3¾	1

SIZES OF CANS—FRUITS AND VEGETABLES

Size of Can	Average Net Weight Per Can	Approx. Cups per Can
No. 1 tall	1 pound	2 cups (1 pint)
No. 2	1 pound 4 ounces	2½ cups
No. 2½	1 pound 12 ounces	3½ cups
No. 5	3 pounds 8 ounces	1¾ quarts
No. 10	6 pounds 10 ounces	3¼ quarts

SIZES OF CANS—JUICES

No. 2	1 pint 2 fluid ounces	2½ cups
No. 3 Cylinder	1 quart 14 fluid ounces	5¾ cups
No. 10	3 quarts	12 cups (3 qts.)

Dehydrated Foods

Dehydrated foods are fresh foods from which water and the inedible parts such as peels, cores, seeds, stems and bones have been removed.

The foods are thoroughly cleaned and then dried by scientifically controlled processes designed to retain much of the original food value, flavor and texture.

Dehydrated products, because of their reduced weight and bulk, save considerable storage space and therefore are part of the food supply of the Navy.

When stored in airtight, insect- and moisture-proof containers, dehydrated products will keep in moderate temperatures for indefinite periods of time. This is made possible because the moisture content has been reduced to a degree where the micro-organisms such as the yeasts, molds and bacteria, which cause spoilage in foods, cannot thrive. However, there are still some micro-organisms present on the food, in an inactive state, which remain inactive until moisture is restored to the product, at which time they again become active and may cause spoilage. It is therefore important that dehydrated products be kept free from moisture until they are ready to be used.

Before they can be used for final preparation in a meal, it is necessary to restore them to as nearly their original state as possible. This is done by restoring to the product the approximate amount of water, through absorption, that was originally removed in the process of dehydration. This process of restoration is termed "reconstitution."

Directions for reconstituting and using the product in various prepared cooked dishes will be found in individual recipes in this book, under their respective classifications. For example, the recipe for Buttered Beets, using dehydrated beets is given on page 292 in the Vegetable Section. The recipe for Applesauce, using dehydrated apple nuggets will be found on page 86, under Fruits.

The dehydrated packaged soup mixes, especially the bean and pea soups, are highly nutritious and in addition can serve as a base for soups to which fresh or canned vegetables and meat may be added.

The flavor and palatability of dehydrated soups is definitely improved when meat stock instead of water is used as the liquid for reconstitution. Powdered bouillon or bouillon type products may be used for the preparation of meat stock when fresh meat and bones are not available. Recipes for the use of powdered bouillon are given on page 251.

Dehydrated milk and dehydrated eggs are supplied in powdered form. Information on powdered eggs and milk, and conversion tables showing the equivalents of fresh and powdered milk and eggs are given on pages 20 and 21.

As the process of dehydration is further developed, changes in the methods of reconstituting and cooking may be somewhat changed. Therefore, it is advisable to strictly follow directions which are supplied by the manufacturer for his respective product.

INFORMATION ON POWDERED EGGS

Powdered eggs are fresh eggs from which water has been removed in the drying process.

The food value of fresh and powdered whole eggs is approximately the same.

After reconstitution, powdered eggs may be used in the same way as fresh eggs. They must be treated the same as fresh eggs removed from the shell. Never let reconstituted eggs stand more than 1 hour unless they are refrigerated

Powdered eggs vary in density. Some are more fluffy than others. It is desirable to use weights, if scales are available, as it is difficult to obtain exact amounts by measuring. Be sure that all measurements are level.

In recipes where dry ingredients are sifted together, powdered egg can be mixed with the dry ingredients. The water required to reconstitute the eggs should then be added to the other liquid in the recipe. This is important.

Always store powdered eggs in a cool, dry place in a tightly covered container, as they absorb moisture when exposed to air. Held at refrigerator temperature (50° F.) or below, powdered eggs (5% moisture content) should give satisfactory results for at least 1 year. Held at high temperatures (80° F. or above) powdered eggs soon become dull and dark in color and develop rancidity and off-flavors. Powdered eggs of low moisture content (2%) are more resistant to deterioration from storage at higher temperature.

TABLE OF EQUIVALENTS FOR FRESH, FROZEN AND POWDERED EGGS

FRESH SHELL EGGS		FROZEN EGGS		POWDERED EGGS			plus WATER
WEIGHT	AMOUNTS (approx.)	WEIGHT	AMOUNTS (approx.)	WEIGHTS		AMOUNTS (approx.)	AMOUNTS
Pounds	1 egg (3 tablespoons).	Pounds	1 egg (3 tablespoons).	Pounds	Ounces	2 tablespoons.	2 to 2½ tablespoons.
1	10 eggs (1 pint)	1	10 eggs (1 pint)	....	4	1 cup	1½ cups.
2	20 eggs (1 quart)	2	20 eggs (1 quart)	....	8	1 pint	1½ pints.
10	100 eggs (1¼ gallons).	10	100 eggs (1¼ gallons).	2	8	1½ quarts	3¾ quarts.

To Reconstitute Powdered Eggs

Sprinkle powdered eggs into cold water, stirring constantly to avoid lumping. Mix until smooth. Never add hot water to powdered eggs.

INFORMATION ON POWDERED AND EVAPORATED MILK

The formulas and recipes in this book specify liquid milk.

Milk may be supplied in the form of fresh liquid milk, powdered whole and evaporated milk reconstituted with water to give an approximate equivalent of fresh milk.

After reconstitution, powdered or evaporated milk can be used in exactly the same manner as fresh milk. No change is necessary in formula or recipe.

Storage

Always store both powdered skim milk and powdered whole milk in a tightly covered container in a cool, dry place. Held at refrigerator temperature (45° F. or below), powdered skim or whole milk of good quality can given satisfactory results for almost 1 year. Held at high temperature (80° F. to 90° F.), powdered whole milk, because of its fat content, may develop rancid flavors rather quickly. Powdered skim milk, in time, will develop off-flavors when stored at high temperatures.

Evaporated milk may develop a musty off-flavor after storage for more than 18 months at room temperature (70° F.). Small solid particles, generally known as "milkstones" may develop. These have no detrimental effect on the use of the milk and are not harmful.

TABLE OF EQUIVALENTS FOR FRESH, EVAPORATED AND POWDERED WHOLE OR SKIM MILK

FRESH LIQUID MILK			EVAPORATED MILK									DRY WHOLE MILK							DRY SKIM MILK						
Weight		Amounts (approx.)	Weight			Amounts (approx.)			Water (to be added) Amounts (approx.)				Weight		Amounts (approx.)		Water (to be added) Amounts (approx.)			Weight		Amounts (approx.)		Water (to be added) Amounts (approx.)		
lbs	oz	pts | qts | gals	lbs	oz | cup		pts | qts | gals			cup | pts | qts | gals				lbs	oz	cups | gals		pts | qts | gals			lbs	oz	cups | qts		pts | qts | gals	
1	1	1 pt		9	1 cup				1 cup					2	½ cup		1 pt				1¾	⅜ cups		1 pt		
2	2	1 qt	1	2		1 pt			1 pt					4	⅞ cup		1 qt				3½	¾ cups		1 qt		
8	8	1 gal	4	7		2 qt			2 qt			1		3½ cups		2 qt				14	3 cups		1 gal		
42	8	5 gal	22	3		2½ gal			2½ gal		5		1½ plus gal		1 gal			4	6	3¾ qts		5 gal		
85		10 gal	44	6		5 gal			5 gal		10		3 plus gal		2 gal			8	12	7½ qts		10 gal		

To Reconstitute Evaporated Milk

Combine equal amounts of evaporated milk and water.

To Reconstitute Powdered Milk

Place measured amount of water in mixing bowl. Sprinkle milk powder into water, slowly, stirring constantly with hand or mechanical whip to properly incorporate the powder.

Stir until milk powder is completely dissolved.

NOTE.—1. A better product, for beverage purposes, is obtained when powdered whole milk is reconstituted and held at refrigerator temperature for about 12 hours before using. Reconstituted milk is a perishable product and must be handled in the same way as fresh milk.

2. For use in coffee or on cereals, reconstitute powdered milk with ½ the amount of water specified in Table, or combine reconstituted milk with evaporated milk.

3. The addition of 2 teaspoons vanilla flavoring and 1 teaspoon salt to 1 gallon reconstituted milk improves the flavor of the milk when used for drinking.

4. Powdered milk can be reconstituted with hot water, if hot milk is desired.

Quick-Frozen Foods

Quick freezing is a method of preserving fruits, vegetables, fish, poultry and meat in the natural state, by subjecting the product to a low temperature for a relatively short period of time.

Advantages of Using Quick Frozen Foods in the Navy

They are packed in convenient-sized containers which can be easily handled and stored.

They have the appearance and flavor of fresh products.

They retain a high per cent of their original vitamin and mineral content.

They are uniform in size and quality.

They are easy to prepare for cooking and serving.

They save shipping space because practically all waste is eliminated before packing.

Storage: All frozen foods are perishable and should be placed under refrigeration immediately upon delivery. The refrigeration temperatures for the various products should be about 0° F. to 8° F. if to be kept for any length of time.

Good circulation of air around the containers is important.

The arrangement of cartons should also be given careful consideration. Products to be used first should be placed so they can be easily and quickly procured.

Defrosting: The length of time necessary for defrosting is dependent upon the type of product and size of the container. In general, vegetables need not be defrosted. Meat and poultry need defrosting so that they may be prepared for cooking. Fruits are thawed but used while still cold. Defrosted products are highly perishable and should be used immediately after they have been thawed.

Cooking: Directions for preparing and cooking frozen vegetables, meats and poultry are given under their respective classification.

Package Directions: Read carefully and follow exactly the directions printed on the container for storing, defrosting and cooking. This is important.

INFORMATION ON FROZEN EGGS

An equivalent amount of frozen whole eggs, frozen egg whites and frozen egg yolks may be used in place of fresh eggs or reconstituted powdered eggs.

Whole eggs may be made from frozen whites and yolks by combining them in proportion of 2 parts whites to 1 part yolks.

Allow frozen eggs to thaw before using. Thawing should take place slowly without application of heat. When thawing is complete, use and treat the same as fresh eggs.

TIME-TABLE FOR DEEP FAT FRYING

	TEMPERATURE	TIME
		Minutes
Doughnuts:		
Cake	380°F. to 390°F.	1½ to 2
Yeast Raised	370°F. to 380°F.	1¾ to 2½
Fish:		
Cakes	370°F. to 375°F.	2 to 3
Clams	365°F. to 370°F.	1 to 3
Fillets (large)	365°F. to 370°F.	4 to 6
Fillets (small)	370°F. to 375°F.	3 to 5
Oysters	355°F. to 360°F.	1 to 4
Scallops	355°F. to 360°F.	3 to 5
Smelts	370°F. to 375°F.	4 to 6
Fruit:		
Bananas	370°F. to 375°F.	1 to 3
Fritters	370°F. to 375°F.	3 to 5
Meat:		
Cutlets (1 inch thick)	345°F. to 350°F.	5 to 8
Chops, breaded	345°F. to 350°F.	5 to 8
Miscellaneous:		
Chinese Noodles	375°F. to 380°F.	1
Croquettes	370°F. to 375°F.	3 to 4
French Toast	360°F.	2 to 3
Poultry:		
Chicken (small pieces)	365°F. to 370°F.	7 to 10
Chicken (large pieces, ½ chicken)	345°F. to 350°F.	8 to 14
Vegetables:		
Asparagus	375°F. to 380°F.	5 to 7
Cauliflower	375°F. to 380°F.	5 to 7
Egg Plant	375°F. to 380°F.	5 to 7
Onions, French Fried	340°F. to 345°F.	5 to 6
Potato Chips	325°F. to 335°F.	4 to 5
Potatoes, French Fried:		
Blanching	365°F. to 375°F.	6 to 8
Browning	395°F. to 400°F.	2 to 3
Potatoes, Shoestring or Julienne	325°F. to 335°F.	6 to 10

OVEN TEMPERATURES

Terms Commonly Used to Describe Oven Temperatures

Term:	Temperature:
Slow	250°F.–350°F.
Moderate	350°F.–400°F.
Hot	400°F.–450°F.
Very hot	450°F.–500°F.

SIZES OF SCOOPS OR DIPPERS

No. Per Quart	Measure	Approx. Weight	Use
30	⅛ cup (2 tablespoons)	1 ounce	Drop cookies
24	⅙ cup (2⅔ tablespoons)	2 ounces	Cream puffs, fritters
20	⅕ cup (3⅕ tablespoons)	2½ to 3 ounces	Muffins, fish balls
16	¼ cup (4 tablespoons)	3 to 3½ ounces	Croquettes
10	⅖ cup (6⅔ tablespoons)	3½ to 4 ounces	Vegetables, desserts
8	½ cup (8 tablespoons)	4 to 4½ ounces	Vegetables, desserts
6	¾ cup (12 tablespoons)	5 ounces	Patties, salads

EQUIVALENTS OF WEIGHTS AND MEASURES

3 teaspoons .... 1 tablespoon

16 tablespoons .... 1 cup

1 cup (standard measuring) .... ½ pint (8 fluid ounces)

2 cups .... 1 pint

2 pints .... 1 quart

4 quarts .... 1 gallon

8 quarts (dry) .... 1 peck

4 pecks .... 1 bushel

16 ounces .... 1 pound

32 ounces .... 1 fluid quart

Mess Kit Spoon (Army) .... 1 tablespoon

No. 55 Dipper (Army) .... 1¾ quarts

No. 56 Dipper (Army) .... 1 quart

Canteen or Mess Kit Cup (Army and Navy) .... 1½ pints

ABBREVIATIONS

A. P. = as purchased   pt. = pint

E. P. = edible portion   qt. = quart

t. or tsp. = teaspoon   gal. = gallon

T. or tbsp. = tablespoon   oz. = ounce

c. = cup   lb. = pound

WEIGHTS AND APPROXIMATE EQUIVALENTS OF SOME COMMON FOODS

	WEIGHTS	APPROX. AMOUNTS
Allspice, ground	1 ounce	4½ tablespoons
Apples, A. P.	1 pound	1 pint, E. P.
Apples, diced	1 pound	1 quart
Apricots, dried, A. P.	1 pound	1½ pints
Bacon, cooked, diced	1 pound	1½ cups
Bacon, uncooked	1 pound	15 to 20 strips
Bacon, uncooked, diced	1 pound	1 pint
Bacon fat, melted	7½ ounces	1 cup
Baking powder	1 ounce	2½ tablespoons
Bananas, sliced	1 pound	1 pint
Beans, dried	1 pound	2⅓ cups
Beans, dried, 1 pound after cooking	2½ pounds	1½ to 1¾ quarts
Beef, cooked, chopped	1 pound	1 pint
Beef, cooked, diced	1 pound	1½ pints
Beef, uncooked, ground	1 pound	1 pint
Boiled dressing, cooked	1 pound	1 pint
Bread, broken	1 pound	½ gallon
Bread, soft, broken	1 pound	2¼ quarts
Bread crumbs, dry	1 pound	1¼ quarts
Bread crumbs, fresh	1 pound	½ gallon
Butter	1 pound	1 pint
Cabbage, chopped or shredded	1 pound	1 quart
Carrots	1 pound	6 small
Carrots, diced, cooked	1 pound	1½ pints
Carrots, raw, diced	1 pound	1½ pints
Celery, diced	1 pound	1 quart
Cheese, diced ¼ inch, or ground	1 pound	3½ cups
Cheese, grated	1 pound	1 quart

WEIGHTS AND APPROXIMATE EQUIVALENTS OF SOME COMMON FOODS

	WEIGHTS	APPROX. AMOUNTS
Chicken, cooked, cubed	1 pound	1½ pints
Chili powder	1 ounce	6 tablespoons
Chocolate	1 pound	16 squares
Chocolate, grated	1 pound	1 quart
	1 ounce	4 tablespoons
Chocolate, melted	1 pound	1 pint
Cinnamon, ground	1 ounce	4½ tablespoons
Clams	1 quart	24 to 40 large
	1 quart	40 to 60 medium
Cloves, ground	1 ounce	¼ cup
Cloves, whole	1 ounce	6 tablespoons
Cocoa	1 pound	4½ cups
Coconut, shredded	1 pound	1¾ quarts
Coffee, coarse grind	1 pound	4¾ cups
Coffee, fine grind	1 pound	1¼ quarts
Cornflakes	1 pound	1 gallon
Cornmeal	1 pound	1½ pints
Corn sirup	11 ounces	1 cup
Corn starch	1 ounce	3 tablespoons
Crab, whole, A. P.	½ pound	½ cup meat
Crab meat, flaked	½ pound	1½ pints
Cracked wheat	1 pound	1½ pints
Cranberries, cooked	1 pound	1 quart
Cranberries, raw	1 pound	1 quart
Cream of tartar	1 ounce	3 tablespoons
Cucumbers, diced	1 pound	1½ pints
Currants, dried	1 pound	1½ pints
Curry powder	1 ounce	4½ tablespoons
Dates, pitted	1 pound	1½ pints

WEIGHTS AND APPROXIMATE EQUIVALENTS OF SOME COMMON FOODS

	WEIGHTS	APPROX. AMOUNTS
Eggs, hard-cooked, chopped	1 pound	2¾ cups
Eggs, whites	(18) 1 pound	1 pint
Eggs, whole	(10) 1 pound	1 pint
Eggs, yolks	(24) 1 pound	1 pint
Flour, white	1 pound	1 quart
French dressing	15 ounces	1 pint
Gelatin, granulated, unflavored	1 ounce	3¼ tablespoons
Gelatin, dessert, flavored	1 pound	2⅓ cups
Ginger, ground	1 ounce	5 tablespoons
Grapefruit, size 54	1	1½ cups sections
Ham, cooked, diced	1 pound	1½ pints
Hominy grits	1 pound	1½ pints
Honey	11 ounces	1 cup
Horse-radish, prepared	1 ounce	2 tablespoons
Jam	1 pound	1½ cups
Lemons	4 to 5	1 cup juice
Lemon juice	1 ounce	2 tablespoons
Lemon juice powder, synthetic	3 ounces plus 1 quart water.	1 quart
Lemon rind	1 ounce	¼ cup
Lettuce, A. P. (average head)	9 ounces	1 medium head
Lettuce, broken, 2-inch pieces	1 pound	½ gallon
Macaroni, 1-inch pieces, uncooked	1 pound	1¼ quarts
Macaroni, 1 pound, after cooking	5 pounds	2¼ quarts
Maple tablets, imitation	2 tablets	1 teaspoon flavoring
	12 tablets	2 tablespoons flavoring
Mayonnaise	1 pound	1 pint
Milk, evaporated, No. 1 tall can	14½ ounces	1⅔ cups
Milk, liquid	8 ounces	1 cup
Milk, powdered	1 pound	2½ cups

WEIGHTS AND APPROXIMATE EQUIVALENTS OF SOME COMMON FOODS

	WEIGHTS	APPROX. AMOUNTS
Molasses	11 ounces	1 cup
Mushrooms, fresh, sliced	1 pound	1¾ quarts
Mustard, dry	1 ounce	4½ tablespoons
Mustard, prepared	1 ounce	¼ cup
Noodles, uncooked	1 pound	2¼ quarts
Noodles, 1 pound, after cooking	4½ pounds	3½ quarts
Nutmeats	1 pound	1 quart
Nutmeg, ground	1 ounce	3½ tablespoons
Oats, rolled	1 pound	4¾ cups
Oats, rolled, cooked	1 pound	3 to 3½ cups
Oil	7½ ounces	1 cup
Onions, chopped	1 pound	1½ pints
Onions, dehydrated	2 ounces	1 cup
Onions, dehydrated, reconstituted	2 ounces plus 1 quart water.	1 pound chopped onions
Oranges	8 medium	1 quart sections
	3 average size	1 cup juice
Orange rind	1 ounce	¼ cup
Oysters	1 quart	24 to 40 large
	1 quart	60 to 100 small
Paprika	1 ounce	4½ tablespoons
Parsley, chopped	3 ounces	1 cup
Peaches, canned, sliced, drained	1 pound	1 pint
Peanut butter	1 pound	1¾ cups
Peas, cooked	1¼ pounds	1 pint
Peas, green or yellow, split	1 pound	2¼ cups
Peas, 1 pound dried, after cooking	2½ pounds	5½ cups
Pepper, ground	1 ounce	3½ tablespoons
Peppers, green, chopped	1 pound	1 quart
Pickles, chopped	1 pound	1½ pints
Pickles, sweet relish	1 pound	2¾ cups
Pimientos, chopped	1 (7-ounce) can	1 cup
Pineapple, diced or tidbits	1 pound	1 pint

WEIGHTS AND APPROXIMATE EQUIVALENTS OF SOME COMMON FOODS

	WEIGHTS	AMOUNTS (approx.)
Pineapple, fresh	2 pounds	1 pineapple
Potatoes, cooked, diced	1 pound	2½ cups
Potatoes, mashed	1 pound	1 pint
Raisins, seedless	1 pound	1½ pints
Rice, uncooked	1 pound	1 pint
Rice, 1 pound, after cooking	3 pounds 6 ounces	½ gallon
Sage	1 ounce	½ cup
Salmon, flaked	1 pound	1 pint
Salt	1 ounce	2 tablespoons
Shortening	1 pound	1 pint
Soda	1 ounce	2 tablespoons
Spaghetti, 2-inch pieces, uncooked	1 pound	1¼ quarts
Spaghetti, 1 pound, after cooking	3 pounds	½ gallon
Spinach, raw, chopped	1 pound	1 gallon
Sugar, brown	1 pound	1½ pints
Sugar, confectioner's	1 pound	3½ cups
Sugar, granulated	1 pound	1 pint
Tapioca, pearl	1 pound	3½ cups
Tapioca, quick-cooking	1 pound	2¾ cups
Tea	1 pound	1½ quarts
Tomatoes, fresh, diced	1 pound	1 pint
Tuna fish, flaked	1 pound	1 pint
Turnips, raw, diced	1 pound	1½ pints
Vanilla	1 ounce	2 tablespoons
Vanilla tablets, imitation	1 tablet / 6 tablets	1 teaspoon flavoring / 2 tablespoons flavoring
Vinegar	1 ounce	2 tablespoons
Wheat cereal, granulated	1 pound	1½ pints
Yeast, compressed	½ ounce	1 cake

Cookery Terms

Bake: To cook by dry heat in an oven. When applied to meats it is called *Roasting*.

Baste: To moisten foods while cooking, especially while roasting meat. Melted fat, meat drippings, stock, water or water and fat may be used.

Beat: To make a mixture smooth or to introduce air by using a lifting motion with spoon or whip.

Blanch: To rinse with boiling water, drain, and rinse in cold water. Used for rice, macaroni and other pastes to prevent sticking.

To cook in hot deep fat for a short time until clear but not brown. Used for potatoes.

Blend: To mix thoroughly two or more ingredients.

Boil: To cook in a liquid which bubbles actively during the time of cooking. The boiling temperature at sea level is 212°F. When applied to eggs, the terms "hard-cooked" and "soft-cooked" are used.

Braise: To brown meat or vegetables in a small amount of fat, then to cook slowly, covered, at simmering temperature (185°F. to 210°F.) in a small amount of liquid. The liquid may be juices from meat, or added water, milk, or meat stock.

Bread: To dip appropriate food into an egg-milk mixture and then into fine dry crumbs.

Broil: To cook under or over direct heat to *grill*. *Oven-broil:* to cook in an oven, uncovered. No liquid is added. *Pan-broil:* to cook uncovered on a hot griddle or in hot pan, removing grease as it accumulates. No liquid is added.

Candy: To cook in sugar or sirup.

Caramelize: To heat sugar or foods containing sugar until sugar melts and a brown color and characteristic flavor develop.

Chill: To place in a refrigerator or cool place until cold.

Chop: To cut into pieces with a knife or chopper.

Coat: To cover entire surface of food with a given mixture.

Cream: Mixing until smooth, sugar, shortening and other ingredients to incorporate air so that resultant mixture increases appreciably in volume and is thoroughly blended.

Cube: To cut into approximately ¼ to ½ inch squares.

Cut In Shortening: To combine firm shortening and flour with pastry blender or knife.

Dice: To cut into ¼ inch or smaller cubes.

Dissolve: To mix a solid dry substance with a liquid until solid is in solution.

Dredge: To sprinkle or coat with flour, sugar, or meal.

Fricassee: To cook by braising; usually applied to fowl, or veal cut into pieces.

Frizzle: To cook in a small amount of fat until food is crisp and curled at the edges.

Fry: To cook in hot fat. When a small amount of fat is used, the process is known as *pan-frying* or *sauteeing;* when food is partially covered *shallow frying;* when food is completely covered, *deep-fat frying.*

Grill: See *Broil.*

Larding: To cover uncooked lean meat or fish with strips of fat, or to insert strips of fat with a skewer.

Marinate: To cover with French dressing and to let stand for a short length of time.

Milk, liquid: Refers to fresh fluid milk or evaporated or powdered milk reconstituted to the equivalent of fresh fluid milk.

Mince: To cut or chop into very small fine pieces using knife or chopper.

Mixing: To unite two or more ingredients.

Oven-broil: See *Broil.*

Pan-broil: See *Broil.*

Pan-fry: See *Fry.*

Parboil: To boil in water until partially cooked.

Peel: To remove skin, using a knife or peeling machine.

Render: To melt fat trimmed from meats by heating slowly at low temperature.

Roast: See *Bake.*

Sauté: See *Fry.*

Scallop: To bake food, usually cut in pieces, with a sauce or other liquid.

Score: To cut shallow slits or gashes in surface of food with knife, fork or other implement.

Sear: To brown the surface of meat by a short application of intense heat to develop flavor and improve appearance.

Shred: To cut or tear into thin strips or pieces using a knife or a shredder attachment.

Simmer: To cook in liquid at a temperature just below the boiling point (185°F. to 210°F.).

Steam: To cook in steam with or without pressure.

Steep: To let stand in hot liquid below boiling temperature to extract flavor, color or other qualities from a specific food.

Stew: To simmer in liquid to cover or in smaller amount.

Sugar: Refers to granulated unless otherwise specified in recipe.

Toast: To brown surface of a food by application of direct heat.

Toss: To mix lightly. Usually used for salad ingredients.

Truss: To bind or fasten together.

Whip: To beat rapidly to increase volume by incorporating air.

The Recipes

Information

Recipes are important. They are valuable as a guide to menu planning and to the preparation of food of high quality.

The recipes in this book have been selected and tested particularly for Navy use. They comprise a wide variety of foods based mainly upon the issues for a Navy ration.

To obtain the desired results it is advisable to have a copy of the recipe at hand during food preparation. The recipe should be read several times in order to become thoroughly familiar with the contents before starting to prepare the food, and directions should be carefully followed.

WHAT TO KNOW ABOUT THESE RECIPES

The recipes have been calculated on the basis of 100 portions.

Blank Column

A blank column on the right side of the recipe has been reserved for the commissary steward to insert the calculations needed for supplies which apply to his respective mess. On page 3, in the Knickerbocker Bean Soup recipe, the use of the blank column is demonstrated. These calculations should be made in pencil so that changes can easily be made when necessary.

Yield and Portion

The yield for each recipe is given in weights or amounts (measures) and both are specified when considered necessary. This applies also to the individual portion. Because of the variability in equipment and conditions under which the food must be prepared, the *approximate* weights and amounts, rather than the exact weights and amounts, are specified.

If the size of the portions are too large, or too small, for a given mess, the size of the portions should be regulated to suit the needs of the men.

Seasonings

Seasonings have an important place in the Navy diet as they help to relieve monotony and make the food more palatable and interesting.

A good cook uses seasonings wisely and varies them often. The amounts of seasonings included in various recipes throughout the book are on the "mild side," designed to suit the average taste. Over-seasoning is as undesirable as under-seasoning. Salt and pepper should be used with discretion. Seasonings such as parsley, green pepper, garlic, and pimiento may be omitted, when not available, without affecting the flavor of the food too much.

Weights and Measures

Ingredients are designated in both *weights* and *amounts* (measures). The *amount* specified for each ingredient is comparable to its *weight* and should be used only when scales for weighing are not available. More accurate results can be expected if the ingredients can be weighed instead of measured.

Amounts (measures) of ingredients are designated in teaspoons, tablespoons, cups, pints, quarts and gallons.

The *8-ounce* standard measuring cup graduated in ¼'s, ⅓'s, and ½'s is used as a basis for the cup measurements.

For ingredients using 1 cup (½ pint) or more, the amount is expressed in terms of pints, quarts, and gallons.

Ladles, dippers and scoops, of definite measure, are also necessary for making accurate measurements (page 24).

All ingredients in these recipes are based on *LEVEL* measurements. These must be made *accurately* in order to obtain best results.

Tables of Weights and Measures are given on page 24.

A.P. and E.P.

A.P. refers to the net weight of a product "as purchased" in its natural state, parts of which are considered not edible.

For example, the net weight of a crate of grapefruit is approximately 74 pounds, as purchased (A.P.). The peelings weigh about 29 pounds, leaving an "edible portion" (E.P.), of 45 pounds.

Notes

The *NOTE* appearing below the recipe contains valuable information pertaining to the recipe. It frequently contains suggestions on methods of preparation and should be carefully read before preparing the recipe.

Variations

Variations of the basic recipe are valuable because they show how the basic recipe can be easily changed into a different recipe by the substitution of one or more ingredients. Variations in this way help to relieve monotony in the diet.

Each variation is listed in the index as a separate recipe.

Time and Temperatures

The length of time for cooking is given in each recipe, and should be carefully noted. This information is particularly helpful as a guide in meal planning.

Specific temperatures for cooking and baking in the oven are also given.

Tables containing general information on preparation and cooking-time for cereals, sauces, fruits, vegetables and meat are given in each respective section.

These recipes have been developed and tested at altitudes less than 5,000 feet. The temperature of boiling water referred to in these recipes is 212° F.

Simmering temperatures range between 180° F. and 210° F.

Average room temperature is considered to be 68° F. to 70° F.

Beverages
Coffee

Roasted coffee is a delicate and perishable product. Whether ground or in the bean, unless vacuum packed in tin, coffee requires careful handling. It loses both flavor and strength on contact with air.

Store coffee, tightly covered, in a cool, dry place. Avoid storing it near foods which have strong odors. Roasted coffee readily absorbs foreign odors, and these make themselves apparent in the finished brew.

If coffee in the bean is procured for general mess use, grind only the quantity required just previous to using it each time the brew is made.

Navy coffee has been expertly blended and roasted. If a few simple rules for making coffee are followed, a rich and enjoyable brew may be expected.

General Rules

Always use clean equipment.
Rinse urn bag with fresh cold water before using.
Measure coffee and water accurately.
Use freshly drawn cold water which has been brought to a rapid bubbling boil for brewing coffee.
Keep coffee covered while brewing.
Hold finished coffee at temperature of 185° F. to 190° F. until served. Never allow finished coffee to boil.
Remove grounds as soon as coffee is made. Seepage from coffee grounds impairs the good flavor and aroma.
Use fresh coffee for each brew. Never use any portion of used coffee grounds a second time.
Make coffee fresh as needed. Never allow more than an hour to elapse between making and serving the coffee.

Care of Urn Equipment

Keep all parts of urn equipment scrupulously clean.

Rinse urn thoroughly with clear, hot water after each use.
Wash urn twice every 24 hours using urn brush, hot water, and washing soda. Use approximately 1 tablespoon washing soda for each quart water. Never use soap or soap powder.
Rinse urn thoroughly several times with clear, hot water. Be sure that all traces of washing soda are removed.
Remove coffee faucet on urn daily. Scrub all parts thoroughly with brush, hot water, and washing soda. Rinse throughly with clear, hot water. Insert long, thin coffee pipe brush and scrub inside of faucet pipe and plug at bottom of inner liner thoroughly. Rinse with clear, hot water.
Clean gauge glasses at least twice each week using gauge glass brush, hot water, and washing soda. Rinse thoroughly with clear, hot water.
Rinse urn bag in clear, cold water after each use. Keep bag submerged in cold water at all times when not in use. Renew cloth bag frequently.
If filter basket is used, wash and dry all parts thoroughly after each use.

Care of Glass Coffee-Makers

Wash upper and lower bowls in clear, hot water after each use.
Rinse filter cloth in clear, cold water. Keep submerged in cold water when not in use. Renew frequently. Scald new filter cloth. Rinse in cold water before using.
Dry outside of upper and lower bowls before placing over heat. Never allow empty bowl to remain on heat.
Scrub out tube of upper bowl regularly with stiff brush to remove all coffee stains.
Place coffee-maker on rubber, asbestos, or cork mat after removing from heating unit. Heat-resistant glass may break if placed while hot on a cold surface.

METHODS OF MAKING COFFEE

Urn Bag Method

Yield: Approx. 6 gallons.

Portion: 1 cup (approx. 8 ounces).

INGREDIENTS	100 PORTIONS			PORTIONS
	WEIGHTS		AMOUNTS (approx.)	
	Pounds	Ounces		
Water, freshly drawn, cold	---	---	6¼ gallons	
Coffee, regular Navy grind	3	---	3¾ quarts	

Pour water into hot water boiler. Heat to boiling temperature.

Fill jacket of coffee urn with water ¾ full as indicated on the gauge glass. Maintain temperature of this water at 185° F. to 190° F.

Rinse urn bag with clear, cold water. Place in position in empty urn, in which coffee is to be made, making sure that both the urn bag and urn ring are correct size.

Place coffee in urn bag.

Draw off boiling water, 1 gallon at a time. Pour slowly in circular motion over coffee in bag. Keep covered between pouring of each gallon of water to keep heat and aroma in the coffee brew.

Repour 4 gallons brewed coffee over coffee grounds.

Remove urn bag and coffee grounds, immediately after all the brewed coffee has dripped through.

Draw off 1 gallon brewed coffee. Repour into urn to insure uniform strength throughout the brew.

Hold finished coffee at temperature of 185° F. to 190° F. until served.

Empty coffee grounds from urn bag. Rinse bag thoroughly in clear, cold water. Keep submerged in cold water until used again.

NOTE.—1. If urn is not equipped with hot water boiler, heat water for brewing coffee in a separate utensil.

2. The jacket water is used to keep coffee warm and *must not* be used for brewing the coffee.

3. In making larger quantities of coffee, repour ⅔ of the brew over coffee grounds.

Bag Method

Pour water into large kettle. Heat to boiling temperature.

Place coffee in large, clean bag made of washed, unbleached muslin.

Tie top of bag securely and loosely to permit swelling of coffee. Tie with cord long enough to fasten to handles of kettle to facilitate removal.

Place bag of coffee in boiling water. Tie cord to handles of kettle.

Reduce heat to keep water below boiling temperature.

Submerge bag with stick or paddle. Push up and down to force water through grounds.

Cover kettle. Allow bag to remain in water 10 to 15 minutes, depending on strength of brew desired.

Lift bag out of brew. Hold over kettle until thoroughly drained.

Remove bag. Empty coffee grounds immediately. Wash bag in clear, cold water. Keep submerged in cold water until used again.

Hold finished coffee at temperature of 185° F. to 190° F. until served.

NOTE.—1. Use kettle in which coffee is made for coffee only.

2. Renew coffee bag frequently.

Filter or Drip Method

Yield: Approx. 6 gallons

Portion: 1 cup (approx. 8 ounces)

INGREDIENTS	100 PORTIONS			..........PORTIONS
	WEIGHTS		AMOUNTS (approx.)	
	Pounds	*Ounces*		
Water, freshly drawn, cold......	---	---	6¼ gallons..........	
Coffee, fine grind................	3	...	3¾ quarts..........	

Pour water into hot water boiler. Heat to boiling temperature.

Fill jacket of coffee urn with water ¾ full as indicated on the gauge glass. Maintain temperature of this water at 185° F. to 190° F.

Place filter paper evenly and smoothly over perforations in clean, dry filter basket.

Spread coffee evenly over filter paper so that no coffee goes under the paper.

Insert water spreader, or sieve, over coffee in filter basket. Place basket in position over empty coffee urn.

Draw off boiling water, 1 gallon at a time. Pour slowly in circular motion over coffee in basket. Keep covered between pouring of each gallon of water to keep heat and aroma in coffee brew.

Remove filter basket, after all water has dripped through.

Draw off 1 gallon brewed coffee. Repour into urn to insure uniform strength throughout the brew.

Hold finished coffee at temperature of 185° F. to 190° F. until served.

Empty coffee grounds from filter basket. Wash and dry all parts thoroughly.

NOTE.—Some filter devices are equipped with a very fine mesh sieve and do not require filter paper. Use same procedure for brewing coffee. Do not omit filter paper in equipment designed for its use.

Coffee Prepared With Cream and Sugar

Yield: Approx. 6 gallons.

Portion: 1 cup (approx. 8 ounces).

INGREDIENTS	100 PORTIONS			..........PORTIONS
	WEIGHTS		AMOUNTS (approx.)	
	Pounds	*Ounces*		
Milk, evaported	2	12	3 No. 1 tall (14½ oz.) cans (1¼ quarts).	
Water, hot	....	....	1 quart	
Sugar	4	...	½ gallon	
Coffee brew, hot..................	....	....	6 gallons	

Combine milk and water. Dissolve sugar in coffee. Pour milk into coffee. Mix thoroughly.

NOTE.—1½ pounds (1¼ quarts) powdered skim milk and 1½ quarts water may be used in place of 3 No. 1 cans (1¼ quarts) evaporated milk and 1 quart water.

Percolator Method

(For small amounts)

Yield: 6 cups.   Portion: 1 cup (approx. 8 ounces).

INGREDIENTS	6 PORTIONS			............PORTIONS
	WEIGHTS		AMOUNTS (approx.)	
	Pounds	*Ounces*		
Water, freshly drawn, cold......	....	....	6½ cups	....
Coffee	....	....	7½ tablespoons	....

Measure water into pot. Insert basket of percolator into pot. Measure coffee into basket.

Place pot over heat. Heat water to boiling temperature. Allow water to percolate through coffee about 10 minutes.

NOTE.—Clean and rinse percolator thoroughly after each use.

Vacuum-Type Coffee Maker Method

(For small amounts)

Yield: 8 (8-ounce) cups.   Portion: 1 cup (approx. 8 ounces).

INGREDIENTS	8 PORTIONS			............PORTIONS
	WEIGHTS		AMOUNTS (approx.)	
	Pounds	*Ounces*		
Water, freshly drawn, cold......	....	....	½ gallon	....
Coffee, fine grind....................	....	3½	¾ cup	....

Pour water into lower bowl. Place over heat and bring to a boil. Do not fill lower bowl. Leave air space of 1 to 2 inches below neck.

Moisten filter cloth and tie tightly over filter. Place in seat of funnel, or if using glass rod, place in position. Put in coffee.

When water in lower bowl is boiling, insert upper glass bowl into lower bowl with slight twist so that a perfect seal forms at neck of bowl. Water will start going from lower to upper bowl almost immediately. As soon as all the water, except a small amount below bottom of tube, has risen, stir coffee well and leave on heat about 2 minutes longer.

Remove from heat and place on rubber, asbestos, or cork mat. As the bowl cools, a vacuum is created and the filtered coffee flows into the lower bowl in only a few seconds.

Remove the funnel with a gentle side to side motion. The coffee is now ready to serve. Keep hot but do not allow it to boil.

NOTE.—1. Most of the vacuum-type coffee makers are made of glass, although there are some made of part glass and metal, all metal, or part plastic.

2. Directions supplied by different manufacturers of vacuum coffee makers vary, depending on type of grind, amount of coffee to be used, and on differences in the construction of the coffee maker.

Iced Coffee

Prepare coffee brew. Cool. Stir in sufficient cracked ice to chill.

Serve with or without cream.

NOTE.—1. If coffee is to be sweetened, add sugar while brew is still hot.

2. Coffee may be brewed double strength and, while still hot, sufficient ice added to chill thoroughly.

Tea

Tea must be made just previous to serving. The tea leaves must never be boiled as this impairs the flavor and gives the tea a bitter taste.

Hot Tea

Yield: Approx. 6 gallons.

Portion: 1 cup (approx. 8 ounces).

INGREDIENTS	100 PORTIONS			..........PORTIONS
	WEIGHTS		AMOUNTS (approx.)	
	Pounds	*Ounces*		
Water, freshly drawn, cold......	....	....	6¼ gallons	....
Tea	....	6	1¼ pints	....

Place tea in muslin bag large enough to hold about three times the amount specified to allow for swelling of tea.

Tie top of bag with cord long enough to be fastened to handle of kettle to facilitate removal.

Measure water into kettle. Heat to boiling temperature. Turn off heat.

Drop tea bag into water. Tie cord to handle of kettle. Cover. Steep 5 to 7 minutes, depending upon strength of brew desired.

Remove bag. Serve tea in preheated pitchers.

Iced Tea

Use 7 ounces (1⅓ pints) tea and 6¼ gallons water. Prepare brew. Sweeten tea when hot, using approximately 4 ounces (½ cup) sugar for each gallon of tea.

Cool. Stir in enough cracked ice to chill. Serve with lemon.

CHOCOLATE SIRUP

Yield: Approx. 1 gallon.   Portion: Approx. 1½ ounces.

INGREDIENTS	100 PORTIONS			............Portions
	WEIGHTS		AMOUNTS (approx.)	
	Pounds	Ounces		
Cocoa	2	....	2¼ quarts	
Sugar	3	....	1½ quarts	
Salt	....	½	1 tablespoon	
Water, boiling	....	....	1¼ gallons	
Vanilla	....	1	2 tablespoons	

Mix together cocoa, sugar and salt. Stir in enough boiling water to form a smooth paste. Add remaining water. Boil 5 minutes. Add vanilla.

NOTE.—1. This sirup can be kept under refrigeration for several days.

2. 3 pounds (48 squares) chocolate, melted, may be used in place of 2 pounds (2¼ quarts) cocoa.

3. Chocolate sirup may be used as a sauce for ice cream or puddings, or for making cocoa and chocolate milk.

HOT COCOA

Yield: Approx. 6¼ gallons.   Portion: 1 cup (approx. 8 ounces).

INGREDIENTS	100 PORTIONS			............Portions
	WEIGHTS		AMOUNTS (approx.)	
	Pounds	Ounces		
Milk, liquid	....	....	5½ gallons	
Cocoa	1	8	1½ quarts	
Sugar	3	....	1½ quarts	
Salt	....	⅙	1 teaspoon	
Water	....	....	1½ quarts	

Heat milk to boiling temperature over hot water or in steam-jacketed kettle. Do not boil.

Combine cocoa, sugar and salt. Add water gradually to make a smooth paste. Heat to boiling temperature.

Stir cocoa sirup into milk. Beat thoroughly with wire whip.

COCOA OR CHOCOLATE MILK

Yield: Approx. 6¼ gallons.   Portion: 1 cup (approx. 8 ounces).

INGREDIENTS	100 PORTIONS			........Portions
	WEIGHTS		AMOUNTS (approx.)	
	Pounds	Ounces		
Chocolate Sirup (page 39)........	10	....	1¼ gallons	
Milk, liquid	....	....	5 gallons	

Hot: Add Chocolate Sirup to milk which has been heated to boiling temperature and stir thoroughly.

Cold: Add Chocolate Sirup to chilled milk. Stir thoroughly.

NOTE.—Reconstituted evaporated or powdered milk may be used.

Lemon Juice Powder, Synthetic

Navy issue lemon juice powder, synthetic, can be used satisfactorily, when properly reconstituted with water, in place of fresh lemon juice specified in the recipes and bakery formulas. Three ounces lemon juice powder, synthetic dissolved in 1 quart water is equivalent to 1 quart juice of fresh lemons.

Composition

This product is a mixture of dried pure lemon juice with corn sirup, dextrose, citric acid, ascorbic acid (vitamin C), tricalcium phosphate, and oil of lemon.

The synthetic powder will make six times as much beverage by volume as the straight lemon juice powder and will result in substantial saving of space and containers. Sufficient ascorbic acid has been added so that a 12-ounce serving of the beverage will furnish approximately 60 per cent of the daily requirement of vitamin C.

It is not possible to incorporate sufficient oil of lemon in the powder to give the maximum desired flavor without impairing keeping qualities. Therefore, in using synthetic lemon juice powder in the bakery products, puddings and fillings specifying lemon juice, it is often desirable to supplement the powder with additional oil of lemon.

The addition of Navy issue lemon oil flavoring to puddings, custards, fillings and other products in which synthetic lemon juice powder is used, gives a more pleasing flavor.

Use from ½ to 1 teaspoon of lemon oil flavoring to 1 pint of pudding or filling.

LEMONADE

(Using Lemon Juice Powder, Synthetic)

Yield: Approx. 6¼ gallons.   Portion: 1 cup (approx. 8 ounces).

INGREDIENTS	100 PORTIONS			........Portions
	WEIGHTS		AMOUNTS (approx.)	
	Pounds	Ounces		
Lemon juice powder	....	12	1⅔ cups	
Sugar	5	....	2½ quarts	
Water, cold	....	....	6 gallons................	

Dissolve the lemon juice powder and sugar in water. Serve.

NOTE.—Do *not* use these crystals in hot or warm water.

Variations

Citrus Concentrates

Citrus concentrates may be used in place of lemons or oranges. They should be diluted according to directions on the package, adding sugar if so indicated. Follow directions carefully.

Fruit Lemonade

Fresh or canned fruit juices, or sirups from canned fruits such as apricot, peach, cherry, plum, pear and pineapple may be used to advantage in making fruit lemonade.

Use 1 gallon fruit sirup in place of 2 gallons water and reduce amount of sugar to suit the taste.

Grape Lemonade

Use 1 gallon grape juice and ½ gallon pineapple juice for equal amounts of cold water.

LEMONADE
(Using lemons)

Yield: Approx. 6¼ gallons.   Portion: 1 cup (approx. 8 ounces).

INGREDIENTS	100 PORTIONS			............PORTIONS
	WEIGHTS		AMOUNTS (approx.)	
	Pounds	*Ounces*		
Sugar	6	....	¾ gallon	
Water, hot	....	....	1 gallon	
Water, cold	....	....	5 gallons	
Lemon juice	....	....	1½ quarts (24 lemons)	
Ice	....	....	To chill	

Dissolve sugar in hot water. Add to cold water. Stir in lemon juice and ice.

FRUIT PUNCH

Yield: Approx. 6¾ gallons.   Portion: 1 cup (approx. 8 ounces).

INGREDIENTS	100 PORTIONS			............PORTIONS
	WEIGHTS		AMOUNTS (approx.)	
	Pounds	*Ounces*		
Tea, sweetened, cold	....	....	4 gallons	
Apricot sirup	....	....	½ gallon	
Peach sirup	....	....	2½ gallons	
Lemon juice	....	....	¾ gallon (48 lemons)	

Prepare sweetened cold tea according to recipe for Iced Tea (page 38).

Combine fruit juices and sweetened cold tea. Stir thoroughly. Add enough ice to chill.

NOTE.—9 ounces lemon juice powder, synthetic, added to ¾ gallon of water may be used in place of fresh lemon juice.

TOMATO JUICE

Yield: Approx. 6 gallons.   Portion: 1 cup (approx. 8 ounces).

| INGREDIENTS | 100 PORTIONS | | ....PORTIONS |
	WEIGHTS	AMOUNTS (approx.)	
	Pounds	*Ounces*		
Tomato juice, canned	53	....	8 No. 10 cans............ (6 gallons).	
Salt	....	1	2 tablespoons	
Pepper	....	....	1 teaspoon	

Combine tomato juice, salt and pepper. Chill.
NOTE.—Tomato juice may be served unseasoned.

Variations

Tomato Juice Cocktail

Season tomato juice with ¼ cup onion juice, 2 tablespoons Worcestershire sauce and ½ cup lemon juice.

Tomato-Sauerkraut Juice Cocktail

Combine tomato juice with juice from canned sauerkraut or sauerkraut juice, in the proportion desired.

Cereals

Breakfast Cereals

Cereals and cereal products have an important place in the Navy menu, as they are a good source of food energy.

In addition to furnishing food energy, the whole grain cereals and restored breakfast cereals supply valuable vitamins, minerals and protein. Some of the refined cereals have been restored by the manufacturers to the nutritive value of the whole grain cereals by the addition of minerals and synthetic vitamins.

When cereals are served with milk, or milk and fruit, the protein, mineral and vitamin content of the meal is desirably increased.

There are three main types of breakfast cereals on the market:

1. Regular Cereals

This class includes rolled oats, corn meal, farina, cracked whole wheat and others which require complete cooking. These cereals are served hot.

2. Quick-Cooking Cereals

These cereals have been partially cooked before packaging and require a relatively short period of further cooking before eating. These are also served hot.

Cooked cereals may be used in meat loaves or added to soups. When placed into pans and chilled until firm, cooked cereals such as corn meal and farina may be sliced and fried and served with sirup, powdered sugar or fruit sauce.

3. Prepared or "Ready to Eat" Cereals

These comprise the packaged, dry cereals made from grains such as wheat, corn, rice, barley and rye. They are fully cooked and flavored before packaging. They are available in different forms such as granular, flaked, puffed and shredded.

If necessary or desirable, they can be reheated and recrisped by removing from the package and placing them into baking pans, in a slow oven (325° F.) about 5 minutes.

Macaroni, Noodles, Spaghetti and Rice

Macaroni, noodles and spaghetti are made from a base of hard wheat flour. Some noodles contain egg in addition.

Macaroni and spaghetti can be cooked in long sticks or in pieces, 1 to 2 inches long. If the ends of the long sticks are first dipped into boiling water, they will soften so that the entire mass can be gradually submerged and cooked in coils.

Macaroni, noodles, spaghetti and rice need to be cooked in large amounts of rapidly boiling, salted water, using approximately 4 times as much water as cereal. The product should be drained well immediately after cooking.

Macaroni, noodles, spaghetti and rice when combined with meat, cheese, eggs or milk can be used as a main dish. In this way, these cereals serve as an alternate for meat. A salad or one or two vegetables should be served in addition.

DIRECTIONS FOR COOKING BREAKFAST CEREALS

100 Portions

| CEREAL | APPROXIMATE QUANTITY | | SALT | WATER | COOKING TIME | | APPROXIMATE PORTIONS | |
	Weight	Amount			Steam-Jacketed Kettle	Double Boiler	Weight	Amount
	Pounds	Gallons	Table-spoons	Gallons	Minutes	Minutes	Ounces	Cup
Regular:								
Rolled Oats	6	1¾	6	5	20	30–45	5–6	⅔
Wheat Cereals.	6	1⅛	6	5	20	30–45	5–6	⅔
Cornmeal	6	1⅛	6	6	20–30	60	6–7	¾
Hominy Grits .	6	1⅛	6	6	20–30	60	6–7	¾
Quick-Cooking:								
Rolled Oats	6	1¾	6	4¾	5	5–10	5–6	⅔
Wheat Cereals.	6	1⅛	6	4¾	5	5–10	5–6	⅔
Whole Wheat Cereals........	6	1⅛	6	4¾	5	5–10	5–6	⅔

In Steam-jacketed Kettle

Rolled Oats (Regular)

Add salt to water. Heat to boiling temperature.

Add oats to water gradually, stirring to prevent lumping.

Stir only 1 or 2 times during cooking, to change position of cereal so that heat can penetrate evenly.

Cook at very "slow boil" until done.

Wheat Cereals (Regular)

Add salt to water. Heat to boiling temperature.

Stir cereal gradually into boiling water. Continue stirring until thickened.

Cook at very "slow boil" until done.

Hominy Grits and Cornmeal (Regular)

Add salt to water. Heat to boiling temperature.

Stir cereal gradually into boiling water. Continue stirring until thickened.

Cook at very "slow boil" until done.

In Double Boiler

Rolled Oats, Wheat Cereals, Hominy Grits, Cornmeal (Regular)

Place water in top of double boiler. Add salt. Heat to boiling temperature.

Stir in cereal gradually. Continue stirring until thickened.

Place top of double boiler over bottom, filled to ⅔ capacity with boiling water.

Cook, without stirring, the required length of time or until done.

NOTE.—Stir Rolled Oats only the required number of times, and add only required amount of water, otherwise a gummy cooked product will result.

300 or More Portions in Steam Jacketed Kettle

Granular Cereals

Start cooking process of cereals in cold water. Fill kettle with specified amount of cold water. Measure accurately. Stir in cereal, carefully mixing with water to form a smooth mixture.

Turn on steam. Continue stirring until cereal comes to boiling temperature and is thickened.

Stir only 1 or 2 times during cooking to change position of cereal, so that heat can penetrate evenly.

Cook about 30 minutes or until done.

Rolled Oats

Follow same method as used for preparing 100 portions in steam-jacketed kettle.

BOILED RICE

Portion: 4 to 5 ounces (approx. ½ cup).

INGREDIENTS	100 PORTIONS			............PORTIONS
	WEIGHTS		AMOUNTS (approx.)	
	Pounds	Ounces		
Salt	....	5	10 tablespoons	
Water	....	....	4 gallons	
Rice	10	....	1¼ gallons	

Add salt to water. Heat to boiling temperature.

Wash rice thoroughly. Drain. Stir slowly into rapidly boiling water.

Cook about 20 to 30 minutes or until rice is tender. Do not stir.

Drain well. Rinse with hot water. Drain.

Place in slow oven (250° F.) to dry and keep hot.

NOTE.—1 pound (1 pint) melted butter may be added just before serving.

BOILED MACARONI, NOODLES OR SPAGHETTI

Portion: 5 to 6 ounces (¾ to 1 cup).

INGREDIENTS	100 PORTIONS			............PORTIONS
	WEIGHTS		AMOUNTS (approx.)	
	Pounds	Ounces		
Salt	....	4	½ cup	
Water	....	....	8 gallons	
Macaroni	8	....	2½ gallons	

Add salt to water. Heat to boiling temperature.

Stir in macaroni. Reheat to boiling temperature, stirring until boiling begins. Stir occasionally thereafter to prevent sticking.

Cook about 20 minutes or until macaroni is tender. Drain well.

NOTE.—1. Blanch macaroni only if it is to be used in a salad.

2. 9 pounds (2¾ gallons) spaghetti or 6 pounds (3¼ gallons) noodles may be cooked in same way as macaroni. Spaghetti is usually broken into 2 to 3-inch pieces before cooking.

3. Combine with Cheese Sauce (page 210), Tomato Sauce (page 218) or use as desired.

4. Avoid overcooking.

Cheese

Cheese, being a milk product in concentrated form, takes exceedingly high rank on the list of essential foods in the Navy. It is high in proteins, vitamins and minerals. It is an excellent source of calcium.

In combination with spaghetti, macaroni, noodles or rice it serves well as a main dish on the dinner or supper menu.

BAKED MACARONI AND CHEESE

Portion: 8 ounces (approx. 1 cup).

INGREDIENTS	100 PORTIONS			............PORTIONS
	WEIGHTS		AMOUNTS (approx.)	
	Pounds	Ounces		
Salt	....	5	10 tablespoons	
Water, boiling	....	....	10 gallons	
Macaroni	10	....	3 gallons	
Cheese, American cheddar, shredded.	8	....	2 gallons	

Add salt to water. Heat to boiling temperature.

Stir in macaroni. Cook 20 minutes or until tender. Drain well.

Place ½ the macaroni in well greased baking pans. Cover with ½ the cheese. Add remaining macaroni. Sprinkle remaining cheese on top.

Bake in moderate oven (350°F.) 25 minutes or until cheese is thoroughly melted.

CHEESE SOUFFLE

Portion: Approx. 2½-inch square.

Ingredients	100 Portions			........Portions
	Weights		Amounts (approx.)	
	Pounds	*Ounces*		
Eggs, well beaten	4	8	45 (2¼ quarts)	
Milk, liquid	....	....	3¾ gallons	
Paprika	....	....	6 tablespoons	
Worcestershire sauce	....	....	½ cup	
Salt	....	3	6 tablespoons	
Butter or other fat, melted	....	6	¾ cup	
Bread	9	....	100 slices	
Cheese, American cheddar, grated.	6	....	1½ gallons	

Combine eggs and milk.

Add paprika, Worcestershire sauce, salt and fat.

Trim crusts from bread. Place layer of bread on bottom of greased baking pan.

Sprinkle with cheese. Arrange alternate layers of bread and cheese until all is used.

Add milk mixture. Allow to stand 15 minutes.

Bake in moderate oven (350°F.) 30 to 40 minutes or until firm.

NOTE.—Before baking set pan of souffle in pan of hot water to insure smooth texture and bake.

MACARONI AND CORN AU GRATIN WITH BACON

Portion: Approx. 8 ounces; 1 slice bacon.

INGREDIENTS	100 PORTIONS			..........PORTIONS
	WEIGHTS		AMOUNTS (approx.)	
	Pounds	Ounces		
Milk, liquid	....	....	1¼ gallons	
Butter or other fat, melted	1	4	1¼ pints	
Flour	....	10	2½ cups	
Salt	....	4	½ cup	
Pepper	....	....	1 teaspoon	
Mustard, dry	....	½	2¼ tablespoons	
Paprika	....	½	2¼ tablespoons	
Cheese, American cheddar, chopped.	2	8	2⅛ quarts	
Water	....	....	4 gallons	
Salt	....	1	2 tablespoons	
Macaroni	4	....	1¼ gallons	
Corn, cream style	25	---	20 No. 2 cans (3¼ gallons).	
Bacon	6		100 strips	

Heat milk to boiling temperature.

Blend fat, flour, salt, pepper, mustard and paprika to a smooth paste. Stir into milk. Cook until thickened, stirring constantly.

Remove from heat. Add cheese and stir until melted.

Add salt to 4 gallons water. Heat to boiling temperature. Stir in macaroni. Cook 20 minutes or until tender.

Combine macaroni, cheese sauce and corn.

Pour into greased baking pans.

Bake in moderate oven (350°F.) 25 minutes.

Broil bacon until it begins to curl. Place over top of macaroni 5 minutes before end of baking period.

NOTE.—1. Whole kernel corn should be drained before adding to mixture. Reserve liquid for cheese sauce.

2. Spaghetti may be used in place of macaroni.

MACARONI WITH TOMATOES AND CHEESE

Portion: 8 ounces (approx. 1 cup).

INGREDIENTS	100 PORTIONS			..........PORTIONS
	WEIGHTS		AMOUNTS (approx.)	
	Pounds	Ounces		
Tomatoes	12	12	2 No. 10 cans (6½ quarts).	
Onions, chopped	....	12	2½ cups	
Celery, leaves, chopped	....	1½		
Sugar	....	9	1⅛ cups	
Pepper	....	....	1 tablespoon	
Salt	....	3½	7 tablespoons	
Butter	....	8	½ pint	
Cheese, American cheddar, shredded.	4	2	1 gallon	
Salt	....	1	2 tablespoons	
Water	....	....	8 gallons	
Macaroni	8	....	2½ gallons	

Cook together tomatoes, onions, celery leaves, sugar, pepper and 3½ ounces salt 20 minutes. Remove from heat.

Add butter and cheese to hot tomato mixture. Stir until cheese is melted.

Add 1 ounce salt to water. Heat to boiling temperature. Stir in macaroni. Cook 20 min-utes or until tender. Drain well.

Combine sauce and macaroni. Place in greased baking pans. Bake in moderate oven (350°F.) 25 minutes.

NOTE.—Noodles or spaghetti may be used in place of macaroni.

MACARONI REPUBLIC

Portion: Approx. 1 cup.

INGREDIENTS	100 PORTIONS			...........PORTIONS
	WEIGHTS		AMOUNTS (approx.)	
	Pounds	Ounces		
Milk, liquid	....	....	4½ quarts	
Butter, melted	1	8	1½ pints	
Pimiento, finely chopped.........	2	....	1½ quarts	
Salt	....	10	½ cup	
Pepper	....	4	1½ teaspoons	
Celery salt	....	....	1½ teaspoons	
Mustard, dry	....	....	1½ teaspoons	
Cheese, American cheddar, grated.	3	....	¾ gallon	
Eggs, beaten	3	10	36 (3½ pints)	
Salt	....	4	½ cup	
Water	....	....	9 gallons	
Macaroni	6	....	2 gallons	
Bread, cubed	2	4	1¼ gallons	
Paprika	....	....	To garnish	

Heat milk to boiling temperature. Add butter, pimiento, salt, pepper, celery salt and mustard. Remove from heat.

Add cheese. Stir until melted. Add eggs, stirring constantly.

Add ½ cup salt to water. Heat to boiling temperature.

Stir in macaroni. Cook 20 minutes or until tender. Drain well.

Combine bread and macaroni. Stir into milk mixture.

Place in greased baking pans. Sprinkle top with paprika.

Bake in slow oven (325°F.) about 25 to 30 minutes, or until firm.

CHEESE STRATS

Portion: Approx. 8 ounces.

INGREDIENTS	100 PORTIONS			..........PORTIONS
	WEIGHTS		AMOUNTS (approx.)	
	Pounds	Ounces		
Bread, day-old	12	....	8 (1½-pound) loaves	....
Cheese, American cheddar, shredded.	9	8	2¼ gallons	....
Eggs, slightly beaten	8	....	80 (1 gallon)	....
Milk, liquid	....	....	3¼ gallons	....
Paprika	....	½	2¼ tablespoons	....
Salt	....	2½	5 tablespoons	....
Pepper	....	¼	2¾ teaspoons	....

Trim crusts from bread and cut into 1-inch cubes.

Arrange ½ of bread in bottom of baking pans. Cover with cheese. Place remaining bread cubes on top.

Combine eggs, milk, paprika, salt and pepper.

Pour mixture over bread and cheese, letting it soak into bread 45 minutes.

Bake in moderate oven (350°F.) about 1 hour, or until custard is set and bread is puffed and brown.

Serve immediately.

SPAGHETTI LOAF

Yield: Approx. 36 pounds.   Portion: Approx. 6 ounces.

INGREDIENTS	100 PORTIONS			..........PORTIONS
	WEIGHTS		AMOUNTS (approx.)	
	Pounds	Ounces		
Cheese, American cheddar, shredded.	7	....	1¾ gallons	....
Milk, liquid	....	....	5½ quarts	....
Salt	....	4	½ cup	....
Pepper	....	....	1 teaspoon	....
Onions, minced	....	8	1½ cups	....
Eggs, beaten	2	13	28 (5½ cups)	....
Spaghetti	7	....	2¼ gallons	....
Salt	....	1½	3 tablespoons	....
Water	....	....	7 gallons	....

★ 50

Melt cheese in milk over boiling water or in steam-jacketed kettle. Add 4 ounces salt. Stir in pepper and onions.

Add eggs slowly, stirring vigorously. Remove from heat.

Add 1½ ounces salt to water. Heat to boiling temperature.

Stir in spaghetti. Cook 20 minutes or until tender. Drain well.

Combine spaghetti and cheese sauce. Pour into greased loaf pans.

Bake in moderate oven (350°F.) 1 hour.

NOTE.—1. 10 ounces (1½ pints) parsley, minced, may be added to sauce.

2. ½ ounce garlic may be cooked with spaghetti. Remove garlic after spaghetti is cooled.

MACARONI AU GRATIN

Portion: 8 ounces (approx. 1 cup).

INGREDIENTS	100 PORTIONS			........PORTIONS
	WEIGHTS		AMOUNTS (approx.)	
	Pounds	Ounces		
Milk, liquid	....	....	2¾ gallons	
Butter or other fat, melted	1	8	1½ pints	
Flour	....	8	1 pint	
Salt	....	3	6 tablespoons	
Pepper	....	....	1 teaspoon	
Salt	....	4	½ cup	
Water, boiling	....	....	9 gallons	
Macaroni	9	....	2¾ gallons	
Cheese, American cheddar, shredded.	8	....	2 gallons	
Bread crumbs, dry	1	8	½ gallon	
Butter, melted	1	8	1½ pints	

Heat milk to boiling temperature.

Blend together fat, flour, salt and pepper to a smooth paste. Stir into milk.

Cook until thickened, stirring constantly.

Add salt to water. Heat to boiling temperature. Stir in macaroni. Cook 20 minutes or until tender. Drain well.

Place macaroni in well greased baking pans. Cover with cheese.

Pour sauce over macaroni and cheese.

Mix together crumbs and butter. Sprinkle over macaroni.

Bake in moderate oven (350°F.) 25 minutes or until crumbs are browned.

Variation

Buttered Macaroni

Cook macaroni in boiling salted water 20 minutes or until tender. Drain well. Add 2 pounds (1 quart) melted butter. Serve with meat in place of potatoes.

NOODLES SCALLOPED WITH CHEESE, TOMATO, AND BACON

Portion: 8 ounces (approx. 1 cup).

INGREDIENTS	100 PORTIONS			............PORTIONS
	WEIGHTS		AMOUNTS (approx.)	
	Pounds	*Ounces*		
Salt	....	4	½ cup	
Water, boiling	....	....	8 gallons	
Noodles	8	....	4½ gallons	
Salt	....	1	2 tablespoons	
Pepper	....	....	2 teaspoons	
Tomatoes	19	2	3 No. 10 cans (2½ gallons).	
Cheese, American cheddar, shredded.	4	2	1 gallon	
Bacon, sliced	2	....	35 to 40 strips	

Add ½ cup salt to water. Heat to boiling temperature.

Stir in noodles. Cook 20 minutes or until tender. Drain well.

Add salt and pepper to tomatoes. Heat to boiling temperature.

Arrange alternate layers of noodles, tomatoes and cheese in greased baking pans. Top with bacon slices.

Bake in moderate oven (350°F.) 20 minutes or until bacon is crisp.

BAKED RICE AND CHEESE

Portion: 8 ounces (approx. 1 cup).

| INGREDIENTS | 100 PORTIONS | | ....PORTIONS |
	WEIGHTS	AMOUNTS (approx.)	
	Pounds | *Ounces*		
Butter or other fat, melted......	1 | 8	1½ pints	
Flour	.... | 12	1½ pints	
Salt	.... | 1	2 tablespoons	
Mustard, dry	.... | ½	2 tablespoons	
Milk, liquid, hot	.... |	5½ quarts	
Cheese, American cheddar, shredded.	6 |	1½ gallons	
Salt	.... | 3	6 tablespoons	
Water, boiling	.... |	3 gallons	
Rice, uncooked, washed............	3 |	1½ quarts	
Bread crumbs, moist..............	1 | 8	¾ gallon	
Butter, melted (for crumbs)..	.... | 8	½ pint	

Blend together fat, flour, salt and mustard to a smooth paste. Add milk. Cook until thickened, stirring constantly. Reduce heat. Add cheese. Stir until melted. Remove from heat.

Add salt to water. Heat to boiling temperature.

Stir in rice. Cook 20 to 30 minutes or until tender. Drain well.

Combine cheese mixture and cooked rice. Place in baking pans. Sprinkle with buttered crumbs.

Bake in slow oven (325°F.) 25 minutes or until crumbs are browned.

SCALLOPED RICE, CHEESE AND EGGS

Portion: Approx. 8 ounces.

INGREDIENTS	100 PORTIONS			..........PORTIONS
	WEIGHTS		AMOUNTS (approx.)	
	Pounds	*Ounces*		
Milk, liquid	....	....	2½ gallons	
Butter or other fat, melted	2	....	1 quart	
Flour	1	...	1 quart	
Salt	....	3	6 tablespoons	
Pepper	....	....	1 teaspoon	
Paprika	....	1	4½ tablespoons	
Cheese, American cheddar, shredded.	2	....	½ gallon	
Rice, uncooked, washed	6	....	¾ gallon	
Salt	....	2	¼ cup	
Water, boiling	....	....	6 gallons	
Eggs, hard cooked, sliced	....	...	48	
Cheese, American cheddar, shredded.	2	....	½ gallon	

Heat milk to boiling temperature.

Blend fat, flour, 3 ounces salt, pepper and paprika to a smooth paste. Stir into hot milk. Cook, stirring constantly, until thickened.

Add 2 pounds cheese. Stir until melted.

Add ¼ cup salt to 6 gallons water. Heat to boiling temperature. Stir in rice. Cook in boiling water for 20 minutes or until tender. Drain well.

Arrange alternate layers of rice, sauce and sliced eggs in greased baking pans.

Sprinkle shredded cheese over top.

Bake in moderate oven (350°F.) 30 minutes or until thoroughly heated through and cheese is browned.

TOMATO RAREBIT

Yield: Approx. 6 gallons.

Portion: Approx. 1 cup.

INGREDIENTS	100 PORTIONS			........PORTIONS
	WEIGHTS		AMOUNTS (approx.)	
	Pounds	Ounces		
Tomatoes	19	2	3 No. 10 cans............ (2½ gallons)	
Butter or other fat, melted.....	5	....	2½ quarts	
Flour	2	....	½ gallon	
Salt	....	6	¾ cup	
Mustard, dry	....	½	2¼ tablespoons	
Cheese, American cheddar, shredded.	15	....	3¾ gallons	
Bread, toasted	....	....	100 slices	

Heat tomatoes to boiling temperature.

Blend together fat, flour, salt and mustard to a smooth paste.

Stir into tomatoes. Cook, stirring constantly, until thickened.

Add cheese. Stir until melted.

Serve immediately on toast.

WELSH RAREBIT

Yield: Approx. 6 gallons.

Portion: Approx. 1 cup.

INGREDIENTS	100 PORTIONS			...........PORTIONS
	WEIGHTS		AMOUNTS (approx.)	
	Pounds	Ounces		
Milk, liquid	....	....	2½ gallons	
Eggs, slightly beaten...............	2	8	25 (1¼ quarts)............	
Salt	....	1½	3 tablespoons	
Mustard, dry	....	1	4½ tablespoons	
Cheese, American cheddar, shredded.	15	....	3¾ gallons	
Bread, toasted	....	....	100 slices	

Heat milk to boiling temperature.

Add eggs, salt and mustard, stirring rapidly and constantly to prevent cooking of the eggs.

Stir in cheese until melted. Remove from kettle. Serve immediately on toast.

Desserts

The dessert is important in both the dinner and supper menu. It rounds out the meal in a satisfactory manner and is one means of controlling the caloric content of the meal.

Serve a light dessert with the heavier meal and a sweeter, richer dessert with the lighter meal. Recipes for pies, other pastries and cakes are found in the bakery section of this book.

APPLE BROWN BETTY

Yield: Approx. 18¾ pounds.

Portion: 3½ ounces (approx. ½ cup).

INGREDIENTS	100 PORTIONS			............PORTIONS
	WEIGHTS		AMOUNTS (approx.)	
	Pounds	*Ounces*		
Bread crumbs, dry	3	8	1¼ gallons	
Apples, diced	8	....	2 gallons	
Sugar, brown	2	8	1¾ quarts	
Nutmeg	....	⅛	1½ teaspoons	
Cinnamon	....	¼	1 tablespoon	
Lemon rind	....	1	¼ cup	
Water	....	....	1½ quarts	
Lemon juice	....	....	¼ cup (1 lemon)	
Butter or other fat, melted	1	10	3¼ cups	

Line greased baking pans with bread crumbs. Cover with a layer of apples.

Mix together sugar, nutmeg, cinnamon and lemon rind. Sprinkle over apples.

Arrange alternate layers of remaining bread crumbs, apples and sugar mixture, making top layer crumbs.

Combine water, lemon juice and butter. Pour over mixture.

Bake in moderate oven (375°F.) 45 to 60 minutes or until top is browned.

NOTE.—Serve hot or cold with hot or cold Lemon Sauce (page 73) or Orange Sauce (page 74).

BAKED CUSTARD

Yield: Approx. 3 gallons.   Portion: 5 ounces (approx. ¾ cup).

INGREDIENTS	100 PORTIONS			........PORTIONS
	WEIGHTS		AMOUNTS (approx.)	
	Pounds	Ounces		
Eggs, whole	4	6	44 (2⅛ quarts)	
Sugar	3	....	1½ quarts	
Salt	....	½	1 tablespoon	
Vanilla	....	3	6 tablespoons	
Milk, liquid	....	....	2¾ gallons	
Nutmeg	....	½	1½ tablespoons	

Blend all ingredients together thoroughly. Pour into baking pans or dishes.

Bake in hot oven (400°F.) about 30 minutes. Cool.

NOTE.—1 pound 1½ ounces powdered eggs and 1⅝ quarts water may be used in place of 4 pounds 6 ounces eggs.

CALIFORNIA CREAM

Yield: Approx. 3⅛ gallons.   Portion: 3 ounces (approx. ½ cup).

INGREDIENTS	100 PORTIONS			........PORTIONS
	WEIGHTS		AMOUNTS (approx.)	
	Pounds	Ounces		
Gelatin	....	4½	⅞ cup	
Milk, liquid	....	....	1⅛ gallons	
Salt	....	....	1½ teaspoons	
Sugar	3	....	1½ quarts	
Egg yolks, slightly beaten......	1	8	36 (1½ pints)	
Egg whites, stiffly beaten	2	....	36 (1 quart)	
Orange juice	....	....	1½ quarts	

Soak gelatin in 1 pint of milk for 10 minutes.

Heat remaining milk to boiling temperature. Add salt.

Mix together sugar and egg yolks. Stir into milk. Cook until mixture coats spoon. Stir in gelatin. Cool.

Stir in orange juice. Fold egg whites in carefully. Chill.

NOTE.—1. Equal parts of powdered egg yolks and water may be used in place of the egg yolks.

2. 3¼ ounces powdered egg white and 1¾ pints water may be used in place of 2 pounds egg whites.

3. Other fruit juices may be used in place of orange juice. Properly diluted fruit concentrates can also be used.

ASSORTED FRUIT GELATIN CUBES

Yield: Approx. 21½ pounds.   Portion: 4 ounces (approx. ½ cup).

| INGREDIENTS | 100 PORTIONS | | | ....PORTIONS |
	WEIGHTS		AMOUNTS (approx.)	
	Pounds	*Ounces*		
Gelatin dessert, raspberry	1	2	2½ cups	
Gelatin dessert, lemon	1	2	2½ cups	
Gelatin dessert, lime	1	2	2½ cups	
Water, boiling	....	....	¾ gallon	
Water or fruit juice, cold	....	....	1½ gallons	

Stir 1 quart boiling water into each of the gelatins, separately, until gelatin is dissolved.

Stir ½ gallon cold water or fruit juice into each. Pour each gelatin into individual shallow pans.

Chill until firm. Cut into ½ to ¾-inch cubes.

Combine different flavored cubes before serving.

NOTE.—1. Serve plain or with cold Custard Sauce (page 72), cold Fruit Sauce (page 73), bananas or berries.

2. Dip knife into warm water to cut gelatin.

ORANGE BAVARIAN

Yield: Approx. 16 pounds.   Portion: 3 ounces (approx. ½ cup).

| INGREDIENTS | 100 PORTIONS | | | ....PORTIONS |
	WEIGHTS		AMOUNTS (approx.)	
	Pounds	*Ounces*		
Gelatin, unflavored	....	2½	½ cup	
Orange juice	....	....	⅔ cup	
Milk, evaporated, icy cold	9	1	10 No. 1 (14½-oz.) cans (1 gallon).	
Sugar	2	6	4⅔ cups	
Lemon juice	....	....	½ cup (2 lemons)	
Salt	....	....	1 teaspoon	
Orange sections, diced	5	....	½ gallon	

Soak gelatin in orange juice for 10 minutes. Place bowl over hot water to dissolve gelatin.

Combine milk and sugar. Whip until fluffy with cold beater.

Add lemon juice, salt and dissolved gelatin. Continue whipping until stiff.

Fold in oranges. Place in refrigerator to chill until firm.

GELATIN BANANA DESSERT

Yield: Approx. 5 gallons.

Portion: 6 to 6¼ ounces (approx. ¾ cup).

| INGREDIENTS | 100 PORTIONS | | ....PORTIONS |
| | WEIGHTS | AMOUNTS (approx.) | |
	Pounds	Ounces		
Water, boiling	....	....	1 gallon	
Gelatin dessert, flavored	4	11	2¾ quarts	
Water, cold	....	....	1½ gallons	
Bananas, ripe	16	....	60 to 75	

Stir boiling water into gelatin until gelatin is dissolved. Add cold water.

Pour gelatin into pans to a depth of about 2 inches. Cool until slightly thickened.

Peel bananas. Arrange rows of whole bananas in cooled gelatin.

Chill until firm. Cut into squares or slices.

NOTE.—1. Other fresh fruits except fresh pineapple may be used with or in place of bananas.

2. Canned fruits, drained, also may be used.

3. Fruit juice from canned fruit should be used in place of water.

4. Bananas are fully ripe when the yellow peel is flecked with brown. Ripe bananas are thoroughly digestible and sweet in flavor.

LEMON SNOW

Yield: Approx. 3⅛ gallons.

Portion: 1⅓ ounces (approx. ½ cup).

| INGREDIENTS | 100 PORTIONS | | ....PORTIONS |
| | WEIGHTS | AMOUNTS (approx.) | |
	Pounds	Ounces		
Gelatin, unflavored	....	4	⅞ cup	
Water, cold	....	....	1½ cups	
Water, hot	...	...	1½ quarts	
Sugar	2	4	1⅛ quarts	
Lemon juice	....	....	1½ cups (6 lemons)	
Egg whites	....	13	16 (1½ cups)	

Soak gelatin in cold water 10 minutes.

Stir gelatin into hot water. Stir in sugar until dissolved.

Stir in lemon juice and chill until slightly thickened. Beat until light.

Beat egg whites to a stiff peak and fold into the mixture. Chill.

NOTE.—1. 1¼ ounces powdered egg white and 1½ cups water may be used in place of 13 ounces of egg whites.

2. Reconstituted powdered or synthetic lemon juice may be used in place of fresh lemon juice.

3. Serve with cold Fruit Sauce (page 73) or cold Custard Sauce (page 72).

PRUNE WHIP

Yield: Approx. 3 gallons.　　　　　　　　　　　Portion: 4 ounces (approx. ½ cup).

INGREDIENTS	100 PORTIONS		.........PORTIONS
	WEIGHTS	AMOUNTS (approx.)	
	Pounds	Ounces		
Prunes, cooked	6	14	3¼ quarts	
Gelatin dessert, orange	2	12	2¼ quarts	
Water, boiling	....	....	¾ gallon	
Sugar	2	....	1 quart	
Water, cold	....	....	2½ quarts	

Remove pits from prunes. Chop prunes very fine.

Dissolve gelatin in boiling water. Add sugar. Stir until dissolved.

Add cold water and prune pulp. Chill.

Place in mixer bowl. Whip until thick and fluffy. Chill until firm.

NOTE.—1. Serve with Whipped Evaporated Milk Topping (page 75) or cold Vanilla Sauce (page 76).

2. 2½ pounds (5 cups) apricots, chopped, may be used in place of 2½ pounds prunes.

3. An equivalent amount of fruit juice may be used in place of water.

FRUIT AND RICE COMPOTE

Yield: Approx. 30½ pounds.　　　　　　　　　　Portion: 5 ounces (approx. ½ cup).

INGREDIENTS	100 PORTIONS		.........PORTIONS
	WEIGHTS	AMOUNTS (approx.)	
	Pounds	Ounces		
Gelatin dessert, strawberry	3	12	¾ gallon	
Water, boiling	....	....	¾ gallon	
Sugar	1	4	2½ cups	
Fruit juices, mixed	....	....	¾ gallon	
Pineapple, canned, cut in wedges.	6	8	1 No. 10 can (3¼ quarts).	
Apricots, quartered	3	4	½ No. 10 can (1½ quarts).	
Rice, cooked	5	....	¾ gallon	

Dissolve gelatin in boiling water. Add sugar, stirring until dissolved. Add juice.

Chill until slightly thickened. Fold in fruits and rice.

Place in pans. Chill until firm.

NOTE.—Serve with Whipped Evaporated Milk Topping (page 75) or cold Custard Sauce (page 72).

RICE PUDDING WITH RAISINS

Yield: Approx. 3 gallons.   Portion: Approx. ½ cup.

| INGREDIENTS | 100 PORTIONS | | | ....PORTIONS |
| | WEIGHTS | | AMOUNTS (approx.) | |
	Pounds	Ounces		
Milk, liquid	---	---	4 gallons	
Rice	4	---	½ gallon	
Sugar	4	....	½ gallon	
Salt	....	1½	3 tablespoons	
Raisins	2	11	½ gallon	
Butter	....	8	½ pint	

Heat milk to boiling temperature in steam-jacketed kettle or in top of double boiler.

Wash rice. Stir into milk. Let simmer about 45 minutes or until rice is tender. Stir occasionally.

Stir in sugar, salt, raisins and butter.

Pour mixture into greased baking pans.

Bake in moderate oven (350°F.) about 30 minutes.

RICE CUSTARD PUDDING

Yield: Approx. 3⅛ gallons.   Portion: 5 ounces (approx. ½ cup).

| INGREDIENTS | 100 PORTIONS | | | ....PORTIONS |
| | WEIGHTS | | AMOUNTS (approx.) | |
	Pounds	Ounces		
Milk, liquid	....	....	3 gallons	
Rice, cooked	3	6	½ gallon	
Sugar	2	8	1¼ quarts	
Butter or shortening, melted	1	....	1 pint	
Eggs, whole	2	....	20 (1 quart)	
Salt	....	1	2 tablespoons	
Cinnamon	....	¼	1 teaspoon	
Nutmeg	....	¼	1 teaspoon	
Vanilla	....	2	¼ cup	

Heat milk to boiling temperature. Stir in remaining ingredients. Mix thoroughly. Pour into greased baking pans.

Bake in moderate oven (375°F.) about 1 hour.

Serve with Vanilla Sauce (page 76) or Lemon Sauce (page 73).

NOTE.—8 ounces powdered eggs and 1 cup water may be used in place of 2 pounds eggs.

BREAD PUDDING

Yield: Approx. 3 gallons.

Portion: 4 ounces (approx. ½ cup).

INGREDIENTS	100 PORTIONS			..........PORTIONS
	WEIGHTS		AMOUNTS (approx.)	
	Pounds	Ounces		
Milk, liquid	....	....	3 gallons	
Bread cubes	2	8	1¼ gallons	
Sugar	2	8	1¼ quarts	
Butter or shortening, melted	1	....	1 pint	
Eggs, beaten lightly	2	....	20 (1 quart)	
Salt	....	3	6 tablespoons	
Vanilla	....	2	¼ cup	

Mix all ingredients together thoroughly.

Pour into greased baking pans 2 to 2½ inches deep.

Bake in moderate oven (375° F.) about 1 hour.

NOTE.—8 ounces powdered eggs and 1½ pints water may be used in place of 2 pounds eggs.

Variations

Chocolate Bread Pudding

Heat milk to boiling temperature.

Add 1 pound (4½ cups) cocoa or 1½ pounds chocolate, melted, before mixing with other ingredients.

Raisin Bread Pudding

Add 3 pounds (2¼ quarts) seedless raisins to bread mixture.

Caramel Bread Pudding

Use brown sugar in place of granulated sugar.

BUTTERSCOTCH PUDDING

63 ★

Yield: Approx. 4 gallons.

Portion: 5 ounces (approx. ⅔ cup).

INGREDIENTS	100 PORTIONS			..........PORTIONS
	WEIGHTS		AMOUNTS (approx.)	
	Pounds	Ounces		
Sugar, brown	5	....	3¾ quarts	
Butter	2	8	1¼ quarts	
Salt	...	3	6 tablespoons	
Cornstarch	1	4	3¾ cups	
Water	....	....	1¼ quarts	
Milk, liquid	....	....	4½ gallons	
Vanilla	....	2½	5 tablespoons	

Combine sugar, butter and salt. Cook over low heat until sugar is melted.

Blend together cornstarch and water to a smooth paste.

Heat milk to boiling temperature. Stir cornstarch paste into milk. Mix until smooth.

Add sugar-butter mixture. Mix thoroughly.

Cook in double boiler or steam-jacketed kettle about 30 to 40 minutes, or until thick and smooth. Remove from heat. Cool slightly. Stir in vanilla.

Serve cold.

Variations

Walnut Butterscotch Pudding

Add 1 pound (1½ pints) chopped walnuts with the vanilla. Other nuts, chopped, may be used.

Coconut Topping

Sprinkle shredded, dry or fresh, coconut on top of pudding.

CHOCOLATE PUDDING

Yield: Approx. 3½ gallons.   Portion: 6½ ounces (approx. ½ cup).

| INGREDIENTS | 100 PORTIONS | | | ....PORTIONS |
| | WEIGHTS | | AMOUNTS (approx.) | |
	Pounds	Ounces		
Milk, liquid	....	....	2¾ gallons	
Chocolate	2	4	36 squares	
Sugar	7	8	3¾ quarts	
Salt	....	1½	3 tablespoons	
Flour	2	8	2½ quarts	
Eggs, whole	4	....	40 (½ gallon)	
Butter	1	....	1 pint	
Vanilla	....	1	2 tablespoons	

Heat together 2 gallons milk and chocolate to boiling temperature.

Mix together sugar, salt, flour, remaining milk and eggs to a smooth paste. Stir into milk and chocolate mixture. Cook about 30 to 40 minutes or until thickened, stirring constantly. Stir in butter and vanilla. Cool.

NOTE.—1 pound powdered eggs and 1½ quarts water may be used in place of 4 pounds eggs.

VANILLA CREAM PUDDING

Yield: Approx. 3⅛ gallons.   Portion: 4½ ounces (approx. ½ cup).

| INGREDIENTS | 100 PORTIONS | | | ....PORTIONS |
| | WEIGHTS | | AMOUNTS (approx.) | |
	Pounds	Ounces		
Milk, liquid	....	....	3 gallons	
Sugar	2	8	1¼ quarts	
Flour	1	4	1¼ quarts	
Salt	....	½	1 tablespoon	
Eggs, whole, slightly beaten	2	....	20 (1 quart)	
Egg yolks, slightly beaten	1	12	42 (1¾ pints)	
Vanilla	....	4	½ cup	

Heat milk to boiling temperature. Combine sugar, flour and salt. Stir into milk.

Cook, stirring constantly, about 20 to 30 minutes or until thickened. Remove from heat.

Add eggs and egg yolks, stirring constantly. Add vanilla. Pour into containers to chill before serving.

NOTE.—1. 8 ounces powdered eggs and 1½ pints water may be used in place of 2 pounds eggs.

2. Equal parts of powdered egg yolk and water may be used in place of the egg yolks.

3. 10 ounces cornstarch may be used in place of 1¼ pounds flour.

Variations

Coconut Cream Pudding

Stir in 1 pound 4 ounces (1⅞ quarts) shredded coconut.

Cherry Cream Pudding

Omit vanilla. Stir in 1 quart cherries, 2 ounces (¼ cup) lemon juice and 1 ounce (2 tablespoons) almond extract.

TAPIOCA CREAM
(Pearl tapioca)

Yield: Approx. 3⅛ gallons.   Portion: Approx. ½ cup.

INGREDIENTS	100 PORTIONS			..........PORTIONS
	WEIGHTS		AMOUNTS (approx.)	
	Pounds	*Ounces*		
Tapioca, pearl	1	12	1½ quarts	
Water, cold	....	....	To cover	
Milk, liquid, hot...................	....	....	2½ gallons	
Eggs, slightly beaten.............	2	....	20 (1 quart).............	
Sugar	3	8	1¾ quarts	
Salt	....	1	2 tablespoons	
Vanilla	....	1	2 tablespoons	

Soak tapioca in cold water to cover 6 to 8 hours or overnight.

Drain. Add hot milk. Cook 1½ to 2 hours or until clear.

Combine eggs, sugar and salt. Add tapioca mixture, stirring constantly.

Continue cooking slowly, only until egg is cooked.

Remove from heat. Stir in vanilla.

NOTE.—1. Overcooking after egg is added will cause mixture to curdle.

2. Serve pudding cold, plain, or garnish with canned or fresh fruits or jams.

3. Equal parts of powdered egg and water may be used in place of eggs.

TAPIOCA CREAM
(Quick-cooking tapioca)

Yield: Approx. 3 gallons.   Portion: Approx. ½ cup.

INGREDIENTS	100 PORTIONS		..........PORTIONS
	WEIGHTS	AMOUNTS (approx.)	
	Pounds	Ounces		
Egg yolks, slightly beaten........	....	8	12 (1 cup)................	
Milk, liquid	....	....	2⅝ gallons	
Tapioca, quick-cooking	1	8	4½ cups	
Sugar	3	....	1½ quarts	
Salt	....	1	2 tablespoons	
Egg whites, stiffly beaten........	....	10	12 (1¼ cups)................	
Vanilla	....	1	2 tablespoons	

Stir egg yolks into ¾ gallon milk. Heat remaining milk to boiling temperature.

Stir egg yolk mixture, tapioca, sugar and salt into hot milk.

Cook rapidly 5 minutes, stirring constantly. Remove from heat.

Fold in egg whites. Add vanilla. Chill.

NOTE.—1. Serve plain or garnish with canned or fresh fruits or jam.

2. Equal parts of powdered egg yolk and water may be used in place of egg yolks.

3. 1 ounce powdered egg white and 1⅛ cups water may be used in place of 10 ounces egg whites.

Variations

Creamy Tapioca With Chocolate Sauce

Serve chilled Tapioca Cream with Chocolate Sauce (page 72). Garnish with chopped nuts or shredded coconut.

Banana or Peach Fancy

Fold slices of ripe bananas or peaches, fresh or canned, drained, into cooled Tapioca Cream. Chill. Serve with Chocolate Sauce (page 72) or sirup from canned peaches.

APPLE TAPIOCA PUDDING
(Pearl tapioca)

Yield: Approx. 3¼ gallons.   Portion: Approx. ½ cup.

INGREDIENTS	100 PORTIONS			............PORTIONS
	WEIGHTS		AMOUNTS (approx.)	
	Pounds	Ounces		
Tapioca, pearl	1	12	1½ quarts	
Water, cold	....	....	To cover	
Water, hot	....	....	1½ gallons	
Salt	....	1½	3 tablespoons	
Sugar	7	....	3½ quarts	
Nutmeg	....	....	1½ tablespoons	
Cinnamon	....	....	1 tablespoon	
Apples, thinly sliced.................	15	....	3¾ gallons	
Lemon juice	....	....	1 cup (4 lemons)..........	
Butter	½	....	½ pint	

Soak tapioca in cold water 6 to 8 hours or overnight.

Drain. Add hot water and salt. Cook 1½ to 2 hours or until clear.

Combine sugar, nutmeg and cinnamon.

Arrange tapioca, apples, and sugar mixture in baking pans in alternate layers, making apple and sugar mixture the top layer.

Add lemon juice. Dot with butter.

Bake in moderate oven (350°F.) 35 to 45 minutes or until apples are tender.

Serve hot or cold.

NOTE.—Serve plain or with cream or Hard Sauce (page 73).

Ice Cream

Ice Cream should be a "regular" on the Navy menu. In addition to being one of America's favorite desserts, ice cream is nourishing and economical.

The following directions, if carefully observed, will be helpful in producing ice cream of good quality.

Keep the freezer, utensils used in measuring the ingredients, ice cream cans and all other equipment scrupulously clean and properly sterilized.

Weigh or measure all ingredients accurately to insure uniformity, proper texture and pleasing flavor in the finished product.

Follow directions carefully.

It is important that the correct "overrun" be reached before the batch is drawn off from the freezer. The "overrun" which refers to the increase in volume, obtained by whipping air into the mix during the freezing process, may vary from 80% to 100%. An "overrun" of 100% is most commonly used in commercial practice.

A simple way to determine "overrun" is as follows: Weigh 1 cupful of the original mix, deducting the weight of the cup. When it is determined that the proper "overrun" has been reached, weigh 1 cupful of the ice cream and again determine the net weight. If the weight of the ice cream is just 50% of the weight of the original mix, the proper "overrun" of 100% has been obtained. For example, if the cup of mix originally weighed 8 ounces, the sample taken just before the batch is drawn should weigh 4 ounces. Ice cream with too much "overrun" will melt rapidly and show many air bubbles in the melted product.

Keep the blades of the freezer sharp and properly adjusted since faulty adjustment allows a thin layer of cream to freeze along the inside wall of the freezer. This tends to insulate the batch from the refrigerant and lengthens the freezing time and decreases the "overrun."

Store the ice cream in a hardening cabinet or room at 10° F. below 0° F.

When serving, have the dispensing cabinet at 6° F. Use a "rolling" motion with the scoop. Digging or pushing the scoop into the ice cream will compress it and reduce the number of servings per gallon.

ICE CREAM

Yield: Approx. 5 gallons (2½ gallons mix with 100% overrun).
Portion: No. 12 scoop: 6 portions to 1 quart, 120 to 5 gallons; No. 16 scoop: 8 portions to 1 quart, 160 to 5 gallons.

INGREDIENTS	100 PORTIONS			.... PORTIONS
	WEIGHTS		AMOUNTS (approx.)	
	Pounds	*Ounces*		
Ice cream mix, dry......................	9	....	....	....
Water, cold	....	....	1¾ gallons	....

Combine the mix and water. Whip together at temperature ranging from 40° F. to 70° F. in an electric mixer or with a wire whip. Cool to 40° F. before placing in freezer.

Fill freezer half full. Begin freezing at 15° F. below 0° F.

Open wide the refrigerant valve. Allow mix to freeze from 3 to 6 minutes, depending upon the temperature of the refrigerant.

Start to whip mix when hard enough to "string" across the opening in head of a perpendicular freezer, or when it is slightly less than the consistency for drawing in a horizontal freezer.

Turn off refrigerant. Whip mix 4 to 5 minutes, to double the volume by incorporating air. If the temperature rises above 10° F. the mix may thin out. Open refrigerant valve until mix is hard enough to draw.

When the maximum overrun is obtained, draw off immediately the thick ice cream into cans chilled in hardening cabinet to the same temperature as the ice cream when drawn.

Store in hardening cabinet at about 10° F. below 0° F.

NOTE.—1. If unflavored mix is used, dissolve 12 vanilla flavoring tablets in 1 quart of the water and add to mix with remaining water.

2. Ice cream softens at 12° F. to 15° F. because of the sugar content.

3. Temperatures of 40° F. to 70° F. are satisfactory for mixing the powder and water.

4. Ice cream liquid mix may be held in a refrigerator for 8 hours or longer.

5. Add fruits or fruit juices just before mix is drawn off. When fruits or chocolate are to be added, decrease the quantity of liquid mix by an equivalent amount.

Variations

To 2½ gallons of mix, add the following flavors:

Apricot Ice Cream

1 No. 10 can (6 pounds 14 ounces) (3¼ quarts) apricots, mashed through a coarse sieve
1 teaspoon yellow coloring
1 teaspoon orange coloring

Banana Nut Ice Cream

4 pounds 8 ounces (12 to 16) ripe bananas, peeled and mashed
1 teaspoon yellow coloring
12 ounces (1½ pints) English walnuts or pecans, chopped or ground
NOTE.—Peel and mash bananas just before using to prevent discoloration.

Cherry Ice Cream

½ No. 10 can (3 pounds 6 ounces) (2 quarts) cherries, crushed
1 ounce strawberry-red coloring

Cherry Nut Ice Cream

1 quart cherries, crushed
½ ounce wild cherry extract
½ ounce strawberry-red coloring
12 ounces (1½ pints) nuts, chopped

Chocolate Ice Cream I

½ No. 10 can (1½ quarts) double-strength chocolate sirup

Chocolate Ice Cream II

Mix thoroughly 1½ quarts to ⅜ gallon (1⅛ to 1¾ pounds) cocoa with 2½ quarts of the water for ice cream mix. Add with remaining water to dry ice cream mix. Freeze.

Coffee Ice Cream

Use 6½ pints coffee brew in place of 6½ pints water and add to dry ice cream mix.

Date Nut Ice Cream

1 pound 8 ounces (1½ pints) dates, chopped
12 ounces (1½ pints) English walnuts, chopped

Grape Ice Cream

8 ounces (1 cup) grape juice
1½ ounces (3 tablespoons) grape flavoring
½ tablespoon grape coloring

Peach Ice Cream

½ No. 10 can (3 pounds 3 ounces) (1½ quarts) peaches, mashed through a coarse sieve
2 ounces (4 tablespoons) peach extract
1 teaspoon orange coloring

Pineapple Ice Cream

2 quarts crushed pineapple
1 teaspoon lemon coloring

Pineapple Grape Ice Cream

1 quart crushed pineapple
1 quart grape juice

Pistachio Ice Cream

1 pound (1 quart) cashew nuts, ground
1 ounce (2 tablespoons) pistachio extract
1 teaspoon green coloring

Strawberry Ice Cream

1½ No. 10 cans (9 pounds 15 ounces) (1¼ gallons) strawberries
OR
5 quarts fresh or frozen strawberries, crushed
1 teaspoon strawberry-red coloring

Maple Ice Cream

Dissolve 32 maple flavoring tablets in 1 pint hot water. Add with cold water to dry ice cream mix. Freeze.

Maple Walnut or Walnut Ice Cream

1 to 2 ounces (2 to 4 tablespoons) maple flavoring

1 pound (1 quart) English walnuts
      OR
2 pounds (½ gallon) black walnuts

Chop or grind nuts fine. Add in the last 3 minutes of freezing.

NOTE.—1. Pecans or cashews may be used. Care must be taken to see that they are free from shells.

2. To bring out the flavor of the nuts. soak nut meats in sugar sirup about 10 hours before using.

ICE CREAM

(Using powdered whole milk and powdered eggs)

Yield: Approx. 5 gallons.

Portion: No. 12 scoop: 6 portions to 1 quart, 120 to 5 gallons; No. 16 scoop: 8 portions to 1 quart, 160 to 5 gallons.

INGREDIENTS	100 PORTIONS			..........PORTIONS
	WEIGHTS		AMOUNTS (approx.)	
	Pounds	Ounces		
Cornstarch	....	8	1 pint	
Sugar	5	....	2½ quarts	
Salt	....	1½	3 tablespoons	
Eggs, whole, powdered	....	11	¾ quart	
Milk, whole, powdered	4	....	3½ quarts	
Water, cool	....	....	3¼ gallons	
Vanilla	....	2	¼ cup	

Mix together cornstarch, sugar and salt. Combine powdered eggs and milk.

Reconstitute with water the same as for powdered milk or eggs (pages 20 and 21). Stir into cornstarch mixture.

Cook over boiling water or in steam-jacketed kettle about 20 minutes, stirring occasionally.

Cool completely. Add vanilla. Freeze.

NOTE.—1. 12 vanilla tablets, reconstituted, may be used in place of vanilla.

2. Mixture may have curdled appearance while cooking. This will disappear in freezing.

3. This Ice Cream formula can be used as basis for other flavors.

SHERBETS

Yield: Approx. 5 gallons.   (Using prepared sherbet mix).

Portion: No. 12 scoop: 6 portions to 1 quart, 120 to 5 gallons; No. 16 scoop: 8 portions to 1 quart, 160 to 5 gallons.

Mix ingredients and freeze in the same manner as ice cream. It may be necessary to freeze for 8 minutes before shutting off the refrigerant.

Lemon Sherbet

2 pounds lemon sherbet mix
10 pounds (1¼ gallons) sugar
25 pounds (12½ quarts) water

Lemon and Grape Sherbet

2 pounds lemon sherbet mix
10 pounds (1¼ gallons) sugar
23 pounds (11½ quarts) water
3 pounds (1½ quarts) grape juice

Lemon and Raspberry Sherbet

2 pounds lemon sherbet mix
10 pounds (1¼ gallons) sugar
25 pounds (12½ quarts) water
½ No. 10 can (approx. 1½ quarts) raspberry puree

Orange Sherbet

2 pounds 8 ounces orange sherbet mix
9 pounds (1 gallon) sugar
21 pounds (10½ quarts) water

Lemon and Strawberry Sherbet

2 pounds lemon sherbet mix
4 pounds 4 ounces (½ gallon) sugar
21 pounds (10½ quarts) water
1 No. 10 can (6 pound 10 ounce) (3¼ quarts) strawberries
        OR
3 quarts frozen strawberries

Orange and Apricot Sherbet

2 pounds 8 ounces orange sherbet mix
9 pounds (1 gallon) sugar
21 pounds (10½ quarts) water
1 No. 10 can (6 pound 10 ounce) (3¼ quarts) apricots, unsweetened, crushed

Orange and Pineapple Sherbet

2 pounds 8 ounces orange sherbet mix
9 pounds (1 gallon) sugar
21 pounds (10½ quarts) water
½ No. 10 can (3 pounds 5 ounces) (1½ quarts) crushed pineapple

Dessert Sauces

BUTTERSCOTCH SAUCE

Yield: Approx. 1½ gallons.　　　　　Portion: Approx. 4 tablespoons (2 ounces).

INGREDIENTS	100 PORTIONS			.... PORTIONS
	WEIGHTS		AMOUNTS (approx.)	
	Pounds	Ounces		
Sugar, brown	10	....	7½ quarts	
Water	....	....	1 quart	
Sirup, corn	3	....	1 quart	
Butter	....	8	1 cup	
Milk, evaporated	4	8	5 No. 1 tall (14½ oz.) cans (1½ gallon).	

Combine sugar, water and syrup. Cook to temperature of 234°F. or until a few drops form a soft ball when dropped into cold water.

Remove from heat. Cool to 180°F. to prevent curdling.

Add butter and milk slowly, stirring constantly. Beat until thick.

Cool completely before serving.

NOTE.—Serve on Baked Custard (page 57) or Ice Cream (page 68).

CHOCOLATE SAUCE

Yield: Approx. 1½ gallons.　　　　　　　Portion: Approx. 4 tablespoons (2 ounces).

| INGREDIENTS | 100 PORTIONS | | ....Portions |
| | WEIGHTS | AMOUNTS (approx.) | |
	Pounds	Ounces		
Sugar	6	....	¾ gallon	
Cocoa	1	8	1¾ quarts	
Water	....	....	1½ pints	
Sirup, corn	1	6	1 pint	
Milk, evaporated	7	4	8 No. 1 tall (14½ oz.) cans (3⅓ quarts).	
Vanilla	....	1½	3 tablespoons	

Mix together sugar and cocoa. Stir in water and corn sirup.

Cook to temperature of 234°F. or until a few drops form a soft ball when dropped into cold water.

Remove from heat. Combine milk and vanilla and stir into cocoa mixture, gradually.

NOTE.—Serve warm or cold on ice cream, custards or rice.

Variation

Chocolate Mint Sauce

Add ½ teaspoon essence of peppermint when sauce has completely cooled.

CUSTARD SAUCE

Yield: Approx. 1½ gallons.　　　　　　　Portion: Approx. 4 tablespoons (2 ounces).

| INGREDIENTS | 100 PORTIONS | | ....Portions |
| | WEIGHTS | AMOUNTS (approx.) | |
	Pounds	Ounces		
Milk, liquid	....	....	1½ gallons	
Cornstarch	....	3	9 tablespoons	
Sugar	1	8	1½ pints	
Salt	....	¼	½ tablespoon	
Eggs, slightly beaten	1	8	15 (1½ pints)	
Vanilla	....	1	2 tablespoons	

Heat milk to boiling temperature.

Mix together thoroughly cornstarch, sugar and salt. Add to hot milk, stirring constantly. Cook 30 minutes, stirring frequently.

Stir in eggs rapidly. Cook 1 minute longer.

Remove from heat and cool to 160°F. Stir in vanilla.

NOTE.—4 ounces powdered eggs and 1½ cups cold water may be used in place of 1 pound eggs.

HARD SAUCE

Yield: 6 pounds.   Portion: 1 ounce (approx. 1½ to 2 tablespoons).

| INGREDIENTS | 100 PORTIONS | | .... PORTIONS |
| | WEIGHTS | AMOUNTS (approx.) | |
	Pounds	Ounces		
Butter, softened	2	....	1 quart	
Sugar, confectioner's, sifted	4	....	2½ quarts	
Vanilla	....	2	¼ cup	

Beat butter until creamy. Add sugar and vanilla gradually.

Whip until smooth.

Pack in waxed paper-lined bread tins or square molds.

Chill in refrigerator until firm.

Lift from pans. Slice.

NOTE.—1. Serve with hot or cold steamed pudding, Baked Apples (page 86), Dutch Apple Pie (page 404) or Mince Pie (page 408).

2. Hard Sauce may be served without chilling until firm.

LEMON SAUCE

Yield: Approx. 1½ gallons.   Portion: Approx. 4 tablespoons (2 ounces).

| INGREDIENTS | 100 PORTIONS | | ....PORTIONS |
| | WEIGHTS | AMOUNTS (approx.) | |
	Pounds	Ounces		
Sugar	4	4	½ gallon	
Cornstarch	....	8	¾ pint	
Salt	....	....	½ teaspoon	
Nutmeg	....	....	½ teaspoon	
Water, boiling	....	....	4½ quarts	
Butter	....	8	1 cup	
Lemon rind, grated	....	....	1½ tablespoons	
Lemon juice	....	....	1¼ cups	

Combine sugar, cornstarch, salt and nutmeg.

Stir into water slowly.

Heat to boiling temperature. Cook about 5 minutes or until thickened, stirring constantly.

Stir in butter, lemon rind and juice.

Reheat to boiling temperature.

NOTE.—An excellent sauce for vanilla pudding, fruit fritters and left-over cake.

Variations

Cherry Sauce

Use cherry juice in place of water.

Fruit Sauce

Use fruit juice in place of water. Add crushed fruit, if desired.

ORANGE SAUCE

Yield: Approx. 1½ gallons.   Portion: Approx. 4 tablespoons (2 ounces).

| INGREDIENTS | 100 PORTIONS | | | ....PORTIONS |
| | WEIGHTS | | AMOUNTS (approx.) | |
	Pounds	Ounces		
Sugar	4	6	2¼ quarts	
Cornstarch	....	7	1⅓ cups	
Salt	....	....	¾ teaspoon	
Cinnamon	....	....	¾ teaspoon	
Water, boiling	....	....	1 gallon	
Butter	1	4	2½ cups	
Orange rind, grated	....	2½	10 tablespoons	
Orange juice	....	....	2½ pints	
Lemon juice	....	....	6 tablespoons (1½ lemons)	

Combine sugar, cornstarch, salt and cinnamon. Stir into water slowly.

Heat to boiling temperature. Cook about 5 minutes or until thickened, stirring constantly.

Stir in butter, orange rind, orange juice and lemon juice. Reheat to boiling temperature.

NOTE.—A very desirable and popular sauce for cornstarch and rice puddings, fruit fritters and left-over cake.

PINEAPPLE SAUCE

Yield: Approx. 1½ gallons.   Portion: Approx. 4 tablespoons (2 ounces).

| INGREDIENTS | 100 PORTIONS | | | ....PORTIONS |
| | WEIGHTS | | AMOUNTS (approx.) | |
	Pounds	Ounces		
Cornstarch	....	5	1 cup	
Sugar (variable, depending upon sweetness of the fruits).	2	4	4½ cups	
Pineapple, crushed, and juice, or other fruits.	10	....	1½ gallons	

Mix together cornstarch and sugar. Stir into crushed pineapple.
Cook until clear.

NOTE.—Ginger may be added to the sauce for extra zest. Add approximately 1 tablespoon of powdered ginger with the cornstarch and sugar.

WHIPPED EVAPORATED MILK TOPPING

Yield: Approx. 2¼ quarts.   Portion: Approx. 1½ tablespoons.

METHOD I

| INGREDIENTS | 100 PORTIONS | | ....PORTIONS |
	WEIGHTS	AMOUNTS (approx.)	
	Pounds *Ounces*		
Milk, evaporated	1 13	2 No. 1 tall (14½ oz.) cans (3⅓ cups).	....
Gelatin, flavored	....	3 tablespoons	....
Sugar, powdered	 3	6 tablespoons	
Vanilla	 1	2 tablespoons	....

Heat milk to boiling temperature. Do not boil. Add gelatin to milk. Stir until dissolved. Chill until icy cold. Whip quickly, with cold beater, until stiff.

Fold sugar and vanilla into whipped milk.

Serve immediately on desserts, salads or beverages.

METHOD II

| INGREDIENTS | 100 PORTIONS | | ....PORTIONS |
	WEIGHTS	AMOUNTS (approx.)	
	Pounds *Ounces*		
Milk, evaporated, icy cold........	1 13	2 No. 1 tall (14½ oz.) cans (3⅓ cups).	....
Sugar	 3	6 tablespoons	
Lemon juice	....	6 tablespoons (1 lemon)	

Combine milk and sugar.

Whip until fluffy with cold beater.

Add lemon juice. Continue whipping until stiff.

NOTE.—1. Evaporated milk, beater and container in which milk is to be whipped should be thoroughly chilled to give best results in whipping.

2. Whip milk as quickly as possible and in a small amount at a time.

3. Use whipped milk immediately.

4. Evaporated milk, when whipped, triples in volume.

MAPLE FLAVOR
(Using maple flavoring tablets)

Yield: 1 pint.

| INGREDIENTS | 100 PORTIONS | | ....PORTIONS |
	WEIGHTS	AMOUNTS (approx.)	
	Pounds *Ounces*		
Flavoring tablets, maple..........	....	4	....
Water, boiling	....	1 pint	

Add tablets to water. Stir until dissolved. Cool before using.

NOTE.—1. Maple flavor can be used "to taste" in baking and other foods.

2. For cream type icing 1 teaspoon of maple flavor per pound of icing gives a pleasing flavor.

VANILLA FLAVOR
(Using vanilla tablets, imitation)

1 vanilla tablet, imitation, is equivalent to 1 teaspoon liquid vanilla flavor.

6 vanilla tablets, imitation, are equivalent to 1 fluid ounce (2 tablespoons) vanilla flavor.

Dissolve the required number of tablets specified in the liquid portion of the recipe.

MAPLE SIRUP

Yield: Approx. 2 gallons. Portion: ¼ cup (approx. 2 ounces).

INGREDIENTS	100 PORTIONS			............PORTIONS
	WEIGHTS		AMOUNTS (approx.)	
	Pounds	Ounces		
Flavoring tablets, maple	....	....	16	
Water, boiling	....	....	1 gallon	
Sugar, granulated	12	....	1½ gallons	
Sugar, brown	4	....	¾ gallon	

Dissolve tablets in boiling water.

Add sugars. Heat to boiling temperature, stirring to dissolve sugars. Cool before using.

NOTE.—4 pounds (¾ gallon) granulated sugar may be used in place of 4 pounds (¾ gallon) brown sugar.

VANILLA SAUCE

Yield: Approx. 1½ gallons. Portion: Approx. 4 tablespoons (2 ounces).

INGREDIENTS	100 PORTIONS			............PORTIONS
	WEIGHTS		AMOUNTS (approx.)	
	Pounds	Ounces		
Sugar	2	4	4½ cups	
Cornstarch	....	4	¾ cup	
Salt	....	....	½ teaspoon	
Water, boiling	....	....	1¼ gallons	
Butter, melted	1	....	1 pint	
Vanilla	....	3	6 tablespoons	

Mix together sugar, cornstarch and salt. Stir into water until mixture is smooth.

Heat to boiling temperature. Cook 3 to 4 minutes or until thickened.

Stir in butter and vanilla. Chill.

NOTE.—Serve with custards.

Eggs

Eggs are valuable not only for their excellent protein but for their contribution of vitamins and minerals, especially iron, calcium and phosphorous.

Because of their high nutritive value and ease in preparation and cooking, the Navy menu should be planned to include the equivalent of 1 egg per man per day.

Eggs may be prepared in various delicious ways and served as the main dish of the meal or used as an ingredient in sauces, salads, meat loaves and desserts.

SOFT-COOKED EGGS

Place eggs in cooking vessel.
Cover completely with boiling water.
Cook 3 to 5 minutes, according to desired degree of firmness.
Drain. Serve immediately.

HARD-COOKED EGGS

Place eggs in cooking vessel.
Cover completely with boiling water.
Heat to boiling temperature.
Cook 10 to 12 minutes. Drain.

STEAMER-COOKING OF EGGS

Place eggs in steamer trays. Close steamer. Turn on steam full.
Steam 3 to 5 minutes for soft-cooked eggs and 15 minutes for hard-cooked eggs.
Remove from steamer. Serve immediately.

NOTE.—To cool eggs quickly, plunge in cold water.

POACHED EGGS

Grease skillet. Fill with boiling water.
Add 1 teaspoon salt and 1 tablespoon vinegar to each quart of water.
Break eggs, carefully, into a cup. Slip into water.
Add only enough eggs to float easily in water.
Cover skillet. Let eggs simmer slowly.
Cook about 3 to 5 minutes or until whites are set and yolks are covered with white film.
Lift out with perforated skimmer.

NOTE.—Serve on toast, plain or with Tomato Sauce (page 218), on spinach, or on Beef Hash (page 150) or Corned Beef Hash (page 150).

FRIED EGGS

Portion: 2 eggs.

INGREDIENTS	100 PORTIONS			............PORTIONS
	WEIGHTS		AMOUNTS (approx.)	
	Pounds	Ounces		
Bacon or other fat..........	1	....	1 pint	....
Eggs, whole	20	....	200	....
Salt and pepper..........	....	....	To taste	....

Heat fat on fry top range or in frying pans.
Break two eggs at a time into cup or bowl and slip onto fry top.

Cook until whites are done.
Lift from fry top into flat steam table pans. Serve immediately.

SCRAMBLED EGGS

Portion: Approx. 5 ounces.

INGREDIENTS	100 PORTIONS			............PORTIONS
	WEIGHTS		AMOUNTS (approx.)	
	Pounds	Ounces		
Eggs, whole, slightly beaten	15	....	150 eggs (2 gallons) ..	
Salt	....	3	6 tablespoons	
Pepper	....	¼	¾ tablespoon	
Milk, liquid	....	....	¾ gallon	
Butter or other fat, melted	2	8	1¼ quarts	

Combine eggs, salt, pepper and milk.

Heat fat on fry top range or in frying pans. Add egg mixture.

Cook slowly, stirring constantly until soft but firm.

NOTE.—Remove eggs from heat before completely cooked. Cooking continues for few minutes after removal.

Variations
Steam Table Method

Place uncooked egg mixture into hot steam table pans 15 minutes before serving.

Set pans in steam table. Stir frequently while eggs are cooking.

Oven Method

Place uncooked egg mixture into baking pans.

Bake in slow oven (325° F.) about 15 to 20 minutes. Stir every 4 to 5 minutes until eggs are properly coagulated.

Remove from oven while eggs are still soft. Eggs will continue to cook slightly after removal from oven.

SHIRRED EGGS

Portion: 2 eggs.

INGREDIENTS	100 PORTIONS			PORTIONS
	WEIGHTS		AMOUNTS (approx.)	
	Pounds	Ounces		
Eggs, whole	20	....	200	
Butter or other fat, melted	1	....	1 pint	
Salt	....	1½	3 tablespoons	
Pepper	....	....	1 teaspoon	

Break eggs whole and place in greased baking or muffin pans.

Pour fat over eggs. Sprinkle with salt and pepper.

Bake in moderate oven (350° F.) about 10 minutes, or until whites are firm.

Variation

Shirred Eggs with Bacon

Place cooked, diced bacon in bottom of pans before dropping in the eggs.

SCRAMBLED EGGS

(Using powdered eggs)

Portion: Approx. ½ cup.

INGREDIENTS	100 PORTIONS		.... PORTIONS
	WEIGHTS	AMOUNTS (approx.)	
	Pounds	Ounces		
Eggs, whole, powdered............	6	....	2 gallons	
Water, cool	....	....	2½ gallons	
Salt	....	3	6 tablespoons...............	
Pepper	....	....	1 tablespoon	
Fat, melted	3	....	1½ quarts	

Stir powdered eggs into 1½ gallons water. Stir vigorously with whip to prevent lumping until a perfectly smooth mixture is obtained.

Add remaining water, salt and pepper. Stir until mixture is smooth. Let stand about 20 minutes.

Pour fat into frying pans or roasting pans. Heat fat. Add eggs.

Cook, slowly, over *low* heat until eggs are properly coagulated, stirring occasionally.

Remove from heat while eggs are still soft. Eggs will continue to cook slightly after removal from heat.

NOTE.—1. It is desirable to prepare 25 portions of Scrambled Eggs at one time. However, if care is taken and directions carefully followed, 100 portions can be prepared satisfactorily at one time.

2. Do not prepare Scrambled Eggs more than 10 minutes before serving. Eggs toughen upon standing.

3. Powdered eggs need to be carefully reconstituted. Always use *cool* water for reconstituting.

4. Powdered eggs are highly perishable after water has been added and should not stand longer than 1 hour after reconstitution.

5. The flavor of Scrambled Eggs made from powdered eggs can be greatly improved by the addition of diced, cooked bacon or ham, sausage, luncheon meat or cheese.

Variations

Scrambled Eggs and Diced Bacon

12 pounds bacon, diced, cooked until crisp and brown, may be added to eggs before cooking. Use fat from cooked bacon for cooking eggs.

Scrambled Eggs and Ham

12 pounds cooked ham, diced, may be added to eggs before cooking.

Scrambled Eggs and Luncheon Meat

12 pounds luncheon meat, diced, may be added when eggs are partially cooked. Continue cooking until eggs are properly coagulated. Stir occasionally.

Scrambled Eggs and Pork Sausage

16 pounds pork sausage, cooked, diced, may be added to eggs when eggs are partially cooked. Continue cooking until eggs are properly coagulated. Stir occasionally. Use fat from cooked sausage for cooking eggs.

Scrambled Eggs and Cheese

8 pounds (7 quarts) American cheddar cheese, diced, may be added to eggs when eggs are partially cooked. Continue cooking until eggs are properly coagulated. Stir occasionally.

CREAMED EGGS

Yield: Approx. 5 gallons.　　　　　　　　　　　Portion: 1 cup (approx. 8 ounces).

INGREDIENTS	100 PORTIONS			............PORTIONS
	WEIGHTS		AMOUNTS (approx.)	
	Pounds	Ounces		
Milk, liquid	....	....	3 gallons	
Butter or other fat, melted......	3	....	1½ quarts	
Flour	1	8	1½ quarts	
Salt	....	3	6 tablespoons	
Pepper	....	....	1 teaspoon	
Eggs, hard-cooked, quartered	....	....	96 (1½ gallons)	

Heat milk to boiling temperature.

Blend together fat, flour, salt and pepper to smooth paste.

Stir into milk. Heat to boiling temperature. Cook, stirring constantly, until thickened.

Pour sauce over eggs. Mix lightly.

NOTE.—Serve on toast or cooked rice.

Variation

Creamed Ham and Eggs

10 pounds ham, cooked, cubed may be used in place of 50 eggs.

OMELET

Portion: Approx. 4 ounces.

INGREDIENTS	100 PORTIONS			............PORTIONS
	WEIGHTS		AMOUNTS (approx.)	
	Pounds	Ounces		
Eggs, whole	19	....	192 (2¾ gallons)	
Flour	....	10	2½ cups	
Salt	....	1½	3 tablespoons	
Pepper	....	....	1 teaspoon	
Milk, liquid	....	....	1¼ quarts	
Butter or other fat, melted......	1	....	1 pint	

Separate eggs. Beat yolks until light.

Beat whites until stiff, but not dry.

Stir flour, salt and pepper into yolks. Mix until smooth. Stir in milk.

Fold yolk mixture lightly but thoroughly into whites.

Heat fat bubbling hot in large frying or omelet pans. Pour in egg mixture.

Cover. Cook slowly over low heat about 20 minutes or until bottom of omelet is well browned.

Uncover. Place in moderate oven (350° F.) to dry top.

Remove from oven. Fold omelet with spatula.

Slide onto hot serving pans. Serve immediately.

NOTE.—May be served with Creole Sauce (page 213).

FRENCH TOAST

Portion: 2 slices

INGREDIENTS	100 PORTIONS			----------PORTIONS
	WEIGHTS		AMOUNTS (approx.)	
	Pounds	Ounces		
Eggs, beaten lightly	3	9	36 (3½ pints)	
Milk, liquid	---	---	¾ gallon	
Salt	---	1	2 tablespoons	
Sugar	---	10	1¼ cups	
Bread, day old	---	---	200 slices	

Mix together eggs, milk, salt and sugar, until sugar is dissolved.

Dip slices of bread into egg mixture. Let stand 2 to 3 minutes. Coat each slice thoroughly.

Fry on hot, greased griddle or in hot, deep fat at 360° F. for 2 to 3 minutes or until browned.

NOTE.—1. Serve with maple sirup, jam, jelly, confectioners' or granulated sugar.

2. 14 ounces powdered eggs and 2 pounds 12 ounces (1⅜ quarts) water may be used in place of 3 pounds 9 ounces eggs.

Fruits

Fruits should appear frequently on the menu as they furnish important food essentials and also add variety, color and refreshing flavor to the meal.

Fruits are supplied to the Navy in the fresh state or as quick-frozen, canned and dried.

They fit into all three main meals of the day. They can be served at breakfast alone or in combination with cereal. For dinner or supper they may be used as a first course or as a salad or dessert.

Fresh and canned fruits may be combined to vary flavor and texture.

Fruit compotes, made of a combination of two or three cooked fruits, make a pleasing light dessert for the main meal of the day.

Fruit juices may be served as a first course at breakfast or in place of soup or as the main beverage of the dinner or supper meal.

Discoloration and How to Prevent It

Certain fruits, when peeled and cut, will discolor readily when exposed to air even for a very short time, unless the cut surfaces are protected from direct contact with the air.

Discoloration in apples and pears can be avoided by placing the cut pieces in a solution of salt and water for a very few minutes just before using, allowing 1 teaspoon of salt to 1 quart of cold water. Discoloration in avocados, bananas and peaches can best be retarded by dipping the cut pieces into, or sprinkling them with fresh or canned grapefruit juice, lemon or orange juice or canned pineapple juice. These fruits should not be peeled or cut until time to use them. Fully ripe fruit does not discolor as rapidly as under-ripe fruit.

Storage

Fruit is a perishable product and careful consideration should be given to storage. Some fruits require different temperatures and lengths of time for storage than others.

Since fruit is at its best for flavor, texture and digestibility when fully ripe, it should be served when ripe and care should be taken in meal planning to use the fruit on hand which ripens first.

To Fully Ripen Bananas

To obtain *fully ripe* bananas, the green-tipped or the all-yellow fruit should be held at room temperature, 68° F. to 70° F., until the peels are well flecked with brown.

In *fully ripe* bananas the starch has been converted into fruit sugars. Bananas are then at their best for flavor and digestibility and for use in fruit cups, salads, drinks, desserts, pies and *all bakery* products.

FRESH FRUIT GUIDE

FRUIT	SEASON	APPROXIMATE WEIGHT	UNITS
Apples	All year	44-lb. box or bushel	138 medium per box.
Apricots	May to August	25-lb. lug	312 per lug.
Avocados	All year	13-lb. crate	16 medium per crate.
Bananas	All year	65-lb. stems or 40-lb. box	9 hands or 145 fingers on stem. 8 hands or 110 fingers in box.
Berries:			
Blackberries	May, June, July	Pint and quart boxes in crates.	6 servings per quart.
Blueberries	May to August	½ pint, pint and quart boxes in crates.	9 to 10 servings per quart.
Raspberries (Red and Black).	May to August	½ pint, pint and quart boxes in crates.	8 to 10 servings per quart.
Strawberries	December to July	Pint and quart boxes in crates.	5 to 8 servings per quart.
Cherries (sweet)	May to July	15-lb. box	Portions determined by use.
Cranberries	September to January	25-lb. box	Portions determined by use.
Figs	June to August	10-lb. box	40 per box.
Grapefruit	All year	68- to 85-lb. box	36 to 126 per box.
Grapes	June to January	Climax basket or 28-lb. lug.	Portions determined by use.
Lemons	All year	78-lb. box	360 medium per box.
Melons:			
Cantaloupe or Honeyball.	May to September	83-lb. crate	36 average size per crate 2 servings per melon.
Casaba or Persian	July to November	42-lb. crate	6 average size per crate. 8 servings per melon.
Honeydew	June to December	40-lb. crate	8 to 9 melons per crate. 6 to 8 servings per melon.
Watermelon	May to October	18 to 40 lbs. each	15 to 20 servings per melon.
Oranges	All year	76- to 90-lb. box	96 to 324 per box. 4 gallons juice.
Peaches	June to October	Bushel basket or 18-lb. box.	Portions determined by use.
Pears	July to April	46-lb. box	120 medium per box.
Pineapple	All year	70-lb. crate	12 to 36 per crate.
Plums and Prunes	June to October	½ bushel, 28-lb. crate	208 average size per crate.
Rhubarb	All year	15- to 20-lb. box or 5-lb. carton.	Portions determined by use.
Tangerines	November to May	Half box	200 average size per box.

CANNED FRUIT GUIDE

Weights and Yields of Canned Fruits

Product—Type—Style	Size of Can	Net Weight Per Can	Approx. Count Per Can	Size of Portion	Average Portions Per Can	Approx. No. Cans for 100 Portions
Apples, heavy pack	No. 2	1 lb. 2 ozs.	....	....	....	....
	No. 10	6 lbs.	....	....	....	....
Applesauce	No. 2	1 lb. 4 ozs.	....	4 ozs.	5	20
	No. 10	6 lbs. 11 ozs.	....	4 ozs.	27	4
Apricots, halves	No. 2½	1 lb. 14 ozs.	18 to 24	3 halves	7	15
	No. 10	6 lbs. 12 ozs.	84	3 halves	28	3½
Blackberries	No. 2	1 lb. 4 ozs.	....	4 ozs.	5	20
	No. 10	6 lbs. 10 ozs.	....	4 ozs.	26	4
Cherries—Red Sour Pitted	No. 2	1 lb. 3 ozs.	....	....	....	....
	No. 10	6 lbs. 11 ozs.	....	....	....	....
Cranberry Sauce	No. 10	7 lbs. 5 ozs.	....	3 ozs.	39	2½
Figs	No. 2½	1 lb. 14 ozs.	18	3 figs	6	16
	No. 10	7 lbs.	100	3 figs	35	3
Fruit Cocktail	No. 2½	1 lb. 14 ozs.	....	4 ozs.	7	15
	No. 10	6 lbs. 12 ozs.	....	4 ozs.	27	4
Fruits for Salad	No. 2½	1 lb. 14 ozs.	....	4 ozs.	7	15
	No. 10	6 lbs. 12 ozs.	....	4 ozs.	27	4
Grapefruit	No. 2	1 lb. 4 ozs.	....	4 ozs.	4	25
	No. 10	6 lbs. 9 ozs.	....	4 ozs.	26	4
Grapefruit Juice	No. 2	18 ozs.	....	5 ozs.	3	35
	No. 10	3 quarts	....	5 ozs.	18	5½
Orange Juice	No. 2	18 ozs.	....	5 ozs.	3	35
	No. 10	3 quarts	....	5 ozs.	18	5½
Peaches, Clingstone	No. 2½	1 lb. 14 ozs.	10	2 halves	5	20
	No. 10	6 lbs. 14 ozs.	66	2 halves	33	3
Peaches, Freestone, halves	No. 2½	1 lb. 14 ozs.	10	2 halves	4	25
	No. 10	6 lbs. 14 ozs.	50	2 halves	25	4
Pears, halves	No. 2½	1 lb. 14 ozs.	8	1 half	8	12½
	No. 10	6 lbs. 12 ozs.	28	1 half	28	3½
Pineapple, sliced	No. 2½	1 lb. 14 ozs.	8	1 slice	8	12½
	No. 10	6 lbs. 12 ozs.	28	1 slice	28	3½
Pineapple, crushed	No. 2½	1 lb. 14 ozs.	....	4 ozs.	7	15
	No. 10	6 lbs. 14 ozs.	....	4 ozs.	28	3½
Pineapple Juice	No. 2	18 ozs.	....	5 ozs.	3	35
	No. 10	3 qts. 2 ozs.	....	5 ozs.	18	5½
Plums, whole	No. 10	6 lbs. 14 ozs.	38	2 plums	19	5
Prunes, prepared	No. 2	1 lb. 14 ozs.	30	5 prunes	6	17
	No. 10	6 lbs. 14 ozs.	185	5 prunes	35	3
Raspberries	No. 2	1 lb. 5 ozs.	....	4 ozs.	5	20
	No. 10	6 lbs. 14 ozs.	....	4 ozs.	28	3½

DIRECTIONS FOR COOKING DRIED FRUITS
100 Portions

Portion: 3 ounces.

FRUIT	WEIGHT (POUNDS)	WATER AMOUNT (APPROX.)	METHOD	SUGAR AMOUNT (APPROXIMATE)
Apples	9	To cover	Heat to boiling temperature. Cook 40 minutes.	None needed. Add 1 ounce to each pound of apples, if desired.
Apricots	9	To cover	Heat to boiling temperature. Cook 30 to 40 minutes.	Allow 2 ounces to each pound of apricots.
Figs	9	To cover	Heat to boiling temperature. Cook 20 to 30 minutes.	Allow 1 ounce to each pound of figs. Add during last 15 minutes of cooking.
Peaches	9	To cover	Heat to boiling temperature. Cook 35 to 45 minutes.	Allow 1 ounce to each pound of peaches.
Pears	8	To cover	Heat to boiling temperature. Cook 25 to 35 minutes.	Allow 1 ounce to each pound of pears.
Prunes	11	To cover	Heat to boiling temperature. Cook 45 to 60 minutes.	None needed. Add 2 ounces to each pound of prunes, if desired.

Rinse fruit. Drain before adding cooking water. Cook in covered vessel.

Stir in sugar only during last 5 minutes of cooking.

NOTE.—1. Remove cores in apples and pears before cooking.

2. Excellent for use in cakes, cookies, pies and puddings.

APPLESAUCE

Portion: 4 to 5 ounces (approx. ⅔ cup).

INGREDIENTS	100 PORTIONS			............PORTIONS
	WEIGHTS		AMOUNTS (approx.)	
	Pounds	*Ounces*		
Apples, fresh, A. P.	48	....		
Water	....	....	Small amount	
Sugar	6	....	¾ gallon	
Lemon juice	....	....	¾ cup (3 lemons)	

Wash and core apples. Cut in quarters.

Place in cooking vessel. Add enough water to prevent sticking.

Cook 45 to 60 minutes or until tender. Press through fine sieve.

Stir in sugar and lemon juice.

NOTE.—Apples may be peeled, cooked, and mashed or pressed through fine sieve.

Variation

Spiced Applesauce

Add ¾ ounce (3 tablespoons) cinnamon and ½ ounce (2 tablespoons) ground cloves to hot applesauce.

APPLESAUCE

(Using dehydrated apple nuggets)

Portion: Approx. 4 ounces (approx. ½ cup).

INGREDIENTS	100 PORTIONS			............PORTIONS
	WEIGHTS		AMOUNTS (approx.)	
	Pounds	Ounces		
Apple nuggets, dehydrated.....	3	8	1¼ gallons................	
Water, hot	----	----	3⅜ gallons................	
Sugar	2	8	1¼ quarts	
Cinnamon	----	½	2 tablespoons	

Mix together apple nuggets, water and sugar. Cover. Heat, slowly, to boiling temperature, stirring occasionally.

Let simmer 1 hour, stirring occasionally. Stir in cinnamon.

NOTE.—1. Nutmeg may be used in place of cinnamon, or spices may be omitted.

2. A better product is obtained by continuous stirring during the cooking period.

Variation

Stewed Apples

Proceed as for Applesauce but cook for 30 minutes instead of 1 hour.

BAKED APPLES

Portion: 1 apple.

INGREDIENTS	100 PORTIONS			............PORTIONS
	WEIGHTS		AMOUNTS (approx.)	
	Pounds	Ounces		
Apples, size 100, A. P...........	----	----	100	
Sugar	7	----	¾ gallon	
Salt	----	----	2 teaspoons	
Cinnamon	----	----	2 teaspoons	
Water	----	----	2½ quarts	

Wash and core apples. Place in baking pans.

Stir sugar, salt and cinnamon into water until sugar is dissolved. Pour over apples.

Bake in moderate oven (350° F.) 1 to 1½ hours.

Baste with sirup several times during cooking. Add more water if necessary.

NOTE.—1. Serve with Hard Sauce (page 73).

2. Cover if apples begin to brown before being thoroughly done.

Variation

Stuffed Baked Apples

Before baking, stuff apples with a mixture of 2 pounds 12 ounces (½ gallon) chopped dates and 1 pound 8 ounces (1½ quarts) chopped nut meats.

BUTTERED APPLES

Portion: Approx. 5 ounces (approx. ¾ cup).

INGREDIENTS	100 PORTIONS			..........PORTIONS
	WEIGHTS		AMOUNTS (approx.)	
	Pounds	*Ounces*		
Apples, A. P.	20	....		
Water	....	....	1¼ quarts	
Butter, melted	1	4	2½ cups	
Sugar	3	4	6½ cups	
Salt	....	2	¼ cup	

Wash apples. Cut into sections and remove cores. Arrange sections in baking pans. Cover bottom of pans with water.

Brush apples with butter. Sprinkle with sugar and salt. Cover.

Bake in moderate oven (350° F.) 20 minutes.

Remove cover.

Increase temperature of oven to 400° F. Continue baking about 15 minutes or until apples are tender and lightly browned.

Add more water as it evaporates.

NOTE.—Serve with pork or as a dessert.

ESCALLOPED APPLES

Portion: 4 to 5 ounces (approx. ⅔ cup).

INGREDIENTS	100 PORTIONS			..........PORTIONS
	WEIGHTS		AMOUNTS (approx.)	
	Pounds	*Ounces*		
Apples, A. P.	30	....		
Sugar, brown	1	4	3¾ cups	
Nutmeg	...	½	1¾ tablespoons	
Salt	...	½	1 tablespoon	
Butter, melted	2	...	1 quart	
Bread crumbs, soft	2	12	1½ gallons	
Lemon juice	....	....	1 pint (8 lemons)	
Water or fruit juice	....	....	1¼ gallons	

Wash apples. Cut into wedges. Core and peel. Mix together sugar, nutmeg, salt, butter and crumbs.

Cover bottoms of greased baking pans with layer of crumbs.

Place apples and crumb mixture in alternate layers with bread crumb layer on top.

Combine lemon juice and water or fruit juice. Pour over apples.

Bake in moderate oven (350° F.) 1¼ to 1½ hours.

NOTE.—Serve with meats or as a dessert.

BAKED APPLE RINGS

Portion: 4 rings. (approx. 4½ ounces).

INGREDIENTS	100 PORTIONS			............PORTIONS
	WEIGHTS		AMOUNTS (approx.)	
	Pounds	Ounces		
Apples, medium-sized, A. P....	35	....	....	....
Butter or other fat, melted....	1	8	1½ pints	....
Sugar, brown	2	8	1¾ quarts	....
Water, boiling	....	....	1 pint	....

Wash and core apples. Slice in rings ½ inch thick. Arrange, slightly overlapping, in greased baking pans.

Stir fat and sugar into water until sugar is dissolved. Pour over apples.

Bake in moderate oven (350° F.) 30 to 40 minutes or until tender. Baste apples with sirup occasionally.

NOTE.—Serve with meats.

BAKED BANANAS

Portion: 1 whole or 2 half bananas.

INGREDIENTS	100 PORTIONS			...........PORTIONS
	WEIGHTS		AMOUNTS (approx.)	
	Pounds	Ounces		
Bananas, firm	25 to 30	....	100	....
Butter, melted	1	4	2½ cups	....
Salt	....	....	As desired	....

Peel bananas. Place in well greased baking pans. Brush well with butter. Sprinkle lightly with salt.

Bake in moderate oven (375° F.) 15 to 18 minutes or until tender.

NOTE.—1. Serve very hot as vegetable, or as dessert with Custard Sauce (page 72) or Lemon Sauce (page 73).

2. Test for doneness of bananas by piercing with fork.

3. Bananas may be baked until almost done, then placed in broiler to brown.

Variations

Bananas Baked with Maple Sirup

Brush bananas with lemon juice. Pour sirup over bananas, allowing ¾ to 1 cup for every 6 bananas. Bake as for Baked Bananas.

Serve hot as a sweet entree with beef or ham or with cream as a hot dessert.

Bananas Baked with Sugar (Glazed)

Sprinkle white or brown sugar lightly over bananas. Add cinnamon if desired. Bake as for Baked Bananas.

Serve hot as an entree with beef, ham, chicken or turkey.

Bananas Baked with Cranberries

Pour cranberry sauce over bananas allowing 1 cup for every 6 bananas. Bake as for Baked Bananas.

Serve hot with beef, chicken or turkey.

Bananas Baked with Jelly or Jam

Spread tart jelly or jam over bananas allowing 1 to 2 tablespoons for each banana.

Bake as for Baked Bananas. Serve hot as a sweet entree or as a dessert.

BANANA FRITTERS

Yield: 200 medium sized.   Portion: 2 fritters.

INGREDIENTS	100 PORTIONS		..........PORTIONS
	WEIGHTS	AMOUNTS (approx.)	
	Pounds	Ounces		
Flour	4	4	4¼ quarts	
Baking powder	....	4	10 tablespoons	
Salt	....	4	½ cup	
Sugar	1	12	3½ cups	
Eggs, beaten	1	4	12 (1¼ pints)	
Milk, liquid	....	....	1¾ quarts	
Shortening, melted	....	6	¾ cup	
Bananas, firm	15 to 20	....	50 to 65....................	
Flour for rolling	1	....	1 quart	

Mix together flour, baking powder, salt and sugar.

Combine eggs, milk and shortening. Stir into dry ingredients until batter is smooth.

Peel bananas. Cut each into 3 or 4 diagonal pieces. Roll in flour.

Dip into batter, completely coating banana with batter.

Fry in hot deep fat (375° F.) 4 to 6 minutes, turning frequently to brown evenly.

Drain 1 or 2 minutes on absorbent paper. Serve immediately.

NOTE.—Serve very hot with sugar, sugar and cinnamon, sirup, Lemon Sauce (page 73) or Orange Sauce (page 74).

APPLE CRANBERRY SAUCE
(Using dehydrated apple nuggets and dehydrated cranberries)

Yield: Approx. 2 gallons.   Portion: Approx. ¼ cup.

INGREDIENTS	100 PORTIONS		..........PORTIONS
	WEIGHTS	AMOUNTS (approx.)	
	Pounds	Ounces		
Apple nuggets, dehydrated....	1	....	½ gallon	
Cranberries, flaked, dehydrated.	....	9	2¼ pints	
Water, hot	....	....	1½ gallons	
Sugar	4	....	½ gallon	

Soak apple nuggets and cranberries in water 30 minutes.

Add sugar. Cover. Heat, slowly, to boiling temperature. Let simmer 30 minutes, stirring occasionally. Cool.

CRANBERRY AND ORANGE RELISH

Yield: Approx. 13 pounds.

Portion: 2 ounces (approx. ¼ cup).

| INGREDIENTS | 100 PORTIONS | | ....PORTIONS |
	WEIGHTS	AMOUNTS (approx.)	
	Pounds	Ounces		
Cranberries, A. P.	5	....	1¼ gallons	
Oranges	5	....	10 whole	
Sugar	5	....	2½ quarts	
Salt	....	....	½ teaspoon	

Pick-over cranberries. Wash. Drain.

Quarter oranges. Remove seeds. Combine cranberries and oranges. Chop fine.

Stir in sugar and salt until dissolved. Chill.

NOTE.—1 pound (1½ pints) raisins, chopped, may be added.

CRANBERRY SAUCE

Yield: Approx. 2 gallons.

Portion: 2 ounces (approx. ¼ cup).

| INGREDIENTS | 100 PORTIONS | | ....PORTIONS |
	WEIGHTS	AMOUNTS (approx.)	
	Pounds	Ounces		
Cranberries, A. P.	5	....	1¼ gallons	
Sugar	5	....	2½ quarts	
Water	....	....	2½ quarts	

Pick-over cranberries. Wash. Drain.

Combine sugar and water. Heat to boiling temperature. Cook 5 minutes.

Add cranberries. Cook slowly about 5 minutes or until all the skins pop open. Do not stir.

Pour into container. Cool.

Variation

Molded Strained Cranberry Sauce

Pick-over cranberries. Wash. Drain. Add water.

Heat to boiling temperature. Cook until all the skins pop open.

Strain through fine sieve. Stir in sugar.

Heat to boiling temperature. Cook 5 minutes.

Skim. Pour into molds or pans. Chill until firm.

CRANBERRY SAUCE
(Using sliced, dehydrated cranberries)

Yield: Approx. 2 gallons.   Portion: Approx. ¼ cup.

INGREDIENTS	100 PORTIONS			..........PORTIONS
	WEIGHTS		AMOUNTS (approx.)	
	Pounds	*Ounces*		
Cranberries, sliced, dehydrated.	1	....	3½ pints	
Water, hot	....	....	1½ gallons	
Sugar	7	....	3½ quarts	

Soak cranberries in water 45 minutes. Add sugar. Cover.

Heat, slowly, to boiling temperature, stirring occasionally.

Let simmer about 15 minutes or until tender. Serve hot or cold.

CRANBERRY SAUCE
(Using flaked, dehydrated cranberries)

Yield: Approx. 2 gallons.   Portion: Approx. ¼ cup.

INGREDIENTS	100 PORTIONS			..........PORTIONS
	WEIGHTS		AMOUNTS (approx.)	
	Pounds	*Ounces*		
Cranberries, flaked, dehydrated.	1	....	1 quart	
Sugar	8	8	4¼ quarts	
Water, hot	....	....	¾ gallon	

Mix together cranberries and sugar thoroughly.

Stir in water. Cover. Heat, slowly, to boiling temperature, stirring gently.

Cook 1 to 2 minutes. Pour into pans. Cool until firm.

CRANBERRY SAUCE
(Using whole, dehydrated cranberries)

Yield: Approx. 2 gallons.   Portion: Approx. ¼ cup.

INGREDIENTS	100 PORTIONS			..........PORTIONS
	WEIGHTS		AMOUNTS (approx.)	
	Pounds	*Ounces*		
Cranberries, whole, dehydrated.	1	....	1½ quarts	
Water, hot	....	....	1½ gallons	
Sugar	7	....	3½ quarts	

Soak cranberries in water 45 minutes or until berries are softened. Add sugar. Cover.

Heat, slowly, to boiling temperature. Let simmer 15 minutes, stirring occasionally. Serve hot or cold.

FRUIT CUP

Yield: Approx. 3 gallons.

Portion: 5 ounces (approx. ½ cup).

INGREDIENTS	100 PORTIONS			..........PORTIONS
	WEIGHTS		AMOUNTS (approx.)	
	Pounds	Ounces		
Pineapple, diced	13	6	2 No. 10 cans (1½ gallons).	
Pears, sliced	6	10	1 No. 10 can (3¼ quarts).	
Peaches, sliced	6	10	1 No. 10 can (3¼ quarts).	
Oranges, diced	4	....	8 medium (1 quart)	
Grapefruit sections, halved	6	9	1 No. 10 can (3¼ quarts).	
Sugar	1	8	1½ pints	
Lemon rind, grated	....	1	¼ cup	

Combine all ingredients. Chill thoroughly before serving.

NOTE.—1. Add diced apple, sliced ripe banana, grapefruit sections, grapes, diced melons or other fresh fruits when available.

2. Use fruit sirups in fruit-ades or sauces.

BAKED RHUBARB

Portion: 4 to 5 ounces (approx. ⅔ cup).

INGREDIENTS	100 PORTIONS			..........PORTIONS
	WEIGHTS		AMOUNTS (approx.)	
	Pounds	Ounces		
Rhubarb, A. P.	35	....		
Salt	....	½	1 tablespoon	
Sugar	10	....	1¼ gallons	
Water	....	....	1¾ quarts	

Remove rhubarb leaves. Do not peel stalk. Wash. Cut in 1-inch pieces. Place in baking pans.

Stir salt and sugar into water. Pour over rhubarb.

Bake in moderate oven (350° F.) 5 to 10 minutes or until tender.

NOTE.—Cinnamon or nutmeg may be added if desired.

Fish

Fish deserves a prominent place on the menu. It is an excellent source of protein. One average portion of fish will furnish, daily, ¼ to ½ the protein required by an adult. Fish also supplies important vitamins and minerals needed daily in the diet.

Types of Fish

The fat content of fish varies with the species and to some extent with the season. As a rule, fat fish are preferable for baking and broiling. The lean fish are best for boiling, steaming, and chowders. Both fat and lean fish can be fried.

Cleaning and Preparing Fresh Fish

Most fish have a season during the year when fresh varieties are particularly abundant. Although today's market provides almost any kind of fish, fresh or frozen, already cleaned and dressed, some information on cleaning and preparing fresh fish for cooking is desirable.

How to Clean Fresh Fish

Soak the fish in water for a few minutes. Scales are more easily removed from a wet fish. Remove from water. Hold the fish firmly near the base of the tail. Scrape off the scales with a scaler or a knife held vertically as it is moved over the fish, scraping from the tail toward the head, taking care to get off all scales near the base of the fins and head.

Cut a slit in the belly of the fish from the head to tail. Remove the viscera. Cut around the pelvic fins and remove them. Cut off the tail. Cut off head, including pectoral fins, removing these with the head.

Cut into the flesh of the fish at each side of the base of the large back fin. Grasp the rear part of the fin and give a quick pull forward toward the head of the fish. This will remove both fin bones and fin. The anal or ventral fin is removed in the same manner, first cutting the flesh around the fin. Fins should never be trimmed off with shears or knife.

Wash the fish in cold running water, removing any remaining viscera and membranes. The fish is now ready for cooking. Large fish may be cut crosswise into steaks.

To Fillet or Bone Fish

With a sharp knife, cut down the flesh just behind the head until the knife reaches the backbone. Turn the knife flat and cut the flesh along the backbone to the tail. Lift off the whole side of the fish in one piece. Turn the fish over and loosen the meat from the other side in the same manner. Take out any small bones that remain near the shoulders after the fillets have been cut away.

Cover fish bones and head with water. Heat to boiling temperature. Let simmer 1 hour to form a stock to use in fish chowders or fish recipes requiring a liquid.

To Skin Fish

Place the fillet with the skin side down on a flat surface. Loosen the skin from the flesh at the tail end by pushing forward a sharp knife held flat against the skin. Grasp the separated skin and flesh together and hold tight against the knife while loosening the skin.

The fish need not be scaled first.

Storage

Fresh Fish: Fresh fish, including shell fish, are highly perishable and will spoil within a few hours if left exposed to warm temperatures.

Fresh fish should be iced immediately after being caught and kept on ice until ready to use. It should not be kept longer than 2 to 3 days.

Frozen Fish: Frozen fish may be held in cold storage for several months.

Frozen fish should not be defrosted until ready to prepare for cooking. Never allow frozen fish to thaw and re-freeze. Follow instructions for defrosting as specified on the container.

Salted Fish: Salting is a method of preserving fish, with relatively large quantities of salt. Salted fish may be purchased whole, in fillets or shredded. Some fish are lightly salted merely to preserve them for a short period of time until they reach the consumer. These can be de-salted and cooked in the same manner as fresh fish. Salted fish are perishable and should be stored in a clean, dry, cool place.

Smoked Fish: Smoked fish are perishable and should be stored in a clean, dry, cool place until ready to use.

Canned Fish: Canned fish will keep for an indefinite period as long as the seal of the can is not broken. Canned fish should be stored in a dry, cool place.

Cooking

Fillets and steaks are sometimes lightly salted, when packaged at the fisheries, in which case additional salt may not be required in cooking. Season, to taste, before serving.

Cooked, left-over fish must be placed in refrigerator as soon as cool enough to handle after serving. Use left-over fish within 24 hours.

COMMONLY AVAILABLE FISH

KIND	TYPE	SEASON	COOKING METHODS
Salt Water:			
Barracuda	Lean	Feb.-June	Broil, bake, boil or steam.
Bluefish	Lean	All year	Broil, bake, fry.
Butterfish	Fat	April-Dec.	Broil, fry.
Cod	Lean	All year	Broil, bake, boil or steam, chowder.
Croaker	Lean	Feb.-Nov.	Broil, bake, pan-fry, boil, chowder.
Flounder	Lean	All year	Broil, bake, pan-fry, chowder.
Grouper	Lean	Nov.-April	Broil, bake, boil or steam, chowder.
Haddock	Lean	All year	Broil, bake, boil or steam, chowder.
Hake	Lean	All year	Bake, boil or steam, chowder.
Halibut	Fat	All year	Broil, bake, boil or steam, chowder.
Herring	Fat	All year	Broil, bake, boil or steam, pan-fry.
Mackerel	Fat	April-Nov.	Broil, bake.
Pollock	Lean	All year	Broil, bake, boil or steam, chowder.
Rockfish	Lean	All year	Broil, bake.
Salmon	Fat	All year	Broil, bake, boil or steam.
Scup (porgy)	Lean	Jan.-Nov.	Broil, bake, pan-fry.
Sea Bass	Fat	All year	Broil, bake, boil or steam, pan-fry, chowder.
Sea Trout	Fat	April-Nov.	Broil, bake, pan-fry.
Shad	Fat	Dec.-July	Broil, bake.
Smelt	Fat	Sept.-May	Broil, fry.
Snapper, red	Lean	All year	Broil, bake, boil or steam.
Spanish Mackerel	Fat	Nov.-April	Broil, bake, pan-fry.
Striped Bass	Fat	All year	Broil, bake, fry.
Swordfish	Lean	July-Sept.	Broil, bake.
Tuna	Fat	All year	Broil, bake, boil or steam.
White Perch	Lean	All year	Broil, bake, boil or steam, fry, chowder.
Whiting	Lean	May-Dec.	Broil, bake, fry.
Fresh Water:			
Blue Pike	Lean	March-Dec.	Broil, bake, boil or steam, fry, chowder.
Lake Trout	Fat	April-Nov.	Broil, bake, boil or steam, fry.
Whitefish	Fat	April-Dec	Broil, bake, fry.
Yellow Perch	Lean	All year	Broil, bake, boil or steam, fry, chowder.
Yellow Pike	Lean	All year	Broil, bake, boil or steam, fry, chowder.
Shellfish:			
Clams	Lean	All year	Broil, bake, boil or steam, deep-fry, chowder.
Crabs	Lean	All year	Broil, bake, boil or steam, pan-fry, chowder.
Lobsters	Lean	All year	Broil, bake, boil or steam, chowder.
Oysters	Lean	Sept.-April	Bake, broil, steam, fry, chowder.
Scallops	Lean	All year	Bake, boil or steam, fry.
Shrimp	Lean	All year	Bake, boil, steam, fry, chowder.

NOTE.—Fry refers to both pan-fry and deep-fry.

BAKED FILLET OF FLOUNDER

Portion: Approx. 4 ounces.

| INGREDIENTS | 100 PORTIONS | | | ....PORTIONS |
| | WEIGHTS | | AMOUNTS (approx.) | |
	Pounds	Ounces		
Butter or other fat, melted.....	2	....	1 quart	
Onions, chopped	4	....	¾ gallon............................	
Salt	....	4	½ cup	
Pepper	....	1	3½ tablespoons	
Flounder fillets	25	....		

Place fillets in greased baking pans.

Combine fat, onions, salt and pepper, mixing thoroughly. Pour over fish.

Bake in slow oven (325°F.) about 25 minutes.

NOTE.—Other fish fillets may be used.

BAKED WHOLE FISH

Portion: Approx. 5 to 6 ounces.

| INGREDIENTS | 100 PORTIONS | | | ....PORTIONS |
| | WEIGHTS | | AMOUNTS (approx.) | |
	Pounds	Ounces		
Fish, whole, A. P.	56	....	16 whole	
Salt	....	5	10 tablespoons	
Paprika	....	1¼	5 tablespoons	
Butter or other fat, melted.....	2	....	1 quart	

Split and clean fish. Wash thoroughly. Wipe with clean cloth.

Place skin side down on greased shallow baking pan.

Combine salt, paprika and fat. Brush on fish.

Bake in hot oven (375°F.) 30 to 40 minutes until fish is browned and flaked from bone.

NOTE.—Trout, Spanish Mackerel, Whitefish, Bluefish, Haddock, Flounder or Red Salmon may be used.

STUFFING FOR BAKED WHOLE FISH

Yield: Approx. 10 pounds.   Portion: ½ cup (approx. 3 ounces).

INGREDIENTS	100 PORTIONS			........Portions
	WEIGHTS		AMOUNTS (approx.)	
	Pounds	Ounces		
Onion, minced	1	4	3¾ cups	
Celery, diced	....	8	1 pint	
Butter or other fat, melted.....	2	....	1 quart	
Bread cubes, soft	8	....	4½ gallons	
Lemon juice	....	....	1 pint	
Salt	....	4	½ cup	
Pepper	....	....	2 teaspoons	

Fry onions and celery in fat until clear.

Combine bread, lemon juice, salt and pepper.

Stir in onion, celery and fat. Mix well.

Stuff fish. Bake.

BAKED STUFFED FISH FILLETS

Portion: Approx. 5 ounces.

INGREDIENTS	100 PORTIONS			........Portions
	WEIGHTS		AMOUNTS (approx.)	
	Pounds	Ounces		
Fish, fillets, skinned	30	---	------------	
Bread stuffing	10	---	2½ gallons ------------	
Salt	---	2	¼ cup ------------	
Pepper	---	¼	1 tablespoon ------------	
Bacon, sliced	1	---		

Cut fillets into 4- to 5-inch pieces. Place mound of stuffing on each portion.

Roll. Tie with string or fasten with toothpicks. Place in well greased baking pans.

Sprinkle with salt and pepper. Place ⅓ strip of bacon on each roll.

Bake in moderate oven (375° F.) 30 minutes.

NOTE.—Serve with Tomato Sauce (page 218).

BAKED FISH WITH TOMATOES

Portion: Approx. 6 ounces

INGREDIENTS	100 PORTIONS			.... PORTIONS
	WEIGHTS		AMOUNTS (approx.)	
	Pounds	*Ounces*		
Fish, fillets or steaks	30	---		
Onions, chopped	---	8	1½ cups	
Celery, chopped	2	---	½ gallon	
Peppers, green, chopped	---	8	1 pint	
Butter or other fat	---	8	1 cup	
Salt	---	3	6 tablespoons	
Pepper	---	¼	1 tablespoon	
Flour	---	4	1 cup	
Tomatoes	12	8	2 No. 10 cans (6½ quarts).	

Cut fish in 3- to 4-inch pieces. Place in greased baking pans.

Fry onions, celery, and green pepper in fat until tender.

Stir in salt, pepper, and flour. Add tomatoes. Heat to boiling temperature. Let simmer until mixture is slightly thickened.

Pour sauce over fish. Bake in moderate oven (350° F.) 1 hour. Serve sauce with fish.

NOTE.—Any fish suitable for baking may be used. See chart (page 95).

BROILED FISH

Portion: Approx. 5 ounces

INGREDIENTS	100 PORTIONS			.... PORTIONS
	WEIGHTS		AMOUNTS (approx.)	
	Pounds	*Ounces*		
Fish, fillets or steaks	30	---		
Oil, salad	---	---	1 pint	
Salt	---	2½	5 tablespoons	
Pepper	---	¼	1 tablespoon	
Parsley, chopped fine	---	3	1 cup	

Cut fish into 3- to 4-inch pieces.

Combine oil, salt, pepper, and parsley. Dip each portion of fish in oil mixture.

Place fish on preheated broiler pan or in shallow baking pans about 2 inches from flame.

Broil 10 to 15 minutes or until fish is browned. Baste fish while cooking.

NOTE.—1. If skin is left on fillet, fish should be placed skin side down in pan.

2. Serve with Creole Sauce (page 213), Mock Hollandaise Sauce (page 214), or Drawn Butter Sauce (Page 214).

Variation

Oven-Broiled Fish

Prepare fish. Place in shallow baking pans.

Bake in moderate oven (375° F.) 30 to 40 minutes. Baste fish while baking.

DEEP FAT FRIED FISH

Portion: Approx. 5 ounces.

INGREDIENTS	100 PORTIONS			.... PORTIONS
	WEIGHTS		AMOUNTS (approx.)	
	Pounds	Ounces		
Fish, fillets or steaks	30	---		
Eggs, slightly beaten	1	8	15 (1½ pints)	
Milk, liquid	---	---	1 pint	
Salt	---	2½	5 tablespoons	
Pepper	---	¼	1 tablespoon	
Bread crumbs, dry	2	---	2½ quarts	

Cut fillets into 3- to 4-inch pieces.

Combine eggs, milk, salt and pepper. Mix thoroughly.

Dip fish in egg mixture. Roll in bread crumbs. Cover completely.

Fry in deep fat at 375° F. 4 to 6 minutes or until browned.

Drain on absorbent paper. Serve immediately.

Variation

Pan-Fried Fish

Omit eggs and milk. Sprinkle fish with salt and pepper. Dredge with flour. Roll in bread crumbs or cornmeal.

Pan-fry in hot fat allowing 3 to 4 minutes cooking for each side. Turn to insure even browning. Drain on absorbent paper. Serve immediately.

Breaded Baked Fish Fillets

Place breaded fillets in single layer in well greased baking pans.

Place ½ slice bacon on top of each fillet.

Bake in moderate oven (375° F.) 30 minutes or until tender and browned.

CODFISH BALLS

Portion: 2 (2½ to 3-ounce) balls.

INGREDIENTS	100 PORTIONS			............PORTIONS
	WEIGHTS		AMOUNTS (approx.)	
	Pounds	*Ounces*		
Potatoes, mashed	20	....	2½ gallons	
Codfish, canned	10	....	1¼ gallons	
Butter or other fat, melted......	....	10	1¼ cups	
Eggs, slightly beaten	2	....	20	
Salt	....	....	To taste	

Mix together potatoes, fish, fat and eggs. Salt to taste.

Form into balls or cakes using a No. 20 ice cream scoop.

Fry in deep fat at 375°F. for 2 minutes or until light golden brown.

NOTE.—1. Fish balls may be rolled in bread crumbs, crackermeal, cornmeal or flour before frying.

2. Amount of salt added varies with salt in potatoes and fish.

CREAMED CODFISH

Yield: Approx. 5 gallons.   Portion: ⅔ cup (approx. 6 ounces).

INGREDIENTS	100 PORTIONS			............PORTIONS
	WEIGHTS		AMOUNTS (approx.)	
	Pounds	*Ounces*		
Codfish, cooked, flaked	15	....	1¾ gallons	
Cream Sauce, medium............ (page 208), hot	....	....	4 gallons	
Eggs, beaten	2	....	20 (1 quart)	

Mix together codfish and cream sauce.

Add eggs, stirring rapidly to prevent cooking.

NOTE.—Serve on toast or rice or in casseroles with buttered crumbs.

BOILED FINNAN HADDIE

Portion: Approx. 4 ounces.

INGREDIENTS	100 PORTIONS			...........PORTIONS
	WEIGHTS		AMOUNTS (approx.)	
	Pounds	*Ounces*		
Finnan Haddie, fillets............	25	....	....	
Water, cold	....	....	To cover	
Milk, liquid	....	....	¾ gallon	
Butter or other fat	....	6	¾ cup	

Place fillets in baking pans. Cover with water.

Heat to boiling temperature. Let simmer about 10 minutes. Pour off water.

Add milk. ·Heat, slowly, to boiling temperature.

Dot with butter and serve.

Variation

Steamed Finnan Haddie

Place fillets in pans. Place in steamer. Steam about 15 minutes or until tender. Sprinkle lightly with pepper.

NOTE.—Fish may be placed over boiling water, covered tightly and steamed until done.

ESCALLOPED FISH

Portion: Approx. 5 ounces.

INGREDIENTS	100 PORTIONS			...........PORTIONS
	WEIGHTS		AMOUNTS (approx.)	
	Pounds	*Ounces*		
Fish, cooked, flaked	15	....	1¾ gallons	
Cream Sauce, medium thick (page 209).	....	....	1½ gallons	
Salt	....	2	¼ cup	
Pepper	....	½	1¾ tablespoons	
Bread crumbs, dry	4	....	1¼ gallons	

Combine fish, cream sauce, salt and pepper.

Arrange fish mixture and bread crumbs in alternate layers in greased baking pans.

Sprinkle surface with crumbs.

Bake in moderate oven (375°F.) 25 minutes.

FISH CAKES

Portion: 2 (3-inch) cakes.

INGREDIENTS	100 PORTIONS			............PORTIONS
	WEIGHTS		AMOUNTS (approx.)	
	Pounds	Ounces		
Fish, cooked, flaked	20	....	2½ gallons	
Potatoes, mashed, unseasoned.	20	....	2½ gallons	
Eggs, slightly beaten	1	4	16 (1½ pints)..............	
Bread crumbs, dry, fine	2	12	3½ quarts	
Salt	....	3	6 tablespoons	
Pepper	....	....	1½ teaspoons	
Flour	1	...	1 quart..............	

Combine fish, potatoes, eggs, crumbs, salt, and pepper.

Place in refrigerator to chill thoroughly.

Shape into 3-ounce cakes, 3 inches in diameter and 1 inch thick. Roll in flour.

Fry in hot, deep fat at 375°F. about 2 to 3 minutes.

Drain on absorbent paper.

NOTE.—1. Any cooked fish may be used.

2. Serve with Tomato Sauce (page 218).

TUNA FISH A LA KING

Portion: Approx. 5 ounces.

INGREDIENTS	100 PORTIONS			............PORTIONS
	WEIGHTS		AMOUNTS (approx.)	
	Pounds	Ounces		
Peppers, green, chopped	1	....	1 quart	
Mushrooms, chopped	2	....	3½ quarts	
Butter or other fat, melted.....	....	8	½ pint	
Cream Sauce, medium.............. (page 213).	....	....	1¼ gallons	
Tuna fish, flaked	16	....	21 No. 1 (12-oz.) cans (2 gallons).	
Pimientos, chopped	1	14	2 (15-ounce) cans (4½ cups).	

Fry green peppers and mushrooms in fat about 5 minutes or until tender.

Stir in cream sauce, tuna and pimientos. Reheat.

NOTE.—Serve hot on toast.

SALMON LOAF

Portion: Approx. 6 ounces

INGREDIENTS	100 PORTIONS			............PORTIONS
	WEIGHTS		AMOUNTS (approx.)	
	Pounds	*Ounces*		
Salmon	24	---	24 No. 1 cans (3 gallons).	
Celery, diced	1	---	1 quart	
Onions, chopped	1	---	1½ pints	
Butter or other fat	1	---	1 pint	
Milk and salmon liquor	---	---	½ gallon	
Bread crumbs, dry	3	8	1 gallon	
Salt	---	1	2 tablespoons	
Pepper	---	¼	1 tablespoon	
Tabasco sauce	---	---	1 tablespoon	
Lemon juice	---	---	1 pint (8 lemons)	
Lemon rind, grated	---	1	¼ cup	
Egg yolks, beaten	1	---	24 (1 pint)	
Egg whites, stiffly beaten	1	6	24 (1½ pints)	

Drain salmon. Reserve liquor. Remove bones and skin. Flake.

Fry celery and onions in fat until clear.

Combine salmon, celery, onions, milk, and bread crumbs. Stir in salt, pepper, tabasco sauce, lemon juice, lemon rind, and egg yolks. Mix well.

Fold in egg whites. Pack mixture in well greased baking pans.

Bake in moderate oven (350° F.) 1 hour or until firm.

NOTE.—1. Use all the salmon liquor drained from salmon.

2. Serve with Egg Sauce (page 210) or Pimento Sauce (page 210).

Variations

Tuna Fish Loaf

Use 24 pounds (24 1-pound cans, 3 gallons) tuna fish in place of salmon.

Salmon Croquettes

Chill salmon mixture thoroughly.

Make croquettes using a No. 16 scoop. Shape and crumb for frying. Chill thoroughly.

Fry in hot, deep fat at 375° F. about 5 minutes or until golden brown.

STEAMED CLAMS

Scrub clams. Wash under running water to remove sand.

Place in large kettle. Add 1 quart water for each bushel of clams.

Cover closely. Heat to boiling temperature.

Cook until shells open. Remove from heat immediately.

Serve hot, in shells, with melted butter and cups of liquor from kettle.

NOTE.—1. Clams removed from shells may be breaded and fried.

2. Chopped clams may be used in Clam Cakes. See recipe for Fish Cakes (page 102).

BOILED HARD SHELL CRAB

Portion: 1 (approx. 8-ounce) crab; ½ cup meat (approx. 4 ounces).

Select only live crabs for cooking.

Plunge into rapidly boiling salted water (1 tablespoon salt to 1 quart water).

Cover. Heat to boiling temperature. Cook 20 minutes.

Drain. Plunge in cold water to cool thoroughly.

Break off claws and tail, or apron. Open shells by wedging strong, sharp knife at the tail end.

Remove spongy substance (gills, stomach and intestines) from between sides of top shell and body.

Remove meat. Flake.

Crack claws with cracker or small hammer.

Remove meat.

NOTE.—1. Use meat for salads, or in creamed and au gratin dishes.

2. Before using crab meat, examine it carefully for any small pieces of gristle or shell.

Variation

Steamed Crabs

Combine 3 parts water with 1 part vinegar and pour small amount, enough to create sufficient steam, into steam-jacketed kettle. Heat to boiling temperature. Place live, active crabs in kettle or steamer and cook, covered, until shells have turned red.

DEVILED CRAB

Portion: 4 to 6-ounce individual Deviled Crab.

INGREDIENTS	100 PORTIONS			............PORTIONS
	WEIGHTS		AMOUNTS (approx.)	
	Pounds	Ounces		
Crabmeat, flaked	16	....	2 gallons	
Milk, liquid	..	....	4½ quarts	
Butter or other fat, melted	1	8	1½ pints	
Flour	....	12	1½ pints	
Salt	....	2	¼ cup	
Mustard, dry	....	....	1 tablespoon	
Lemon juice	....	....	½ cup (2 lemons)	
Worcestershire sauce	....	....	2 tablespoons	
Bread crumbs, fine	2	....	1 gallon	

Examine crabmeat carefully for any small pieces of gristle or shell.

Remove cartilage or any solid particles from crabmeat. Flake.

Heat milk to boiling temperature.

Blend together fat, flour, salt and mustard to a smooth paste.

Stir into milk. Cook 5 to 10 minutes or until thickened.

Stir in lemon juice, Worcestershire sauce and crabmeat.

Stuff thoroughly scrubbed crab shells with mixture or place in greased baking pans. Cover with crumbs.

Bake in moderate oven (375°F.) about 10 minutes or until crumbs are browned.

BOILED LIVE LOBSTER

Portion: ¾ to 1-pound lobster in shell.

Select live lobster for cooking.

Hold lobster firmly just behind the claws and plunge head first into boiling salted water (1 tablespoon salt to 1 quart water).

Reheat to boiling temperature. Cook for 25 to 30 minutes or until lobsters turn bright red.

Drain. Remove lobsters.

Pull tail back from body. Split under side of shell with sharp knife. Lay open.

Remove sac (called "lady") and black intestinal vein running from head to tail. Do not remove coral and greenish liver.

Crack claws with cracker or small hammer.

NOTE.—1. Serve with melted butter or Tartare Sauce (page 218).

2. Lobster meat may be used for creamed or au gratin dishes or salad.

Variation

Cold Boiled Lobster

Plunge cooked hot lobster into cold water. Chill before splitting.

Serve with mayonnaise (page 237).

BROILED LIVE LOBSTER

Portion: ¾ to 1-pound lobster in shell.

Place lobster on its back. Cross long claws and hold firmly.

Make a deep incision through the entire body from the mouth to the tail.

Remove sac and black intestinal vein running from head to tail. Do not remove coral and greenish liver. Crack claws.

Place lobster, shell side down, in baking pan or on broiler tray.

Brush with melted butter or oil. Sprinkle lightly with salt, pepper and paprika.

Broil about 20 minutes or until meat is tender and the shell red.

NOTE.—1. Serve with drippings from lobster, melted butter and quartered lemon.

2. Select only live lobsters for broiling.

3. Crack claws with nut cracker or small hammer.

OYSTERS CREOLE

Portion: 4 ounces (approx. ½ cup).

INGREDIENTS	100 PORTIONS			............PORTIONS
	WEIGHTS		AMOUNTS (approx.)	
	Pounds	Ounces		
Onions, grated or chopped........	1	....	1½ pints	
Butter or other fat, melted......	2	....	1 quart	
Flour	....	4	½ pint	
Salt	....	4	½ cup	
Tomato juice	....	....	1 No. 10 can (3 qts.)	
Tabasco sauce	....	1	2 tablespoons	
Oysters, selects	....	....	3 gallons	

Fry onions in fat until clear. Stir in flour and salt and blend to a smooth paste. Add tomato juice and tabasco sauce.

Heat to boiling temperature. Cook until slightly thickened, stirring constantly.

Add oysters. Let simmer until edges of oysters curl.

NOTE.—1. Serve hot on toast.

2. 4 ounces (1⅓ cups) minced parsley may be stirred in after oysters are cooked.

FRIED OYSTERS

Portion: 6 to 7 oysters.

INGREDIENTS	100 PORTIONS			............PORTIONS
	WEIGHTS		AMOUNTS (approx.)	
	Pounds	Ounces		
Oysters, selects	....	....	4 gallons	
Salt	....	2	¼ cup	
Pepper	....	½	1¾ tablespoons	
Eggs, whole	....	9½	6 (1 cup)	
Milk, liquid	....	....	1⅔ cups	
Cracker meal	3	....	1 gallon	

Remove any foreign particles or shell clinging to oysters.

Mix together salt, pepper, eggs and milk.

Place oysters into egg and milk mixture. Remove oysters, individually. Coat each oyster thoroughly with meal.

Fry in hot deep fat at 375° F. 3 to 4 minutes or until crisp and brown.

Drain on absorbent paper. Serve immediately.

OYSTERS JAMBALAYA

Portion: Approx. 8 ounces, with rice.

INGREDIENTS	100 PORTIONS			............PORTIONS
	WEIGHTS		AMOUNTS (approx.)	
	Pounds	Ounces		
Oyster liquor or stock	....	....	2 gallons	
Butter or other fat	2	....	1 quart	
Flour	....	8	1 pint	
Salt	.....	2	¼ cup	
Cayenne	....	¼	¾ tablespoon	
Tomatoes	12	12	2 No. 10 cans (1½ gallons).	
Ham, cooked, diced	6	....	4½ quarts	
Oysters, standards...............	....	....	3 gallons	
Rice, cooked, hot (page 44)....	21	....	3⅛ gallons	

Strain and heat oyster liquor to boiling temperature.

Blend together fat, flour, salt and cayenne. Stir into hot liquor.

Cook until thickened, stirring constantly.

Add tomatoes, ham and oysters. Cook slowly about 10 minutes or until edges of oysters curl. Serve hot over cooked rice.

CREAMED SHRIMPS

Portion: Approx. 6 ounces.

INGREDIENTS	100 PORTIONS			............PORTIONS
	WEIGHTS		AMOUNTS (approx.)	
	Pounds	Ounces		
Egg yolks, beaten	1	....	24 (1 pint)	
Cream Sauce, medium, hot (page 208).	....	....	1¾ gallons	
Eggs, hard-cooked, diced	3	....	30	
Salt	....	2	¼ cup	
Pepper	....	½	1¾ tablespoons	
Shrimps, cooked, cleaned	20	....	4 gallons	

Stir egg yolks into cream sauce. Add hard-cooked eggs, salt and pepper.

Stir in the shrimps. Heat to boiling temperature. Simmer gently 10 minutes.

NOTE.—10 No. 5 cans (4 gallons) shrimps may be used in place of 20 pounds fresh shrimps, cooked, cleaned.

SHRIMP CHOP SUEY

Portion: 8 ounces (approx. 1 cup).

INGREDIENTS	100 PORTIONS			..........PORTIONS
	WEIGHTS		AMOUNTS (approx.)	
	Pounds	*Ounces*		
Shrimps, A. P.	20	....	2½ gallons E. P.	
Water	....	....	To cover	
Pork drippings, melted	1	8	1½ pints	
Onions, chopped	3	....	2¼ quarts	
Peppers, green, chopped	2	....	½ gallon	
Celery, chopped	4	....	1 gallon	
Tomatoes, fresh, cubed	6	....	¾ gallon	
Salt	....	1½	3 tablespoons	
Pepper	....	¼	¾ tablespoon	
Bean sprouts, drained	12	12	2 No. 10 cans (6½ quarts).	
Fish stock or water	....	....	2 gallons	
Butter or other fat, melted	1	....	1 pint	
Flour	....	8	1 pint	
Soy sauce	....	....	1 quart	
Rice, cooked (page 44)...........	21	....	3⅛ gallons	

Cover shrimps with water. Heat to boiling temperature.

Cook 20 minutes. Drain. Plunge into cold water to cool quickly.

Remove shell. Remove black vein with sharp pointed knife. Wash thoroughly.

Fry in drippings 10 minutes.

Add onions, green pepper, celery, tomatoes, salt and pepper. Simmer 10 minutes. Add bean sprouts.

Heat fish stock or water to boiling temperature.

Blend together fat and flour to a smooth paste. Stir into stock.

Cook about 10 minutes or until slightly thickened, stirring constantly.

Stir in Soy sauce. Add sauce to shrimp mixture. Reheat.

Serve with the cooked rice.

NOTE.—1. 6 No. 5 cans of shrimp may be used in place of fresh shrimp.

2. 1 No. 10 can tomatoes may be used in place of fresh tomatoes.

SHRIMPS CREOLE

Portion: Approx. 8 ounces.

INGREDIENTS	100 PORTIONS			..........PORTIONS
	WEIGHTS		AMOUNTS (approx.)	
	Pounds	Ounces		
Shrimps, A. P.	20	....	2½ gallons E. P.	....
Water	....	....	To cover	....
Tomatoes	10	....	1½ No. 10 cans (1¼ gallons).	....
Creole Sauce (page 213).......	....	....	1 gallon	....
Peas	6	10	1 No. 10 can (3¼ quarts).	....
Salt	....	2	¼ cup	....
Cayenne	....	¼	¾ tablespoon	....
Rice, cooked, hot (page 44)	21	....	3⅛ gallons	....

Cover shrimps with water. Heat to boiling temperature.

Cook 20 minutes. Drain. Plunge into cold water to cool quickly.

Remove shell. Remove black vein with sharp pointed knife. Wash thoroughly.

Combine shrimps, tomatoes, creole sauce, peas, salt and cayenne.

Heat to boiling temperature. Let simmer 10 minutes.

Serve with boiled rice.

NOTE.—6 No. 5 cans (12 pounds) (2½ gallons) shrimps may be used in place of raw shrimps.

Meat

Meat is one of the most important components of the meal. It supplies a large proportion of the nutrients necessary in a well-balanced menu.

In addition to its contribution of vitamins, minerals, protein and food energy, it has a distinctive savory value. The appearance and aroma of a well-cooked piece of meat helps to stimulate the flow of digestive juices and is thus an aid to digestion.

Storage of Meat

Meat is a perishable product and must be treated as such.

Place fresh meat under refrigeration immediately upon receiving it. Place it so that air can circulate freely around it. Store fresh meat at 32° F. to 34° F.

Optimum temperature for storing frozen meats, either boneless or bone-in, is 0° F. or lower, preferably lower.

Place left-over meat in a refrigerator as soon as it is cool enough to handle and definitely plan to use it within 24 to 36 hours.

Smoked and salted meat should also be stored in a refrigerator.

Selection of Cuts

Make a study of the carcass so that it may be cut economically and advantageously. Cuts of meat differ in tenderness according to the location in the carcass. These differences make it desirable to use certain cuts for each method of cooking.

Selection of cuts is possible in the Navy, because of the number of carcasses available. The use of all cuts, irrespective of tenderness, for a single purpose is neither necessary nor desirable.

Choose, carefully, the cuts of meat for each respective use to obtain the most satisfactory results. Select the tender cuts for steaks, chops and oven roasts, the less tender cuts for braising and stews, and the least tender for ground meat.

If both tender and less tender cuts are used for the same purpose, the tender cuts are overcooked and unpalatable before the less tender pieces are edible. In addition, it is not good economy to use a tender cut, which is expensive, when a less tender, less expensive cut will serve the same purpose and will give satisfactory results.

Cut the pieces of meat for roasting or braising of approximately uniform size so that the smaller pieces will not overcook before the larger ones are done. It is preferable to cut the pieces of meat for braising and roasting as large as possible, because this reduces the amount of shrinkage. If the pieces are not all the same size, put the largest cuts on to cook first.

Cooking Temperatures

A relatively low, constant temperature is recommended for cooking all cuts of meat regardless of the method.

The advantages of using a low, constant temperature are: less cooking loss, more servings, juicier meat, more tender meat, more uniform cooking, less fuel consumption although longer cooking time, less attention required and less splattering of the oven in roasting.

Degree of Doneness

Avoid overcooking meat. The longer meat is cooked the greater the shrinkage and loss in flavor and juiciness.

The stage of doneness depends on the kind of meat and personal preference.

A meat thermometer is recommended as the most accurate means of determining when roasted meat is done. The exterior appearance cannot be used as a guide to doneness. The thermometer should be inserted to the center of the largest muscle in the cut. The meat then is roasted until the thermometer reading indicates the desired degree of doneness.

Carving Cooked Meat

After cooking, let meat "set" about 30 minutes. This allows the meat to become firm. Hold the meat firmly and carve across the grain with a sharp knife. Keep the meat hot, before and after carving, when it is to be served hot.

Time-Table

Time-tables are based on the relation of time to weight, allowing a certain number of minutes per pound of meat at a given temperature. They are useful for estimating the time at which meat must be started in order to be done in time for the meal. Time-tables will be found under the various methods of cooking.

Seasoning

Large cuts of meat may be seasoned at any time. The most convenient time is at the beginning of the cooking stage. Salt does not penetrate more than 1 inch below the surface and any juices drawn out by it enrich the gravy. Salt will penetrate small pieces of meat fairly well.

Boning

It is desirable to remove bones in roasts before cooking to facilitate the carving of the cooked product.

Larding

To improve the flavor of lean cuts of meat, fat may be inserted into the meat with a larding needle, or slices of cod fat, suet or pork back may be placed on the top of the cuts before cooking.

FATS

Fats are important sources of calories. All fat should be used to good advantage. Excess fat from carcass meat should be rendered. Drippings from bacon, sausage, lamb, pork, and beef should be strained and held in a refrigerator to use for cooking.

Prepare Fat for Rendering

Use Only Fresh Fat: Fat should be rendered daily. If fat must be kept over night, hold it in refrigerator in largest pieces possible.

Trim Fat Carefully: Remove all lean meat, tough membranes, bones, cartilages, blood, and dirt.

Cut Into Strips For Grinding: Strips of fat will feed through grinder more easily than cubes. Do not cut until ready to render.

Grind Through Coarse Plate: Ground fat will render more quickly, render more uniformly, and will provide 10 to 15 per cent more rendered fat.

Render Immediately: Ground fat and small pieces of fat are highly perishable and should be rendered promptly.

Where to Render Fat

Top Of Stove: Preferred for small quantities of fat.

Steam-Jacketed Kettle: Preferred for large quantities of fat. Render with lid off and steam valve wide open.

Immersion Heat Unit Fryer: Suitable for rendering a small quantity of fat. Add fresh fat for rendering only when fat in fryer is hot from previous use. Do not heat fat in fryer to render a small quantity of additional fat, since each heating lowers the smoke point.

How to Render Fat

Put Ground Fat in Container: Use roasting pan, top of double-boiler or steam-jacketed kettle. Do not pack. Loose fat renders more quickly. Fat from beef, lamb, pork, and veal may be rendered separately, or together, in any proportions available.

Render Slowly: Low temperatures help to provide a high quality rendered fat. Avoid hot spots on stove where fat is likely to scorch.

Stir Frequently: Stirring prevents fat from sticking, shortens rendering time and assures a higher quality product.

Render Until Done: When completely rendered, the cracklings have separated and are a mixture of grayish white and light brown color.

Do Not Overcook: Overcooking impairs flavor and lowers the smoking point of rendered fat. Temperature of fat during rendering should not exceed 250° F.

Handling Rendered Fat

Pour Off Immediately After Rendering: The rendered fat may take on a roast meat flavor if allowed to remain with the cracklings too long after rendering.

Strain Through Cloth: Place clean cheesecloth in strainer over container. Dip and pour fat and cracklings into cloth, slowly. Press cracklings to remove fat.

Cool At Room Temperature: Allow fat to cool at room temperature in clean container.

Stir Occasionally: Stir rendered fat a few times while hardening to improve its texture.

Recovering Fat Drippings

Pour Off Excess Fat: Fat drippings not used for gravy should be saved.

Strain Fat Through Cloth: Straining assures more satisfactory fat for cooking purposes.

Cool At Room Temperature: Allow fat to cool slowly at room temperature in suitable container. If there is water in the fat it will settle to the bottom. The straight fat can then be removed.

Blending and Storage of Fats

Mixing Fats: Rendered fat from beef, lamb, pork, and veal and fat drippings may be kept separate or poured into the same container, if desired. When two or more kinds of fat are poured into the same container, they should be mixed thoroughly.

Store in Covered Containers: Cover fat to keep out light and air; like heat they are enemies of fat.

Store in Cool Place: As soon as the fat has cooled, place it in the refrigerator and hold it until ready to be used. Prevent accumulation of old stock.

BASIC METHODS OF MEAT COOKERY

There are two basic methods for cooking meat.

1. By *Dry Heat*: The more tender cuts of meat which can be roasted, broiled or fried are cooked by this method.

2. By *Moist Heat*: The less tender cuts, which contain more connective tissue and need longer cooking, in water or steam, to soften the connective tissue and make the meat more tender are cooked by this method. Braising and simmering are the two main ways of cooking meat by the *moist heat* method.

How to Roast

Season with salt and pepper: This may be done before, during, or at the end of the roasting period.

Place roast on rack, if available, in the pan, fat side up: As fat melts it runs over and through the meat, so basting is unnecessary.

Do not sear: Searing does not keep in the juices. Meat and gravy will be nicely browned without searing.

Do not add water: At constant temperature, the drippings will not burn. If the heat cannot be kept constant, a small amount of water may be necessary.

Do not cover: If covered, the meat will be surrounded by steam, making it a pot roast.

Roast at constant temperature (325° F.): Roasting in a slow oven reduces shrinkage and increases flavor, juiciness and tenderness.

Turn boneless roast: A boneless roast will cook more uniformly if turned once or twice during cooking.

Roast until done: Time required for roasting depends on the kind of meat, oven temperature and degree of doneness desired. See Time-Table for roasting.

ROASTING

(Meat Cuts for Roasting)

BEEF	LAMB	PORK	VEAL
		Fresh	
Inside (Top) Round.	Leg, boneless.	Leg, boneless.	Leg, boneless.
Outside (Bottom) Round.	Loin, boneless.	Loin, boneless.	Loin, boneless.
Knuckle (Tip).	Rack, boneless.	Boston Butt.	Rib, boneless.
Tenderloin.	Shoulder, boneless.	Picnic, boneless.	Shoulder, boneless.
Sirloin-Rump Butt.	Loaf (Ground Lamb).	Spareribs.	Loaf (Ground Veal).
Loin Strip.			
Boneless Rib.		*Smoked*	
Inside Chuck.		Ham.	
Shoulder Clod.		Picnic.	
Loaf (Ground Beef).		Shoulder Butt.	

TIME-TABLE FOR ROASTING

(Oven Temperature 325° F.)

KIND OF MEAT	WEIGHTS	APPROXIMATE COOKING TIME PER POUND		
		RARE	MEDIUM	WELL DONE
	Pounds	*Minutes*	*Minutes*	*Minutes*
Beef, boneless	6 to 8	25 to 30	30 to 35	35 to 40
Lamb, boneless	3 to 6	Never rare	35 to 40	40 to 45
Pork, boneless	4 to 6	Always well done.		45 to 50
Veal, boneless	4 to 6	Always well done.		40 to 45
Ham, smoked	8 to 10	Always well done.		30
Ham, smoked	10 to 12	Always well done.		25
Ham, smoked	12 to 14	Always well done.		20
Ham, smoked	14 to 16	Always well done.		20
Ham, smoked, picnic	4 to 8	Always well done.		35 to 45

(Internal Temperatures With Oven Temperature at 325° F.)

KIND OF MEAT	STAGE OF DONENESS	MEAT THERMOMETER READING	APPROXIMATE COOKING TIME PER POUND	
			BONELESS	BONE-IN
			Minutes	*Minutes*
Beef	Rare	140° F.	25 to 30	15 to 20
Beef	Medium	160° F.	30 to 35	20 to 25
Beef	Well done	170° F.	35 to 40	25 to 30
Veal	Well done	170° F. to 180° F.	40 to 45	30 to 35
Lamb	Medium	170° F.	35 to 40	25 to 30
Lamb	Well done	180° F.	40 to 45	30 to 35
Pork, fresh	Well done	185° F.	45 to 50	30 to 35
Pork, smoked	Well done	170° F.	25 to 35	20 to 30

How to Broil

Turn heat to highest point: Proper distance of meat from heat assures a moderate temperature.

Place steak in broiler: Place 1-inch steak 2 inches from heat and 2-inch steak 3 inches from heat.

Broil until top side is evenly browned: The meat will be about half done at this point.

Season browned side with salt and pepper: Salt is added after browning, to reduce the loss of juices.

Turn, brown and season second side: Only one turning is necessary, as searing does not keep in juices.

Broiling time: Size and thickness of steaks and chops determine the broiling time. See Time-Table for broiling.

Serve hot: Broiled meat should be served on hot plates as soon after cooking as possible.

How to Griddle-Broil

Place meat on ungreased griddle: Enough fat cooks out of meat to keep it from sticking.

Brown and turn: This develops the flavor and insures more even cooking.

Season with salt and pepper: Season each side after browning.

Turn occasionally: This insures even cooking.

Cook at moderate temperature: A moderate temperature helps to retain the juice in the meat and prevents over-browning.

Scrape away surplus fat as it collects: Meat should griddle-broil, not fry.

Do not add water. Do not cover: Meat will braise in the presence of moisture.

Cook to desired doneness: Time for griddle-broiling will be approximately ½ the time for broiling a similar cut of equal thickness.

Serve hot: Broiled meat should be served on hot plates as soon after cooking as possible.

MEAT CUTS FOR BROILING AND FOR PAN-BROILING

(Tender cuts)

BEEF	LAMB	PORK	VEAL
Top Round Steak (Inside).	Leg Steaks.	*Fresh* Fresh pork is not broiled or pan-broiled.	Veal is not broiled or pan-broiled.
Sirloin Tip Steak (Knuckle).	Sirloin Chops.		
Filet Mignon (Tenderloin).	Loin Chops.	*Smoked*	*Variety Meats*
Top Sirloin Steak (Sirloin Butt).	Rib Chops.	Ham, sliced.	Liver, sliced. (Beef, Lamb, Pork, Veal.)
Rib Steak (Spencer Roll).	Shoulder Chops.	Bacon, sliced.	
Inside Chuck Steak (Chuck Roll).		Shoulder Butt, sliced.	

TIME-TABLE FOR BROILING

(Moderate Broiling Temperature)

KIND OF CUT	THICKNESS	APPROXIMATE COOKING TIME		
		RARE	MEDIUM	WELL DONE
Beef:	*Inches*	*Minutes*	*Minutes*	*Minutes*
Individual boneless steaks	½	6	10	15
	1	15	20	25
	1½	25	30	35
	2	35	45	50
Patties	1	15	20	25
Lamb:				
Leg chops	½	Never rare	10	15
Shoulder chops	1	Never rare	20	25
Double loin and rib chops	1½	Never rare	25	30
Patties	1	Never rare	20	25
Pork:				
Ham slice	½	Always well done.		20
	1	Always well done.		25
Bacon	⅛	Always well done.		4 to 5

NOTE.—Time for griddle-broiling is approximately one-half the time for broiling.

How to Fry

1. Griddle-Frying

Dredge meat in flour, if desired: Meat for frying should be sliced thin.

Brown quickly on both sides, in small amount of hot fat: This differs from griddle-broiling in which no fat is added.

Season with salt and pepper: Season each side after browning.

Turn occasionally: This insures even cooking.

Do not cover: If meat is covered it will braise.

Cook at moderate temperature until done: Frying gives crisply browned exterior, and fine flavored, but less tender product than braising.

2. Deep Fat Frying

Keep temperature of fat under 380° F.: Follow recipe directions for deep fried foods.

Proper Care of Frying Fat

Proper care of frying fat is important to flavor, quality, wholesomeness and the economical production of fried foods.

Temperature Control: Fat should never be heated to a temperature above 400° F. It will burn or scorch and break down chemically. This impairs the flavor and quality and shortens the life of the fat.

Use a thermostat or a thermometer to control the temperature. Check at regular intervals to be sure the readings are accurate.

Regulate the heat on gas heated equipment to prevent the flame from flaring up around the sides of the kettle above the surface of the fat. Hot fat splashed on a still hotter surface burns and scorches.

In electrically heated equipment, carefully clean the heating elements to keep them free from burnt fat and food particles which may cause non-uniform heating.

Adjust the burners frequently and periodically. Poor adjustment produces unsatisfactory temperatures.

Turnover: Fat is absorbed by the food in the frying process. Therefore, the original amount of fat in the kettle is reduced and fresh fat must be added to replace the absorbed fat. This replacement is called "turnover." A rapid "turnover" reduces the amount of fat to be discarded.

Any frying fat will break down when it is held at frying temperatures. The more stable frying fats break down least.

With a large amount of frying fat, in proportion to the amount of food being fried in the kettle, there is an excess of fat being held at frying temperatures. Also, fat absorbed in fried food is small in proportion to the total amount of fat in the kettle, and "turnover," therefore, is slow. These factors lead to fat breakdown.

For best results use a frying kettle which is not too large for the amount of food being fried and use the smallest quantity of fat possible.

Use the fat level ordinarily indicated on the equipment for best results. If a fat level is not indicated, about ½ kettle of fat allows ample room for frying without the fat bubbling or foaming over the top as food is added.

Cleaning the Fat: Strain or filter off burnt food particles which collect in the fat after each frying period. An accumulation causes excessive smoking and shortens the frying life of the fat.

The simplest method for removing burnt particles is to strain the fat through several thicknesses of cheese cloth.

When this method does not entirely clear the fat, it can be drawn off into a separate container, after heating it to a temperature below 212° F., and carefully sprinkling the surface with water. As the water settles to the bottom, it carries down very fine particles of burnt food which are suspended throughout the fat. The clear fat can then either be poured off from the water and remaining sediment, or the water and sediment can be drawn off from the bottom of the container by means of a spigot device.

Cleaning Equipment: Clean frying kettles once each week.

Scrub kettles with a wire brush and hot water and soap or washing powder. Be sure that no soap or washing powder remains. Rinse kettles thoroughly with clean water.

When to Replace Frying Fat: Taste fried food daily in order to determine the point at which fat in the kettle should be discarded and replaced. If foods begin to have a noticeable flavor of used fat, the fat should be discarded for frying purposes.

How to Make a Stew

Cut meat in small pieces: To avoid bone splinters, do not chop unboned meat with a cleaver.

A boneless stew is more desirable than one with bones.

Season with salt and pepper: Salt will penetrate small pieces, so season at start of cooking.

Brown meat on all sides in hot fat, if desired: A browned stew has more flavor than a light stew.

Cover meat with hot or cold water: Boiling water does not seal in juices. Cover meat entirely with water so it will cook uniformly.

Cover kettle and cook at simmering temperature: Meat will have more flavor and more juice when simmered at 185°F. to 200°F.

Cook until tender: Meat will be done when it is tender, about 2 to 2½ hours.

Add vegetables before meat is done: Vegetables should be added just long enough before the meat is done for them to become tender. Follow recipe directions.

How to Cook in Water (Simmering)

Cover meat with water: Water may be hot or cold. It should entirely cover the meat to insure uniform cooking.

Season with salt and pepper: Spices or herbs may be added for extra flavor.

Cover kettle and cook meat until tender: Meat will be done when it is tender.

Cook at simmering (not boiling) temperature: Simmering retains juices, increases flavor, and leaves meat firm for carving.

Add vegetables, if desired: Vegetables should cook just long enough to be tender for best nutritive value, flavor and texture.

MEAT CUTS FOR STEWING AND FOR COOKING IN WATER
(Less tender cuts)

BEEF	LAMB	PORK	VEAL
		Fresh	
Flank Meat.	Shoulder, boneless or bone-in.	Spareribs.	Shoulder, boneless or bone-in
Shank Meat.	Breast, boneless or bone-in.	Pigs Feet.	Breast, boneless or bone-in.
Boneless Neck.	Shank, boneless or bone-in.	Hocks.	Neck, boneless or bone-in.
Boneless Brisket.	Neck, boneless or bone-in.		Shank, boneless or bone-in.
Boneless Plate.	(Large cuts of lamb are not cooked in water.)	*Smoked*	Flank, boneless or bone-in.
Rib Fingers.		Bacon.	(Large cuts of veal are not cooked in water.)
Hanging Tender.		Ham.	*Variety Meats*
		Picnic.	Heart, Tongue, Kidneys.
		Shoulder Butt.	

TIME-TABLE FOR COOKING MEAT IN WATER

KIND OF CUT	AVERAGE WEIGHT	APPROXIMATE COOKING TIME PER POUND
	Pounds	*Minutes*
Ham, smoked	8 to 10	30
Ham, smoked	10 to 12	25
Ham, smoked	12 to 14	20
Ham, smoked	14 to 16	20
Ham, smoked, picnic	4 to 8	35 to 45
Beef, corned	4 to 6	40 to 50
Beef, fresh	4 to 6	40 to 50

How to Braise

Season with salt and pepper: Herbs, spices, and certain vegetables may be added for variety in flavor during the cooking process.

Brown meat on all sides in hot fat: Browning develops aroma, flavor, and color.

Add very little liquid: Meat and gravy will have better flavor and color when a small amount of liquid is added.

Cover closely: This retains steam and helps to make the meat tender.

Use oven, top of range or steam-jacketed kettle: The cooking utensil should remain covered.

Cook at low temperature: A simmering temperature decreases shrinkage and increases juiciness and flavor.

Cook until tender: Size, thickness and kind of meat influence the cooking time. When meat is tender it is done. Follow recipe directions.

MEAT CUTS FOR BRAISING
(Less tender cuts, except pork)

BEEF	LAMB	PORK	VEAL
		Fresh	
Outside (Bottom) Round.	Shoulder, boneless or bone-in.	Loin Chops.	Shoulder, boneless or bone-in
Heel of Round.	Breast, boneless or bone-in.	Leg Steaks.	Breast, boneless or bone-in.
Rump Butt.	Shank, boneless or bone-in.	Shoulder Steaks.	Shank, boneless or bone-in.
Boneless Flank.	Neck, boneless or bone-in.	Spareribs.	Neck, boneless or bone-in.
Shoulder Clod.		Hocks.	Flank.
Inside Chuck.			*Variety Meats*
Boneless Neck.			Liver.
Chuck Tender.			Hearts.
Boneless Plate.			Kidneys.
Boneless Brisket.			
Shank Meat.			

TIME-TABLE FOR BRAISING MEAT

(Simmering temperature)

KIND OF CUT	AVERAGE WEIGHT or THICKNESS	APPROXIMATE COOKING TIME
Beef:		
Steaks, boneless	½ to ¾ inch	1 to 1½ hours.
Swiss steak	1 to 1½ inches	2 to 3 hours.
Pot roast or "soft" roast..............	6 to 8 pounds	3 to 4 hours.
Fricassee	2-inch pieces	2 to 3 hours.
Veal:		
Cutlets (chops or steaks)	½ to ¾ inch	45 to 60 minutes.
Breaded slices	½ to ¾ inch	45 to 60 minutes.
Fricassee	2-inch pieces	1½ to 2 hours.
Lamb:		
Chops	½ to ¾ inch	45 to 60 minutes.
Fricassee	2-inch pieces	1½ to 2 hours.
Pork:		
Chops and steaks	½ to ¾ inch	45 to 60 minutes.
Fricassee	2-inch pieces	1½ to 2 hours.
Spareribs	Individual servings	1½ to 2 hours.

BEEF: BONELESS, FROZEN

Beef, fresh, frozen, boneless is made from the entire side of beef (hindquarter and forequarter). It is packed in fiber boxes containing approximately 50 pounds as follows:

Roasting and Frying Beef .... 40% of the side
Stewing and Boiling Beef .... 30% of the side
Chopped Beef .... 30% of the side

Defrosting Frozen, Boneless Beef

When facilities are available, frozen boneless beef should be allowed to defrost gradually at temperatures ranging from 36° F. to 38° F. There will be occasions, however, when limited time or lack of facilities will make it necessary to thaw the meat at room temperatures even though it means increased loss of meat juices. The meat should remain in the boxes just as it comes from the meat packing plant. The boxes furnish good insulation which permits all the meat to thaw uniformly.

An alternative emergency method for thawing this product outside of refrigeration is to open the boxes and distribute the wrapped pieces in the cover and bottom of the box.

The meat will be less likely to discolor if allowed to remain in original wrapping while thawing.

Where electric meat cutters (band saws) are available, the time between issue and use of frozen boneless beef can be speeded up by using the meat cutter to:

Cut frozen boneless roasts into steaks.

Cut stewing and boiling meat into small pieces for stewing.

Cut bricks of chopped beef into small pieces so they will defrost more quickly. Ground meat dishes are more satisfactory when the bricks are thoroughly mixed together after thawing.

Cooking Frozen Stewing and Boiling Beef

Since stewing and boiling beef is cooked in the presence of moisture it makes no great difference whether or not this meat is defrosted before cooking. Simply cut it into pieces of a suitable size, cook at a *simmering temperature,* and allow additional time for the cooking process.

Roasting Frozen Beef

Frozen, boneless beef can be roasted satisfactorily without being defrosted before it is put in the oven. A very low oven temperature (250° F.) *must* be maintained; otherwise the meat will become burned and charred on the outside before the inside is thawed and cooked. Frozen meat requires approximately twice as long to roast at 250° F. as fresh chilled or completely defrosted meat at 325° F.

CANNED MEATS

A wide variety of canned meat products are provided for use when the supply of fresh meats is limited, unavailable, or impractical. Because they require less storage space than an equivalent amount of fresh meat, canned meats are desirable. In addition, with the exception of canned whole ham and canned sliced, dried beef, canned meats procured for Navy use are sterile and require no refrigeration. This releases valuable refrigerator space for provisions requiring it.

Canned meats require heating only before serving. They may be eaten cold. In order to reheat the meat, the best method is to heat the unopened can in boiling water. However, because of the danger of handling hot cans and the possibility of the contents spattering when the can is opened, it is advisable to place the meat in roasting pans and reheat in an oven.

Canned meats are served as they come prepared or can be used in all recipes which specify cooked meat as one of the ingredients. They can be used in place of fresh meat in some recipes. When canned meats are so used, allowance must be made for the fact that the meats are completely cooked to begin with, and the cooking period specified for fresh meat must be reduced.

ROAST BEEF

Portion: Approx. 4 ounces.

INGREDIENTS	100 PORTIONS			............PORTIONS
	WEIGHTS		AMOUNTS (approx.)	
	Pounds	*Ounces*		
Beef, bone-in	60	....	....	....
OR				
Beef, boneless	42	....	....	....
Salt	....	8	1 cup	....
Pepper	....	1	3½ tablespoons	....

Cut beef into 6 to 8-pound pieces.

Rub with salt and pepper.

Place fat side up in roasting pans. Do not stack or crowd roasts.

Roast at constant temperature in slow oven (325° F.) approximately 3 hours (about 30 minutes per pound per piece) or until roasts are the desired degree of doneness.

Remove roasts from oven. Carve across the grain in ⅛-inch slices.

Note.—1. Serve with gravy.

2. Serve with Yorkshire Pudding.

YORKSHIRE PUDDING

Portion: 1 piece (approx. 2 x 2 inches).

INGREDIENTS	100 PORTIONS			..........Portions
	WEIGHTS		AMOUNTS (approx.)	
	Pounds	*Ounces*		
Flour	6	....	1½ gallons	
Salt	....	3	6 tablespoons	
Eggs, unbeaten	4	12	48 (2½ quarts)	
Milk, liquid	....	....	5½ quarts	
Beef fat (from roasts), melted	....	....		

Sift together flour and salt. Stir eggs into flour. Mix thoroughly.

Add milk gradually. Beat until smooth and bubbles form.

Cover bottom of baking pans with fat. Heat in hot oven (400°F.)

Pour mixture to depth of ½ inch into the pans. Bake in moderate oven (350°F.) 45 minutes.

Cut in squares and serve with roast beef.

ROAST BEEF WITH SAVORY BROWN GRAVY

(Using roast beef, canned)

Portion: Approx. 6 ounces.

INGREDIENTS	100 PORTIONS			..........Portions
	WEIGHTS		AMOUNTS (approx.)	
	Pounds	*Ounces*		
Fat, melted	1	8	1½ pints	
Flour	1	8	1½ quarts	
Meat Stock (page 251)	---	---	3 gallons	
Salt		1½	3 tablespoons	
Pepper		¼	1 tablespoon	
Beef, roast, canned	30	---	5 6-pound cans	

Blend together fat and flour. Cook until flour is browned, stirring constantly.

Add stock slowly, stirring constantly. Cook until thickened and smooth. Stir in salt and pepper.

Cut canned roast beef into 6-ounce portions. Arrange in roasting pans. Cover with gravy.

Heat in moderate oven (350° F.) 30 minutes.

NOTE.—1. Use all natural juices of canned meat as part of meat stock for making gravy.

2. Meat stock may be made with 6 ounces powdered bouillon or 48 bouillon cubes dissolved in 3 gallons boiling water.

BEEF, SPANISH STYLE

(Using roast beef, canned)

Portion: Approx. 6 ounces.

INGREDIENTS	100 PORTIONS			............Portions
	WEIGHTS		AMOUNTS (approx.)	
	Pounds	Ounces		
Onions, dehydrated....................	---	15	½ gallon..................	....
Water, for onions....................	---	---	1 gallon..................	....
Beef, roast, canned....................	36	---	6 6-pound cans..........	....
Salt....................	---	3	6 tablespoons..........	....
Pepper....................	---	¼	1 tablespoon..........	....
Paprika....................	---	½	2¼ tablespoons..........	....
Tomatoes....................	19	2	3 No. 10 cans (2½ gallons).	....

Soak onions in water 20 minutes.

Place beef and beef juices in roasting pans. Sprinkle with salt, pepper and paprika.

Combine tomatoes and onions. Pour over meat.

Cook in slow oven (300° F.) 30 to 45 minutes or until beef is thoroughly heated through.

NOTE.—Handle meat carefully as canned beef breaks up easily.

BARBECUED BEEF

(Using roast beef, canned)

Portion: Approx. 5 ounces.

INGREDIENTS	100 PORTIONS			............Portions
	WEIGHTS		AMOUNTS (approx.)	
	Pounds	Ounces		
Beef, roast, canned....................	24	---	4 6-pound cans..........	....
Barbecue Sauce (page 207)....	---	---	2 gallons..........	....

Break up meat into small pieces. Add to sauce. Heat to boiling temperature.

NOTE.—Serve on mashed potatoes, cooked rice, or cooked noodles, over corn bread or on bread or toast.

POT ROAST OF BEEF (BRAISED BEEF)

Portion: 4 to 5 ounces.

INGREDIENTS	100 PORTIONS			..........PORTIONS
	WEIGHTS		AMOUNTS (approx.)	
	Pounds	*Ounces*		
Beef, bone-in .... OR	60	....	....	
Beef, boneless	42	....	....	
Beef fat	....	8	1 cup	
Salt	....	6	¾ cup	
Pepper	....	½	1¾ tablespoons	
Beef Stock (page 251) or water, hot.	....	....	1 quart	
Onions, chopped	5	....	3¾ quarts	

Cut beef into 6 to 8-pound pieces.

Cook in fat until meat is browned on all sides, turning frequently.

Add salt, pepper, stock or water and onions.

Let simmer in tightly covered kettle or cook in slow oven (300° F.) 3 hours or until tender. Turn meat 2 or 3 times while cooking. Add small amounts of liquid as needed.

Remove from pans and slice across the grain in ⅛-inch slices.

NOTE.—1. Onions may be cooked in fat until brown, if desired.

2. Heavy utensils are best for cooking pot roasts.

3. Serve with Brown Gravy (page 212) if desired.

Variations

Beef A La Mode

Add 3 pounds (¾ gallon) diced carrots, 2 pounds (1½ quarts) diced onions and 1 No. 10 can (3¼ quarts) tomatoes to the pot roast 30 to 45 minutes before the meat is done. Serve the vegetables in the gravy as a sauce over the sliced meat.

Braised Beef with Vegetables

Use 45 pounds bone-in or 31 pounds boneless beef. Add 3 pounds each of sliced carrots, onions, celery and turnips to pot roast allowing 30 to 40 minutes for cooking before roast is done.

Beef Pot-Roast, Spiced

Use highly seasoned, spiced and diluted vinegar, for the liquid on the pot roast and in making the gravy.

Beef Pot-Roast, Yankee

Add diced carrots, sliced onions, parsley, bay leaves, thyme and tomatoes to beef pot-roast.

Garlic may be used.

BEEF AND GRAVY

(Using beef and gravy, canned)

Portion: 5 to 6 ounces

INGREDIENTS	100 PORTIONS		............Portions
	WEIGHTS	AMOUNTS (approx.)	
	Pounds	*Ounces*		
Beef and gravy, canned............	36	---	17 34-ounce cans............	

Place beef and gravy in roasting pans to thickness of 2 inches.

Heat in moderate oven (350° F.) 1½ hours.

NOTE.—1. Handle meat carefully. It is tender and breaks easily and should not be stirred more than necessary.

2. Serve with mashed potatoes, cooked noodles, or cooked rice.

Variation

Pork and Gravy

Use 36 pounds (17 34-ounce cans) pork and gravy, canned, in place of beef and gravy, canned.

BEEF AND GRAVY WITH TOMATO DUMPLINGS

(Using beef and gravy, canned)

Portion: Approx. 6 ounces

INGREDIENTS	100 PORTIONS		..........Portions
	WEIGHTS	AMOUNTS (approx.)	
	Pounds	*Ounces*		
Beef and gravy, canned..........	36	---	17 34-ounce cans...........	
Meat Stock (page 251)...........	---	---	1 gallon............	
Flour...........	6	---	1½ gallons..........	
Baking powder...........	---	4½	¾ cup............	
Salt...........	---	2¼	4½ tablespoons.........	
Shortening.........	---	4	½ cup...........	
Tomato juice.........	6	---	1 No. 10 can (¾ gallon).	

Place beef and gravy in roasting pans. Add stock. Heat, slowly, to boiling temperature.

Combine flour, baking powder, salt, and shortening. Blend together thoroughly.

Add tomato juice. Mix to a soft dough.

Drop dumpling dough in 1-ounce portions on hot meat mixture.

Cover roasting pans, closely. Cook 10 minutes or until dumplings are tender.

NOTE.—1. Meat stock may be made with 2 ounces powdered bouillon or 16 bouillon cubes dissolved in 1 gallon boiling water.

2. Plain Dumplings may be used in place of Tomato Dumplings.

Variation

Pork and Gravy with Tomato Dumplings

Use 36 pounds (17 34-ounce cans) pork and gravy, canned, in place of beef and gravy, canned.

BEEF AND GRAVY WITH VEGETABLES

(Using beef and gravy, canned)

Portion: Approx. 10 ounces

INGREDIENTS	100 PORTIONS			............PORTIONS
	WEIGHTS		AMOUNTS (approx.)	
	Pounds	Ounces		
Carrots, dehydrated.............	1	4	1½ quarts................	
Water, for carrots.................	---	--	¾ gallon................	
Potatoes, Julienne style, dehydrated.	3	..	1 gallon	
Water, for potatoes.............	---	---	1¾ gallons............	
Onions, dehydrated	---	4	1 pint................	
Water, for onions......	..	..	1 quart................	
Salt........	---	3	6 tablespoons............	
Pepper....................... ..	---	---	2 teaspoons............	
Beef and gravy, canned..........	29	12	14 34-ounce cans........	

Soak carrots in ¾ gallon water 45 minutes. Cover. Heat, slowly, to boiling temperature, about 45 minutes. Let simmer 10 minutes or until tender. Drain.

Soak potatoes in 1¾ gallons water 45 minutes. Cover. Heat, slowly, to boiling temperature, about 45 minutes. Let simmer 10 minutes or until tender. Drain.

Soak onions in 1 quart water 20 minutes. Heat to boiling temperature. Let simmer until all liquid is cooked off.

Combine carrots, potatoes, onions, salt, and pepper. Mix well. Place in baking pans. Pour beef and gravy over vegetables.

Heat in moderate oven (350° F.) 30 to 45 minutes.

NOTE.—Reserve liquid drained from vegetables for use in soups or gravies.

Variation

Pork and Gravy with Vegetables

Use 30 pounds (14 34-ounce cans) pork and gravy, canned, in place of beef and gravy, canned.

FRENCH POT ROAST

Portion: 5 to 6 ounces.

INGREDIENTS	100 PORTIONS		............PORTIONS
	WEIGHTS	AMOUNTS (approx.)	
	Pounds / *Ounces*		
Beef, boneless	40 /	....	....
Onions, finely chopped...........	2 /	1½ quarts	....
Salt	.... / 6	¾ cup	....
Pepper	.... / 1	3½ tablespoons	....
Flour	3 /	¾ gallon	....
Tomato catsup	.... /	½ gallon	....
Beef Stock (page 251)	.... /	As needed	....
Potatoes, white, E.P.	15 /	....	....

Cut meat into 3-inch cubes.

Combine meat, onion, salt and pepper. Cook in slow oven (300° F.) 20 to 30 minutes.

Stir in flour. Cook until brown. Stir in tomato catsup. Add enough stock to cover roasts.

Reduce heat to 200° F. to 250° F. Cook until meat is tender.

Cut potatoes French style. Add to roast 40 minutes before end of cooking period.

NOTE.—Use less tender cuts of meat.

SIMMERED BEEF

Portion: Approx. 5 ounces.

INGREDIENTS	100 PORTIONS		............PORTIONS
	WEIGHTS	AMOUNTS (approx.)	
	Pounds / *Ounces*		
Beef, bone-in	60 /	....	....
OR			
Beef, boneless	42 /	....	....
Water	.... /	....	....
Salt	.... / 8	1 cup	....
Pepper	.... / 1	3½ tablespoons	....
Onions, peeled, whole...........	2 /	8 (medium sized).....................	....
Bay leaves	.... /	15	....

Cut meat into 5-pound pieces.

Place in kettle without stacking or overlapping. Add water only up to surface of meat.

Add salt, pepper, onions and bay leaves.

Cover tightly. Let simmer about 3 to 4 hours or until beef is tender. Remove from kettle. Reserve broth. Carve across grain.

NOTE.—Serve with potatoes boiled in beef broth or with Horse-radish Sauce (page 210).

GRIDDLE-BROILED STEAKS

Portion: 1 (6-ounce) steak.

INGREDIENTS	100 PORTIONS			..........PORTIONS
	WEIGHTS		AMOUNTS (approx.)	
	Pounds	*Ounces*		
Beef, bone-in	60	....		
OR				
Beef, boneless	42	....		
Salt	....	8	1 cup	
Pepper	....	1	3½ tablespoons	

Cut meat into 6-ounce steaks ½ to ¾ inch thick.

Broil steaks on heated griddle until browned on both sides. Turn steaks frequently to insure even cooking.

Cook to desired degree of doneness. Avoid overcooking.

Sprinkle with salt and pepper, just before serving.

NOTE.—1. If steaks lack fat, grease griddle slightly with beef suet.

2. Steaks may be cooked on griddle until brown on both sides, then placed on racks in open baking pans in slow oven (300° F.) and cooked to desired degree of doneness.

3. Serve with French Fried Onions (page 307) or Steak Butter Sauce (page 217).

BRAISED BEEF STEAKS

Portion: 1 (6-ounce) steak.

INGREDIENTS	100 PORTIONS			..........PORTIONS
	WEIGHTS		AMOUNTS (approx.)	
	Pounds	*Ounces*		
Beef, bone-in	60	....		
OR				
Beef, boneless	42	....		
Flour	2	....	½ gallon	
Salt	....	6	¾ cup	
Pepper	....	½	1¾ tablespoons	
Fat	2	....	1 quart	
Water	....	....		

Cut meat into 6-ounce steaks ½ to ¾ inch thick.

Mix together flour, salt and pepper. Roll steaks in flour.

Cook in fat until browned on both sides.

Add water to cover bottom of pan to depth of 1 inch. Cover tightly. Bake in slow oven (300°F.) 1 to 1½ hours or until tender.

Variations

Country Style Beef Steaks

Prepare steaks and serve with Cream Gravy.

Beef Steaks Smothered with Onions

Brown beef steaks. Cover with 25 pounds (4¾ gallons) of partly cooked onions instead of water. Cover. Cook until steaks are tender.

127★

SWISS BEEF STEAKS

Portion: 1 (6-ounce) steak.

INGREDIENTS	100 PORTIONS			..........PORTIONS
	WEIGHTS		AMOUNTS (approx.)	
	Pounds	*Ounces*		
Beef, bone-in	60	...		
OR				
Beef, boneless	42	....		
Flour	2	....	½ gallon	
Salt	....	6	¾ cup	
Pepper	...	½	1¾ tablespoons	
Fat	2	...	1 quart	
Tomatoes	12	12	2 No. 10 cans (6½ quarts).	
Onions, sliced	6	....	4½ quarts	
Salt	....	1	2 tablespoons	
Flour (for gravy)	1	...	1 quart	
Water, cold	....	....		

Cut meat into 6-ounce steaks 1 to 1½ inches thick.

Sift together flour, salt and pepper. Pound into steaks.

Cook steaks in fat until browned on both sides. Place in roasting pans.

Add tomatoes. Cover with onion slices. Sprinkle with 1 ounce salt.

Cover pans. Cook in slow oven (300°F.) 3 hours or until steaks are tender.

Drain liquid from Swiss steaks. Make a paste of flour and water. Stir into steak liquid. Cook until thickened. Pour over steaks. Reheat.

Variation

Spanish Beef Steaks

Add 6 pounds (1½ gallons) sliced or chopped green peppers to the tomatoes and onions. Prepare as for Swiss Steaks.

BEEF STEW

Portion: 10 ounces (approx. 1 cup).

INGREDIENTS	100 PORTIONS			............PORTIONS
	WEIGHTS		AMOUNTS (approx.)	
	Pounds	*Ounces*		
Beef, bone-in	40	....		
OR				
Beef, boneless	28	....		
Salt	....	6	¾ cup	
Pepper	....	½	1¾ tablespoons	
Flour	1	8	1½ quarts	
Fat	1	8	1½ pints	
Beef Stock (page 251) or water.	....	....	4 gallons	
Peas, fresh or frozen.............	5	....	2½ quarts	
Tomatoes	12	12	2 No. 10 cans (6½ quarts).	
Onions, small, quartered........	6	....	1½ gallons	
Carrots, sliced or cubed.........	6	....	1½ gallons	
Potatoes, cubed	12	....	2 gallons	
Celery, diced	5	....	1¼ gallons	
Flour (for gravy)	1	....	1 quart	
Water, cold	....	....	1½ pints	
Salt, as desired	....	....		
Pepper, as desired.................	....	....		

Cut meat into 1 to 2-inch cubes.

Mix together salt, pepper and flour. Dredge meat in flour. Cook in fat until browned, stirring constantly.

Add 4 gallons stock or water. Cover. Let simmer 2½ to 3 hours or until tender.

Cook peas in small amount of water 10 to 15 minutes. Drain.

Add remaining vegetables to meat mixture. Cook 40 to 45 minutes.

Blend together flour and water to a smooth paste. Drain stock from meat and thicken with paste. Heat to boiling temperature stirring constantly. Add salt and pepper, as desired.

Pour gravy over meat and vegetables. Reheat. Garnish with cooked peas.

Variations

Ham or Lamb Stew

Use ham or lamb in place of beef. Do not flour ham. Omit salt if ham is used. Reduce cooking time to 2 hours for ham.

129★

Beef, Ham or Lamb Pie with Biscuits

Place stew in baking pans. Cover with Biscuits (page 361) or biscuit crust. Bake in hot oven (425° F.) until browned.

Beef, Ham or Lamb Pie with Mashed Potato Crust

Place stew in baking pans. Cover with seasoned mashed potatoes. Bake in hot oven (425° F.) until browned.

NOTE.—Mashed sweet potatoes may be used for ham pie.

Beef, Ham or Lamb Stew with Dumplings

Add dumplings or noodles 15 to 20 minutes before stew has finished cooking.

Beef, Ham or Lamb Pie with Pie Crust

Place stew in baking pans. Cover with pie crust. Bake in hot oven (425° F.) until browned.

Beef or Lamb Ragout

Prepare as beef stew. Omit vegetables except tomatoes, onions, green peppers and celery.

Paprika, Worcestershire sauce, bay leaves and parsley may be used for seasoning.

Beef, Ham or Lamb Stew with Rice

Prepare stew. Serve with cooked barley or cooked rice.

Beef or Lamb Stew, Spiced

Omit all vegetables in stew. Add ½ gallon vinegar, 2 pounds (1½ quarts) brown sugar, 1 ounce (4½ tablespoons) cinnamon, 16 bay leaves and 1 pound (1½ pints) sliced onions to the liquid covering meat.

Cover pans. Let simmer 2½ to 3 hours or until meat is tender. Drain liquid from meat and serve as gravy.

BEEF FRICASSEE

Portion: 6 to 8 ounces.

INGREDIENTS	100 PORTIONS			............PORTIONS
	WEIGHTS		AMOUNTS (approx.)	
	Pounds	Ounces		
Beef, bone-in	50	....		
OR				
Beef, boneless	35	....		
Salt	....	8	1 cup	
Pepper	....	1	3½ tablespoons	
Fat	4	....	½ gallon	
Beef Stock (page 251) or water.	....	....	1 gallon	
Onions, chopped	5	....	3¾ quarts	
Celery, chopped	3	....	¾ gallon	
Carrots, diced	3	....	¾ gallon	

Cut meat into 2-inch pieces.

Sprinkle with salt and pepper. Cook in fat until browned on all sides.

Add small amount of stock or water. Cover.

Bake in moderate oven (350°F.) approximately 3 hours. Add more liquid as needed.

Add chopped vegetables about 40 to 45 minutes before meat has finished cooking.

Variation

Lamb Fricassee

Use same weight of lamb in place of beef. Prepare as for Beef Fricassee.

BEEF STEW

(Using roast beef, canned)

Portion: Approx. 8 ounces

INGREDIENTS	100 PORTIONS			.........PORTIONS
	WEIGHTS		AMOUNTS (approx.)	
	Pounds	*Ounces*		
Carrots, dehydrated	1		1 quart . ..	
Water, for carrots . . -		..	¾ gallon......... ..	.... -
Potatoes, diced, dehydrated ...	3		1 gallon	....
Water, for potatoes.............		..	1¾ gallons............	.| ....
Onions, dehydrated ... .. - ..	...	10	1¼ quarts.......	... .
Water, for onions ....| -	...	2½ quarts.......	....|.................
Beef, roast, canned	24		4 6-pound cans	... . -
Fat. . .. - .... - ...	2		1 quart	.	....
Salt...... . _	..	5	10 tablespoons............	....
Pepper.		½	1¾ tablespoons .	.| .. ..
Worcestershire sauce .... -	.	.	6 tablespoons..	... .
Tomatoes.	12	12	2 No. 10 cans (6½ quarts).	... - .. .. - ....
Meat Stock (page 251)........ .| ---	---	1½ quarts...	.|.......... .....

Soak carrots in ¾ gallon water 45 minutes. Cover. Heat, slowly, to boiling temperature, about 45 minutes. Drain. Reserve liquid.

Soak potatoes in 1¾ gallons water 45 minutes. Cover. Heat, slowly, to boiling temperature, about 45 minutes. Drain. Reserve liquid.

Soak onions in 2½ quarts water 20 minutes. Drain. Reserve liquid.

Cut beef into 1- to 1½-inch pieces. Cook in fat until browned. Add salt, pepper, Worcestershire sauce, tomatoes, and stock.

Add cooked carrots, potatoes, and onions. Heat to boiling temperature. Let simmer 20 minutes.

NOTE.—Meat stock may be made with ¾ ounce powdered bouillon or 6 bouillon cubes dissolved in 1½ quarts boiling water. Use liquid drained from vegetables.

BEEF GOULASH

Portion: 6 to 8 ounces.

INGREDIENTS	100 PORTIONS			............Portions
	WEIGHTS		AMOUNTS (approx.)	
	Pounds	*Ounces*		
Beef, bone-in	50	....	....	....
OR				
Beef, boneless	35	....	....	....
Onions, chopped or sliced........	5	....	3¾ quarts	....
Beef or bacon fat........................	1	....	1 pint	....
Garlic, minced	....	....	3 cloves	....
Salt	....	4	½ cup	....
Paprika	....	1	4½ tablespoons	....
Tomatoes	12	12	2 No. 10 cans (6½ quarts).	....
Flour	....	....	....	....

Cut meat into 1-inch cubes.

Cook onions in fat until clear. Add meat. Cook until browned.

Add garlic, if available, salt and paprika.

Add tomatoes. Cover pans tightly. Let simmer about 3 hours or until beef is tender. Add more liquid as needed.

Drain liquid from meat. Stir in enough flour to thicken slightly.

Combine gravy and meat. Reheat.

NOTE.—1. 1¼ gallons stock or water may be used in place of tomatoes.

2. Serve goulash with or on cooked rice.

Variation

Lamb or Veal Goulash

An equivalent amount of lamb or veal may be used in place of beef.

BEEF PIE

(Using roast beef, canned)

Portion: Approx. 8 ounces

INGREDIENTS	100 PORTIONS			.... PORTIONS
	WEIGHTS		AMOUNTS (approx.)	
	Pounds	*Ounces*		
Potatoes, diced, dehydrated...	4		1½ gallons...............	....
Water, for potatoes.....			4½ gallons...............	....
Onions, dehydrated....	1		½ gallon...............	....
Water, for onions...			1 gallon...............	....
Fat, melted.....	2		1 quart...	.. ..
Flour_ . _	2	2	4½ cups............	....
Salt....		4	½ cup....	....
Pepper..		½	1¾ tablespoons	....
Water, drained from vegetables.			2⅛ gallons...............	
Beef, roast, canned....	30		5 6-pound cans...	....
Pie Dough (page 399)............	5		....	....

Soak potatoes in 4½ gallons water 45 minutes. Cover. Heat, slowly, to boiling temperature, about 45 minutes. Drain. Reserve liquid.

Soak onions in 1 gallon water 20 minutes. Drain. Reserve liquid.

Blend fat, flour, salt, and pepper to a smooth paste. Stir into water drained from vegetables.

Heat to boiling temperature. Cook for 15 minutes or until thickened.

Cut beef into 1- to 1½-inch pieces. Add beef, beef juices, potatoes, and onions to gravy. Place in baking pans.

Roll pie dough ⅛ to ¼ inch thick. Perforate. Place over beef mixture.

Bake in hot oven (450° F.) 15 to 20 minutes.

NOTE.—1. If water drained from vegetables does not measure 2¼ gallons, add additional water to make the quantity required.

2. Biscuits or Biscuit Dough (page 361) may be used in place of Pie Dough.

Variations

Luncheon Meat Pie

30 pounds (5 6-pound cans) luncheon meat, canned, may be used in place of beef, roast, canned.

KIDNEY AND BEEF PIE

Portion: Approx. 8 ounces.

INGREDIENTS	100 PORTIONS			............PORTIONS
	WEIGHTS		AMOUNTS (approx.)	
	Pounds	Ounces		
Kidneys	10	....		
Water	....	....		
Beef, bone-in	35	....		
OR				
Beef, boneless	25	....		
Salt	....	6	¾ cup	
Pepper	....	½	1¾ tablespoons	
Flour	2	....	½ gallon	
Bacon fat or other fat	1	....	1 pint	
Water	....	....	3½ quarts	
Biscuit Dough (page 361)	....	....		

Slice kidneys. Wash in cold water.

Cover with water. Heat and let simmer in closely covered kettle about 45 minutes or until tender. Drain.

Cut meat into 1 to 2-inch pieces.

Combine salt, pepper and part of the flour. Dredge beef in flour mixture. Cook in fat until browned.

Add ¾ gallon water. Bake in slow oven (300°F.) 1 to 1½ hours or until tender.

Blend together remaining flour and water into smooth paste.

Drain liquid from beef. Thicken with paste.

Combine kidneys, beef, and gravy. Place in baking pans.

Cover with biscuit dough rolled ½ inch thick. Bake in hot oven (425°F.) 15 to 20 minutes or until top is browned.

BEEF LOAF

Portion: Approx. 5 ounces.

INGREDIENTS	100 PORTIONS			............PORTIONS
	WEIGHTS		AMOUNTS (approx.)	
	Pounds	*Ounces*		
Beef, bone-in	45	....	....	
OR				
Beef, boneless	31	....	....	
Onions, finely chopped	3	....	3¾ quarts	
Celery, finely chopped	3	....	¾ gallon	
Bread crumbs, soft	5	....	2½ gallons	
Salt	....	6	¾ cup	
Pepper	....	½	1¾ tablespoons	
Eggs, slightly beaten	4	12	48 (2½ quarts)	
Beef Stock (page 251)	....	....	2 to 3 quarts	
Bacon fat	....	....	....	

Grind beef. Combine meat, onions, celery, bread crumbs, salt, pepper, eggs and stock. Mix lightly but thoroughly.

Shape into loaves, about 12 x 4 x 3 inches. Place in greased roasting pans.

Roast uncovered at constant temperature in slow oven (325° F.) 1½ hours or until done.

NOTE.—1. Meat, onions and celery may be ground together.

2. Serve with Tomato Sauce (page 218) or Barbecue Sauce (page 207).

3. Amount of beef stock used depends on quantity of moisture in the bread.

GRIDDLE-BROILED BEEFBURGERS

Portion: 2 (3½-ounce) patties.

INGREDIENTS	100 PORTIONS			............PORTIONS
	WEIGHTS		AMOUNTS (approx.)	
	Pounds	*Ounces*		
Beef, bone-in .... OR	55	....	....	
Beef, boneless	38	....	....	
Onions, ground	5	....	3¾ quarts	
Salt	....	6	¾ cup	
Pepper	....	½	1¾ tablespoons	
Water	....	....	2½ quarts	

Cut beef into cubes. Grind.

Combine beef with onions, salt, pepper and water. Mix together lightly, but thoroughly.

Shape into 3 to 3½-ounce patties 1 inch thick.

Broil on heated griddle about 10 minutes or until the desired degree of doneness. Turn to insure even cooking.

NOTE.—1. Serve immediately with or without gravy, or Barbecue Sauce (page 207) or Tomato Sauce (page 218).

2. Barbecue Sauce or catsup may be used for part or all of the water in recipe.

Variations

Lamburgers

Use lamb in place of beef.

Baked Beefburgers or Lamburgers

Prepare uncooked beefburgers or lamburgers. Arrange in baking pans. Cook uncovered without turning, in slow oven (325°F.) about 45 minutes or to desired degree of doneness.

BEEF AND PORK LOAF

Portion: Approx. 6 ounces.

INGREDIENTS	100 PORTIONS			............PORTIONS
	WEIGHTS		AMOUNTS (approx.)	
	Pounds	*Ounces*		
Beef, ground	25	....	....	
Pork, ground	6	....	....	
Eggs, slightly beaten	1	....	10 (1 pint)	
Rolled oats, cooked	....	....	2 gallons (2½ lbs. A. P.).	
Onions, chopped fine	1	...	1½ pints	
Salt	....	6	¾ cup	
Pepper	....	¼	1 tablespoon	

Combine ingredients. Mix thoroughly. Pack lightly into greased loaf pans.

Bake in slow oven (325° F.), at constant temperature, about 1½ hours or until there is no trace of pink meat left.

Remove from pans. Slice and serve hot.

NOTE.—1. Use liquid from meat loaf for gravy.

2. Serve with Barbecue Sauce (page 207) or Tomato Sauce (page 218).

Variation

Ham and Beef Loaf

Use ground smoked ham in place of pork.

BEEF LOAF

(Using roast beef, canned)

Portion: Approx. 7 ounces

INGREDIENTS	100 PORTIONS			.............PORTIONS
	WEIGHTS		AMOUNTS (approx.)	
	Pounds	*Ounces*		
Onions, dehydrated		8	1 quart	
Water, for onions			½ gallon	
Milk, powdered, whole		10	2¼ cups	
Water, for milk			2½ quarts	
Eggs, powdered, whole		14	3½ cups	
Water, for eggs			1½ quarts	
Beef, roast, canned	36		6 6-lb. cans	
Bread crumbs	3	12	4½ quarts	
Salt		3½	7 tablespoons	
Pepper		¼	1 tablespoon	

Soak onions in ½ gallon water 20 minutes.

Stir powdered milk into 2½ quarts water until completely dissolved.

Sprinkle powdered eggs into 1½ quarts water, stirring constantly to avoid lumping. Mix until smooth.

Grind beef coarsely or break into very small pieces.

Combine all ingredients. Mix together thoroughly. Pack into greased loaf pans.

Bake in moderate oven (350° F.) 30 to 45 minutes.

NOTE.—Serve with Spanish Sauce (page 217), Tomato Sauce (page 218), or Tomato Puree Sauce (page 219).

BEEF CHEESEBURGERS

Portion: 2 buns with approx. 5 ounces beef and 1¼ ounces cheese.

| INGREDIENTS | 100 PORTIONS | | ....Portions |
	WEIGHTS	AMOUNTS (approx.)	
	Pounds / *Ounces*		
Beef, bone-in	45 /	....	
OR			
Beef, boneless	31 /	....	
Salt	.... / 6	¾ cup	
Pepper	.... / ½	1¾ tablespoons	
Buns, round	.... /	200	
Cheese, American cheddar. sliced.	10 /	....	
Mayonnaise (page 237).........	4 /	½ gallon	
Pickle relish	2 /	1 quart	

Cut beef into small pieces. Grind. Combine meat with salt and pepper. Mix well.

Form into 200 flat patties, 2½ ounces each or 5 to the pound.

Broil on heated griddle, or oven-broil until the desired degree of doneness.

Split and toast buns. Spread top halves with mayonnaise. Cover lower halves with slice of cheese.

Place lower half under broiler or in moderate oven (350° F.) until cheese is melted.

Cover cheese with hot meat pattie. Spread with relish. Cover with top half of bun.

Serve immediately.

GRIDDLE-BROILED SALISBURY STEAKS

Portion: 2 (3½-ounce) patties.

| INGREDIENTS | 100 PORTIONS | | ....Portions |
	WEIGHTS	AMOUNTS (approx.)	
	Pounds / *Ounces*		
Beef, bone-in	45 /	....	
OR			
Beef, boneless	31 /	....	
Bread crumbs, soft...........	7 /	3½ gallons	
Onions, ground or grated	6 /	3¾ quarts	
Salt	.... / 6	¾ cup	
Pepper	.... / ¼	¾ tablespoon	
Beef Stock (page 251), water	.... /	¾ gallon	
OR			
Milk, liquid..................	.... /	2¾ quarts	

Cut beef into small pieces. Grind.

Mix together all ingredients lightly, but thoroughly.

Shape into 3 to 3½-ounce patties 1 inch thick.

Broil on heated griddle about 12 minutes or until the desired degree of doneness. Turn to insure even cooking. Serve immediately.

NOTE.---1. Barbecue Sauce (page 207) or catsup may be used for part or all of the water.

2. Serve beef patties with Brown Gravy (page 212) if desired.

BEEF MEAT BALLS

Portion: 4 (2-ounce) meat balls.

INGREDIENTS	100 PORTIONS			............PORTIONS
	WEIGHTS		AMOUNTS (approx.)	
	Pounds	Ounces		
Bread, dry	6	....	1½ gallons	
Water	....	....	As needed	
Beef, bone-in .... OR	45	....	....	
Beef, boneless	31	....	....	
Eggs, whole	1	....	10 (1 pint)	
Onions, chopped fine................	5	....	3¾ quarts	
Salt	....	6	¾ cup	
Pepper	....	½	1¾ tablespoons	
Beef Stock (page 251)................	....	....	1 quart	

Soak bread in water. Press out water and discard.

Cut beef into small cubes. Grind.

Mix bread and ground meat together with remaining ingredients lightly, but thoroughly.

Form into 2-ounce meat balls (8 balls to 1 pound).

Place in greased baking pans. Bake in hot oven (400°F.) until browned on all sides.

Add small amount of stock. Cover pans tightly.

Bake in slow oven (300°F.) about 30 minutes.

NOTE —Serve with Brown Gravy (page 212) or Tomato Sauce (page 218).

Variation

Veal Meat Balls

Use veal in place of beef.

BEEF PATTIES WITH TOMATO PUREE SAUCE

(Using roast beef, canned)

Portion: 5 to 6 ounces with sauce.

INGREDIENTS	100 PORTIONS			.... PORTIONS
	WEIGHTS		AMOUNTS (approx.)	
	Pounds	*Ounces*		
Onions, dehydrated	---	4	1 pint	
Water for onions	---	---	1 quart	
Beef, roast, canned	36	---	6 6-pound cans	
Bread crumbs, dry	5	8	1¾ gallons	
Eggs, powdered	1	2	1⅛ quarts	
Mustard, dry	---	2	½ cup	
Salt	---	3	6 tablespoons	
Pepper	---	½	1¾ tablespoons	
Fat, melted	1	---	1 pint	
Tomato Puree Sauce, hot (page 219)	---	---	2½ gallons	

Soak onions in 1 quart water 20 minutes. Drain.

Grind beef with fine blade on grinder, or break into fine pieces. Add bread crumbs, eggs, mustard, onions, salt, and pepper. Mix thoroughly.

Shape into 5-ounce patties. Place in single layer in greased roasting pans. Brush with melted fat.

Bake in moderate oven (350° F.) 20 minutes. Pour hot Tomato Puree Sauce over patties. Continue cooking 10 minutes.

MEAT SAUCE FOR SPAGHETTI

Yield: Approx. 5 gallons.   Portion: ¾ to 1 cup.

INGREDIENTS	100 PORTIONS			..........PORTIONS
	WEIGHTS		AMOUNTS (approx.)	
	Pounds	*Ounces*		
Bacon drippings	....	4	½ cup	
Onions, minced	5	....	3¾ quarts	
Celery, diced	1	4	1¼ quarts	
Garlic, mashed	....	5		
Beef, coarsely ground	20	....		
Parsley	....	½	1 cup	
Salt	....	6	¾ cup	
Pepper	....	1	3½ tablespoons	
Mushrooms, sliced	1	4	2¼ quarts	
Tomatoes	19	2	3 No. 10 cans (2½ gallons).	
Tomato juice	6	....	1 No. 10 can (¾ gallon).	
Tomato paste	7	2	1 No. 10 can (¾ gallon).	
Beef Stock (page 251)	....	....	½ gallon	

Cook together slowly bacon drippings, onions, celery and garlic until thoroughly browned. Cook beef until browned. Add onion mixture. Place in steam-jacketed kettle.

Stir in parsley, salt, pepper and mushrooms. Add tomatoes, tomato juice, tomato paste and stock.

Mix ingredients thoroughly. Let simmer 3 hours.

Combine with hot cooked spaghetti. Let stand 10 to 15 minutes before serving.

NOTE.—1. 1 No. 10 can (¾ gallon) tomato puree may be used in place of tomato paste.

2. Garlic salt may be used in place of clove of garlic. Reduce salt, to taste.

MEAT SAUCE AND SPAGHETTI

(Using roast beef, canned)

Portion: Approx. 7 ounces.

INGREDIENTS	100 PORTIONS			.... PORTIONS
	WEIGHTS		AMOUNTS (approx.)	
	Pounds	*Ounces*		
Onions, dehydrated	---	8	1 quart	
Water, for onions	---	--	½ gallon	
Bacon, sliced	2	--		
Beef roast, canned	12	---	2 6-lb. cans	
Flour	--	5	1¼ cups	
Salt	---	2	¼ cup	
Pepper	--	1	3½ tablespoons	
Tomatoes	12	12	2 No. 10 cans (6½ quarts).	
Worcestershire sauce	--	---	3 tablespoons	
Salt	--	2½	5 tablespoons	
Water, boiling	---	---	3½ gallons	
Spaghetti	8	---		

Soak onions in water 20 minutes.

Cut bacon into 1-inch pieces. Fry until brown. Remove bacon from fat.

Break beef into small pieces. Add meat and onions to fat. Cook until browned.

Stir flour, 2 ounces salt and pepper into meat mixture until thoroughly blended.

Heat tomatoes to boiling temperature. Add to meat mixture. Add bacon and Worcestershire sauce.

Let simmer 20 to 30 minutes or until mixture thickens.

Add 2½ ounces salt to water. Heat to boiling temperature. Stir in spaghetti. Cook 20 minutes or until tender. Drain well.

Pour hot sauce over spaghetti. Let stand 10 minutes before serving.

BEEF STUFFED PEPPERS

Portion: 1 pepper (approx. 1 cup (8 ounces) filling).

INGREDIENTS	100 PORTIONS			..........PORTIONS
	WEIGHTS		AMOUNTS (approx.)	
	Pounds	*Ounces*		
Peppers, green, large	....	....	100	....
Water, boiling...........................	....		To cover..........................	....
Salt...	....	4	½ cup...............................	....
Bread crumbs	8	....	2½ gallons	....
OR				
Rice, cooked	13	8	2 gallons	....
Onions, chopped	2	8	½ gallon	....
Salt	....	2	¼ cup	....
Pepper	....	¼	1 tablespoon	....
Beef, cooked, chopped..............	21	....	4 gallons	....
Beef Stock (page 251)...............	....	....	½ gallon	....

Select peppers of uniform size. Wash and cut into halves. Remove seeds and white membrane.

Cover with boiling water. Add ½ cup salt. Cook 3 to 5 minutes. Drain.

Mix bread or rice with onions, salt and pepper.

Add chopped beef and stock. Mix thoroughly. Fill pepper halves. Place in greased baking pans.

Bake in moderate oven (350° F.) 20 to 30 minutes.

NOTE.—1. The amount of meat stock necessary depends on dryness of bread. Use only enough to moisten the bread.

2. Serve with Tomato Sauce (page 218).

Variation

Pork, Ham, Veal, Chicken or Turkey Stuffed Peppers

The same weight of pork, ham or veal and other ingredients may be used in place of beef for Stuffed Peppers.

Use 12 pounds of chicken or turkey with 6 pounds of pork or veal.

Omit salt when ham is used.

BEEF CHILI CON CARNE

Portion: 8 ounces (approx. 1 cup).

INGREDIENTS	100 PORTIONS			............PORTIONS
	WEIGHTS		AMOUNTS (approx.)	
	Pounds	*Ounces*		
Chili beans, small red............	6	12	1 No. 10 can (¾ gallon).	
Beef, bone-in	35	....		
OR				
Beef, boneless	25	....		
OR				
Beef, cooked	18	....		
Garlic, crushed	....	....	4 cloves	
Beef fat	1	....	1 pint	
Beef Stock (page 251)	....	....	2 gallons	
Pepper, cayenne	....	....	1 tablespoon	
Chili powder	....	3	1⅛ cups	
Salt	....	6	¾ cup	
Tomatoes	6	6	1 No. 10 can (¾ gallon).	

Press ⅔ of beans through food chopper. Leave remainder whole.

Cut meat into ½-inch cubes or grind.

Cook crushed garlic in fat until yellow. Add meat. Cook until brown.

Add enough stock to cover. Stir in cayenne pepper, chili powder and salt.

Cover pans tightly. Let simmer 3 hours or until meat is tender. Add remainder of stock as needed to keep meat covered.

Mix ground beans, remaining whole beans and tomatoes with meat. Heat to boiling temperature. Serve immediately.

Variation

Veal Chili Con Carne

Veal may be used in place of beef.

BEEF WITH SPANISH RICE

(Using roast beef, canned)

Portion: Approx. 6 ounces.

INGREDIENTS	100 PORTIONS			............Portions
	WEIGHTS		AMOUNTS (approx.)	
	Pounds	*Ounces*		
Onions, dehydrated............	1	...	½ gallon............	
Water, for onions............	...	...	1 gallon............	
Fat, melted............	1	8	1½ pints............	
Rice, uncooked............	6	...	¾ gallon............	
Beef, roast, canned......	12	...	2 6-pound cans............	
Tomatoes............	25	8	4 No. 10 cans (3¼ gallons).	
Water, boiling............	...	...	1 gallon............	
Salt............	...	3	6 tablespoons............	
Pepper............	...	¼	1 tablespoon............	

Soak onions in 1 gallon water 20 minutes. Cook in fat until clear.

Wash rice. Drain well.

Cut beef into 1-inch pieces: Combine beef, beef juices, onions, rice, tomatoes, water, salt, and pepper. Mix well.

Heat to boiling temperature. Let simmer 30 to 40 minutes or until rice is tender, adding more liquid as mixture thickens, if needed.

Variations

Corned Beef with Spanish Rice

Use 12 pounds beef, corned, canned, in place of beef, roast, canned.

Ham with Spanish Rice

Use 12 pounds left-over or trimmings from whole ham, canned, in place of beef, roast, canned.

Vienna Sausage with Spanish Rice

Use 12 pounds sausage, Vienna style, canned, cut in ½-inch pieces or ground coarsely in place of beef, roast, canned.

Luncheon Meat with Spanish Rice

Use 12 pounds luncheon meat, canned, cut into 1-inch pieces or ground coarsely in place of beef, roast, canned.

145 ★

BEEF STUFFED CABBAGE ROLLS

Portion: 2 (3-ounce) rolls.

INGREDIENTS	100 PORTIONS			..........PORTIONS
	WEIGHTS		AMOUNTS (approx.)	
	Pounds	*Ounces*		
Beef, ground	20	....		
Salt	....	5	10 tablespoons	
Pepper	....	½	1¾ tablespoons	
Onions, minced	2	....	1½ quarts	
Rice, uncooked	3	....	1½ quarts	
Cabbage leaves, fresh, large	....	....	200	
Beef Stock (page 251)	....	....	2¼ gallons	

Combine meat, salt, pepper, onions and rice thoroughly and shape into 200 loosely formed balls.

Dip cabbage leaves into boiling water or soften slightly in steamer, so they will roll.

Wrap each meat and rice roll securely in a cabbage leaf.

Place in baking pans. Add beef stock.

Cover. Bake in moderate oven (350° F.) 1½ hours or until rice is cooked.

NOTE.—1. 2¼ gallons tomato juice may be used in place of beef stock.

2. An excellent way to use cabbage and vary the use of ground meat.

SLICED DRIED BEEF AND MACARONI

Portion: 8 ounces (approx. 1 cup).

INGREDIENTS	100 PORTIONS			..........PORTIONS
	WEIGHTS		AMOUNTS (approx.)	
	Pounds	*Ounces*		
Salt	....	2	¼ cup	
Water, boiling	....	....	4½ gallons	
Macaroni, uncooked	4	8	5½ quarts	
Beef, dried, sliced	8	....	2 gallons	
Milk, liquid	....	....	5 gallons	
Fat, melted	2	....	1 quart	
Flour	2	....	½ gallon	
Pepper	....	½	1¾ tablespoons	
Cheese, American cheddar, shredded.	4	....	1 gallon	

Add salt to water. Heat to boiling temperature. Stir in macaroni. Heat to boiling temperature.

Cook about 20 minutes or until macaroni is tender. Drain.

Cut beef into small pieces. Heat milk to boiling temperature.

Blend together fat and flour to a smooth paste. Stir into milk. Cook, stirring constantly, until thickened.

Add pepper. Stir in dried beef. Let simmer 10 minutes. Add cheese.

Stir until cheese is completely melted. Serve creamed beef over macaroni.

NOTE.—Soak meat in warm water 15 to 20 minutes if too salty.

DICED BEEF IN BROWN SAUCE

Portion: 8 ounces (approx. 1 cup).

INGREDIENTS	100 PORTIONS			............PORTIONS
	WEIGHTS		AMOUNTS (approx.)	
	Pounds	Ounces		
Onions (optional), chopped......	5	....	3¾ quarts	
Beef fat, melted........	2	....	1 quart	
Flour	2	....	½ gallon	
Beef Stock (page 251)	....	....	3 gallons	
Beef, cooked, diced........	23	....	4¼ gallons	
Salt, as desired........	....	....		
Pepper, as desired	....	....		
Bread, toasted .... OR	....	....	100 slices	
Rice, cooked	20	8	4 gallons	

Cook onions in fat until clear. Stir in flour and mix thoroughly. Cook until flour is browned, stirring constantly.

Heat stock to boiling temperature. Add gradually to flour mixture, stirring constantly. Cook until mixture boils vigorously. Remove from heat.

Add diced beef, salt and pepper as desired. Reheat.

Serve over toast or cooked rice.

NOTE.—1. Beef may be either roast, pot roast or steak.

2. Lamb may be used in place of beef.

CREAMED SLICED DRIED BEEF

Portion: 8 ounces (approx. 1 cup).

INGREDIENTS	100 PORTIONS			..........PORTIONS
	WEIGHTS		AMOUNTS (approx.)	
	Pounds	*Ounces*		
Beef, dried, sliced....................	7	....	1¾ gallons	
Milk, liquid	....	....	5 gallons	
Fat, melted	2	....	1 quart	
Flour	2	8	2½ quarts	
Pepper	....	½	1¾ tablespoons	
Bread, toasted	....	....	100 slices	

Cut beef into small pieces. Heat milk to boiling temperature.

Blend together fat and flour to a smooth paste. Stir into milk.

Cook, stirring constantly, until thickened.

Add pepper. Stir in beef.

Let simmer about 10 minutes. Serve over toast.

NOTE.—Soak meat in warm water 15 to 20 minutes if too salty.

SLICED DRIED BEEF SCALLOPED WITH POTATOES

Portion: 12 ounces (approx. 1½ cups).

INGREDIENTS	100 PORTIONS			..........PORTIONS
	WEIGHTS		AMOUNTS (approx.)	
	Pounds	*Ounces*		
Beef, dried, sliced....................	8	....	2 gallons	
Potatoes, A.P.	48	....	....	
Onions, chopped	2	....	1½ quarts	
Flour	....	12	1½ pints	
Salt	....	6	¾ cup	
Pepper	....	¼	¾ tablespoon	
Butter or other fat, melted.....	1	8	1½ pints	
Milk, liquid	....	....	2½ gallons	

Cut beef into small pieces.

Peel potatoes. Slice in 1/16 to 1/8-inch slices.

Arrange dried beef, potatoes and onions in alternate layers in baking pans.

Mix together flour, salt and pepper. Sprinkle over beef mixture.

Pour melted butter over beef. Pour milk over mixture.

Bake in moderate oven (375°F.) about 1 hour or until potatoes are soft.

BEEF CROQUETTES

Portion: 2 croquettes.

INGREDIENTS	100 PORTIONS			............PORTIONS
	WEIGHTS		AMOUNTS (approx.)	
	Pounds	*Ounces*		
Beef, cooked, ground................	25	....	3 gallons	
Salt	....	2	¼ cup	
Pepper	....	¼	1 tablespoon	
Onions, finely chopped............	5	....	3¾ quarts	
Fat	2	8	1¼ quarts	
Flour	2	....	½ gallon	
Beef Stock (page 251), hot........	....	....	½ gallon	
Eggs, slightly beaten............	3	....	30 (1½ quarts)...........	
Bread crumbs	5	....	1½ gallons	
Milk, liquid	....	....	1 quart	
Eggs, beaten	1	....	10 (1 pint)................	
Flour	....	....	....	
Bread crumbs	....	....	....	

Combine ground beef, salt and pepper.

Cook onions in fat until clear.

Add 2 pounds flour. Mix thoroughly. Stir into heated stock gradually, stirring constantly. Heat to boiling temperature.

Cool. Stir in eggs and bread crumbs. Add beef and mix thoroughly.

Chill in refrigerator until firm.

Mix together milk and eggs.

Shape meat into croquettes. Roll in flour. Dip into egg and milk mixture. Roll in crumbs.

Fry in hot deep fat at 375° F. 4 to 5 minutes or until evenly browned on all sides. Serve immediately.

NOTE.—Lamb or veal may be used in place of beef.

Variation

Beef, Lamb or Veal "Croquette" Loaf

Place "croquette" mixture in well greased baking pans. Bake in slow oven (325° F.) 45 to 60 minutes.

Cut in squares or slices for serving.

BAKED BEEF HASH

Portion: 8 ounces (approx. 1 cup).

INGREDIENTS	100 PORTIONS			............PORTIONS
	WEIGHTS		AMOUNTS (approx.)	
	Pounds	Ounces		
Beef, boneless, cooked, diced...	23	....	4¼ gallons	
Potatoes, cooked, diced	20	....	3 gallons	
Onions, chopped	5	...	3¾ quarts	
Salt	....	4	½ cup	
Pepper	....	¼	¾ tablespoon	
Beef Stock (page 251)............	....	....	2 gallons	

Combine meat, potatoes, onions, salt, pepper and stock. Mix well.

Spread mixture in well greased baking pans. Bake in slow oven (325° F.) about 1 hour.

Cut hash into squares for serving.

NOTE.—1. Fresh ground beef may be used to make up the deficiency if there is not sufficient cooked beef. Increase the cooking time. Use ⅓ more uncooked boneless meat than cooked, to allow for shrinkage.

2. 24 pounds (4 6-pound cans) beef, roast, canned, or beef, corned, canned, may be used.

3. Barbecue Sauce (page 207) may be used in place of beef stock.

Variations

Baked Tongue Hash

The same weight tongue, canned, may be used in place of beef.

Baked Lamb, Pork, Veal, Ham, Chicken or Turkey Hash

The same weight of cooked lamb, pork, ham or veal, or 15 pounds cooked chicken or turkey may be used in place of beef. Omit salt in ham hash.

Baked Corned Beef Hash

The same weight of cooked corned beef, diced, may be used in place of beef.

Baked Luncheon Meat Hash

The same weight luncheon meat, canned, may be used in place of beef.

SIMMERED BEEF TONGUE

Portion: 5 to 6 ounces.

| INGREDIENTS | 100 PORTIONS | | ....Portions |
	WEIGHTS	AMOUNTS (approx.)	
	Pounds | *Ounces*		
Tongue, fresh or smoked	60 |		
Water	.... |		

Cover tongues with water. Heat to boiling temperature.

Cover tightly. Let simmer 3 to 4 hours or until tongues are tender. Drain.

Plunge into cold water. Remove skin and trim base of tongues.

NOTE.—1. Cool tongues in water in which they were cooked if served cold. If tongues are to be served hot, trim and return to cooking water. Reheat.

2. Add 6 ounces (¾ cup) salt to water for cooking fresh tongue.

3. Spices and chopped vegetables such as onions, carrots and green peppers may be added for seasonings.

4. Slice tongue, hot or cold. Serve with Horse-radish Sauce (page 210).

Variation

Tongue A La Maryland

Prepare tongue. Remove skin. Reheat with canned cherries to which spices and bay leaves have been added. Serve hot.

Breaded Tongue

Use prepared tongue, fresh or canned. Slice. Dip in breading. Pan-fry until browned.

Tongue with Raisin Sauce

Use hot prepared tongue, fresh or canned. Slice. Serve with Raisin Sauce (page 216).

BRAISED BEEF HEARTS

Portion: 5 to 6 ounces.

| INGREDIENTS | 100 PORTIONS | | ....Portions |
	WEIGHTS	AMOUNTS (approx.)	
	Pounds | *Ounces*		
Hearts, beef	40 |		
Onions, minced	1 |	1½ pints	
Beef drippings	.... | 12	1½ cups	
Salt	.... | 6	¾ cup	
Pepper	.... | ½	1¾ tablespoons	
Carrots, diced	1 |	1 quart	
Beef Stock (page 251)	.... |	2 gallons	
Flour	.... | 4½	1¼ cups	
Water	.... |	1½ cups	

Wash hearts. Remove arteries, veins and valves. Wash.

Cook onions in beef drippings until clear.

Place hearts in roasting pan. Add onions and drippings, salt, pepper, carrots and stock. Cover tightly. Simmer or bake in slow oven (300° F.)

3 to 4 hours or until tender.

Strain liquid from hearts. Blend flour and water to a smooth paste. Stir into liquid from meat. Cook until thickened, stirring constantly.

Carve hearts across grain. Serve with gravy.

BEEF HEARTS STUFFED AND BRAISED

Portion: Approx. 8 ounces.

INGREDIENTS	100 PORTIONS			..........PORTIONS
	WEIGHTS		AMOUNTS (approx.)	
	Pounds	*Ounces*		
Hearts, beef	35	....	....	
Salt	....	6	¾ cup	
Pepper	....	½	1¾ tablespoons	
Onions, chopped	....	5	1 cup	
Celery, diced	1	....	1 quart	
Fat	1	8	1½ pints	
Bread crumbs, soft, coarse...	8	....	4 gallons	
Poultry seasoning (optional)	....	1	....	
Eggs, slightly beaten	1	8	15 (1½ pints)	
Beef Stock (page 251), hot......	....	....	....	

Wash hearts in warm water. Remove arteries, veins and valves. Drain and sprinkle inside with 3 ounces salt and ¼ ounce pepper.

Cook onions and celery in 1 pound fat. Add bread crumbs, remaining salt, pepper and poultry seasoning. Remove from heat.

Add slightly beaten eggs and enough hot stock to moisten. Mix lightly. Fill hearts with hot stuffing. Pack loosely. Tie or sew, if needed.

Cook hearts in remaining fat until browned. Place in roasting pans. Add just enough stock to cover bottom of pan. Cover tightly.

Bake in slow oven (300°F.) 3 to 4 hours or until tender. Add more stock during cooking if necessary.

Remove hearts. Slice across grain in ½-inch slices so stuffing will be in center of slice.

NOTE.—1. Serve with Brown Gravy (page 212) if desired.

2. Fruit Dressing (page 199) may be used to stuff hearts.

3. Hearts may be rolled in flour before frying, if desired.

4. 1 ounce (⅓ cup) parsley, finely chopped, may be added to dressing.

CORNED BEEF, BAKED

Portion: 5 to 6 ounces.

INGREDIENTS	100 PORTIONS			..........PORTIONS
	WEIGHTS		AMOUNTS (approx.)	
	Pounds	*Ounces*		
Corned beef, canned...............	35	....	....	
Beef Stock (page 251)............	....	....	....	

Place corned beef in roasting pans. Add enough stock to cover bottom of pan. Cover.

Cook in slow oven (325° F.) 30 minutes.

NOTE.—Barbecue Sauce (page 207) may be used in place of stock.

CORNED BEEF

Yield: Approx. 55 pounds.

INGREDIENTS	100 PORTIONS			............Portions
	WEIGHTS		AMOUNTS (approx.)	
	Pounds	Ounces		
Beef	50	....	....	
Salt	4	....	½ gallon	
Sugar, brown	1	8	4½ cups	
Saltpeter	....	1½		
Water	....	....	2½ gallons	

Select fresh meat, preferably covered with fat layers, from brisket, plate, chuck or round.

Cut into 5 to 6-pound pieces of uniform size.

Cover bottom of thoroughly clean curing vat with a ¼-inch layer of salt.

Arrange alternate layers of meat and salt in vat, covering top layer of meat with a thick layer of salt. Pack meat as closely as possible.

Heat water to boiling temperature. Add sugar and saltpeter, stirring until dissolved.

Cool liquid until lukewarm. Pour over meat.

Keep meat entirely under brine. Weight down with loose cover.

Store in refrigerator at 34° F. to 38° F.

Repack meat on the 4th and 8th days, reversing the individual pieces and the order of the cuts, so that the curing mixture will penetrate the meat evenly. Let meat stand 15 to 20 days.

NOTE.—1. A clean wooden tub or barrel, earthenware crock or galvanized curing vat may be used.

2. Corned Beef is ready for use after 10 days, but 15 to 20 days is preferable for curing.

3. Keep meat in brine until used.

4. Use only fresh meat for corning. Meat which has begun to spoil is unwholesome and will probably sour during corning process.

CORNED BEEF SCRAMBLE

Portion: 6 to 8 ounces (approx. 1 cup).

INGREDIENTS	100 PORTIONS			.... Portions
	WEIGHTS		AMOUNTS (approx.)	
	Pounds	Ounces		
Corned beef, canned................	20	....	....	
Peppers, green	1	....	1 quart	
Onions	1	....	1½ pints	
Fat, melted	....	8	1 cup	
Corn, whole kernel, drained...	13	4	2 No. 10 cans (1½ gallons).	
Rice, cooked (page 44)	27	....	4 gallons	

Chop together corned beef, green peppers and onions.

Cook in fat until corned beef is browned, stirring frequently.

Stir in corn and cooked rice. Heat thoroughly. If necessary add the liquor from corn.

Serve in mounds.

SIMMERED CORN BEEF

Portion: 4 to 5 ounces.

INGREDIENTS	100 PORTIONS			............PORTIONS
	WEIGHTS		AMOUNTS (approx.)	
	Pounds	Ounces		
Beef, corned, boneless...............	42	....	....	....
Water, cold	....	....	....	....

Cut meat into 5-pound pieces.

Place in kettle without stacking or over-lapping. Cover with cold water.

Heat to boiling temperature. Let simmer 4 to 6 hours or until meat is tender. Add cold water from time to time to solidify fat.

Skim grease from top of water to prevent possibility of discoloration.

Test each piece of meat for doneness after 3½ to 4 hours of cooking. Remove each piece as soon as it is tender, to prevent overcooking.

Submerge all pieces in cold water fat side down, at least 15 minutes, to bleach and solidify fat and prevent shrinkage.

Serve immediately. If necessary to hold several hours, immerse pieces in lukewarm, mildly salted water at temperature of 98°F.

NOTE.—1. Equipment may be such that cold water can be added to the vats or kettles which overflow into a trap, thereby automatically skimming the cooking water.

2. Pieces of exactly the same size may vary 15 minutes in cooking time.

Variation

New England Boiled Dinner

Peel and cut into about 1-inch cubes 10 pounds turnips, 10 pounds carrots, 10 pounds parsnips and 20 pounds potatoes. Add to corned beef and let simmer in the stock 20 to 25 minutes before beef is done. Add 20 pounds cabbage, washed and cut into small wedges, 10 to 15 minutes before meat is done. Cook uncovered.

NOTE.—1. Small white onions, whole and peeled, may be added together with turnips, carrots, parsnips and potatoes.

2. Vegetables, if small-sized, may be left whole, halved or quartered, instead of being cut into 1-inch cubes. Add about 5 minutes to cooking time.

CORNED BEEF HASH, BAKED

Portion: 6 to 8 ounces.

INGREDIENTS	100 PORTIONS			...........PORTIONS
	WEIGHTS		AMOUNTS (approx.)	
	Pounds	Ounces		
Corned beef hash, canned...........	50	....	....	....
Beef Stock (page 251).................	....	....	....	....

Place corned beef hash in roasting pans. Add enough stock to cover bottom of pan. Cover.

Heat in slow oven (325° F.) 30 minutes.

Variations

Corned Beef Hash and Tomatoes

Combine 40 pounds corned beef hash and 12¾ pounds (6½ quarts) tomatoes. Heat thoroughly about 45 minutes.

Corned Beef Hash with Eggs

Remove 35 pounds corned beef hash from cans. Slice. Place in greased roasting pans. Bake in slow oven (325° F.) 30 minutes.

Fry eggs for 100 portions. Place 1 egg on top of each slice of hash and serve.

NOTE.—Hash may be shaped into mounds for individual servings. Place in well greased pans. Press a cavity in top.

Drop 1 egg into each cavity with small amount of butter. Sprinkle with salt and pepper.

Bake in slow oven (325° F.) until eggs are cooked and hash is browned.

★154

BAKED CORNED BEEF WITH MASHED POTATOES

(Using corned beef, canned)

Portion: Approx. 5 ounces.

INGREDIENTS	100 PORTIONS			............PORTIONS
	WEIGHTS		AMOUNTS (approx.)	
	Pounds	*Ounces*		
Milk, powdered, whole	1	---	3½ cups	
Water, for milk	---	---	¾ gallon	
Onions, dehydrated	---	4	1 pint	
Water, for onions	---	---	1 quart	
Potatoes, diced, dehydrated ...	5	---	7¼ quarts	
Water, for potatoes...............	---	---	3 gallons..............	
Butter, melted	1	---	1 pint	
Salt	---	1	2 tablespoons	
Beef, corned, canned	18	---	3 6-pound cans	
Bread crumbs, dry	1	8	½ gallon	
Eggs, powdered, whole	---	6	1½ cups	

Stir milk into ¾ gallon water until completely dissolved.

Soak onions in 1 quart water 20 minutes.

Soak potatoes in 3 gallons water 45 minutes. Cover. Heat, slowly, to boiling temperature about 45 minutes. Let simmer until tender. Drain. Reserve liquid.

Mash potatoes until smooth. Stir in, slowly, butter, salt and ½ gallon milk. Beat thoroughly. Keep hot.

Break corned beef into small pieces. Add bread crumbs, powdered eggs, onions and remaining ¼ gallon milk.

Place beef mixture in greased roasting pans in layers 2 inches deep. Cover with layer of mashed potatoes.

Bake in moderate oven (350° F.) 30 minutes or until browned.

NOTE.—1. Use liquid drained from potatoes as part of water to reconstitute milk.

2. The amount of milk used in mashed potatoes may vary. Use only enough to make mashed potatoes of proper consistency.

CORNED BEEF AND SPAGHETTI WITH CHEESE

(Using corned beef, canned)

Portion: Approx. 8 ounces.

INGREDIENTS	100 PORTIONS			.... PORTIONS
	WEIGHTS		AMOUNTS (approx.)	
	Pounds	*Ounces*		
Salt	---	2½	5 tablespoons	
Water, boiling	---	---	4 gallons	
Spaghetti	5	---		
Salt	---	2	¼ cup	
Pepper	---	¼	1 tablespoon	
Tomatoes	12	12	2 No. 10 cans (6½ quarts).	
Beef, corned, canned	12	..	2 6-pound cans	
Cheese, sliced	1	8		

Add 2½ ounces salt to water. Heat to boiling temperature. Stir in spaghetti.

Cook 20 minutes or until tender. Drain well.

Add 2 ounces salt and pepper to tomatoes. Heat to boiling temperature.

Cut corned beef into ¼-inch slices. Place in bottom of greased baking pans.

Cover with layer of spaghetti. Pour tomatoes over entire surface.

Arrange slices of cheese over top of tomatoes.

Bake in moderate oven (350° F.) 30 to 45 minutes.

Variations

Roast Beef and Spaghetti With Cheese

Use 12 pounds (2 6-pound cans) beef, roast, canned, in place of 12 pounds beef, corned, canned.

Luncheon Meat and Spaghetti With Cheese

Use 12 pounds (2 6-pound cans) luncheon meat, canned, in place of 12 pounds beef, corned, canned.

ROAST LAMB

Portion: Approx. 5 ounces.

INGREDIENTS	100 PORTIONS			............PORTIONS
	WEIGHTS		AMOUNTS (approx.)	
	Pounds	*Ounces*		
Lamb, bone-in	60	....	....	
OR				
Lamb, boneless	42	....	....	
Salt	....	8	1 cup	
Pepper	....	1	3½ tablespoons	

Use legs, loins, rack and shoulders cut into 4 to 6-pound pieces.

Rub with salt and pepper.

Place, fat side up, in roasting pans. Fill pans, without stacking or crowding roasts.

Roast, uncovered, at constant temperature in slow oven (325°F.) about 4 hours. Allow 40 to 45 minutes per pound. Cook without water.

Remove roasts from pans. Carve across the grain in thin slices.

NOTE.—1. Serve lamb very hot or thoroughly chilled. It is not palatable when lukewarm.

2. Serve roast lamb with gravy.

3. Lamb roasts may be rubbed with garlic for additional flavor.

BRAISED LAMB

Portion: 4 to 5 ounces.

INGREDIENTS	100 PORTIONS			............PORTIONS
	WEIGHTS		AMOUNTS (approx.)	
	Pounds	*Ounces*		
Lamb, bone-in	60	....	....	
OR				
Lamb, boneless	42	....	....	
Lamb fat or other fat	....	8	1 cup	
Salt	....	6	¾ cup	
Pepper	....	½	1¾ tablespoons	
Meat Stock (page 251) or water, hot.	....	....	1 quart	
Onions, chopped (optional) ...	5	....	3¾ quarts	

Cut lamb into 4 to 6-pound pieces.

Cook, in fat, until lamb is browned on all sides. Turn to insure even browning.

Add salt, pepper and small amount of stock or water and chopped onions, if desired.

Let simmer, in tightly covered kettle, or cook in slow oven (300° F.) 3 hours or until tender. Turn meat several times while cooking. Add small amounts of liquid, as needed.

Remove meat from pans. Slice across the grain in thin slices. Keep hot.

NOTE.—Serve with Brown Gravy (page 212).

Lamb A La Mode

Add 3 pounds (¾ gallon) diced carrots, 2 pounds (1½ quarts) diced onions, and 1 No. 10 can (3¼ quarts) tomatoes to the braised lamb 30 to 45 minutes before meat is done. Serve the vegetables in the gravy as a sauce.

Lamb Braised with Vegetables

Use 45 pounds bone-in or 31 pounds boneless lamb. Add 3 pounds each of sliced carrots, onions, celery and turnips to braised lamb allowing 40 to 45 minutes for cooking before meat (roast) is done.

GRIDDLE-BROILED LAMB CHOPS

Portion: 2 (approx. 4-ounce) chops.

INGREDIENTS	100 PORTIONS			............PORTIONS
	WEIGHTS		AMOUNTS (approx.)	
	Pounds	*Ounces*		
Lamb, bone-in	65	....	....	....
Salt	....	6	¾ cup	....
Pepper	....	½	1¾ tablespoons	....

Cut lamb into 4-ounce chops ¾ inch thick.

Broil on heated griddle. Turn to insure even cooking. Cook until browned on both sides and desired degree of doneness is obtained. Avoid overcooking. Place in slow oven (300° F.) until ready to serve.

Sprinkle with salt and pepper just before removing from oven. Serve immediately.

NOTE.—1. Chops may be cooked until browned on both sides on heated griddle, then stacked on end in open baking pans, placed in slow oven (300° F.) and cooked to desired degree of doneness.

2. If meat is lacking in fat, grease the griddle with fat to prevent sticking.

3. Lamb chops should be served very hot.

FRIED LAMB CHOPS

Portion: 2 (4-ounce) chops.

INGREDIENTS	100 PORTIONS			............PORTIONS
	WEIGHTS		AMOUNTS (approx.)	
	Pounds	*Ounces*		
Lamb, bone-in	65	....	....	....
Salt	....	6	¾ cup	....
Pepper	....	½	1¾ tablespoons	....
Lamb or other fat....................	2	....	1 quart	....

Cut lamb into 4-ounce chops ½ to ¾ inch thick.

Sprinkle with salt and pepper.

Pan-fry until light brown. Turn to insure even cooking.

NOTE.—1. Lamb should be served very hot.

2. Serve with Brown Gravy (page 212).

BRAISED LAMB CHOPS

Portion: 2 (approx. 4-ounce) chops.

INGREDIENTS	100 PORTIONS			.........PORTIONS
	WEIGHTS		AMOUNTS (approx.)	
	Pounds	*Ounces*		
Lamb, bone-in	65	....	....	
Salt	....	8	1 cup	
Pepper	....	1	3½ tablespoons	

Cut lamb into 4-ounce chops ½ inch thick.

Cook on heated griddle, or in pan on top of stove, or in hot oven (450° F.) 10 minutes or until chops are browned on both sides. Sprinkle with salt and pepper.

Stack on end in baking pans. Cover pans tightly. Cook in slow oven (300° F.) about 30 minutes.

NOTE.—For additional flavor, before cooking, let lamb chops stand about 2 hours in French Dressing (page 242) to which finely minced onions have been added.

Variations

Country Style Lamb Chops

Prepare braised chops and serve with Cream Gravy (page 212).

Lamb Chops with Barbecue Sauce or Tomato Sauce

Prepare braised chops and serve with Barbecue Sauce (page 207) or Tomato Sauce (page 218).

SAVORY LAMB

Portion: Approx. 6 ounces.

INGREDIENTS	100 PORTIONS			.........PORTIONS
	WEIGHTS		AMOUNTS (approx.)	
	Pounds	*Ounces*		
Lamb, bone-in	45	....	....	
OR				
Lamb, boneless	31	....	....	
Bacon, diced....................	10	....	1¼ gallons	
Flour	1	8	1½ quarts	
Salt	....	4	½ cup	
Pepper	....	½	1¾ tablespoons	
Onions, sliced	5	....	1 gallon	
Lemons, juice, and peels cut into strips.	....	....	9	

Trim all excess fat from lamb. Cut meat into 1- to 2-inch cubes.

Fry bacon until light brown but not crisp.

Mix together flour, salt and pepper. Dredge lamb cubes in flour. Cook in pan with bacon and bacon fat until browned.

Add sliced onions, lemon juice and lemon rind.

Cook slowly in steam-jacketed kettle or in slow oven (325° F.) 1½ hours or until lamb is tender. Stir occasionally.

159★

IRISH LAMB STEW

Portion: 8 ounces (approx. 1 cup).

INGREDIENTS	100 PORTIONS			...........PORTIONS
	WEIGHTS		AMOUNTS (approx.)	
	Pounds	*Ounces*		
Lamb, bone-in	40	....	....	
OR				
Lamb, boneless	28	....		
Salt	....	6	¾ cup	
Pepper	....	½	1¾ tablespoons	
Onions, chopped	....	8	1½ cups	
Meat Stock (page 251) or water.	....	....	3 gallons	
Potatoes, cubed	12	....	1¾ gallons	
Onions, quartered	6	....	1½ gallons	
Carrots, 1 to 2-inch pieces.....	8	....	2 gallons	
Peas	5	....	2½ quarts	
Flour	2	....	½ gallon	
Water	....	....	1½ quarts	

Trim all excess fat from lamb. Cut meat into 1- to 2-inch cubes. Add salt, pepper, and onions.

Add stock or water. Cover tightly. Let simmer 2 to 2½ hours or until meat is tender.

Add vegetables before meat is tender. Allow 45 to 60 minutes for potatoes and onions to cook. Allow 30 minutes for carrots. Prepare and cook peas separately.

Blend flour and water to a smooth paste.

Drain stock from stew and thicken with paste. Reheat.

Combine gravy with meat and vegetables.

Heat to, boiling temperature. Garnish with cooked peas just before serving.

NOTE.—One of the following vegetables or combinations may be added, if desired: turnips and celery; celery, green peppers and summer squash; lima beans and turnips; onions, apples and celery; okra, tomatoes and celery; carrots, onions and green beans; kidney beans, celery and onions. (See Time-Table for cooking vegetables (page 282).)

Variation

Irish Beef or Veal Stew

Beef or veal may be used in place of lamb.

LAMB CURRY

Portion: ¾ to 1 cup curry. Approx. 1 cup cooked rice.

INGREDIENTS	100 PORTIONS			........PORTIONS
	WEIGHTS		AMOUNTS (approx.)	
	Pounds	*Ounces*		
Flour	2	....	½ gallon	
Bacon fat or other fat, melted..	4	....	½ gallon	
Milk, liquid	....	....	1½ gallons	
Meat Stock (page 251)..........	....	....	2 gallons	
Salt	....	6	¾ cup	
Pepper, cayenne	....	....	¼ teaspoon	
Curry powder	....	6	1½ cups	
Cinnamon	....	....	1 teaspoon	
Cloves	....	....	1 teaspoon	
Nutmeg	....	....	1 teaspoon	
Allspice	....	....	1 teaspoon	
Onions, minced	3	8	2½ quarts	
Apples, sliced	6	....	1½ gallons	
Lamb, cooked, cubed..........	23	....	4¼ gallons	
Rice, cooked	27	....	4 gallons	

Blend together flour and 2 pounds fat. Combine milk and stock. Heat to boiling temperature. Stir in flour mixture.

Heat to boiling temperature. Cook about 3 minutes.

Combine remaining fat, salt, pepper, curry powder, cinnamon, cloves, nutmeg, and allspice.

Add onions, apples and lamb. Cover tightly. Cook slowly 30 to 45 minutes. Stir in Cream Sauce.

Reheat lamb curry to boiling temperature. Serve on or around mound of hot rice.

NOTE.—Lamb curry may be made from fresh lamb by cooking it cubed as for stew. Use 31 pounds boneless lamb if meat is to be cooked.

Variation

Veal, Chicken or Turkey Curry

Use same weight of veal or 15 pounds cooked chicken or turkey, in place of lamb.

GRIDDLE-BROILED LAMB PATTIES

Portion: 2 (approx. 3½-ounce) patties.

INGREDIENTS	100 PORTIONS			..........PORTIONS
	WEIGHTS		AMOUNTS (approx.)	
	Pounds	*Ounces*		
Lamb, bone-in	45	....	....	....
OR				
Lamb, boneless	31	....	....	....
Bread crumbs, soft	7	....	3½ gallons	....
Onions, minced	5	....	3¾ quarts	....
Salt	....	5	10 tablespoons	....
Pepper	....	¼	¾ tablespoon	....
Meat Stock (page 251) or water.	....	....	¾ gallon	....

Cut lamb into small cubes. Grind.

Mix together all ingredients lightly, but thoroughly. Shape into 3 to 3½-ounce patties 1 inch thick.

Broil on heated griddle about 12 minutes or to the desired degree of doneness. Turn to insure even cooking. Serve immediately.

NOTE.—1. Barbecue Sauce (page 207) or Tomato Sauce (page 218) may be used for part or all of the water.

2. Serve lamb patties with or without gravy.

Variation

Baked Lamb Patties

Prepare lamb patties. Arrange in roasting pans. Bake, uncovered without turning, in slow oven (325° F.) about 45 minutes or to desired degree of doneness.

ROAST PORK

Portion: Approx. 5 ounces.

INGREDIENTS	100 PORTIONS			..........PORTIONS
	WEIGHTS		AMOUNTS (approx.)	
	Pounds	*Ounces*		
Pork cuts, bone-in..................	55–60	....	....	....
OR				
Pork cuts, boneless	42	....	....	....
Salt	....	8	1 cup	....
Pepper	....	1	3½ tablespoons	....

Cut pork into 6 to 8-pound pieces. Rub with salt and pepper.

Place in roasting pans with fat side up. Fill pans, without stacking or crowding.

Roast, uncovered without addition of water, in slow oven (325°F.) about 4½ to 5 hours or until well done. Allow 45 to 50 minutes per pound per roast. Reduce cooking time if smaller roasts are used.

Remove roasts about 1 hour before serving. Let stand about 30 minutes before carving. Carve roast, across grain, in thin slices. Keep hot.

NOTE. 1. Serve with Brown Gravy (page 212) and applesauce, stewed or baked apples, apple rings, cranberries, or tart jelly.

2. Roast pork may be served with Bread Dressing (page 199).

BRAISED PORK CHOPS OR STEAKS

Portion: 2 (approx. 4-ounce) steaks.

INGREDIENTS	100 PORTIONS			........PORTIONS
	WEIGHTS		AMOUNTS (approx.)	
	Pounds	*Ounces*		
Pork chops or steaks..............	55–65	....	....	....
OR				
Pork, boneless	45	....	....	....
Salt	....	8	1 cup	....
Pepper	....	·¼	¾ tablespoon	....
Meat Stock (page 251) or water.	....	....	....	....

Cut meat into 4-ounce chops or steaks ¾ inch thick. Sprinkle with salt and pepper.

Cook on heated griddle about 10 minutes or until evenly browned on both sides.

Stack in roasting pans, bone side down on end. Cover with stock or water. Cover pan tightly.

Bake in slow oven (325° F.) 45 to 60 minutes or until tender.

NOTE.—1. Chops may be served with Brown Gravy (page 212).

2. Chops may be browned in oven instead of on griddle.

Variations

Country Style Pork Chops or Steaks

Braised chops or steaks may be served with Cream Gravy (page 212).

Pork Chops or Steaks with Barbecue or Creole Sauce

Barbecue Sauce (page 207) or Creole Sauce (page 213) may be used in place of water on browned meat for braising.

FRIED PORK CHOPS OR STEAKS

Portion: 2 (approx. 4-ounce) chops or steaks.

INGREDIENTS	100 PORTIONS			........PORTIONS
	WEIGHTS		AMOUNTS (approx.)	
	Pounds	*Ounces*		
Pork chops or steaks..............	55–65	....	....	....
OR				
Pork, boneless	45	....	....	....
Flour	2	....	½ gallon	....
Salt	....	6	¾ cup	....
Pepper	....	¼	¾ tablespoon	....

Cut meat into chops or steaks ½ inch thick.

Mix together flour, salt and pepper. Dredge chops or steaks in flour.

Pan-fry in small amount of fat until well done and evenly browned. Turn to insure even cooking.

NOTE.—Serve with Brown Gravy (page 212). Beef Stock (page 251), vegetable liquor, or water may be used in making gravy.

163★

BREADED PORK CHOPS OR STEAKS

Portion: 2 (approx. 4-ounce) chops.

INGREDIENTS	100 PORTIONS			............PORTIONS
	WEIGHTS		AMOUNTS (approx.)	
	Pounds	Ounces		
Pork chops or steaks............	50–60	....	....	
OR				
Pork, boneless	42	....	....	
Salt	....	8	1 cup	
Pepper	....	½	1¾ tablespoons	
Flour	2	....	½ gallon	
Milk, liquid	....	....	½ gallon	
Eggs, beaten	2	....	20 (1 quart)..................	
Bread crumbs	2	....	2½ quarts	

Cut meat into 4-ounce chops or steaks about ⅜ inch thick. Sprinkle with salt and pepper. Dredge with flour.

Combine milk and eggs. Mix well. Dip chops into egg mixture and then into bread crumbs.

Fry in hot deep fat at 350°F. about 7 to 10 minutes or until chops are browned. Place chops, on end, in baking pans and bake in slow oven (325°F.) for 30 to 40 minutes.

NOTE.—1. Breaded pork chops may be braised by cooking in small amount of fat until browned, then stacked on end, bone side down, in baking pans, covered tightly and baked in slow oven (325°F.) 45 minutes.

Breaded pork chops may be pan-fried. Turn to insure even cooking.

2. Serve with Tomato Sauce (page 218) or Brown Gravy (page 212).

BRAISED SPARERIBS

Portion: 8 to 10 ounces.

INGREDIENTS	100 PORTIONS			............PORTIONS
	WEIGHTS		AMOUNTS (approx.)	
	Pounds	Ounces		
Spareribs	65	....	....	
Salt	....	10	1¼ cups	
Pepper	....	½	1 tablespoon	
Meat Stock (page 251) or water.	....	....	....	

Cut spareribs into 4-rib pieces weighing about 8 to 10 ounces each.

Place in roasting pans. Stack as little as possible. Bake uncovered in hot oven (400°F.) until browned.

Sprinkle with salt and pepper. Add just enough stock or water to cover bottom of pan.

Cover and bake in slow oven (325° F.) 1½ to 2 hours or until ribs will slip from meat.

Variations

Braised Spareribs with Sauerkraut

Place sauerkraut in greased baking pans and cover with spareribs which have been cooked until browned.

Add small amount of stock or water. Bake in slow oven (325° F.) 1½ to 2 hours or until ribs are done.

Braised Spareribs with Barbecue Sauce

Pour Barbecue Sauce (page 207) over the ribs after they have been browned. Bake. Baste several times with the sauce.

PORK CHOP SUEY

Portion: Approx. 8 ounces chop suey. Approx. 6 ounces rice.

INGREDIENTS	100 PORTIONS			.........PORTIONS
	WEIGHTS		AMOUNTS (approx.)	
	Pounds	*Ounces*		
Pork cuts, bone-in	35	....	....	
OR				
Pork, boneless	25	....	....	
Meat Stock (page 251) or water.	....	....	1 gallon	
Salt	....	6	¾ cup	
Pepper	....	¼	¾ tablespoon	
Onions, thinly sliced	4	....	1 gallon	
Celery, cut in strips	8	....	2 gallons	
Cornstarch	....	11	1 pint	
Bean sprouts	13	4	2 No. 10 cans (1½ gallons).	
Soy sauce	....	....	1 pint	
Rice, cooked	27	....	4 gallons	

Cut meat into cubes or strips 1 x ½ x ¼ inch. Cook until browned. Cover with stock or water. Add salt and pepper. Let simmer 1 hour.

Add onions and celery to meat. Continue cooking 30 minutes.

Make a smooth paste of cornstarch and part of water from sprouts.

Drain liquid from meat and vegetables. Stir cornstarch into hot liquid.

Add cooked meat, bean sprouts and soy sauce. Cook until thickened.

Serve chop suey on cooked rice.

Variation

Beef or Veal Chop Suey

Beef or veal may be used in place of pork. Cook meat in 1 pound (1 pint) fat until browned.

PORK LOAF

(Using pork sausage meat, canned)

Portion: Approx. 4 ounces.

INGREDIENTS	100 PORTIONS			........PORTIONS
	WEIGHTS		AMOUNTS (approx.)	
	Pounds	*Ounces*		
Onions, dehydrated..........	1	12	1¾ quarts..................	..
Water, for onions................	---	---	1½ gallons.................	
Eggs, powdered, whole...........	---	6	1½ cups..................	
Onion juice or water....	. .	---	2¼ cups...................	
Milk, powdered, whole...........	---	3	¾ cup..................	
Onion juice or water................	..	---	1½ pints................	
Sausage meat, pork, canned...	17	---	8 34-ounce cans..........	..
Salt.............................	---	1	2 tablespoons............	
Cracker crumbs.................	5	..	2½ gallons...............	

Soak onions in 1½ gallons water 20 minutes. Drain. Reserve liquid.

Stir powdered eggs into 2¼ cups liquid drained from onions, stirring constantly to avoid lumping. Mix until smooth.

Stir powdered milk into 1½ pints liquid drained from onions or water until dissolved, stirring to prevent lumping.

Mix together sausage meat, salt, and cracker crumbs. Add onions, eggs, and milk. Mix until well blended.

Shape into loaves. Pack in greased loaf pans.

Bake, uncovered, in moderate oven (350° F.) 45 minutes.

NOTE.—Bulk sausage meat or ground sausage links may be used.

KINDS OF SMOKED HAM

Commercial Ham

The commercial, domestic, or regular-cure smoked ham has a low salt content and is suitable for baking (roasting) without parboiling or soaking beforehand.

Cutting Smoked Commercial Hams Before Cooking: The following method of preparing commercial hams in the butcher shop, before they are turned over to the cooks, is recommended for several reasons:

The hams will require less space in the oven.
They will be easier to carve.
The shanks can be held back for seasoning purposes.
The surplus fat can be rendered and used for frying and baking.
It eliminates the possibility of cooking sour hams, because it provides a definite check on the interior of the ham around the leg bone.

Directions for Cutting: Defrost ham completely before preparation for cooking, if ham is frozen.

Remove hock at stifle joint, leaving as much meat as possible on the cushion section. (Store hock in refrigerator until needed.)

Trim off outside skin and remove surplus fat, exceeding one-half inch, covering outside of ham.

Take out aitch bone.

Loosen meat around knuckle ends of leg (round) bone.

NOTE.—An alternate method is to remove the aitch bone after cooking, since it can be taken out easier then. This prevents checking the ham for sourness unless a ham trier is used.

Carving Cooked Smoked Ham: It is assumed that the smoked ham was prepared before cooking as indicated in the paragraph "Cutting Smoked Commercial Hams Before Cooking." As a result the shank, aitch bone, skin and surplus fat from the outside of the ham have already been removed. The ham contains only the leg bone. Allow ham to "set" for 30 minutes, then proceed as follows:

Remove knuckle section by cutting through meat to leg bone on each side of ham. Remove knee cap from this section. Lift out leg bone.

Split cushion of ham into inside and outside sections.

The preceding method of splitting the cooked ham provides 3 boneless pieces of uniform size. These may be carved across the grain either by hand or on the electric slicing machine.

Overseas Ham

The overseas ham has a high salt content. It is usually shankless and, when it is to be used within a few weeks after leaving the packer, it may be wrapped in paper like the commercial ham. When it is to be shipped overseas, or is to be held for a long period of time without refrigeration, it is put in a cloth bag and packed for export.

When the overseas ham has been out of cure for only a short time, it may be cooked whole, if it is first parboiled for about 1 hour, or soaked overnight in cold water.

When these have been out of cure for a month or longer, at temperatures which may exceed 100° F., it is almost impossible to cook the ham whole and have a palatable product, even after soaking or parboiling before cooking.

Since it is difficult to tell how long the ham has been out of cure, or at what temperatures it was stored, it is recommended that the overseas ham be cut into slices not over 1 inch (preferably ½ inch) in thickness before cooking. The slices can be parboiled twice and then cooked in numerous ways. See recipes on pages 171 and 173.

Ham, Canned, Whole

Canned whole hams are prepared from cured, smoked hams which have been completely skinned, boned, and closely trimmed. They are packed and cooked in hermetically sealed cans. These hams, including natural juices, weigh from 8 to 14 pounds.

Canned hams are perishable. Each can is marked *"Perishable—Keep Under Refrigeration"* and must be held under refrigeration of 50° F. or lower.

Canned ham is cooked ready to eat as it is packed. It may be sliced for sandwiches, or, reheated, used as the meat item for a meal. Reheating enhances the flavor of the ham. The natural juices in the can should be used as a base for soups, gravies, and for flavoring vegetables.

BAKED HAM
(Commercial)

Portion: 4 to 5 ounces.

INGREDIENTS	100 PORTIONS			........PORTIONS
	WEIGHTS		AMOUNTS (approx.)	
	Pounds	*Ounces*		
Hams, commercial	60	....	....	....

Prepare commercial hams for cooking (page 167).

Place hams, fat side up, in roasting pans. Fill pans but do not stack or crowd hams.

Roast, uncovered and without water, at constant temperature in slow oven (325° F.) according to the cooking schedule.

NOTE.—If ham is to be served cold, let stand until cool enough to handle. Place in refrigerator until ready to be served.

Cooking Schedule

WEIGHT OF HAM	COOKING TIME
Pounds	*Hours*
16 to 18.................	4½ to 5
12 to 15................	3½ to 4½
10 to 12................	3 to 3½
8 to 10................	3

BAKED HAM

(Using whole ham, canned)

Portion: 4 to 5 ounces.

INGREDIENTS	100 PORTIONS			...........PORTIONS
	WEIGHTS		AMOUNTS (approx.)	
	Pounds	*Ounces*		
Ham, canned, whole......	25–31	...	....	....

Place hams, fat side up, in roasting pans. Add all natural juice from the cans.

Add water to cover bottom of pans.

Roast, uncovered, in slow oven (325° F.) allowing 12 to 15 minutes per pound.

Variation

Glazed Baked Ham

Pack brown sugar on fat surface of ham before baking. Use 1 pound, 6 ounces (1 quart) brown sugar for 25 pounds ham.

If desired, cloves may be inserted in fat surface before sugar is packed on. Remove cloves before carving.

BAKED HAM
(Commercial simmered and baked)

Portion: 4 to 5 ounces.

INGREDIENTS	100 PORTIONS			...........PORTIONS
	WEIGHTS		AMOUNTS (approx.)	
	Pounds	*Ounces*		
Hams, commercial	60	....	....	....
Water	....	...	To cover	

Prepare commercial hams for cooking (page 167).

Place in steam-jacketed kettle or cooking vessel.

Cover with water. Cover kettle. Let simmer approximately ½ the total cooking time.

Remove hams from water. Place, fat side up, in roasting pans. Fill pans but do not stack or crowd hams.

Roast, uncovered and without water, at constant temperature, in moderate oven (325° F.) for the remaining half of the total cooking time.

NOTE.—If ham is to be served cold, let stand until cool enough to handle. Place in refrigerator until ready to be served.

Cooking Schedule

WEIGHT OF HAM	TOTAL COOKING TIME
Pounds	*Hours*
16 to 18............................	4
12 to 15............................	3½
10 to 12............................	3
8 to 10............................	2½

SIMMERED (BOILED) HAM

(Commercial)

Portion: 4 to 5 ounces.

INGREDIENTS	100 PORTIONS			..........PORTIONS
	WEIGHTS		AMOUNTS (approx.)	
	Pounds	*Ounces*		
Hams, commercial	60	....	....	....
Water	....	....	To cover	....

Prepare commercial hams for cooking (page 167).

Place in steam-jacketed kettle or cooking vessel.

Cover with water. Cover kettle. Let simmer until tender according to the cooking schedule.

NOTE.—1. If ham is to be served cold, let stand in cooking water until ham is cool enough to handle. Remove from water. Place in refrigerator until ready to be served.

2. Hams should be cooked at a simmering temperature and not at a boiling temperature to prevent hams from breaking or tearing apart.

Cooking Schedule

WEIGHT OF HAM	COOKING TIME
Pounds	*Hours*
16 to 18........................	4
12 to 15........................	3½
10 to 12........................	3
8 to 10........................	2½

HAM SLICES COOKED IN MILK

(Commercial)

Portion: Approx. 6 ounces.

INGREDIENTS	100 PORTIONS			..........PORTIONS
	WEIGHTS		AMOUNTS (approx.)	
	Pounds	*Ounces*		
Ham, bone-in	60	....	....	....
OR				
Ham, boneless	42	....	....	....
Sugar, brown	3	....	2¼ quarts	....
Mustard, dry	....	1	4½ tablespoons	....
Milk, liquid	....	....	3½ quarts	....

Split ham into cushion and knuckle sections. Cut into 6-ounce slices ½ to ¾ inch thick.

Mix brown sugar and mustard. Rub on surface of both sides of ham slices.

Place slices in baking pans. Pour milk over ham.

Cook uncovered in slow oven (325° F.) about 2 hours or until tender.

Serve with the milk sauce over the ham slices.

HAM SLICES COOKED IN MILK
(Overseas)

Portion: 4 to 5 ounces.

INGREDIENTS	100 PORTIONS			.... PORTIONS
	WEIGHTS		AMOUNTS (approx.)	
	Pounds	*Ounces*		
Ham, overseas	60	....		
Water	....	....		
Sugar, brown	3	....	2¼ quarts	
Mustard, dry	....	1	4½ tablespoons	
Milk, liquid	....	....	To cover	

Prepare overseas hams for cooking (page 167).

Place ½-inch thick slices in roasting pans. Cover with cold water. Heat to boiling temperature. Drain.

Cover again with cold water. Heat to boiling temperature. Drain.

Mix together sugar and mustard. Rub on both sides of ham slices.

Place in roasting pans. Cover with milk. Cook, uncovered, in moderate oven (300° F.) about 2 hours or until tender.

NOTE.—Water may be used in place of milk.

Variation

Escalloped Ham and Potatoes

Parboil ham slices twice. Drain off water.

Prepare Escalloped Potatoes (page 314). Arrange layer of uncooked potatoes in roasting pans. Place ham slices over potatoes. Cover with layer of potatoes.

Bake in slow oven (325° F.) for 1½ to 2 hours or until potatoes are tender.

FRIED HAM

Portion: 3 to 6 ounces.

INGREDIENTS	100 PORTIONS			...........PORTIONS
	WEIGHTS		AMOUNTS (approx.)	
	Pounds	*Ounces*		
Ham, bone-in	30–60	....		
OR				
Ham, boneless	21–42	....		

Split hams into cushion and knuckle sections. Cut pieces into ⅜-inch slices.

Cut into 3 to 6-ounce portions, each according to what is to be served with the ham.

Cut fat edge, in several places, on each portion of ham to prevent curling.

Pan-fry ham, slowly, on top of stove, at moderate heat, allowing the fat to collect in pan.

Cook about 10 minutes, turning slices to insure even browning.

NOTE.—If fat from ham smokes, the frying temperature is too high.

GRIDDLE-BROILED HAM

Portion: 3 to 6 ounces.

INGREDIENTS	100 PORTIONS			............PORTIONS
	WEIGHTS		AMOUNTS (approx.)	
	Pounds	*Ounces*		
Ham, bone-in	30–60	....		
OR				
Ham, boneless	21–42	....		

Split hams into cushion and knuckle sections. Cut pieces into ⅜-inch slices.

Cut into portions 3 to 6 ounces each, according to what is to be served with the ham. Cut fat edge in several places to prevent curling.

Broil on heated griddle. Turn to insure even cooking.

Cook about 10 minutes, 5 minutes on each side. Serve immediately.

NOTE.—1. Scrape fat from ham as it accumulates. Keep griddle temperature moderate.

2. Serve with Cream Gravy (page 212), if desired.

3. Serve with eggs or omelet, pancakes, or potatoes. Especially good with escalloped potatoes.

HAM SLICES, SMOTHERED

(Commercial)

Portion: Approx. 6 ounces.

INGREDIENTS	100 PORTIONS			............PORTIONS
	WEIGHTS		AMOUNTS (approx.)	
	Pounds	*Ounces*		
Ham, bone-in	60	....		
OR				
Ham, boneless	42	....		
Water, boiling	....	....		
Cloves, whole	....	¼	1½ tablespoons	
Sugar, brown	1	....	1½ pints	
Onions, chopped	2	....	1½ quarts	
Bread crumbs, dry, fine	5	....	5¼ quarts	
Milk, liquid	....	....	3½ quarts	

Split ham into cushion and knuckle sections. Cut pieces into 6 to 7-ounce slices, ¼ to ½ inch thick.

Place in roasting pans. Cover with boiling water. Let simmer 35 to 40 minutes.

Drain water from meat. Reserve for cooking vegetables.

Sprinkle cloves, sugar, onions and bread crumbs over ham slices. Pour milk over ham.

Bake in slow oven (325°F.) about 45 minutes or until top is browned and crisp.

★ 172

HAM SLICES, SMOTHERED
(Overseas)

Portion: 4 to 5 ounces.

| INGREDIENTS | 100 PORTIONS | | | ....PORTIONS |
| | WEIGHTS | | AMOUNTS (approx.) | |
	Pounds	Ounces		
Ham, overseas	60	....		
Water	...	...		
Cloves, whole	...	¼	1½ tablespoons	
Sugar, brown	1	....	1½ pints	
Bread crumbs, dry	5	....	6¼ quarts	
Onion, chopped fine	2	....	1½ quarts	
Milk, liquid	....	....	1 gallon	

Prepare overseas hams for cooking (page 167).

Place slices in roasting pans. Cover with water. Heat to boiling temperature. Drain.

Cover again with cold water. Heat to boiling temperature. Drain.

Cover with hot water. Let simmer 35 to 45 minutes. Drain.

Place cloves, sugar, onions and bread crumbs over ham slices. Add milk.

Bake in moderate oven (300° F. to 350° F.) about 45 minutes or until top is browned and crisp.

GRIDDLE-BROILED HAM AND MEAT PATTIES

Portion: 4 to 5 ounces.

| INGREDIENTS | 100 PORTIONS | | | ....PORTIONS |
| | WEIGHTS | | AMOUNTS (approx.) | |
	Pounds	Ounces		
Ham, ground	10	....		
Meat (beef, lamb, pork or veal), ground.	20	....		

Mix together ham and other meat. Shape into 3 to 3½-ounce patties.

Broil on heated griddle slowly, 12 to 15 minutes or until well done and browned on outside. Keep temperature below smoking point of fat. Turn meat to insure even cooking. Serve immediately.

NOTE.—Serve ham and meat patties with Brown Gravy (page 212).

Variation

Baked Ham and Meat Patties

Mix meat and shape into patties about 5 to 1 pound. Arrange in baking pans.

Cook at constant temperature in slow oven (325° F. to 350° F.) 25 to 30 minutes or until well done.

Serve with Cream Gravy (page 212).

HAM AND PORK LOAF

Portion: Approx. 5 ounces.

INGREDIENTS	100 PORTIONS			........Portions
	WEIGHTS		AMOUNTS (approx.)	
	Pounds	Ounces		
Pork, lean, ground..........	18	....	....	....
Ham, smoked, ground..........	12	....	....	....
Onions, minced	3	....	1½ quarts	....
Bread crumbs	4	....	1¼ gallons	....
Salt	....	4	½ cup	....
Pepper	....	¼	¾ tablespoon	....
Eggs, slightly beaten..........	3	....	30 (1½ quarts)..........	....
Milk, liquid	....	....	½ gallon	....

Combine pork, ham and onions.

Add crumbs, salt, pepper, eggs and milk. Mix well.

Shape into loaves about 12 x 4 x 3 inches. Place in greased roasting pans.

Roast, uncovered, without adding water, in slow oven (325° F.) 2 to 2½ hours or until well done.

NOTE.—1. Serve with Cream Gravy (page 212) if desired.

2. Pork, ham and onions may be ground together or separately.

HAM SCALLOPED WITH APPLES

Portion: Approx. 6 ounces.

INGREDIENTS	100 PORTIONS			........Portions
	WEIGHTS		AMOUNTS (approx.)	
	Pounds	Ounces		
Ham, cooked, chopped..........	20	....	2½ gallons	....
Apples, sliced	20	....	3½ gallons	....
Sugar, brown	4	....	¾ gallon	....
Cloves, whole	....	¾	4½ tablespoons	....
Fruit juice or water..........	....	....	1½ quarts	....

Arrange alternate layers of ham, apples, sugar and cloves in baking pans. Cover with fruit juice or water.

Bake in slow oven (300°F.) 1½ hours.

HAM AND LIMA BEAN SCALLOP

Portion: Approx. 8 ounces.

| INGREDIENTS | 100 PORTIONS | | | ....PORTIONS |
| | WEIGHTS | | AMOUNTS (approx.) | |
	Pounds	Ounces		
Beans, lima. dried...............	12	....	1¾ gallons	
Water	....	....	To cover	
Ham, cooked, cubed...............	20	....	....	
Salt	....	2	¼ cup	
Pepper	....	....	2 teaspoons	

Pick over and wash beans. Cover with water. Soak 4 hours.

Heat to boiling temperature. Let simmer 1 hour or until almost tender, being careful not to break skins.

Add ham, salt and pepper.

Place mixture in greased baking pans. Bake in slow oven (325° F.) 1 to 1½ hours.

NOTE.—1 quart molasses or brown sugar and ¾ pound minced onions may be added for flavor.

JAMBALAYA

Yield: Approx. 6 gallons.   Portion: 1 cup (approx. 8 ounces).

| INGREDIENTS | 100 PORTIONS | | | ....PORTIONS |
| | WEIGHTS | | AMOUNTS (approx.) | |
	Pounds	Ounces		
Ham ends and trimmings, cooked.	10	....	....	
Celery, diced	2	....	½ gallon	
Onions, chopped	1	8	4½ cups	
Ham or bacon fat...............	1	....	1 pint	
Rice, uncooked, washed............	3	....	1½ quarts	
Tomatoes	12	12	2 No. 10 cans (6½ quarts).	
Ham Stock (page 254)...............	....	....	2 gallons	
Catsup	....	....	1 pint	
Salt	....	3	6 tablespoons	
Worcestershire sauce	....	....	1 cup	

Cut meat into ½ to ¾-inch cubes.

Fry celery and onions in fat until lightly browned.

Add ham, rice. tomatoes, stock, catsup, salt and Worcestershire sauce.

Heat to boiling temperature. Let simmer, stirring frequently until rice is tender and mixture is thick.

HAM AND NOODLES AU GRATIN

Portion: 4 to 5 ounces.

| INGREDIENTS | 100 PORTIONS | | | ....PORTIONS |
	WEIGHTS		AMOUNTS (approx.)	
	Pounds	Ounces		
Water	....	....	5 gallons	
Noodles	5	....	2¾ gallons	
White Sauce, medium (p. 208)	....	....	4 gallons	
Onions, minced	....	8	1½ cups	
Ham, cooked, ground	14	....		
Butter or other fat	....	4	½ cup	
Bread crumbs, dry, fine	2	....	2½ quarts	

Heat water to boiling temperature. Stir in noodles. Cook 20 minutes or until tender. Do not overcook. Drain.

Combine white sauce and onions.

Arrange alternate layers of noodles, white sauce and ham, in greased baking pans.

Mix together butter and crumbs. Sprinkle over ham mixture.

Bake in moderate oven (350° F.) about 60 minutes.

NOTE.—Macaroni may be used in place of noodles.

HAM BANANA ROLLS WITH CHEESE SAUCE

Portion: 2 rolls.

| INGREDIENTS | 100 PORTIONS | | | ....PORTIONS |
	WEIGHTS		AMOUNTS (approx.)	
	Pounds	Ounces		
Ham, cooked, sliced thin	12	8	200 (1-ounce) slices	
Mustard, prepared	....	....	½ pint	
Bananas, medium	....	....	200	
Cheese Sauce (page 210)	....	....	2½ gallons	

Spread each slice of ham lightly with mustard. Peel bananas and wrap slice of ham around each.

Place in baking pans. Pour Cheese Sauce over bananas and ham.

Bake in slow oven (325° F.) about 30 minutes, or until bananas are tender when pierced with a fork. Serve immediately with any cheese sauce remaining in pan.

Variation

Banana Rolls with Chopped Ham

Peel bananas. Place in greased baking pans. Brush with melted butter. Spread lightly with prepared mustard.

Cover bananas with chopped left-over ham, allowing ¾ to 1 ounce for each portion. Pour Cheese Sauce over bananas. Bake in moderate oven (350° F.) 20 minutes.

Sprinkle with buttered crumbs or paprika.

HAM CROQUETTES

Portion: 2 croquettes.

INGREDIENTS	100 PORTIONS			.... PORTIONS
	WEIGHTS		AMOUNTS (approx.)	
	Pounds	*Ounces*		
Ham, cooked, finely chopped...	25	....		
Salt	....	2	¼ cup	
Pepper	....	½	1¾ tablespoons	
Onions, finely chopped	5	....	3¾ quarts	
Fat	2	....	1 quart	
Flour	2	....	½ gallon	
Ham Stock (page 254) hot	....	....	1¼ gallons	
Eggs, whole	3	....	30 (1½ quarts)	
Bread crumbs, dry	5	....	6¼ quarts	
Flour, for dredging	....	....		
Eggs, slightly beaten	1	....	10 (1 pint)	
Milk, liquid	....	....	3½ cups	
Bread crumbs, dry	....	....		

Mix together ham, salt and pepper.

Fry onions in fat until clear. Stir in flour. Mix well.

Add ham stock. Heat to boiling temperature, stirring constantly. Remove from heat.

Stir in 5 pounds bread crumbs, ham and 1½ quarts eggs. Mix well.

Chill in refrigerator.

Shape into 3 to 3½-ounce croquettes. Roll in flour.

Mix together eggs and milk. Dip croquettes into mixture. Roll in crumbs.

Fry in hot deep fat at 375°F. 3 to 4 minutes, or until evenly browned.

BAKED CANADIAN BACON

Portion: 4 to 5 ounces.

INGREDIENTS	100 PORTIONS			.... PORTIONS
	WEIGHTS		AMOUNTS (approx.)	
	Pounds	*Ounces*		
Canadian bacon	30	....	4 to 5 pieces	
Water	....	....	¾ gallon	

Score surface of bacon with knife. Place in roasting pans. Add water.

Bake in moderate oven (350° F.) until tender, allowing 15 to 20 minutes per pound.

NOTE.—Canadian bacon may be covered with a mixture of 1¼ pounds (3¾ cups) brown sugar and 1 quart orange or pineapple juice before baking.

GRIDDLE-BROILED BACON

Portion: Approx. 2 ounces.

INGREDIENTS	100 PORTIONS			............PORTIONS
	WEIGHTS		AMOUNTS (approx.)	
	Pounds	*Ounces*		
Bacon	25	....		

Remove rind from slabs of bacon, cutting away as little fat as possible. Slice bacon about 8 slices to 1 inch.

Broil slowly on heated griddle. Turn until crisp, but not brittle. Keep temperature below the smoking point of fat.

Variation

Oven-Broiled Bacon

Place slices, slightly overlapping, in shallow baking pans. Place only enough slices to fill length of pan.

Cook in moderate oven (350° F.) without turning until bacon is desired degree of doneness.

Lift bacon from fat and drain on absorbent paper. Serve immediately.

NOTE.—1. Avoid overcooking bacon as the crisper the bacon is cooked, the saltier it tastes and the more readily it breaks.

2. Serve with eggs, omelet, pancakes, or potatoes.

GRIDDLE-BROILED PORK SAUSAGE LINKS

Portion: 2 to 3 ounces.

INGREDIENTS	100 PORTIONS			............PORTIONS
	WEIGHTS		AMOUNTS (approx.)	
	Pounds	*Ounces*		
Pork sausage links...................	35	....		

Broil sausage slowly on heated griddle about 10 to 12 minutes or until browned and well done. Turn sausages to insure even cooking.

NOTE.—1. Keep temperature below smoking point of fat.

2. Serve sausage links with gravy, Barbecue Sauce (page 207), or Tomato Sauce (page 218), if desired.

Variation

Baked Pork Sausage Links

Place sausage links in baking pans and pour in just enough water to cover bottom of pan.

Cover pan tightly and bake in slow oven (325° F.) 15 to 20 minutes.

Remove cover and bake until brown. Turn sausages to insure even browning.

PORK SAUSAGE LINKS (PIGS) IN BLANKETS

Portion: 2 rolls.

INGREDIENTS	100 PORTIONS			............PORTIONS
	WEIGHTS		AMOUNTS (approx.)	
	Pounds	*Ounces*		
Biscuit Dough (page 361).......	8	....		
Pork sausage links..................	35	....		
Eggs, beaten	....	8	5 (1 cup)	
Milk, liquid	....	....	1⅔ cups	

Prepare Biscuit Dough using ½ as much fat as usual. Roll dough on floured surface to ¼ inch thickness. Cut into pieces, each to cover 2 sausage links.

Broil sausage on heated griddle 4 to 5 minutes or until slightly browned.

Roll 2 sausages in pieces of dough (blanket).

Moisten edges and seal.

Mix together eggs and milk. Brush each roll with milk mixture.

Bake in hot oven (400°F.) about 20 minutes or until golden brown.

NOTE.—Serve with Brown Gravy (page 212) or Tomato Sauce (page 218).

PORK SAUSAGE LINKS AND SAUERKRAUT PIE

Portion: Approx. 6 ounces.

INGREDIENTS	100 PORTIONS			............PORTIONS
	WEIGHTS		AMOUNTS (approx.)	
	Pounds	*Ounces*		
Pork sausage links..................	25	....		
Sauerkraut	50	....	8 No. 10 cans (6½ gallons).	
Flour	....	....		
Water, hot	....	....	½ gallon	
Biscuit Dough (page 361).......	....	....		

Broil sausage on heated griddle 10 to 12 minutes or until browned, turning to insure even browning.

Heat sauerkraut to boiling temperature.

Spread half of sauerkraut in bottom of baking pans. Sprinkle lightly with flour. Add another layer of sauerkraut and sprinkle with flour.

Place hot sausage links on top of sauerkraut. Add hot water.

Cover pans with biscuit dough rolled ¼ inch thick.

Bake in hot oven (400° F.) 30 minutes or until browned.

NOTE.—Serve with sweet potatoes or noodles.

GRIDDLE-BROILED PORK SAUSAGE PATTIES

Portion: 2 patties.

INGREDIENTS	100 PORTIONS		............PORTIONS
	WEIGHTS	AMOUNTS (approx.)	
	Pounds / *Ounces*		
Pork sausage, fresh....................	35 /	....	....

Shape sausage meat into 3 to 3½-ounce patties.

Broil slowly on heated griddle about 15 minutes or until patties are browned and cooked well done in the center.

Turn to insure even cooking. Serve immediately.

NOTE.—1. Keep temperature below smoking point of fat.

2. Serve sausage patties with or without gravy.

3. 38 pounds (18 34-ounce cans) pork sausage meat, canned, may be used in place of 35 pounds fresh sausage meat. Cut meat in half lengthwise, then slice.

Variation

Baked Pork Sausage Patties

Shape sausage meat into patties, making about 5 to 1 pound. Arrange in baking pans.

Bake at constant temperature in slow oven (325° F. to 350° F.) 25 to 30 minutes or until well done.

Serve with Cream Gravy (page 212) if desired.

ROAST VEAL

Portion: Approx. 5 ounces.

INGREDIENTS	100 PORTIONS		............PORTIONS
	WEIGHTS	AMOUNTS (approx.)	
	Pounds / *Ounces*		
Veal, bone-in .... OR	60 /	....	....
Veal, boneless	42 /	....	....
Salt	.... / 8	1 cup	....
Pepper	.... / 1	3½ tablespoons	....

Cut veal into 6-pound pieces.

Rub with salt and pepper.

Place fat side up in roasting pans. Fill pans without stacking or crowding.

Roast uncovered, without adding water, at constant temperature in slow oven (325° F.) approximately 4 hours (about 40 to 45 minutes per pound).

Remove roasts from pans just before serving. Carve across the grain in thin slices.

NOTE.—1. Chopped onions and bay leaves may be added before roasting the meat. These should be strained out before making Brown Gravy (page 212).

2. Roast veal may be served with Bread Dressing (page 199).

POT ROAST OF VEAL (BRAISED VEAL)

Portion: Approx. 5 ounces.

INGREDIENTS	100 PORTIONS			............PORTIONS
	WEIGHTS		AMOUNTS (approx.)	
	Pounds	*Ounces*		
Veal, bone-in .... OR	60	....		
Veal, boneless	42	....		
Fat	1	....	1 pint	
Salt	....	6	¾ cup	
Pepper	....	½	1¾ tablespoons	
Meat Stock (page 251) or water, hot.	....	....	1 quart	
Onions, chopped (optional).....	5	....	3¾ quarts	

Cut veal into 6-pound pieces.

Cook in fat until browned on all sides.

Add salt, pepper, small amount of stock or water and onions.

Let simmer in closely covered steam-jacketed kettle or cook in slow oven (300° F.) 3 hours or until tender, depending on size of pieces. Turn several times during cooking. Add small amounts of liquid as needed.

Remove meat from pans and carve across the grain in thin slices.

NOTE.—1. Serve with Brown Gravy (page 212).

2. Onions may be cooked in fat with meat until browned, if desired.

Variations

Veal A La Mode

Add 3 pounds (¾ gallon) diced carrots, 2 pounds (1½ quarts) sliced onions, and 1 No. 10 can (3¼ quarts) tomatoes to braised veal 30 to 45 minutes before meat has finished cooking.

Serve vegetables in the gravy as a sauce over the sliced meat.

Braised Veal with Vegetables

Use 45 pounds bone-in or 31 pounds boneless veal. Add 8 pounds each of sliced carrots, onions, celery and turnips to the braised veal, allowing sufficient time for each to cook, before the meat has finished cooking.

181 ★

VEAL STEW

Portion: Approx. 8 ounces (1 cup).

INGREDIENTS	100 PORTIONS			............PORTIONS
	WEIGHTS		AMOUNTS (approx.)	
	Pounds	Ounces		
Veal, bone-in	40	....	....	
OR				
Veal, boneless	28	....	....	
Flour	1	8	1½ quarts	
Salt	....	6	¾ cup	
Pepper	....	½	1¾ tablespoons	
Fat	1	8	1½ pints	
Meat Stock (page 251) or water, hot.	....	....	....	
Onions, white, quartered....	10	....	2½ gallons	
Celery, large dice....................	10	....	2½ gallons	
Tomatoes	12	12	2 No. 10 cans (6½ quarts).	
Beans, green	18	15	3 No. 10 cans (2½ gallons).	
Flour	1	....	1 quart	
Water	....	....	1½ pints	

Cut meat into 1 to 2-inch cubes.

Mix together 1½ pounds flour, salt and pepper. Roll meat in mixture. Cook in fat until browned, stirring constantly.

Cover with stock or water. Cover kettle tightly. Let simmer about 2 hours or until tender.

Add onions and celery 1 hour before end of cooking period. Add tomatoes and green beans 15 minutes before end of cooking period.

Drain stock from meat and vegetables. Mix together flour and water. Stir into stock.

Heat to boiling temperature, stirring constantly.

Pour gravy back over meat and vegetables. Reheat.

Variations

Veal or Pork Pie with Mashed Potato Crust

Use pork in place of veal. Prepare as Veal Stew.

Place in baking pans. Cover with mashed potatoes. Bake in hot oven (425°F.) 15 to 20 minutes or until browned.

Veal or Pork Pie with Biscuit Crust

Use pork in place of veal. Prepare as for Veal Stew. Place in baking pans. Cover with Biscuits (page 361) or with biscuit crust. Bake in hot oven (425° F.) 15 to 20 minutes or until mixture bubbles or biscuits are brown.

Veal or Pork Pie with Pie Crust

Use pork in place of veal. Prepare as Veal Stew.

Place in baking pans. Cover with Pie Crust (page 399). Bake in hot oven (425° F.) 5 to 10 minutes or until browned.

Veal Stew with Rice

Prepare as Veal Stew. Serve with or on cooked rice.

Veal Stew with Dumplings or Noodles

Prepare as Veal Stew. Add Dumplings (page 370) or Noodles (page 45) to stew, allowing sufficient time for them to cook before meat is done.

Spiced Veal Stew

Use 50 pounds bone-in or 35 pounds boneless veal. Omit all vegetables.

Cut meat into 1 to 2-inch cubes. Cook until browned.

Add ½ gallon vinegar, 2 pounds (1½ quarts) brown sugar, 1 ounce (4½ tablespoons) cinnamon, 16 bay leaves, 1 pound (1 quart) sliced onions and liquid to cover meat.

Cover tightly and let simmer 2½ to 3 hours or until meat is tender.

Drain liquid from meat. Serve as gravy, if desired.

VEAL FRICASSEE

Portion: Approx. 8 ounces.

INGREDIENTS	100 PORTIONS		............PORTIONS
	WEIGHTS	AMOUNTS (approx.)	
	Pounds / Ounces		
Veal, bone-in	50 /		
OR			
Veal, boneless	35 /		
Bacon fat or other fat............	3 /	1½ quarts	
Flour	2 / 8	2½ quarts	
Meat Stock (page 251)............	.... /	3 gallons	
Salt	.... / 6	¾ cup	
Pepper	.... / ½	1¾ tablespoons	

Cut meat into 1½ to 2-inch pieces. Add ½ the fat.

Cook in pan on top of stove, or in hot oven (400°F.) about 20 minutes, or until meat is well browned.

Blend together remaining fat and flour to a smooth paste.

Heat stock to boiling temperature.

Stir paste into stock. Cook until thickened, stirring constantly. Add salt and pepper.

Pour mixture over veal. Cover pan tightly.

Bake in slow oven (300°F.) 1½ to 2 hours or until tender.

NOTE.— Serve Veal Fricassee on or with cooked rice (page 44) or cooked noodles (page 45).

Variation

Pork Fricassee

Pork may be used in place of Veal for Fricassee.

Cook pork until browned in its own fat, and add just enough fat to combine with the flour.

BREADED VEAL CUTLETS

Portion: 2 (4-ounce) cutlets.

INGREDIENTS	100 PORTIONS			..........PORTIONS
	WEIGHTS		AMOUNTS (approx.)	
	Pounds	Ounces		
Veal leg, boneless.....................	45	....	....	....
Salt	....	2	¼ cup	....
Pepper	....	¼	¾ tablespoon	....
Milk, liquid	....	....	1 quart	....
Eggs, beaten	1	....	10 (1 pint)..........	....
Flour	2	....	½ gallon	....
Bread crumbs, dry, fine...........	1	8	½ gallon	....

Cut meat into 4-ounce slices ½ inch thick. Sprinkle with salt and pepper.

Combine milk and eggs.

Dredge cutlets in flour. Dip in egg mixture. Cover with bread crumbs.

Fry in hot deep fat at 350° F. 5 to 8 minutes or until cutlets are evenly browned.

Place in baking pan. Cover. Bake in slow oven (325°F.) 1 hour or until well done.

NOTE.—1. For unbreaded cutlet omit egg-wash and crumbing. Pan-fry cutlets until browned. Bake, covered, in a slow oven (325° F.) about 1 hour or until tender and well done.

2. Evaporated milk may be used for dipping instead of milk and egg mixture.

VEAL BIRDS

Portion: 2 Veal Birds.

INGREDIENTS	100 PORTIONS			..........PORTIONS
	WEIGHTS		AMOUNTS (approx.)	
	Pounds	Ounces		
Veal, bone-in	50	....	....	....
OR				
Veal, boneless	35	....	....	....
Salt	....	6	¾ cup	....
Pepper	....	¼	¾ tablespoon	....
Bread Dressing (page 199), moist.	20	....	5 gallons	....
Flour	2	....	½ gallon	....
Fat	4	....	½ gallon	....
Brown Gravy (page 212)........	....	....	1½ gallons	....

Cut veal into 3-ounce rectangular pieces. Sprinkle with salt and pepper.

Spread stuffing on each piece. Roll and fasten with toothpicks. Dip in flour.

Fry in shallow hot fat until browned on all sides.

Place in roasting pans. Add brown gravy.

Cover pans tightly. Bake in slow oven (300° F.) 1 to 1½ hours or until tender and well done.

NOTE.—1½ gallons Tomato Sauce (page 218) may be used in place of gravy.

Variation

Beef or Pork Birds

Beef or pork may be used in place of veal.

VEAL AND PORK LOAF

Portion: Approx. 5 ounces.

INGREDIENTS	100 PORTIONS		............PORTIONS
	WEIGHTS	AMOUNTS (approx.)	
	Pounds	Ounces		
Veal bone-in	35	....	....	....
OR				
Veal, boneless	25	....	....	....
Pork cuts, bone-in	9	....	....	....
OR				
Pork, boneless	6	....	....	....
Bread crumbs, soft................	4	....	2 gallons	....
Onions, finely chopped...........	1	....	1½ pints	....
Celery, finely chopped.........	1	....	1 quart	....
Peppers, green, finely chopped	1	8	1½ quarts	....
Milk, liquid	....	....	3½ quarts	....
Salt	....	8	1 cup	....
Pepper	....	½	1¾ tablespoons	....
Fat, melted	....	....	....	....

Cut veal and pork into small cubes. Grind.

Combine ground veal, pork, bread crumbs, onions, celery, green peppers, milk, salt and pepper. Mix thoroughly.

Shape into loaves about 12 x 4 x 3 inches. Place in greased roasting pans. Brush top of loaves with fat.

Roast, uncovered without adding water, at constant temperature in slow oven (325°F.) 2 hours or until well done. Baste loaves at 20 minute intervals.

NOTE.—1. Well done veal or pork does not retain any pink color. Meat loaf is a roast. Serve hot or cold.

2. If served hot, serve with gravy or Tomato Sauce (page 218).

BRAISED VEAL PATTIES

Portion: 2 patties.

INGREDIENTS	100 PORTIONS			........PORTIONS
	WEIGHTS		AMOUNTS (approx.)	
	Pounds	*Ounces*		
Veal, bone-in	45	....	....	....
OR				
Veal, boneless	31	....	....	....
Bread crumbs, soft..............	7	....	3½ gallons	....
Onions, minced	5	....	3¾ quarts	....
Salt	....	5	10 tablespoons	....
Pepper	....	¼	¾ tablespoon	....
Worcestershire sauce	....	4	½ cup	....
Meat Stock (page 251) or water.	....	....	¾ gallon	....
Fat	2	....	1 quart	....
Water	....	....	....	....

Cut meat into 1 to 2-inch pieces. Grind.

Mix together veal, bread crumbs, onions, salt, pepper, Worcestershire sauce, and stock or water. Mix thoroughly.

Shape into 3 to 3½-ounce patties, 1 inch thick. Fry in hot fat until browned on both sides.

Place in roasting pans. Add small amount of water to cover bottom of pan. Cover pan tightly.

Bake in slow oven (325°F.) approximately 60 minutes or until tender.

NOTE.—1. Barbecue Sauce (page 207) may be used for part of or all of the liquid in Braised Veal Patties.

2. Serve with Barbecue Sauce (page 207) or Tomato Sauce (page 218).

Variation

Braised Pork Patties

Ground pork may be used in place of ½ the ground veal in Veal Patties. Bake until well done.

BRAISED LIVER

Portion: Approx. 5 ounces.

INGREDIENTS	100 PORTIONS			............PORTIONS
	WEIGHTS		AMOUNTS (approx.)	
	Pounds	*Ounces*		
Liver, beef, pork, lamb, or veal.	35	....	....	....
Salt	....	4	½ cup	....
Pepper	....	¼	¾ tablespoon	....
Flour	3	....	¾ gallon	....
Fat	4	....	½ gallon	....
Meat Stock (page 251) or water, hot.	....	....	....	....

Slice liver ⅜ to ½ inch thick. Cut into 5-ounce pieces. Sprinkle with salt and pepper. Dip in flour.

Cook in fat until brown. Reduce temperature.

Add enough stock or water to cover bottom of pans. Cover tightly.

Cook slowly about 20 minutes or until tender.

NOTE.—1. Serve with gravy made from drippings, if desired.

2. Liver may be stacked in roasting pans, with enough stock or water to cover bottom of pan. Bake in slow oven (300° F.) 15 to 20 minutes or until tender.

FRIED LIVER

Portion: Approx. 5 ounces.

INGREDIENTS	100 PORTIONS			............PORTIONS
	WEIGHTS		AMOUNTS (approx.)	
	Pounds	*Ounces*		
Liver, beef, pork, lamb or veal.	35	....	....	....
Salt	....	5	10 tablespoons	....
Pepper	....	¼	¾ tablespoon	....
Flour	2	....	½ gallon	....
Fat	....	....	....	....

Slice liver ⅜ to ½ inch thick. Cut into 5-ounce pieces.

Sprinkle with salt and pepper. Roll in flour.

Fry in fat to desired degree of doneness. Turn to insure even cooking.

NOTE.—1. Cook pork liver until well done, but do not overcook. Too long cooking or cooking at too high temperature hardens liver and impairs the flavor.

2. Liver may be served with grilled bacon, also with fried or French Fried Onions (page 307).

GRIDDLE BROILED LIVER

Portion: Approx. 5 ounces.

| INGREDIENTS | 100 PORTIONS | | | ....PORTIONS |
	WEIGHTS		AMOUNTS (approx.)	
	Pounds	*Ounces*		
Liver, beef, pork, lamb or veal.	35	....		
Fat, melted	1	....	1 pint	
Salt	....	5	10 tablespoons	
Pepper	....	¼	¾ tablespoon	

Slice liver ⅜ to ½ inch thick. Cut into 5-ounce pieces. Dip in fat.

Broil on heated griddle at moderate temperature, 6 to 10 minutes, or until color has changed. Turn to brown evenly on both sides.

Sprinkle with salt and pepper. Serve immediately.

LIVER AND PORK LOAF

Portion: Approx. 6 ounces.

| INGREDIENTS | 100 PORTIONS | | | ....PORTIONS |
	WEIGHTS		AMOUNTS (approx.)	
	Pounds	*Ounces*		
Water	....	....	To cover	
Liver, pork	25	....		
Bread crumbs, dry	5	....	6¼ quarts	
Pork, ground	5	....		
Salt	....	6	¾ cup	
Pepper	....	¼	¾ tablespoon	
Catsup	....	....	1 quart	
Eggs, slightly beaten	3	....	30 (1½ quarts)	
Lemon juice	....	....	1 pint	
Onions, minced	2	....	1½ quarts	

Heat water to boiling temperature. Add liver and let simmer 10 minutes. Drain and grind. Combine all ingredients. Mix thoroughly. Pack lightly into greased loaf pans.

Bake in slow oven (325° F.) about 2 hours or until well done.

Remove from pans. Slice and serve hot.

NOTE.—1. Serve with gravy or Tomato Sauce (page 218), if desired.

2. Mixture may be shaped into 4-ounce patties. Wrap each in bacon slice and oven-broil or braise.

SIMMERED FRANKFURTERS

Portion: 2 to 3 frankfurters.

| INGREDIENTS | 100 PORTIONS | | | ....PORTIONS |
	WEIGHTS		AMOUNTS (approx.)	
	Pounds	*Ounces*		
Frankfurters	35	....	8 to 1 pound..............	
Water	....	....		

Cover frankfurters with water. Heat to boiling temperature.

Let simmer approximately 10 minutes.

Drain and serve hot.

NOTE.—1. Frankfurters may be pan-fried, in a small amount of fat, until browned.

2. Frankfurters may be broiled on heated griddle until evenly browned.

Variations

Frankfurters with Sauerkraut

Use 30 pounds sauerkraut. Heat together frankfurters and sauerkraut thoroughly.

Frankfurters with Baked Beans

Place 25 pounds frankfurters on top of Baked Beans (page 286) about 20 minutes before beans are done. Bake in slow oven (325° F.).

NOTE.—Sausage, Vienna style may be used in place of frankfurters.

FRANKFURTERS IN BLANKETS

Portion: 2 rolls.

| INGREDIENTS | 100 PORTIONS | | | ....PORTIONS |
	WEIGHTS		AMOUNTS (approx.)	
	Pounds	*Ounces*		
Biscuit Dough (page 361)......	10	....		
Frankfurters	25	....	8 to 1 pound.............	
Eggs, slightly beaten............	....	8	5 (1 cup).............	
Milk, liquid	....	....	1⅔ cups	

Prepare Biscuit Dough, using ½ as much fat as usual. Roll dough on floured surface to ¼ inch thickness. Cut into pieces, each to cover 1 frankfurter.

Broil frankfurters on heated griddle until slightly browned.

Roll 1 frankfurter in each piece of dough (blanket). Moisten edges of dough and seal together.

Combine eggs and milk. Brush each roll with egg mixture. Place in greased baking pans.

Bake in hot oven (400° F.) 20 minutes or until golden brown.

NOTE.—Serve hot with Tomato Sauce (page 218), if desired.

Variation

Luncheon Meat, Canned Pork Sausage Links or Vienna Sausage in Blankets

Luncheon meat, canned pork sausage links or Vienna sausage may be used in place of frankfurters in blankets.

Cut luncheon meat in finger length pieces ¾ x ¾ x 3½ inches.

189★

SPANISH FRANKFURTERS

Portion: 2 to 3 frankfurters with sauce.

INGREDIENTS	100 PORTIONS			............PORTIONS
	WEIGHTS		AMOUNTS (approx.)	
	Pounds	Ounces		
Onions, chopped	1	6	1 quart	
Fat	....	8	1 cup	
Vinegar	....	....	1¼ cups	
Sugar, brown	....	8	1½ cups	
Lemon juice	....	....	2½ cups (10 lemons)	
Catsup	....	....	2½ quarts	
Worcestershire sauce	....	....	1 pint	
Mustard, prepared	....	3	¾ cup	
Celery, chopped	1	4	1¼ quarts	
Water	....	....	2½ quarts	
Frankfurters	35	....	8 to 1 pound	

Cook onions in fat until clear. Add vinegar, sugar, lemon juice, catsup, Worcestershire sauce, mustard, celery and water.

Let simmer 30 minutes.

Add frankfurters to sauce. Cover pan tightly. Let simmer about 30 minutes.

BAKED LUNCHEON MEAT

Portion: 5 to 6 ounces.

INGREDIENTS	100 PORTIONS			............PORTIONS
	WEIGHTS		AMOUNTS (approx.)	
	Pounds	Ounces		
Pork luncheon meat	35	....		
Sugar, brown	1	4	3¾ cups	
Orange juice	....	....	1 quart	
Water	....	....	¾ gallon	

Score surface of luncheon meat with knife. Place meat in roasting pans.

Mix together sugar and orange juice. Cover loaves with mixture. Add water.

Bake in moderate oven (350° F.) 45 to 60 minutes.

NOTE.—Luncheon meat may be baked with Barbecue Sauce (page 207) or Tomato Sauce (page 218).

FRIED LUNCHEON MEAT

Portion: 5 to 6 ounces.

INGREDIENTS	100 PORTIONS			............PORTIONS
	WEIGHTS		AMOUNTS (approx.)	
	Pounds	*Ounces*		
Luncheon meat	35	....	....	....
Fat	2	....	1 quart	....

Cut meat into ¼-inch thick slices. Pan-fry in fat until browned on both sides.

Variation

Mustard Grilled Luncheon Meat

Add 1 pound (1 quart) prepared mustard to fat. Pan-fry meat slices in fat and mustard mixture until browned on both sides.

NOTE.—1. Any cold meat, sliced, may be used.

2. Use in sandwiches or as hot meat item in meal.

LUNCHEON MEAT WITH MUSTARD GLAZE

(Using luncheon meat, canned)

Portion: 5 to 6 ounces.

INGREDIENTS	100 PORTIONS			............PORTIONS
	WEIGHTS		AMOUNTS (approx.)	
	Pounds	*Ounces*		
Luncheon meat, canned..........	36	---	6 6-pound cans..........	
Sugar..........	---	4	½ cup..........	
Mustard, dry..........	---	1	4½ tablespoons..........	
Cinnamon..........	---	¼	1½ tablespoons..........	
Corn sirup..........	1	---	1½ cups..........	
Vinegar..........	---	---	1 pint..........	

Score surface of luncheon meat with knife. Place in roasting pans.

Mix together sugar, mustard, cinnamon, corn sirup, and vinegar. Pour mixture over meat.

Bake in moderate oven (350° F.) 1 hour. Baste meat with sirup during baking at least twice.

RICE LUNCHEON MEAT BALLS

(Using luncheon meat, canned)

Portion: 2 (2-ounce) meat balls.

INGREDIENTS	100 PORTIONS			............Portions
	WEIGHTS		AMOUNTS (approx.)	
	Pounds	Ounces		
Luncheon meat, canned............	24	---	4 6-pound cans............	
Rice, uncooked................	5	---	2½ quarts................	
Eggs, powdered...............	1	---	1 quart...............	
Pepper...............	---	¼	1 tablespoon...............	
Tomato juice...............	9	---	3 No. 10 cans (2¼ gallons).	

Break up luncheon meat into small pieces. Add rice, eggs, and pepper. Blend together thoroughly.

Form into 2-ounce meat balls. Place as close together as possible in greased roasting pans.

Add tomato juice to half cover meat balls with juice.

Bake in moderate oven (350° F.) 1 hour.

Pour remaining tomato juice over meat balls. Continue baking 30 minutes.

ESCALLOPED LUNCHEON MEAT AND CORN

(Using luncheon meat, canned)

Portion: Approx. 4 ounces.

INGREDIENTS	100 PORTIONS			............Portions
	WEIGHTS		AMOUNTS (approx.)	
	Pounds	Ounces		
Corn, whole kernel............	13	4	2 No. 10 cans (6½ quarts).	
Milk, liquid............	---	---	2½ gallons............	
Butter or other fat, melted....	2	---	1 quart............	
Flour............	1	12	1¾ quarts............	
Luncheon meat, canned............	18	---	3 6-pound cans............	
Salt............	---	2	¼ cup............	
Pepper............	---	½	1 tablespoon............	
Bread crumbs, fine............	1	8	½ gallon............	
Butter, melted............	1	8	1½ pints............	

Drain corn. Reserve liquid. Heat milk to boiling temperature.

Blend fat and flour to a smooth paste. Stir into milk. Cook 10 minutes or until thickened.

Cut luncheon meat into ½- to ¾-inch cubes. Add meat and corn to sauce. Stir in salt and pepper. Mix thoroughly.

Place in well greased baking pans.

Mix together crumbs and butter. Sprinkle over surface of creamed mixture.

Bake in moderate oven (350° F.) 25 minutes or until crumbs are browned.

NOTE.—1. Use liquid from corn as part of milk to make 2½ gallons.

2. 8 No. 2½ cans (6½ quarts) cream style corn may be used in place of 2 No. 10 cans whole kernel corn.

3. 2 pounds 8 ounces (8¾ cups) milk, powdered, whole, reconstituted with 2½ gallons water may be used in place of 2½ gallons milk.

VIENNA SAUSAGE AND SWEETPOTATOES

(Using sausage, Vienna style, canned)

Portion: Approx. 5 ounces.

INGREDIENTS	100 PORTIONS		............PORTIONS
	WEIGHTS	AMOUNTS (approx.)	
	Pounds	Ounces		
Potatoes, sweet, dehydrated...	5	10	2 gallons............	
Water, for potatoes............	---	---	2½ gallons............	
Sugar...........................	3	12	1¾ quarts............	
Sausage, Vienna style, canned.	22	8	15 24-ounce cans........	
Butter.........................	1		1 pint............	

Soak potatoes in water 45 minutes. Heat slowly, to boiling temperature. Let simmer 30 to 45 minutes until tender.

Drain potatoes, being careful to leave slices whole. Reserve liquid.

Dissolve sugar in liquid drained from potatoes.

Heat to boiling temperature. Let simmer 5 minutes.

Place sausage in baking pans. Cover with sweetpotatoes. Pour sirup over surface. Dot with butter.

Bake in moderate oven (350° F.) 20 minutes.

Poultry

Poultry is purchased either frozen or fresh-killed and chilled, on the basis of dressed weight. It is considered dressed when it has been killed, bled and plucked.

Dressed poultry is not ready to cook until it has been drawn, meaning that the entrails, head and feet have been removed, and then properly prepared for cooking.

Frozen poultry should be stored at 0° F. to 15° F. and never thawed until ready to be used.

Fresh killed poultry should be stored at 31° F. to 33° F. until ready to use.

When purchasing fowl allow 12 ounces per portion dressed weight for turkey and 16 ounces for chicken and duck.

The weight of cooked edible meat of turkey approximates ⅓ of the dressed weight or 5 to 6 ounces per pound. For chicken and duck, the cooked edible meat is equivalent to about ¼ of the dressed weight or 4 ounces per pound.

Preparation for Cooking

Singe and wash the bird thoroughly.

Chop off head.

Pull tendons if necessary and remove shanks at hock joints.

Cut neck skin down center back to the shoulder.

Free neck skin, gullet, windpipe and crop from neck. Pull gullet, windpipe and crop as far out as possible from the body. Be careful not to tear crop. Cut and remove.

Remove neck from body at the shoulder. Cut through the neck muscle, then twist to separate the vertebrae.

Drawing

Make an incision with a sharp pointed knife around the vent.

Cut abdomen through the internal body fat in a straight line from end of breast bone to incision made for vent. Avoid cutting intestinal tract.

Insert finger. Loosen intestines all around the body cavity. Lift lungs from ribs. Remove gizzard and all the entrails intact.

Cut out oil sac on back just above tail; run knife under the valve toward the tail.

Wash carcass, inside and out, quickly but thoroughly. Do not soak.

Separate giblets, gizzard, heart, and liver, from entrails. Carefully cut out bile sac from liver and discard it.

Remove sac attached to heart and cut away blood vessels. Wash heart thoroughly.

Cut into one side of gizzard just to inner sac. Pull walls away from inner sac. Discard sac. Wash gizzard.

NOTE.—1. Giblets should always be used because of their high nutritive value and good flavor. Cook them in a small amount of water until tender. Chop or grind them and add to gravy.

2. Use the bones from uncooked or cooked poultry and the feet, scalded and skinned, for making stock.

Trussing

Cut skin at abdomen above the tail, parallel to the cut made for drawing.

Put drumstick ends through the slits, underneath the strip of skin, to hold leg to body during cooking.

Draw neck skin over front opening onto back.

Fold wings into place.

Preparation of Broilers

Singe and wash thoroughly.

Lay bird on side. Cut off tail. Cut at an angle so that oil sac and vent are included with tail.

Cut from neck down on both sides of backbone.

Remove backbone: grasp head and rip out back, neck and backbone in one piece. Chop off head. Reserve neck and backbone for soup.

Open bird and remove entrails. Lift out lungs.

Flatten bird, breaking or chopping wishbone.

Snap joints to keep bird flattened during cooking.

Separate giblets from entrails. Carefully cut out bile sac from the liver and discard it.

Wash bird quickly but thoroughly. Do not soak.

Disjointing Fryers and Fowls

Cut bird into 12 pieces as follows:

Remove wings at joint next to the body.

Disjoint legs at the back. Cut each leg into 2 portions at knee.

Make an incision through the thin muscle tissue at rear of breast or keel bone. Pass knife forward and upward to the juncture of the last rib and the back. Repeat on opposite side.

Bend back and break at that point.

Remove intestines, giblets and lungs.

Separate breast from ribs and cut into 3 pieces.

TIME-TABLE FOR COOKING POULTRY

| KIND | POUNDS PER BIRD (approx.) | ROASTING | | BRAISING |
		OVEN TEMPERATURE	MINUTES PER POUND (approx.)	MINUTES PER POUND (approx.)
Chicken	3½ to 4	350° F.	35 to 45	40
	4 to 4½	350° F.	35 to 45	40
	4½ to 5	350° F.	35 to 45	....
	5 and over	325° F.	30 to 35	....
Turkey	12 to 14	325° F.	18 to 20	....
	14 to 16	325° F.	With longer time for smaller sizes	18
	16 to 18	325° F.		15
	18 and over	325° F.		....
Duck	4½ to 5½	350° F.	40 to 45	

BRAISED POULTRY

Portion: Approx. ¾ to 1 pound.

| INGREDIENTS | 100 PORTIONS | | | ....PORTIONS |
| | WEIGHTS | | AMOUNTS (approx.) | |
	Pounds	Ounces		
Chicken, frying, drawn	100	....	20	
Flour	4	....	1 gallon	
Salt	....	6	¾ cup	
Pepper	....	1	3½ tablespoons	
Chicken fat or other fat	2	....	1 quart	
Chicken Stock (page 252)	....	....	1 gallon	

Prepare chicken for cooking. Disjoint.

Combine flour, salt and pepper. Dredge chicken in flour.

Cook in fat until well browned. Place in roasting pans. Add enough stock to cover bottom of pan. Cover.

Braise in moderate oven (350°F.) 2½ to 3½ hours or until tender.

Turn and baste several times during braising period.

NOTE.—1. 1 gallon water may be used in place of 1 gallon stock.

2. Roasting chickens may be used in place of frying chickens.

3. Serve with gravy made from liquid drained from braised poultry.

4. Turkey, disjointed and cut into convenient pieces for serving, may be braised in place of chicken.

5. Braising time will vary with type of poultry and size of pieces used.

6. Chicken may be braised in steam-jacketed kettle.

FRIED CHICKEN

Portion: Approx. 1 pound.

INGREDIENTS	100 PORTIONS			............PORTIONS
	WEIGHTS		AMOUNTS (approx.)	
	Pounds	*Ounces*		
Chicken, frying, dressed	125	....	25	
OR				
Chicken, frying, full drawn	100	....	25	
Flour	4	....	1 gallon	
Salt	....	5	10 tablespoons	
Pepper	....	....	2 tablespoons	
Fat, melted	5	....	2½ quarts	
Chicken Stock (page 252)	....	....	To cover bottom of pan	

Prepare chicken for frying. Cut in half through length of the body, or into quarters, depending upon size of chicken.

Mix together flour, salt and pepper.

Dredge or roll chickens in flour mixture. Cover completely. Shake off excess flour.

Cook chicken in fat until browned on all sides.

Place 1 layer deep in roasting pans. Add enough stock to cover bottom of pan to prevent sticking. Cover.

Bake in moderate oven (350°F.) 1½ to 2½ hours or until tender.

NOTE.—1. Chickens may be browned in hot deep fat at 360°F. 5 to 8 minutes then finished off in oven as above.

2. Roasting chickens may be used if cut into quarters instead of halves.

3. Bread crumbs, dried, sifted may be used in place of ½ the flour for dredging.

4. Serve with or without Cream Gravy (page 212).

★196

FRIED CHICKEN, MARYLAND STYLE

Portion: Approx. 1 pound.

INGREDIENTS	100 PORTIONS			............PORTIONS
	WEIGHTS		AMOUNTS (approx.)	
	Pounds	*Ounces*		
Chicken, frying, dressed	125	....	25	
OR				
Chicken, frying, full drawn	100	....	25	
Flour	4	....	1 gallon	
Salt	....	6	¾ cup	
Pepper	....	1	3½ tablespoons	
Eggs, beaten	1	13	18 (1¾ pints)	
Milk, liquid	....	....	½ gallon	
Bread crumbs, fine	4	....	1 gallon	
Chicken fat or other fat, melted.	1	....	1 pint	

Prepare chicken for cooking. Cut into halves or quarters.

Combine flour, salt and pepper. Mix together eggs and milk.

Dredge chicken in flour mixture. Dip in milk. Roll in crumbs and coat thoroughly.

Place into greased roasting pans. Add fat and remaining water.

Bake in moderate oven (350°F.) 1 to 1½ hours or until tender.

Baste during cooking period.

ROAST CHICKEN OR TURKEY OR DUCK

Portion: Approx. ¾ pound chicken or duck.   Approx. 4 to 5 ounces turkey.

INGREDIENTS	100 PORTIONS			............PORTIONS
	WEIGHTS		AMOUNTS (approx.)	
	Pounds	Ounces		
Chicken, roasting, dressed...... OR	125	....	20	
Chicken, roasting, full drawn.	100	....	20	
Salt	....	5	10 tablespoons	
Pepper	....	....	2 teaspoons	
Bread Dressing (page 199)......	14	12	5 gallons	
Chicken fat or other fat, melted.	1	....	1 pint	

Prepare chicken for cooking. Rub cavity of chicken thoroughly with salt and pepper.

Stuff with dressing. Truss. Grease outside of bird with melted fat.

Place in roasting pan. Add enough water to cover bottom of pan.

Roast in slow oven (325°F.) 2½ to 3 hours or until meat is tender. Turn occasionally to brown evenly.

NOTE.—1. To test doneness, grasp drumstick. If joint moves easily or breaks, the ligaments in joint are tender and meat is done.

2. Brush chicken with additional fat, if needed, during roasting to prevent skin from drying.

3. Chickens or turkeys may be stuffed or unstuffed for roasting. For large quantity preparation, roast unstuffed. Bake dressing in greased roasting pan in moderate oven (350° F.) 1 hour. Serve hot with fowl and Chicken Gravy (page 212).

Roast Turkey

Use 85 pounds of turkeys, full drawn.

Prepare for roasting in same manner as chicken. Allow 1 gallon dressing for 16-pound turkey. See Time-Table (page 195) for length of roasting period.

Roast Duck

Use 100 pounds of ducks, full drawn.

Prepare ducks for roasting.

Stuff cavity with 1 apple, quartered, 1 or 2 onions, quartered, and 1 or 2 stalks of celery, or with bread dressing as for chicken.

Prick skin in several places before placing in oven so that fat will run out during roasting. Roast the duck, uncovered, breast side up. Do not turn or baste. Pour off fat during roasting period, if an excess should collect. See Time-Table (page 195) for length of roasting period.

BREAD DRESSING OR STUFFING

Yield: Approx. 25 pounds.   Portion: Approx. 4 ounces.

| INGREDIENTS | 100 PORTIONS | | | ....PORTIONS |
| | WEIGHTS | | AMOUNTS (approx.) | |
	Pounds	*Ounces*		
Bread, day-old, cubed............	20	....	10 gallons	
Thyme	....	....	1 tablespoon	
Sage	....	1	½ cup	
Salt	....	2	¼ cup	
Pepper	....	½	1¾ tablespoons	
Onions, chopped	1	....	1½ pints	
Celery and celery tops, chopped.	5	....	1¼ gallons	
Butter or other fat, melted......	1	8	1½ pints	

Combine bread cubes, thyme, sage, salt and pepper.

Fry onions and celery in fat until clear. Add to bread. Mix lightly but thoroughly.

Place in greased baking pan. Brush with remaining fat.

Bake in moderate oven (350°F.) 1 hour.

NOTE.—1. 4 pounds (1 gallon) dressing will stuff 1 (16 pound) turkey.

2. 1 pound (1 quart) dressing will stuff 1 (4 to 4½-pound) roasting chicken.

3. 8 ounces parsley, minced, may be added.

Variations

Cornbread Dressing

Use an equivalent amount of crumbled cornbread for the bread in Bread Dressing or Stuffing.

Nut Dressing

Use 1 pound any kind of nut, chopped or whole, in Bread Dressing or Stuffing.

Mushroom Dressing

Use 2 pounds mushrooms, chopped or whole, in Bread Dressing or Stuffing. If mushrooms are fresh, cook in fat with celery and onions.

Oyster Dressing

Cook ½ gallon oysters over low heat in oyster liquor until edges begin to curl. Drain. Add to Bread Dressing or Stuffing. Mix carefully.

Fruit Dressing

2 pounds cooked dried prunes or apricots, chopped, or 2 pounds raisins or apples, diced, may be added to Bread Dressing or Stuffing.

199 ★

CHICKEN FRICASSEE

Portion: Approx. ½ to ¾ pound.

INGREDIENTS	100 PORTIONS			............PORTIONS
	WEIGHTS		AMOUNTS (approx.)	
	Pounds	*Ounces*		
Chicken (fowl), dressed............	70	....	14 (5-pound)	
OR				
Chicken (fowl), full drawn.......	52	....		
Flour	3	....	¾ gallon	
Salt	....	6	¾ cup	
Pepper	....	1	3½ tablespoons	
Chicken fat or other fat..........	3	....	1½ quarts	
Water	....	....	To cover	
Flour (for gravy)............	2	....	½ gallon	
Water, cold (for gravy)............	....	....	1 quart	
Milk, liquid	....	....	½ gallon	
Salt (for gravy)............	....	2	¼ cup	

Prepare chickens for cooking. Cut into portions.

Combine flour, salt and pepper. Dredge chicken in flour mixture.

Fry in fat until browned on all sides. Place in kettle and cover with water. Cover kettle.

Let simmer about 3½ to 4 hours or until tender.

Combine flour and water. Blend to a smooth paste.

Drain stock from chicken. Combine milk and enough stock to make 4½ gallons.

Stir paste into stock. Cook, stirring constantly, until thickened. Let simmer 10 to 15 minutes.

Stir in salt. Pour over meat. Reheat.

NOTE.—Serve on cooked rice or mashed potatoes.

CHICKEN STEW

Portion: 6 to 8 ounces.

INGREDIENTS	100 PORTIONS			..........PORTIONS
	WEIGHTS		AMOUNTS (approx.)	
	Pounds	*Ounces*		
Chicken (fowl), dressed...........	65	....	13 (5-pound)	
OR				
Chicken (fowl), full drawn......	49	....		
Celery, coarsely chopped........	2	....	½ gallon	
Onions, coarsely chopped........	2	....	1½ quarts	
Carrots, diced	2	....	½ gallon...........	
Salt	....	6	¾ cup	
Water	....	....	To cover	
Flour	2	....	½ gallon	
Water (for gravy)...........	....	....	1 quart	

Prepare chicken for cooking. Cut into portions or leave whole. Place in kettle.

Add celery, onions, carrots and salt. Cover with water.

Cover tightly. Let simmer 3½ to 4½ hours or until tender.

Combine flour and 1 quart water. Blend to a smooth paste.

Drain stock from meat. Heat to boiling temperature. Stir in flour paste.

Cook, stirring constantly, until thickened. Let simmer about 10 minutes.

Combine meat and gravy. Reheat.

NOTE.—Serve with cooked rice or mashed potatoes.

Variations

Chicken and Biscuit with Gravy

Cook chickens whole. Remove meat from bones.

Scale out (weigh) 4-ounce portions. Place in baking pan.

Cover with thick Cream Gravy (page 212) or Chicken Gravy (page 212). Place unbaked biscuit on each portion of meat.

Bake in hot oven (425° F.) 15 to 20 minutes or until mixture bubbles and biscuits are browned.

NOTE.—1. Biscuit dough rolled ½ inch thick or pie dough rolled ¼ inch thick may be placed over top of mixture in place of individual biscuits.

2. Chicken Pie may be covered with topping of mashed potatoes. Bake in hot oven (425° F.) 10 to 15 minutes until browned.

Chicken Stew with Dumplings or Noodles

Drop dumplings (page 370) by spoonful or noodles into stew. Cover tightly. Cook 15 to 20 minutes.

CHICKEN A LA KING

Yield: Approx. 5 gallons.   Portion: 6 to 8 ounces (approx. 1 cup).

INGREDIENTS	100 PORTIONS			............PORTIONS
	WEIGHTS		AMOUNTS (approx.)	
	Pounds	Ounces		
Milk, liquid	....	....	1 gallon	
Chicken Stock (page 252)	....	....	2 gallons	
Onion juice	....	....	¼ cup	
Mushrooms, sliced	1	4	½ gallon	
Chicken fat or other fat	2	....	1 quart	
Peppers, green, coarsely cut	1	8	1½ quarts	
Flour	1	....	1 quart	
Eggs, slightly beaten	....	13	8 (1½ cups)	
Chicken (fowl), cooked, cut in ½- to ¾-inch cubes.	10	12	2 gallons	
Pimiento, chopped	1	12	1 quart	
Salt	....	1½	3 tablespoons	

Combine milk, chicken stock and onion juice. Heat to boiling temperature.

Fry mushrooms in fat about 5 minutes. Remove from fat.

Cook green peppers in 1 quart of milk and stock mixture 8 to 10 minutes or until peppers are tender. Drain and add liquid to milk mixture.

Stir flour into fat. Blend to a smooth paste. Stir into milk mixture. Cook until thickened, stirring constantly.

Add 1 quart of sauce to eggs, stirring to prevent cooking of eggs.

Add egg mixture to sauce, stirring vigorously.

Stir mushrooms, green peppers, chicken, pimiento and salt into sauce. Reheat.

NOTE.—Serve on toast, split biscuits, cooked rice, noodles or on toasted cornbread.

Variation

Veal a la King

Use 10 pounds (2 gallons) veal, cooked, cut in ½ to ¾-inch cubes in place of chicken for Veal a la king.

CREAMED CHICKEN OR TURKEY

Yield: Approx. 5 gallons.

Portion: 6 to 8 ounces (approx. 1 cup)

| INGREDIENTS | 100 PORTIONS | | | ....PORTIONS |
| | WEIGHTS | | AMOUNTS (approx.) | |
	Pounds	Ounces		
Chicken (fowl), cooked	10	12	2 gallons	
Chicken Stock (page 252)	....	....	2 gallons	
Milk, liquid	....	....	2 gallons	
Chicken fat, or other fat, melted.	2	....	1 quart	
Flour	1	....	1 quart	
Salt	....	1½	3 tablespoons	
Pepper	....	¼	1 tablespoon	

Cut chicken into ¾ to 1-inch cubes.

Combine chicken stock and milk. Heat to boiling temperature.

Blend together fat and flour to a smooth paste. Stir into stock.

Cook, stirring constantly, until thickened. Add chicken. Reheat.

Stir in salt and pepper.

NOTE.—1. 2 gallons turkey, cooked and cubed, may be used in place of chicken.

2. Serve over split biscuits or corn bread, toast, cooked noodles or cooked rice.

Variations

Creamed Chicken or Turkey with Ham

Combine 6 pounds of chicken or turkey, cooked, cubed, with 4 pounds of ham, cooked, cubed.

Creamed Chicken with Eggs

Add 2 dozen coarsely chopped hard-cooked eggs to creamed chicken.

BAKED CHICKEN AND NOODLES

Portion: Approx. 6 ounces.

INGREDIENTS	100 PORTIONS			............PORTIONS
	WEIGHTS		AMOUNTS (approx.)	
	Pounds	*Ounces*		
Salt	....	3	6 tablespoons	
Water, boiling	....	....	5 gallons	
Noodles	7	....	3¾ gallons	
Chicken or other fat............	2	....	1 quart	
Flour	2	....	½ gallon	
Salt	....	4	½ cup	
Pepper	....	½	1¾ tablespoons	
Chicken Stock (page 252) boiling.	....	....	2½ gallons	
Egg yolks.............................	....	6	9 (¾ cup)	
Chicken (fowl), cooked, diced..	10	....	1¾ gallons	
Bread crumbs, fine................	....	12	1½ quarts	
Butter, melted	....	8	½ pint	

Add 3 ounces salt to water. Heat to boiling temperature. Stir in noodles. Cook about 20 minutes or until tender. Drain.

Blend together fat, flour, 4 ounces salt and pepper to a smooth paste. Stir into stock. Heat to boiling temperature. Cook, stirring constantly, until thickened.

Add egg yolks, stirring constantly. Pour sauce over noodles. Stir in chicken. Place in greased baking pans.

Blend together crumbs and butter. Sprinkle over creamed mixture.

Bake in hot oven (400°F.) 30 minutes.

NOTE.—Egg yolks may be omitted.

Variation

Baked Chicken Dinner

Omit noodles and egg yolks.

Add 1 No. 10 can (3¼ quarts) peas, 2 No. 10 cans (6½ quarts) corn and 2 pounds (1½ quarts) onions, chopped, to sauce and meat mixture.

Place in greased baking pans. Sprinkle with buttered crumbs.

Bake in hot oven (400°F.) 30 minutes.

NOTE.—Serve with cooked rice, if desired.

CHICKEN AND VEGETABLE PIE

Yield: Approx. 6 gallons.   Portion: Approx. 8 ounces.

INGREDIENTS	100 PORTIONS			............PORTIONS
	WEIGHTS		AMOUNTS (approx.)	
	Pounds	Ounces		
Chicken Stock (page 252)	....	....	3 gallons	
Chicken fat or other fat, melted.	1	4	1½ pints	
Flour	1	....	1 quart	
Salt	....	2½	5 tablespoons	
Pepper	....	½	1 tablespoon	
Chicken (fowl), cooked, cut in ¾-inch cubes.	10	12	2 gallons	
Potatoes, cooked, cubed.........	3	4	½ gallon	
Peas, cooked	2	8	1 quart	
Carrot strips, cooked...........	1	....	1 quart	
Pie Dough (page 399)......... ...	5	....	....	

Heat stock to boiling temperature.

Blend fat, flour and salt to a smooth paste. Stir into stock. Cook, stirring constantly, until thickened.

Add chicken, potatoes, peas and carrots. Place in baking pans.

Roll pie dough ⅛ to ¼ inch thick. Perforate.

Place over chicken mixture. Bake in hot oven (450°F.) 10 to 15 minutes.

NOTE.—Biscuits or Biscuit Dough (page 361) may be used in place of pie dough.

CHICKEN CROQUETTES

Portion: 2 croquettes.

INGREDIENTS	100 PORTIONS			..........PORTIONS
	WEIGHTS		AMOUNTS (approx.)	
	Pounds	*Ounces*		
Chicken (fowl), cooked, finely chopped.	16	....	4 gallons	
Salt	....	2	¼ cup	
Pepper	....	½	1¾ tablespoons	
Onions, finely chopped...........	4	....	¾ gallon	
Butter or other fat...............	2	....	1 quart	
Flour (for dredging).............	1	8	1½ quarts	
Chicken Stock (page 252).........	....	....	½ gallon	
Eggs, whole	2	8	25 (1¼ quarts).........	
Bread crumbs, dry...............	3	....	3¾ quarts	
Flour	....	....		
Eggs, beaten	1	....	10 (1 pint)................	
Milk, liquid	....	....	1 quart	
Bread crumbs	....	....		

Sprinkle chicken with salt and pepper.

Fry onions in fat until clear.

Add flour and blend to a smooth paste. Stir in stock. Cook until thickened, stirring constantly. Remove from heat. Cool slightly.

Stir in eggs and bread crumbs. Mix thoroughly. Place in refrigerator until chilled.

Shape cold mixture into 3½ to 4-ounce croquettes.

Stir beaten eggs into milk. Mix well. Roll croquettes in flour. Dip in milk mixture. Roll in bread crumbs.

Fry in hot deep fat at 375°F. 3 to 4 minutes or until browned.

NOTE.—Turkey may be used in place of chicken.

Variation

Baked Chicken or Turkey Croquette Loaf

Bake croquette mixture in well greased baking pans in slow oven (325°F.) 1 hour.

Slice or cut in squares for serving.

Gravies and Sauces

Gravies and sauces are a very important part of the meal because they add the finishing flavor to the main dish or dessert. They also extend the main dish, provide contrasting texture and add variety to the menu.

The gravy or sauce must be seasoned exceptionally well and must also be a perfect accompaniment to the meat, fish, vegetable or dessert with which it is to be served.

BARBECUE SAUCE

Yield: Approx. 2 gallons.

Portion: Approx. ⅓ cup.

INGREDIENTS	100 PORTIONS		............PORTIONS
	WEIGHTS	AMOUNTS (approx.)	
	Pounds / Ounces		
Onions, chopped	1 / 8	4½ cups	
Bacon fat or other fat............	2 /	1 quart	
Flour	.... / 4	1 cup	
Mustard prepared	.... / 8	1 pint	
Cloves, ground	.... / ¾	3 tablespoons	
Salt	.... / 2½	5 tablespoons	
Pepper	.... / ½	1¾ tablespoons	
Sugar, brown	.... / 8	1½ cups	
Vinegar	.... /	1 quart.................	
Meat Stock (page 251).........	.... /	½ gallon	
Catsup	.... /	1 gallon	
Worcestershire sauce	.... /	1 pint	

Cook onions in fat until clear and tender.

Mix flour, mustard, cloves, salt, pepper and sugar. Stir into onions and fat.

Add vinegar, stock, catsup and Worcestershire sauce, stirring constantly.

Heat to boiling temperature. Let simmer 15 minutes.

NOTE.—1. 1 gallon fruit juice or juice from sweet pickles may be used in place of vinegar.

2. Serve with meats. May also be used in place of liquid in Beef Loaf (page 135), Stuffed Green Peppers (page 143), or for basting meats while roasting.

THIN CREAM OR WHITE SAUCE
For Cream Soups

Portion: 1/4 cup (approx. 2 ounces).

YIELD	1 GALLON			5 GALLONS			10 GALLONS			... GALLONS
INGREDIENTS	50 PORTIONS			250 PORTIONS			500 PORTIONS			...PORTIONS
	WEIGHTS		AMOUNTS (approx.)	WEIGHTS		AMOUNTS (approx.)	WEIGHTS		AMOUNTS (approx.)	
	Pounds	*Ounces*		*Pounds*	*Ounces*		*Pounds*	*Ounces*		
Butter or other fat, melted.	....	8	1 cup	2	4	1 1/8 quarts	4	8	2 1/4 quarts	
Flour	....	4	1 cup	1	2	4 1/2 cups	2	4	2 1/8 quarts	
Milk, liquid, hot	....	....	1 gallon	....	....	4 1/2 gallons	....	....	9 gallons	
Salt	....	1	2 tablespoons	....	5	10 tablespoons	....	10	1 1/4 cups	
Pepper	....	....	1 teaspoon	....	....	1 1/2 teaspoons	....	....	3 tablespoons	

Blend fat and flour to a smooth paste. Stir rapidly into hot milk. Cook until thickened. Stir constantly. Add salt and pepper.

MEDIUM CREAM OR WHITE SAUCE
For Creamed Vegetables

Portion: 1/4 cup (approx. 2 ounces).

YIELD	1 GALLON			5 GALLONS			10 GALLONS			...GALLONS
INGREDIENTS	50 PORTIONS			250 PORTIONS			500 PORTIONS			...PORTIONS
	WEIGHTS		AMOUNTS (approx.)	WEIGHTS		AMOUNTS (approx.)	WEIGHTS		AMOUNTS (approx.)	
	Pounds	*Ounces*		*Pounds*	*Ounces*		*Pounds*	*Ounces*		
Butter or other fat, melted.	....	12	1 1/2 cups	3	6	6 3/4 cups	6	12	3 1/4 quarts	
Flour	....	6	1 1/2 cups	1	11	6 3/4 cups	3	6	3 1/4 quarts	
Milk, liquid, hot	....	....	1 gallon	....	....	4 1/2 gallons	....	....	9 gallons	
Salt	....	1	2 tablespoons	....	5	10 tablespoons	....	10	1 1/4 cups	
Pepper	....	....	1 1/2 teaspoons	....	....	2 tablespoons	....	1	3 1/2 tablespoons	

Blend fat and flour to a smooth paste. Stir rapidly into hot milk. Cook until thickened. Stir constantly. Add salt and pepper.

MEDIUM THICK CREAM OR WHITE SAUCE
For Escalloped Dishes

Portion: ¼ cup (approx. 2 ounces).

YIELD / INGREDIENTS	1 GALLON 50 PORTIONS Weights (Pounds)	(Ounces)	Amounts (approx.)	5 GALLONS 250 PORTIONS Weights (Pounds)	(Ounces)	Amounts (approx.)	10 GALLONS 500 PORTIONS Weights (Pounds)	(Ounces)	Amounts (approx.)	GALLONS ...PORTIONS Weights	Amounts (approx.)
Butter or other fat, melted.	1	....	1 pint	4	8	2¼ quarts	9	....	1⅛ gallons		
Flour	....	8	1 pint	2	4	2¼ quarts	4	8	1⅛ gallons		
Milk, liquid, hot	....	....	1 gallon	....	....	4½ gallons	....	....	9 gallons		
Salt	....	¼	2½ tablespoons	....	6½	¾ cup	....	12	1½ cups		
Pepper	....	....	2 teaspoons	....	....	3 tablespoons	....	....	6 tablespoons		

Blend fat and flour to a smooth paste. Stir rapidly into hot milk. Cook until thickened. Stir constantly. Add salt and pepper.

THICK CREAM OR WHITE SAUCE
For Croquettes

Portion: ¼ cup (approx. 2 ounces).

YIELD / INGREDIENTS	1 GALLON 50 PORTIONS Weights (Pounds)	(Ounces)	Amounts (approx.)	5 GALLONS 250 PORTIONS Weights (Pounds)	(Ounces)	Amounts (approx.)	10 GALLONS 500 PORTIONS Weights (Pounds)	(Ounces)	Amounts (approx.)	GALLONS ...PORTIONS Weights	Amounts (approx.)
Butter or other fat, melted.	1	8	1½ pints	6	12	3¼ quarts	13	8	6½ quarts		
Flour	....	12	1½ pints	3	6	3¼ quarts	6	12	6½ quarts		
Milk, liquid, hot	....	....	1 gallon	....	....	4½ gallons	....	....	9 gallons		
Salt	....	1½	3 tablespoons	....	7	⅞ cup	....	15	1¾ cups		
Pepper	....	....	2 teaspoons	....	....	3 tablespoons	....	....	6 tablespoons		

Blend fat and flour to a smooth paste. Stir rapidly into hot milk. Cook until thickened, stirring constantly. Stir in salt and pepper.

NOTE.—1. 1 gallon will require cooking from 7 to 10 minutes. Larger quantities require a longer cooking period.

2. Meat stock, vegetable cooking waters and liquor drained from canned vegetables may be used in place of milk. Liquid drained from canned salmon or tuna fish may be used in place of part of milk.

209★

CREAM OR WHITE SAUCE VARIATIONS

SAUCE	ADDITIONAL INGREDIENTS FOR 1 GALLON CREAM SAUCE	AMOUNTS		
		WEIGHTS		AMOUNTS (approx.)
		Pounds	Ounces	
Bacon	Bacon, cooked, diced	1	4	
Caper	Capers, drained	....	....	½ pint
Cheese	Cheese, American cheddar, grated or chopped.	1	8	1¼ quarts
Egg	Eggs, hard-cooked, chopped	....	....	8
Horse-radish	Horse-radish, prepared, drained	....	....	1½ to 2½ cups
	Mustard, dry	....	....	1½ tablespoons
	Paprika	....	....	1 teaspoon
Mushroom	Mushrooms, fresh, sliced OR	1	4	1¾ quarts
	Mushrooms, canned, sliced	....	....	1½ pints
	Onions, minced	....	3	⅔ cup
	Butter (for frying onions)	....	4	½ cup
Parsley	Parsley, finely chopped	....	6	1 pint
Pimiento	Pimientos, diced	....	15	1 (15-oz.) can 1 pint
Pepper	Peppers, red, sweet, chopped	....	2	½ cup
	Peppers, green, sweet, chopped	....	4	1 cup
	Pickle relish or sweet pickles chopped.	....	6	1 cup
	Mustard and celery seed	....	....	½ teaspoon

BECHAMEL SAUCE

Yield: Approx. 2 gallons.   Portion: ¼ cup (approx. 2 ounces).

INGREDIENTS	100 PORTIONS			........PORTIONS
	WEIGHTS		AMOUNTS (approx.)	
	Pounds	Ounces		
Chicken or Veal Stock (page 252)	....	....	1½ gallons	
Milk, liquid	....	....	½ gallon	
Bay leaves	....	....	2	
Onions, chopped	1	....	1½ pints	
Butter or other fat	1	....	1 pint	
Flour	....	8	1 pint	
Thyme	....	....	2 teaspoons	
Salt	....	½	4 teaspoons	
Pepper	....	....	1 teaspoon	

Combine stock and milk. Add bay leaves. Heat to boiling temperature. Remove bay leaves.

Fry onions in fat about 10 minutes or until clear.

Blend together flour, thyme, salt, pepper and onion mixture to a smooth paste.

Stir into hot stock. Cook until slightly thickened, stirring constantly.

NOTE.—1. For a yellow sauce, stir the sauce into beaten yolks of 16 eggs.

2. Thyme and bay leaves may be omitted.

3. Serve with croquettes.

BOUILLON CUBE GRAVY

Yield: Approx. 2 gallons.   Portion: ¼ cup (approx. 2 ounces).

INGREDIENTS	100 PORTIONS			........PORTIONS
	WEIGHTS		AMOUNTS (approx.)	
	Pounds	Ounces		
Water, boiling	....	....	2 gallons	
Bouillon cubes	....	....	30	
Bacon fat, melted	....	....	1 pint	
Flour	1	....	1 quart	

Pour ½ gallon water over bouillon cubes and dissolve.

Add remaining water.

Blend together bacon fat and flour. Cook until browned, stirring constantly.

Gradually add bouillon to flour mixture, stirring constantly.

Heat to boiling temperature.

Cook 5 minutes.

SAVORY BROWN GRAVY

Yield: Approx. 2 gallons.   Portion: Approx. ⅓ cup.

INGREDIENTS	100 PORTIONS			............PORTIONS
	WEIGHTS		AMOUNTS (approx.)	
	Pounds	Ounces		
Fat from meat drippings, melted.	1	....	1 pint	
Flour	1	....	1 quart	
Meat Stock (page 251)	....	....	2 gallons	
Salt	....	1	2 tablespoons	
Pepper	....	....	2 teaspoons	

Blend fat and flour well. Cook until flour is browned, stirring constantly.

Add stock slowly, stirring constantly.

Cook until thickened and smooth. Add salt and pepper.

Variations

Cream Gravy

Use 1 gallon liquid milk in place of 1 gallon meat stock.

Onion Gravy

Slice 2 pounds (1½ quarts) onions and fry until golden brown. Add to gravy.

Vegetable Gravy

Season gravy with 1½ quarts cooked chopped onions, diced celery, diced carrots, and peas.

CHICKEN GRAVY

Yield: Approx. 2 gallons.   Portion: ¼ cup (approx. 2 ounces).

INGREDIENTS	100 PORTIONS			............PORTIONS
	WEIGHTS		AMOUNTS (approx.)	
	Pounds	Ounces		
Chicken Stock (page 252)	....	....	1 gallon	
Milk, liquid	....	....	1⅛ gallons	
Fat from fried chicken, drippings, melted.	1	....	1 pint	
Flour	1	....	1 quart	
Salt	....	1	2 tablespoons	
Pepper	....	....	2 teaspoons	

Combine chicken stock and milk. Heat to boiling temperature.

Blend together fat and flour. Stir into stock. Cook 10 to 15 minutes or until thickened and smooth, stirring constantly.

Stir in salt and pepper.

NOTE —Use drippings from roast chicken for gravy for roast chicken.

CREOLE SAUCE

Yield: Approx. 3 gallons.

Portion: Approx. ½ cup.

INGREDIENTS	100 PORTIONS		...........PORTIONS
	WEIGHTS	AMOUNTS (approx.)	
	Pounds	*Ounces*		
Salt pork, diced	3	....	1 quart	
Onions, chopped	1	5	1 quart	
Celery, chopped	1	....	1 quart	
Bay leaves, minced	....	....	3	
Cloves, whole	....	¼	1½ tablespoons	
Tomatoes	12	12	2 No. 10 cans (6½ quarts).	
Water	....	....	1 gallon	
Sugar	....	8	½ pint	
Flour	....	3	¾ cup	
Water	....	....	½ pint	

Fry salt pork 5 to 10 minutes or until well browned.

Add onions and celery and fry about 5 minutes, until lightly browned.

Add bay leaves and cloves, tied in cloth bag, tomatoes, water and sugar. Let simmer 1 hour.

Blend together flour and ½ pint water to a smooth paste. Stir into sauce. Continue simmering 30 minutes. Remove spice bag.

NOTE.—Serve with omelet, macaroni, fish or meats.

MINT SAUCE

Yield: 1 gallon.

Portion: 2 tablespoons (approx. 1 ounce).

INGREDIENTS	100 PORTIONS		...........PORTIONS
	WEIGHTS	AMOUNTS (approx.)	
	Pounds	*Ounces*		
Mint, fresh, chopped	....	....	½ gallon	
Sugar	1	8	1½ pints.....................	
Vinegar	....	....	¾ gallon	

Remove stems and old leaves from mint. Wash thoroughly.

Drain mint and chop fine. Add sugar and mix.

Let stand about ½ to 1 hour.

Add vinegar. Let stand 1 hour or longer before using.

NOTE.—1. If vinegar is too strong, dilute it with water.

2. An excellent sauce for lamb.

3. Mint or currant jelly may be used in place of Mint Sauce.

MOCK HOLLANDAISE SAUCE

Yield: 1¼ gallons.   Portion: Approx. 1½ tablespoons (¾ ounce)

INGREDIENTS	100 PORTIONS			..........PORTIONS
	WEIGHTS		AMOUNTS (approx.)	
	Pounds	Ounces		
Butter, melted	2	....	1 quart	
Flour	1	....	1 quart	
Milk, liquid, hot	....	....	¾ gallons	
Eggs, beaten	1	13	18 (1¾ pints)	
Lemon juice	....	....	1½ cups (6 lemons)	
Salt	....	1	2 tablespoons	
Pepper	....	....	1 tablespoon	
Paprika	....	....	1 tablespoon	

Blend together fat and flour. Stir into milk. Add eggs and lemon juice gradually, stirring constantly.

Heat to boiling temperature. Add salt, pepper and paprika.

Simmer 20 to 30 minutes. Beat constantly.

DRAWN BUTTER SAUCE

Yield: Approx. 1 gallon.   Portion: 2 tablespoons (approx. 1 ounce).

INGREDIENTS	100 PORTIONS			..........PORTIONS
	WEIGHTS		AMOUNTS (approx.)	
	Pounds	Ounces		
Butter	1	....	1 pint	
Flour	....	8	1 pint	
Water, boiling	....	....	1 gallon	
Salt	....	¾	1½ tablespoons	
Pepper	....	....	1 teaspoon	

Melt about ⅔ of the butter. Stir in flour and blend to a smooth paste.

Add mixture to boiling water. Cook until thickened, stirring constantly.

Add salt, pepper and remaining butter. Mix thoroughly.

NOTE.—This is a particularly good sauce for asparagus, broccoli, boiled new potatoes, baked and broiled fish.

Vaiations

Drawn Butter Sauce with Lemon

Use ½ cup lemon juice in place of ½ cup water. Stir into sauce after it has been thickened.

Drawn Butter Sauce with Chopped Egg

Add 10 hard-cooked eggs, diced or chopped, to Drawn Butter Sauce just before serving.

★214

MUSTARD SAUCE

Yield: Approx. 1 gallon.   Portion: 2 to 3 tablespoons (1 to 1½ ounces).

INGREDIENTS	100 PORTIONS			............PORTIONS
	WEIGHTS		AMOUNTS (approx.)	
	Pounds	*Ounces*		
Mustard, dry	....	7	1 pint	
Sugar	1	....	1 pint	
Flour	....	8	1 pint	
Salt	....	2	¼ cup	
Water, cold	....	....	1 gallon	
Vinegar	....	....	1 quart	
Butter or other fat, melted......	....	2	¼ cup	

Mix together thoroughly mustard, sugar, flour and salt.

Stir in ½ gallon water. Heat to boiling temperature.

Cook 5 minutes or until thickened, stirring constantly.

Heat remaining water to boiling temperature. Stir water and vinegar into mustard mixture.

Heat to boiling temperature. Stir in butter.

Cook until slightly thickened, stirring continuously.

FRESH PINEAPPLE SAUCE

Yield: Approx. 2 gallons.   Portion: ¼ cup (approx. 2 ounces).

INGREDIENTS	100 PORTIONS			............PORTIONS
	WEIGHTS		AMOUNTS (approx.)	
	Pounds	*Ounces*		
Sugar	3	....	1½ pints	
Water	....	....	1 gallon	
Pineapple, fresh, peeled and chopped fine.	8	....	½ gallon	

Combine sugar and water. Heat until sugar is dissolved.

Add pineapple. Heat to boiling temperature. Let simmer until pineapple is clear and tender, stirring occasionally. Serve immediately.

NOTE.—An excellent sauce to serve with baked ham.

215★

RAISIN SAUCE

Yield: 1½ gallons. Portion: 3 tablespoons (approx. 1½ ounces).

| INGREDIENTS | 100 PORTIONS | | | ....PORTIONS |
| | WEIGHTS | | AMOUNTS (approx.) | |
	Pounds	Ounces		
Water, boiling	....	....	1 gallon	
Cloves, whole	....	....	2 tablespoons	
Raisins, seedless	2	5	½ gallon	
Sugar, brown	4	....	¾ gallon	
Flour	....	8	1 pint	
Salt	....	½	1 tablespoon	
Butter, melted	....	8	1 cup	
Catsup	....	....	1½ cups	

Combine water and cloves. Heat to boiling temperature.

Cook 10 minutes. Strain. Add raisins. Cook 5 minutes.

Mix together sugar, flour and salt. Stir into water and mix until smooth.

Heat to boiling temperature. Cook 10 minutes or until thickened. Remove from heat. Stir in butter and catsup.

NOTE.—Serve with baked ham or cold sliced pork.

SPICE SAUCE

Yield: Approx. 2 gallons. Portion: Approx. ⅓ cup.

| INGREDIENTS | 100 PORTIONS | | | ....PORTIONS |
| | WEIGHTS | | AMOUNTS (approx.) | |
	Pounds	Ounces		
Onions, finely chopped	1	....	¾ quart	
Meat Stock (page 251) or water.	....	....	1 gallon	
Worcestershire sauce	....	....	1 cup	
Catsup	....	....	1 pint	
Sugar	....	8	1 cup	
Vinegar	....	....	½ gallon	

Mix together onions, stock or water, Worcestershire sauce, catsup, sugar and vinegar.

Heat to boiling temperature. Cook 5 minutes.
NOTE.—An excellent sauce for meats.

SPANISH SAUCE

Yield: Approx. 2¼ gallons.　　　　　　　　Portion: Approx. ⅓ cup.

INGREDIENTS	100 PORTIONS			............PORTIONS
	WEIGHTS		AMOUNTS (approx.)	
	Pounds	Ounces		
Tomatoes	12	12	2 No. 10 cans (6½ quarts).	
Onions, chopped	1	5	1 quart	
Peppers, green, diced	1	....	1 quart	
Peppers, red, sweet, diced	1	....	1 quart	
Mushrooms, fresh, sliced	1	8	½ gallon	
Butter or other fat	....	8	1 cup	
Flour	....	2	½ cup	
Salt	....	1	2 tablespoons	
Sugar	....	2	¼ cup	
Chili powder	....	....	½ teaspoon	
Water	....	....	½ pint	

Heat tomatoes to boiling temperature.

Fry onions, peppers and mushrooms in fat slowly until soft.

Stir in flour and cook about 2 minutes.

Mix together salt, sugar and chili powder. Add water and stir.

Combine all ingredients, stirring until mixture reaches boiling temperature.

NOTE.—1.　½ pint Meat Stock (page 251) may be used in place of water.

2. Serve with omelet, roast beef, steak, lamb chops or veal roast.

STEAK BUTTER

Yield: Approx. 1½ quarts.　　　　　　Portion: 1 tablespoon (approx. ½ ounce).

INGREDIENTS	100 PORTIONS			............PORTIONS
	WEIGHTS		AMOUNTS (approx.)	
	Pounds	Ounces		
Butter	2	....	1 quart	
Onions, minced	....	8	1½ cups	
Lemon juice	....	....	½ pint (4 lemons)	
Salt	....	1	2 tablespoons	
Pepper	....	....	½ teaspoon	

Beat butter until creamy. Add onions, lemon juice, salt and pepper. Mix thoroughly.

NOTE.—Serve with steak or Beefburgers (page 136).

TARTARE SAUCE

Yield: Approx. ½ gallon. Portion: 1½ tablespoons (approx. ¾ ounce).

| INGREDIENTS | 100 PORTIONS | | ....PORTIONS |
	WEIGHTS	AMOUNTS (approx.)	
	Pounds	*Ounces*		
Capers	....	....	½ cup	
Olives, stoned, chopped	....	....	½ cup	
Pickles, finely chopped	....	3	½ cup	
Onions, finely chopped............	....	1½	¼ cup	
Parsley, finely chopped	....	1	¼ cup	
Mayonnaise (page 237)...........	4	....	½ gallon	

Combine capers, olives, pickles, onion and parsley. Stir into mayonnaise. Mix well.

NOTE.—Serve with fried cod, haddock, halibut, smelts or oysters.

TOMATO SAUCE

Yield: Approx. 2 gallons. Portion: Approx. ⅓ cup.

| INGREDIENTS | 100 PORTIONS | | ....PORTIONS |
	WEIGHTS	AMOUNTS (approx.)	
	Pounds	*Ounces*		
Tomatoes	12	12	2 No. 10 cans (6½ quarts).	
Meat Stock (page 251)..............	....	....	1 gallon	
Sugar	....	4	½ cup	
Garlic	....	....	1 clove	
Bay leaves	....	....	4	
Cloves	....	....	1 tablespoon	
Pepper	....	....	1 tablespoon	
Salt	....	1	2 tablespoons	
Butter, melted or beef drippings.	1	....	1 pint	
Flour	1	...	1 quart	
Vinegar	....	....	1 tablespoon	

Combine tomatoes, meat stock and sugar. Add garlic, bay leaves, cloves, pepper and salt. Heat to boiling temperature.

Blend together butter and flour to a smooth paste. Stir into heated mixture. Add vinegar.

Continue cooking and stirring until mixture is well thickened. Strain.

NOTE.—An excellent sauce for baked fish, veal cutlets and baked stuffed peppers.

TOMATO PUREE SAUCE

Yield: 2½ gallons.   Portion: Approx. ⅓ cup.

INGREDIENTS	100 PORTIONS			...... PORTIONS
	WEIGHTS		AMOUNTS (approx.)	
	Pounds	*Ounces*		
Onions, dehydrated ...		2	1 cup	
Water, for onions			1 pint	
Fat	1	8	1½ pints........	
Tomato puree	13	...	2 No. 10 cans (6½ quarts).	
Sugar	1	8	1½ pints............	
Salt		4	½ cup........	
Pepper		¼	1 tablespoon...........	
Meat Stock (page 251)		...	¾ gallon........	

Soak onions in water for 20 minutes. Drain. Cook in fat until clear.

Add tomato puree, sugar, salt, pepper, and stock. Mix well. Heat to boiling temperature.

NOTE.—1. Especially good sauce to use for baking with meat or fish.

2. Meat stock may be made with 1¾ ounces powdered bouillon or 12 bouillon cubes dissolved in ¾ gallon boiling water.

Salads

Salads have a recognized and important place on the menu and make a nutritious and refreshing contribution to the dinner or supper meal.

Fruit and vegetable salads are the most popular and as such are one of the best means of introducing valuable vitamins, essential minerals and color into the meal.

If a few simple rules for making salads are observed, these salads, selected for the Navy Mess, can be made quickly and easily and served frequently.

Salad Greens

Select salad greens carefully.

Lettuce, endive, romaine, escarole, watercress, young spinach and cabbage offer an abundant choice for the greens which can be best used as a foundation or as one of the main ingredients in the salad itself. Parsley, watercress and the inner tender leaves of curly endive can be used to advantage as a garnish.

Sort, trim, wash and crisp the greens before making the salad. Wash them carefully to free them of sand and earth particles. Drain well.

Cut lettuce and cabbage into strips or pieces or shred them, when they are to be used as one of the main ingredients in the salad.

Place the prepared greens in pans; cover them with wax paper, if available, then with a clean, damp cloth. Place them in a refrigerator to chill and crisp before using. They should be free of excess water and be one of the very last parts of the meal to be prepared.

Fruits and Vegetables

Select these with care and wash them thoroughly. Trim and peel if necessary. Cut them into uniform sizes. Cook the vegetables which need cooking. Place the prepared material, covered, in a refrigerator to be chilled before combining with salad greens and dressing.

Combining the Salad Ingredients

Mix the salad carefully just before serving.

Combine the prepared, chilled ingredients in small amounts at a time. Mix or toss them lightly together. Use a large fork to thoroughly distribute the ingredients and dressing.

The Salad Dressing

The salad dressing is as important as the salad itself. It brings a distinctive flavor to the salad. Each type dressing can take on a new flavor by the addition of various seasonings and herbs.

As a rule, the dressing should be the last ingredient to be added to the salad. This rule should be strictly followed for fruit salads and mixed greens. It should be added just about 5 minutes before placing the salad on the serving counter. An exception may be made for meat, fish, vegetable and potato salads. Adding the dressing to these salads 1 hour in advance of serving, and placing the salad mixture in a refrigerator to be chilled, will greatly improve the flavor of the salad.

The salad dressing, and approximate amount necessary, is specified in each salad recipe.

Serving the Salad

Select as cool place as possible. If necessary to serve from the steam table, place the salad container away from the heat of the steam.

Bring the salad from the refrigerator in small amounts at a time. In this way the salad will be cool, refreshing and the greens will remain fresh and crisp.

Place the salad container in a pan of ice, when possible. This will assure firmness in gelatin mixtures and prevent wilting of the salad greens.

Sprigs of crisp parsley, radish roses, carrot strips or celery curls or other simple garnish, can readily be arranged on top or around the salad. This should be the finishing touch and will add greatly to the attractiveness of the salad.

AVOCADO AND LETTUCE SALAD.

Portion: Approx. ½ cup lettuce (½ avocado).

INGREDIENTS	100 PORTIONS			............PORTIONS
	WEIGHTS		AMOUNTS (approx.)	
	Pounds	*Ounces*		
Avocados, ripe	....	....	50	
Lettuce, coarsely cut	3	....	1½ gallons	
French Dressing (page 239)	....	....	½ gallon	

Cut avocados into halves. Do not peel. Remove stone.

Serve in the peel, with crisp lettuce and French Dressing or Thousand Island Dressing (page 240).

NOTE.—1. Avocados may be peeled and cut into strips or sliced, if desired.

2. Avocados should not be cut until ready to serve as they discolor rapidly. Sprinkling cut pieces with lemon juice will help prevent discoloration.

3. In order to avoid waste, the lettuce and avocados should be placed in separate containers or trays on the serving counter, allowing each man to make his own selection.

BAKED BEAN AND EGG SALAD

Yield: Approx. 5 gallons.   Portion: ¾ cup (approx. 4 ounces).

INGREDIENTS	100 PORTIONS			............PORTIONS
	WEIGHTS		AMOUNTS (approx.)	
	Pounds	*Ounces*		
Beans, baked	12	....	2 gallons	
Celery, diced	5	....	1¼ gallons	
Pickles, sweet, diced	2	8	½ gallon	
Lettuce or chicory	6	....	3 gallons	
Onions, green, chopped	1	4	1 quart	
Eggs, hard-cooked, chopped ...	....	....	36 (2½ quarts)...............	
Salt	....	3	6 tablespoons	
"Boiled" Salad Dressing (page 238).	....	....	To moisten	

Combine beans, celery, pickles, lettuce, onions and eggs. Sprinkle with salt.

Add dressing. Mix together lightly and carefully.

NOTE.—Use large fork for mixing salad in order to avoid mashing the ingredients.

CARROT AND CELERY SALAD

Yield: Approx. 5 gallons.   Portion: ¾ cup (approx. 3 ounces).

| INGREDIENTS | 100 PORTIONS | | | .... PORTIONS |
| | WEIGHTS | | AMOUNTS (approx.) | |
	Pounds	Ounces		
Carrots, shredded	12	....	3 gallons	
Celery, diced	5	....	1¼ gallons	
Lettuce	2	....	1 gallon	
Mayonnaise (page 237)	2	....	1 quart	

Combine carrots, celery and lettuce. Mix thoroughly. Add mayonnaise. Toss lightly and mix until blended.

Variations

Carrot and Raisin Salad

Use 15 pounds (3¾ gallons) carrots, shredded, and 2 pounds raisins, washed.

Beet and Celery Salad

Use 26 pounds (3¾ gallons) cooked or pickled beets, sliced or quartered, in place of carrots.

NOTE.—3 pounds (¾ gallon) onions, sliced, may be used in place of celery.

Carrot, Celery and Apple Salad

Use 5 pounds apples, washed, cored and cubed in place of 5 pounds carrots.

CARDINAL SALAD

Yield: Approx. 5 gallons.   Portion: ⅔ cup (approx. 6 ounces).

| INGREDIENTS | 100 PORTIONS | | | PORTIONS |
| | WEIGHTS | | AMOUNTS (approx.) | |
	Pounds	Ounces		
Beets, cooked, diced	9	4	1½ gallons	
Beans, green, cooked, diced	6	12	1½ gallons	
Peas, cooked	5	....	½ gallon	
Celery, diced	6	....	1½ gallons	
Onions, chopped	1	4	1 quart	
Salt	....	4	½ cup	
Lettuce, coarsely cut	2	....	1 gallon	
Mayonnaise (page 237)	4	....	½ gallon	

Combine beets, green beans, peas, celery and onions.

Sprinkle with salt. Add lettuce and mayonnaise.

Toss lightly until well mixed. Serve immediately.

NOTE.—1. 2 No. 10 cans (1½ gallons) beets, drained, 2 No. 10 cans (1½ gallons) beans, drained, and 1 No. 10 can (3¼ quarts) green peas, drained, may be used in place of fresh beets, peas and beans.

2. Equivalent amounts of other fresh vegetables, cooked or canned vegetables, drained, may be used.

GRAPEFRUIT AND CELERY SALAD

Yield: Approx. 5 gallons.   Portion: ¾ cup (approx. 6 ounces).

| INGREDIENTS | 100 PORTIONS | | | ....PORTIONS |
| | WEIGHTS | | AMOUNTS (approx.) | |
	Pounds	Ounces		
Grapefruit sections, halved	32	....	3 gallons	
Celery, diced	4	....	1 gallon	
Lettuce, coarsely cut	2	....	1 gallon	
Mayonnaise (page 237)	4	....	½ gallon	

Drain grapefruit. Reserve juice.

Mix together grapefruit, celery and lettuce.

Add mayonnaise. Toss lightly until well mixed.

NOTE.—1. Grapefruit juice may be used for fruit punch, fruit cup or as plain fruit juice.

2. Fresh or canned grapefruit may be used.

Variation

Grapefruit and Green Pepper Salad

Use 3½ pounds (1 gallon) green pepper, cut in 1-inch strips in place of celery.

COLE SLAW

Yield: Approx. 5 gallons.   Portion: ¾ cup (approx. 4 ounces).

| INGREDIENTS | 100 PORTIONS | | | ....PORTIONS |
| | WEIGHTS | | AMOUNTS (approx.) | |
	Pounds	Ounces		
Cabbage, shredded	20	....	5 gallons	
Onion, minced	....	5	1 cup	
Peppers, green, diced	1	....	1 quart	
Salt	....	½	1 tablespoon	
"Boiled" Salad Dressing (page 238)	4	....	½ gallon	

Combine cabbage, onion and green pepper. Sprinkle with salt.

Add dressing just before serving. Toss lightly until well mixed.

NOTE.—Diced oranges, grapefruit, pears, apples, pineapple or peaches may be used to vary Cole Slaw. Diced celery, chopped tomatoes, shredded carrots or diced cucumbers also may be used.

Variations

Banana Cole Slaw

30 to 40 ripe bananas, sliced, in place of 2 gallons cabbage, 6 tablespoons lemon juice and ¾ cup prepared mustard, added to above ingredients makes a delicious, different cabbage salad.

Old Fashioned Cole Slaw

Omit onion and green pepper. Add hot "Boiled" Salad Dressing (page 238). Toss lightly to mix well. Cool.

Hot Cabbage Slaw

Omit onion, green pepper, and salt. Mix shredded cabbage with ½ gallon Hot Bacon Dressing (page 238) just before serving.

223 ★

COLE SLAW
(Using dehydrated cabbage)

Portion: Approx. 4 ounces (approx. ⅔ cup).

INGREDIENTS	100 PORTIONS			..........PORTIONS
	WEIGHTS		AMOUNTS (approx.)	
	Pounds	*Ounces*		
Cabbage, dehydrated	2	8	2½ gallons	
Water, cool (for cabbage)	....	....	2¼ gallons	
Onions, dehydrated	1	....	1 quart	
Water, cool (for onions)	....	....	½ gallon	
Salt	....	7½	⅞ cup	
Pepper	....	½	1¾ tablespoons	
Vinegar	....	....	2½ quarts	

Soak cabbage in water 3½ to 4 hours to reconstitute.

Soak onions in water 45 to 60 minutes to reconstitute.

Combine onions, salt, pepper and vinegar. Let stand until cabbage is ready.

Drain all surplus water from cabbage. Combine with onion-vinegar mixture. Serve cold.

NOTE.—1. Long soaking of cabbage at high temperature develops an unsatisfactory flavor and off-color.

2. Place in refrigerator, to soak, if possible. If ice is available, add a small piece to the water in which cabbage is to be soaked.

3. Soaking cabbage for Cole Slaw for a period longer than 4 hours, unless under refrigeration, is not desirable because of the possibility of spoilage.

CHICKEN SALAD

Yield: Approx. 5 gallons.   Portion: ¾ cup (approx. 5 ounces).

INGREDIENTS	100 PORTIONS			..........PORTIONS
	WEIGHTS		AMOUNTS (approx.)	
	Pounds	*Ounces*		
Fowl, cooked (page 201), diced, 60 lbs. A. P.	15 E.P.	....	2¾ gallons	
Celery, diced	6	....	1½ gallons	
Lettuce, coarsely cut	3	....	1½ gallons	
Salt	....	4	½ cup	
Mayonnaise (page 237)	3	....	1½ quarts	

Combine chicken, celery and lettuce.

Sprinkle with salt.

Stir in mayonnaise. Toss until well mixed.

Variation

Veal Salad

15 pounds cooked veal or cooked veal and ham may be used in place of chicken.

★ 224

CUCUMBER AND ONION SALAD

Yield: Approx. 5 gallons.　　　　　　　　　　　　Portion: ¾ cup (approx. 6 ounces).

INGREDIENTS	100 PORTIONS			............PORTIONS
	WEIGHTS		AMOUNTS (approx.)	
	Pounds	Ounces		
Vinegar	....	....	2¾ quarts	
Water	....	....	2¾ quarts	
Sugar	....	12	¾ pint	
Salt	....	3	6 tablespoons	
Pepper	....	....	1¼ tablespoons	
Cucumbers, sliced, chilled	21	....	4 gallons	
Onions, sliced thin	9	8	1¾ gallons	

Mix together vinegar, water, sugar, salt and pepper.

Combine crisp cucumber slices with onions.

Pour vinegar dressing over cucumber and onions.

Serve immediately.

NOTE.—Any of these vegetables alone or in combinations, may be added: radishes, sliced; tomato sections; green sweet pepper, shredded; celery, diced; cauliflower, raw, chopped; carrots, raw, chopped; beets, cooked, sliced.

FRUIT SALAD

Yield: Approx. 5 gallons.　　　　　　　　　　　　Portion: ¾ cup (approx. 5 ounces).

INGREDIENTS	100 PORTIONS			............PORTIONS
	WEIGHTS		AMOUNTS (approx.)	
	Pounds	Ounces		
Apples, A. P.	8	....		
Pineapple, drained, diced	16	....	2 gallons	
Oranges, diced	8	....	½ gallon (16 medium)	
Lettuce, coarsely cut	2	....	1 gallon	
French Dressing (page 239)	....	....	1 quart	

Wash and core apples. Cut into ½-inch cubes.

Combine apples, pineapple, oranges and lettuce.

Just before serving add dressing. Toss lightly and serve immediately.

NOTE.—1. 7 to 8 ripe bananas, sliced (1 quart) may be added just before serving.

2. A combination of any fresh fruits or canned fruits, drained, may be used. Reserve drained juice for fruit punch.

225★

LETTUCE SALAD

Yield: Approx. 5 gallons. Portion: ¾ cup (approx. 3 ounces).

INGREDIENTS	100 PORTIONS			..........PORTIONS
	WEIGHTS		AMOUNTS (approx.)	
	Pounds	Ounces		
Lettuce, coarsely cut	15	....	7½ gallons	
French Dressing (page 239).....	....	....	1½ quarts	

Mix together lettuce and dressing. Toss lightly to mix.

NOTE.—1. Escarole, chicory, watercress, raw spinach and other salad greens may be used.

2. The inner, tender leaves of head lettuce should be used for Hearts of Lettuce Salad.

Variations

Lettuce and Tomato Salad

Mix together 10 pounds lettuce, coarsely cut, and 5 pounds tomatoes, cut in small wedges.

Just before serving add 1 quart French Dressing (page 239).

Tossed Green Salad

7½ gallons coarsely cut escarole, chicory, watercress, raw spinach and other salad greens or a combination of greens may be used in place of lettuce.

Wilted Lettuce Salad

Use ½ gallon Hot Bacon Dressing (page 238) in place of French Dressing. Toss with lettuce just before serving.

Wilted Greens

Use ½ gallon Hot Bacon Dressing (page 238) in place of French Dressing on escarole, chicory or other greens. Toss with greens just before serving.

Chopped raw spinach is especially good served with Hot Bacon Dressing.

ORANGE, GRAPEFRUIT AND BANANA SALAD

Yield: Approx. 4 gallons. Portion: ½ to ¾ cup.

INGREDIENTS	100 PORTIONS			..........PORTIONS
	WEIGHTS		AMOUNTS (approx.)	
	Pounds	Ounces		
Orange sections	20	....	2 gallons	
Grapefruit sections, halved ...	10	....	1 gallon	
Bananas, sliced or diced	8	....	1 gallon	
Celery, diced	1	....	1 quart	
Pimientos, diced (optional)...	....	15	1 (15-ounce) can (1 pint).	
Mayonnaise (page 237)...........	2	....	1 quart	

Combine orange and grapefruit sections. Drain. Peel and slice bananas. Combine with orange and grapefruit.

Add celery and pimiento. Mix thoroughly but lightly to avoid mashing bananas.

Add mayonnaise. Mix just before serving.

NOTE.—This salad may be served on crisp lettuce leaf, or coarsely cut or shredded lettuce may be used as an ingredient.

MACARONI OR SPAGHETTI SALAD

Yield: Approx. 5 gallons.   Portion: ¾ cup (approx. 6 ounces).

| INGREDIENTS | 100 PORTIONS | | | ....PORTIONS |
| | WEIGHTS | | AMOUNTS (approx.) | |
	Pounds	Ounces		
Macaroni, cooked, cold	9	8	1 gallon	
Celery, diced	8	....	2 gallons	
Pimientos, chopped	....	7½	1 cup or ½ (15-oz.) can.	
Onions, minced	....	4	¾ cup	
Lettuce, coarsely cut	2	....	1 gallon	
Eggs, hard-cooked, diced	2	14	30 (½ gallon)	
Salt	....	2	¼ cup	
Mayonnaise (page 237)	2	8	1¼ quarts	

Combine macaroni, celery, pimientos, onions, lettuce and eggs. Sprinkle with salt.

Add mayonnaise. Toss lightly until well mixed.

NOTE.—3 pounds diced, cooked beef, veal or ham may be used in place of eggs.

PINEAPPLE CHEESE SALAD

Yield: Approx. 5 gallons.   Portion: ½ to ¾ cup.

| INGREDIENTS | 100 PORTIONS | | | ....PORTIONS |
| | WEIGHTS | | AMOUNTS (approx.) | |
	Pounds	Ounces		
Pineapple, drained, diced	20	4	2½ gallons	
Lettuce, coarsely cut or shredded.	15	....	7½ gallons	
Cheese, American cheddar, coarsely grated.	1	8	1½ quarts	
Mayonnaise (page 237)	3	....	1½ quarts	

Combine pineapple, lettuce and cheese. Add mayonnaise and mix together lightly.

Variation

Pineapple Coconut Salad

Sprinkle 1 pound (1¾ quarts) grated coconut over top of Pineapple Cheese Salad just before serving.

NOTE.—Dry, shredded coconut soaked in milk, to cover, 1 hour before using and then drained thoroughly, will give appearance and flavor of fresh coconut.

COLD POTATO SALAD

Yield: Approx. 5 gallons.   Portion: ¾ cup (approx. 6 ounces).

INGREDIENTS	100 PORTIONS			.........PORTIONS
	WEIGHTS		AMOUNTS (approx.)	
	Pounds	Ounces		
Potatoes, cooked, sliced	20	....	3⅛ gallons	
Salt	....	6	¾ cup	
Pepper	....	¼	¾ tablespoon	
Oil	....	11	¾ pint	
Vinegar	....	6	¾ cup	
Celery, diced	4	....	1 gallon	
Onions, diced	....	10	1 pint	
Eggs, hard-cooked, chopped....	3	4	36 (2¼ quarts)............	
Mayonnaise (page 237)............	6	....	¾ gallon	
Lettuce, coarsely cut	2	....	1 gallon	

Spread layer of potatoes in bottom of pan. Sprinkle with salt, pepper, oil and vinegar.

Arrange layers of potatoes and seasonings until all are used.

Let stand 1 hour.

Add celery, onion, lettuce, eggs and mayonnaise, just before serving. Mix together lightly.

POTATO SALAD
(Using dehydrated potatoes)

Portion: Approx. 4 ounces.

INGREDIENTS	100 PORTIONS			.........PORTIONS
	WEIGHTS		AMOUNTS (approx.)	
	Pounds	Ounces		
Potatoes, Julienne style, de-hydrated.	5	....	1¾ gallons	
Water (for potatoes)	....	....	2¾ gallons	
Onions, dehydrated	....	8	1½ pints	
Water (for onions)	....	....	1¾ quarts	
Vinegar	....	....	1½ pints	
Salt	....	3	6 tablespoons	
Pepper	....	1	3½ tablespoons	

Soak potatoes in water 45 to 60 minutes to reconstitute. Cover. Heat, slowly, to boiling temperature.

Let simmer 10 to 20 minutes or until tender. Drain thoroughly. Cool.

Stir onions into water and let soak 60 minutes to reconstitute.

Heat to boiling temperature. Let simmer 20 to 25 minutes or until tender. Drain well.

Cool. Add to potatoes.

Add vinegar, salt and pepper. Mix lightly. Sprinkle with paprika or garnish with sprigs of crisp parsley. Serve cold.

NOTE.—1. 1 quart Mayonnaise (page 237) may be used. Omit vinegar in the Potato Salad.

2. 20 eggs, hard-cooked, sliced, or cold scrambled eggs may be added.

PERFECTION SALAD

Yield: 3-gallon mixture.

Portion: 2½-inch square.

INGREDIENTS	100 PORTIONS			............PORTIONS
	WEIGHTS		AMOUNTS (approx.)	
	Pounds	*Ounces*		
Gelatin, lemon flavored	3	4		
Water, hot	....	..	1 gallon	
Water, cold	....	....	3½ quarts	
Celery, diced	3	....	¾ gallon	
Cabbage, chopped fine	3	....	¾ gallon	
Carrots, chopped fine	....	12	¾ quart	
Peppers, green, chopped fine	....	12	¾ quart	
Vinegar	....	....	1½ pints	
Salt	....	....	1 tablespoon	
Lettuce, coarsely cut	6	....	3 gallons	
Mayonnaise (page 237)	4	....	½ gallon	

Dissolve gelatin in hot water. Stir in cold water. Chill until slightly thickened.

Mix together celery, cabbage, carrots, green peppers, vinegar and salt.

Stir vegetable mixture into thickened gelatin. Place into pans. Chill until firm.

Cut into 2½-inch squares. Serve on lettuce with mayonnaise.

HOT POTATO SALAD

Yield: Approx. 6¼ gallons.   Portion: ¾ to 1 cup.

| INGREDIENTS | 100 PORTIONS | | | ....PORTIONS |
| | WEIGHTS | | AMOUNTS (approx.) | |
	Pounds	Ounces		
Bacon, sliced, diced	8	....	1 gallon	....
Potatoes, uncooked, cubed	50	....	6¼ gallons	....
Onions, minced	1	5	1 quart	....
Water	....	....	1¼ gallons	....
Sugar	2	8	1¼ quarts	....
Pepper	....	2	7 tablespoons	....
Mustard, dry	....	5½	1½ cups	....
Salt	....	6	¾ cup	....
Vinegar	....	....	1 quart	....

Fry bacon until lightly browned.

Combine with potatoes, onions, water and sugar.

Stir in pepper, mustard and salt until well mixed. Cover.

Heat to boiling temperature. Cook 20 to 30 minutes, or until potatoes are almost done.

Stir in vinegar, being careful not to mash potatoes. Cook 5 to 10 minutes, or until potatoes are tender but not mushy.

NOTE.—1. 12 ounces (1 quart) crisp parsley, minced, may be added just before serving.

2. 1½ pints caraway seeds may be added, with seasonings, before cooking.

3. Hot potato salad may be served as a main dish with two hot vegetables.

SALMON SALAD

Yield: Approx. 5 gallons.   Portion: ¾ cup (approx. 5 ounces).

| INGREDIENTS | 100 PORTIONS | | | ....PORTIONS |
| | WEIGHTS | | AMOUNTS (approx.) | |
	Pounds	Ounces		
Salmon	20	....	20 No. 1 tall cans (2 gallons).	....
Celery, diced	7	....	1½ gallons	....
Pickles, sweet, chopped	2	....	1½ quarts	....
Lettuce, coarsely cut	2	....	1 gallon	....
Salt	....	3	6 tablespoons	....
Mustard, prepared	....	1	¼ cup	....
Mayonnaise (page 237)	4	....	½ gallon	....

Drain salmon. Remove bones and skin. Flake into large pieces.

Combine salmon, celery, pickles and crisp lettuce. Sprinkle with salt.

Add mustard and mayonnaise. Toss lightly and mix well, being careful not to mash salmon. Garnish with sprigs of crisp parsley.

NOTE.—1. 1 No. 10 can peas (3¾ quarts) drained, may be used in place of celery.

2. Crab flakes, tuna fish, halibut, cod or any firm white fish cooked may be used in place of salmon.

Variation

Salmon Salad Tropical

30 to 40 ripe bananas, sliced or diced, and 1 No. 10 can (3¼ quarts) pineapple, diced, may be used in place of 1 gallon salmon and ½ gallon celery.

Bananas are fully ripe when the yellow peel is flecked with brown.

SHRIMP AND CELERY SALAD

Yield: Approx. 5 gallons.　　　　　　　　　　Portion: ¾ cup (approx. 5 ounces).

INGREDIENTS	100 PORTIONS		............PORTIONS
	WEIGHTS	AMOUNTS (approx.)	
	Pounds / Ounces		
Shrimps, A. P., cooked	20 /	2½ gallons, E. P.	
Lemon juice	.... /	¾ cup	
Celery, diced	6 /	1½ gallons	
Salt	.... / 3	6 tablespoons	
Pepper	.... /	2 teaspoons	
Lettuce, quartered or coarsely cut.	2 /	1 gallon	
Mayonnaise (page 237)....	4 /	½ gallon	

Combine cleaned shrimp, lemon juice and celery. Sprinkle with salt and pepper.

Add mayonnaise. Toss lightly until mixed. Serve on or with crisp, coarsely cut lettuce.

NOTE.—6 No. 5 cans (12 pounds) of shrimps may be used in place of 20 pounds raw shrimps.

Variation

Shrimp and Macaroni Salad

6 pounds A.P. (3½ gallons, cooked) macaroni or spaghetti may be used in place of celery.

231★

ORANGE AND WATERCRESS SLAW

Yield: Approx. 4 gallons.   Portion: Approx. 1 cup.

| INGREDIENTS | 100 PORTIONS | | | ....PORTIONS |
| | WEIGHTS | | AMOUNTS (approx.) | |
	Pounds	Ounces		
Cabbage, shredded	15	....	3¾ gallons	
Onions, chopped	2	....	1½ quarts	
Orange sections, diced	2	8	1 quart	
Mustard, dry	....	....	3 tablespoons	
Salt	....	1	2 tablespoons	
Milk, evaporated	....	....	1 cup	
Vinegar	....	....	1 cup	
Mayonnaise (page 237)	2	....	1 quart	
Watercress	2	6	12 bunches	

Mix together cabbage, onion and oranges.

Stir mustard, salt, milk and vinegar into mayonnaise.

Wash and select watercress carefully. Chop coarse.

Combine cabbage mixture, dressing and watercress.

Toss together lightly. Serve immediately.

NOTE.—25 ripe bananas, sliced or diced may be added.

YELLOW TURNIP AND WATERCRESS SLAW

Yield: Approx. 5 gallons.   Portion: Approx. 1 cup.

| INGREDIENTS | 100 PORTIONS | | | ....PORTIONS |
| | WEIGHTS | | AMOUNTS (approx.) | |
	Pounds	Ounces		
Cabbage, shredded	12	....	3 gallons	
Turnips, yellow, shredded	10	....	2½ gallons	
Mustard, dry	....	....	3 tablespoons	
Salt	....	1	2 tablespoons	
Milk, evaporated	....	....	1 cup	
Vinegar	....	....	1 cup	
Mayonnaise (page 237)	2	....	1 quart	
Watercress	2	6	12 bunches	

Mix together cabbage and turnips.

Stir mustard, salt, milk and vinegar into mayonnaise. Blend thoroughly.

Wash and select watercress carefully. Chop coarse.

Combine cabbage mixture and dressing. Add watercress.

Toss together lightly. Serve immediately.

NOTE.—10 pounds (2½ gallons) carrots, shredded, may be used in place of turnips.

RAW VEGETABLE SALAD

Yield: 5 gallons. Portion: ¾ cup (approx. 3 ounces).

INGREDIENTS	100 PORTIONS			..........PORTIONS
	WEIGHTS		AMOUNTS (approx.)	
	Pounds	Ounces		
Cabbage, shredded	4	....	1 gallon	....
Carrots, shredded	4	....	1 gallon	....
Pepper, green, diced	1	8	1½ quarts	....
Tomatoes, cubed	6	....	¾ gallon	....
Celery, sliced	3	....	¾ gallon	....
Salt	....	4	½ cup	....
Endive, curly, coarsely cut.....	1	8	¾ gallon	....
French Dressing (page 239)	....	....	1 quart	....

Combine cabbage, carrots, green peppers, tomatoes and celery. Sprinkle with salt.

Add endive and dressing just before serving. Toss lightly until well mixed.

NOTE.—A combination of any raw vegetables may be used. Lettuce, spinach, watercress or any greens may be used in place of endive.

Variation

Chef's Salad

Add thinly cut strips of cheese and ham or tongue and arrange in a simple design on top of a combination of salad greens and salad vegetables, such as carrot strips and wedges of tomato. Slices of hard-cooked eggs may also be included in the garnish. Serve with mayonnaise.

NOTE.—This is a good salad for utilizing left-over ham or tongue and serving it in an attractive manner.

WALDORF SALAD

Yield: Approx. 5 gallons.   Portion: ¾ cup (approx. 5 ounces).

| INGREDIENTS | 100 PORTIONS | | | ....PORTIONS |
| | WEIGHTS | | AMOUNTS (approx.) | |
	Pounds	Ounces		
Apples, A. P.	14	....		
Celery, diced	8	....	2 gallons	
Lettuce, coarsely cut	4	....	2 gallons	
Salt	....	1	2 tablespoons	
Mayonnaise (page 237)	2	....	1 quart	

Wash apples. Do not peel. Cut into quarters. Remove core. Dice. Add celery and crisp lettuce. Sprinkle with salt.

Add mayonnaise. Toss lightly and serve immediately.

NOTE.—Apples, cut, discolor when allowed to stand. Prepare salad as near serving time as possible.

Variations

Apple, Celery and Carrot Salad

2 pounds (½ gallon) thinly sliced carrots may be used in place of 2 pounds celery.

Apple, Celery and Raisin Salad

Add 1 pound (1½ pints) raisins to salad.

Banana Waldorf Salad

25 to 30 ripe bananas, sliced or diced, may be used in place of 4 pounds (1 gallon) celery, diced. Bananas are fully ripe when the yellow peel is flecked with brown.

PHILADELPHIA PEPPER RELISH

Yield: Approx. 3 gallons.   Portion: ⅓ to ½ cup.

| INGREDIENTS | 100 PORTIONS | | | ....PORTIONS |
| | WEIGHTS | | AMOUNTS (approx.) | |
	Pounds	Ounces		
Cabbage, finely chopped	8	....	2 gallons	
Peppers, green, finely chopped.	3	....	12 (¾ gallon)	
Peppers, red, finely chopped	3	....	12 (¾ gallon)	
Celery, finely chopped	3	....	¾ gallon	
Celery seed	....	1	4 tablespoons	
Mustard seed	....	¼	1 tablespoon	
Salt	....	1	2 tablespoons	
Sugar, brown	2	....	1½ quarts	
Vinegar (50 grain)	....	....	1 quart	

Mix together cabbage, green peppers, red peppers and celery.

Mix together celery seed, mustard seed, salt and brown sugar. Stir into the vinegar.

Add vinegar mixture to chopped vegetables just before serving.

NOTE.—Serve with roast meat or fried fish.

CORN RELISH

Yield: Approx. 4 gallons.　　　　　　　　　　　　Portion: Approx. ⅔ cup.

INGREDIENTS	100 PORTIONS			........Portions
	WEIGHTS		AMOUNTS (approx.)	
	Pounds	*Ounces*		
Corn, whole kernel, drained...	13	4	2 No. 10 cans (1½ gallons).	
Peppers, green, diced	1	....	1 quart	
Pimiento, chopped	....	12	1½ cups	
Celery, diced	1	....	1 quart	
Onion, minced	1	8	4½ cups	
French Dressing (page 239)......	....	....	1½ quarts	

Mix together corn, green peppers, pimiento, celery and onion.

Add French Dressing. Mix thoroughly.

Let stand in refrigerator for 6 hours until flavor is blended.

NOTE.—1. Serve with meats or fish or as salad.

2. 4 pounds (24 bunches) watercress cut coarse may be added to Relish just before serving.

3. Fresh corn, cooked, cut from cob, may be used in place of canned corn.

DIXIE RELISH

Yield: Approx. 5 gallons.　　　　　　　　　　　　Portion: ½ to ¾ cup.

INGREDIENTS	100 PORTIONS			........Portions
	WEIGHTS		AMOUNTS (approx.)	
	Pounds	*Ounces*		
Cabbage, chopped	12	....	3 gallons	
Celery, diced	4	....	1 gallon	
Peppers, green, chopped........	3	....	¾ gallon	
Onions, chopped	1	....	1½ pints	
Salt	....	4	½ cup	
"Boiled" Salad Dressing (page 238)	6	....	¾ gallon	

Combine cabbage, celery, peppers, onions and salt. Add dressing and mix together lightly.

NOTE.—6 large dill pickles, chopped, add to flavor.

TOMATO ASPIC

Yield: 5 gallons.

Portion: 2½-inch square.

INGREDIENTS	100 PORTIONS			..........PORTIONS
	WEIGHTS		AMOUNTS (approx.)	
	Pounds	Ounces		
Gelatin, unflavored	....	8	1½ cups	
Water, cold	....	....	½ gallon	
Tomatoes	31	14	5 No. 10 cans (4 gallons).	
Onions, chopped	....	5	1 cup	
Salt	....	3	6 tablespoons	
Sugar	....	8	1 cup	
Bay leaves	....	....	3	
Celery stalks and leaves, diced.	1	....	1 quart	
Vinegar	....	....	1½ pints	

Soak gelatin in cold water 10 minutes.

Combine tomatoes, onions, salt, sugar, bay leaves and celery.

Heat to boiling temperature. Cook 10 minutes. Remove from heat and strain. Reserve juice.

Stir gelatin into hot juice until completely dissolved.

Add vinegar. Pour into pans to depth of 1½ inches. Chill until firm.

Cut into 2½-inch squares.

NOTE.—Serve on lettuce with mayonnaise, using 3 pounds lettuce, separated, and ½ gallon mayonnaise.

MAYONNAISE

Yield: Approx. ½ gallon.

Portion: 1 tablespoon.

INGREDIENTS	100 PORTIONS			............PORTIONS
	WEIGHTS		AMOUNTS (approx.)	
	Pounds	Ounces		
Eggs, whole	....	6	4	
Salt	....	¾	1½ tablespoons	
Sugar	....	1	2 tablespoons	
Mustard, dry	....	¼	1½ tablespoons	
Salad oil	1	14	½ gallon	
Vinegar (50 grain)	....	6	¾ cup	

Beat eggs 2 minutes.

Add salt, sugar and mustard. Beat 2 minutes.

Add oil in a fine stream beating constantly. Increase rate of adding oil as mayonnaise emulsion builds up. Add all oil in 10 to 15 minutes.

Add small amount of vinegar if necessary during addition of oil to keep emulsion from breaking. Add remaining vinegar after all oil has been added. Beat 1 more minute.

NOTE.—1. 1½ ounces powdered egg and 4½ ounces (½ cup) cold water may be used in place of 4 whole eggs. In using powdered egg reconstituted with water, have mixing bowl small enough to obtain thorough agitation as oil is being added.

2. 50 grain vinegar is standard Navy issue vinegar containing 5% acetic acid. If higher grain vinegar is used, it must be diluted with water to 50 grain strength. For example:

Dilute 100 grain vinegar with equal volume or weight of water to produce 50 grain vinegar.

Dilute 250 grain vinegar by mixing 1 part vinegar by weight or volume with 4 parts water by weight or volume, to produce 50 grain vinegar.

SOUR CREAM DRESSING

Yield: Approx. ½ gallon.

INGREDIENTS	100 PORTIONS			............PORTIONS
	WEIGHTS		AMOUNTS (approx.)	
	Pounds	Ounces		
Milk, evaporated	3	10	4 No. 1 tall (14½ oz.) cans (1⅔ quarts).	
Sugar	....	8	1 cup	
Salt	....	....	4 teaspoons	
Vinegar	....	....	1 quart	

Combine milk, sugar and salt.

Add vinegar, gradually, stirring briskly with a wire whip until well blended and sugar is dissolved.

NOTE.—1. Add ¼ teaspoon paprika, or dry mustard or ⅛ teaspoon pepper, if desired.

2. Serve cold on slaws or on green salads.

HOT BACON DRESSING

Yield: Approx. 1 gallon.

INGREDIENTS	100 PORTIONS			...........Portions
	WEIGHTS		AMOUNTS (approx.)	
	Pounds	Ounces		
Onions, chopped	1	....	1½ pints	
Bacon, diced	2	....	1 quart	
Water	....	....	1½ quarts	
Vinegar	....	....	1½ quarts	
Sugar	1	4	1¼ pints	
Salt	....	½	1 tablespoon	
Pepper	....	...	1 teaspoon	
Flour	....	6	1½ cups	

Fry together onions and bacon until bacon is crisp and onions are clear. Drain off fat, and reserve.

Combine water and vinegar. Heat to boiling temperature. Add sugar, salt and pepper.

Blend fat and flour to a smooth paste.

Stir into hot liquid. Heat to boiling temperature.

Cook about 10 minutes or until slightly thickened. Add onion and bacon.

Add to salad just before serving.

"BOILED" SALAD DRESSING

Yield: Approx. 1½ gallons.

INGREDIENTS	100 PORTIONS			...........Portions
	WEIGHTS		AMOUNTS (approx.)	
	Pounds	Ounces		
Milk, liquid	....	....	1 gallon	
Flour	....	8	1 pint	
Sugar	....	12	1½ cups	
Mustard, dry	....	1½	6¾ tablespoons	
Salt	....	2	¼ cup	
Eggs, slightly beaten	1	8	15 (¾ quart)	
Butter	....	4	½ cup	
Vinegar	....	....	1 quart	

Heat ¾ gallon milk to boiling temperature. Do *not* boil.

Mix together flour, sugar, mustard and salt. Stir in remaining cold milk to make a smooth paste.

Add paste to hot milk, stirring constantly.

Heat to boiling temperature. Cook, stirring, until thickened.

Add slowly 1 quart dressing to eggs, stirring to prevent cooking of eggs.

Stir egg mixture into cooked dressing. Cook, stirring constantly, 5 to 10 minutes.

Remove from heat. Stir in butter. Cool slightly. Stir in vinegar.

Cool thoroughly before using.

Hold in refrigerator.

FRENCH DRESSING

Yield: Approx. ½ gallon.

INGREDIENTS	100 PORTIONS			..........PORTIONS
	WEIGHTS		AMOUNTS (approx.)	
	Pounds	*Ounces*		
Salt	----	1	2 tablespoons	
Sugar	----	1⅓	2 tablespoons	
Mustard, dry	----	----	1½ tablespoons	
Paprika	----	----	1½ tablespoons	
Salad oil	2	8	1½ quarts	
Vinegar	----	----	2¼ cups	
Onion juice	----	----	2 tablespoons	

Mix together salt, sugar, mustard and paprika. Add oil, vinegar and onion juice.

Place in container. Cover tightly. Shake vigorously before serving.

NOTE.—1. Dressing may be made in mixer or whipped together with wire whip.

2. Lemon juice may be used in place of vinegar.

3. 1 individual clove of garlic may be added, if desired. Remove before using dressing.

Variations

Olive French Dressing

Add 1 pint olives, ripe or green, minced, to 1 gallon French Dressing.

Chiffonade Dressing

Add: 4 hard-cooked eggs, chopped
8 ounces (1 pint) green pepper, chopped
1 (15-ounce) can (1 pint) pimiento, chopped
1 pint catsup
1 tablespoon prepared mustard
1 teaspoon Worcestershire sauce

Curried French Dressing

Add 1 tablespoon curry powder to 1 gallon dressing.

239★

THOUSAND ISLAND DRESSING

Yield: Approx. ½ gallon.

INGREDIENTS	100 PORTIONS			............PORTIONS
	WEIGHTS		AMOUNTS (approx.)	
	Pounds	*Ounces*		
Chili sauce	....	....	½ pint	
Mayonnaise (page 237)	4	....	½ gallon	
Peppers, green, chopped fine.	....	4	1 cup	
Onion, minced	....	1	2 tablespoons	
Worcestershire sauce	....	....	¼ teaspoon	
Eggs, hard-cooked, chopped fine.	....	...	3	
Salt	....	....	1 teaspoon	
Pickles, sweet, chopped fine...	....	3	½ cup	

Stir chili sauce into mayonnaise.

Add peppers, onions, Worcestershire sauce, eggs, salt and pickles.

Mix together thoroughly.

Variation

Russian Dressing

Omit hard-cooked eggs from Thousand Island Dressing.

Sandwiches

Sandwiches serve two purposes in the menu. They provide satisfying nourishment in convenient form in an emergency. They can be served without equipment and can be carried either in made-up form or as separate ingredients.

Sandwiches can be served, on occasion, as a main dish in the meal when served with hot vegetables, a salad and dessert.

Pointers for Making Good Sandwiches

Allow plenty of work space for making sandwiches. Prepare all the materials in advance and have the necessary tools ready and at hand before beginning to make the sandwiches.

Day-old soft bread is preferable.

Place butter in a warm place to soften it. Do not melt. Whip softened butter to a creamy consistency so that it spreads easily and economically. When a soft filling is used, the butter can be mixed with it, thus saving time and one step in the operation of making the sandwich.

Butter one or both slices of bread, spreading from the corners and edges toward the center of the slice, so that the entire surface is covered. Butter prevents the sandwich filling from soaking into the bread.

Make sandwich fillings just before using. Hold them in a refrigerator if they must stand any length of time.

Wrap the sandwiches in wax paper. Place sandwiches in refrigerator until ready to use.

The addition of chopped celery or crisp, shredded lettuce or cabbage, to appropriate soft fillings, makes the sandwich more palatable and increases the food value.

Make Sandwich Filling Just Before Using

Whenever possible, sandwich fillings should not be prepared until just before making the sandwiches. The fillings made with meat, egg, and fish are highly perishable and should not be allowed to remain in warm room temperatures.

When circumstances make it necessary to prepare the fillings and sandwiches 1 to 2 hours before they are to be used, place them in the refrigerator immediately after they have been made, and keep them there until just before using them.

BUTTER AND BREAD FOR SANDWICHES

INGREDIENTS	100 PORTIONS			............PORTIONS
	WEIGHTS		AMOUNTS (approx.)	
	Pounds	*Ounces*		
Butter, softened	2	....	1 quart	....
Milk, evaporated	....	7½	½ No. 1 tall (14½-oz.) can (1 cup).	....
Bread	....	....	200 slices	....

Beat together butter and milk until well blended. Spread on bread slices.

NOTE.—1. Add butter to sandwich mixture instead of spreading separately.

2. The volume of butter will be increased if creamed in an electric mixer.

3. 4 pounds (½ gallon) Mayonnaise (page 237) may be used in place of butter. Any of the following seasonings may be used with the Mayonnaise.

Variations

Added Seasoning

1 pound butter may be seasoned with any of the following ingredients:

Celery, finely chopped	1 cup
Chili sauce or catsup	1 cup
Chives, chopped	¼ cup
Green pepper, chopped	¼ cup
Horse-radish	1 tablespoon
Lemon juice	2 tablespoons
Mustard, prepared	1 tablespoon
Onion, grated	1 tablespoon
Parsely, chopped	½ cup
Pimientos, chopped	¼ cup
Scallions, chopped	¼ cup
Watercress, minced	6 bunches

AMERICAN CHEESE FILLING

Portion: Approx. 2 ounces.

INGREDIENTS	100 PORTIONS			PORTIONS
	WEIGHTS		AMOUNTS (approx.)	
	Pounds	Ounces		
Mustard, prepared	....	1	¼ cup	
Chili sauce	....	8	½ pint	
Mayonnaise (page 237)	1	....	1 pint	
Cheese, American cheddar, ground.	6	....	5¼ quarts	

Mix together mustard, chili sauce and mayonnaise.

Add to cheese and stir until mixture is thoroughly blended and smooth.

NOTE.—1. Cheese warmed to room temperature will blend more quickly and thoroughly.

2. Spread slice of toast with cheese. Grill in broiler. Serve immediately.

CREAM CHEESE AND OLIVE FILLING

Portion: Approx. 2 ounces.

INGREDIENTS	100 PORTIONS			PORTIONS
	WEIGHTS		AMOUNTS (approx.)	
	Pounds	Ounces		
Cheese, cream, softened	9	....		
Milk, evaporated	1	13	2 No. 1 tall (14 ½-oz.) cans (1½ pints).	
Olives, stuffed, chopped fine	3	....	1¾ quarts	

Mix together all ingredients and blend to a smooth paste.

NOTE.—Any of the following may be blended with cream cheese:

Celery, chopped.
Jelly, jam or preserves.
Nuts, chopped.
Peppers, green, chopped.
Pickle, chopped.
Pimiento, diced.
Raisins.
Watercress, minced.

COLD MEAT FILLING

Portion: Approx. 2½ ounces.

INGREDIENTS	100 PORTIONS			.........PORTIONS
	WEIGHTS		AMOUNTS (approx.)	
	Pounds	*Ounces*		
Boiled ham	15–18	....		
Bologna	15–18	....		
Canadian bacon, cooked	15–18	....		
Cervelat	15–18	....		
Corned beef, cooked	15–18	....		
Liverwurst	15–18	....		
Luncheon Meat	15–18	....		
Roast beef	15–18	....		
Roast lamb	15–18	....		
Roast pork	15–18	....		
Roast veal	15–18	....		
Salami	15–18	....		
Spiced ham OR	15–18	....		
Tongue, cooked	15–18	....		

Select 1 or more meats to total 15 to 18 pounds. Slice.

NOTE—1. Cole Slaw (page 223) or chopped raw vegetables, seasoned with salad dressing, may be spread on 1 slice of bread.

2. Slice the bread before removing meat from refrigerator. Meat should not remain in warm room temperatures longer than necessary.

3. Canned meats may be used.

4. Cooked meats may be ground and mixed with chili sauce, prepared mustard, or sweet pickle relish and made into a filling.

PEANUT BUTTER FILLING

Portion: Approx. 2 ounces.

INGREDIENTS	100 PORTIONS			..........PORTIONS
	WEIGHTS		AMOUNTS (approx.)	
	Pounds	*Ounces*		
Peanut butter, softened	10	....	1 gallon	
Butter, softened	1	....	1 pint	
Milk, evaporated	2	4	2½ No. 1 tall (14 ½-oz.) cans (1 quart).	

Mix together peanut butter, butter and milk until smooth.

Variations

Peanut Butter and Cooked Bacon

To 8 pounds (3¼ quarts) peanut butter add 3 pounds (1 quart) chopped cooked bacon.

Peanut Butter and Horse-radish

To 9 pounds (3¾ quarts) peanut butter add 1 pound (1 pint) prepared horse-radish.

Peanut Butter and Chili Sauce

To 8 pounds (3¼ quarts) peanut butter add ½ gallon chili sauce.

Peanut Butter and Jam

To 5 pounds (½ gallon) peanut butter add 7 pounds jam, jelly or applebutter.

Peanut Butter and Ham

To 4 pounds (1¾ quarts) peanut butter add 4 pounds (2¾ quarts) chopped cooked ham and 2 pounds (1¼ quarts) pickle relish.

CORNED BEEF FILLING

Portion: Approx. 2 ounces.

INGREDIENTS	100 PORTIONS			..........PORTIONS
	WEIGHTS		AMOUNTS (approx.)	
	Pounds	*Ounces*		
Corned beef, cooked, ground.	6	....	....	
Eggs, hard-cooked, chopped fine.	5	....	48	
Pickles, sweet, chopped fine....	1	....	1½ pints	
Milk, evaporated	4	8	5 No. 1 tall (14½-oz.) cans (½ gallon).	
Salt	....	1	2 tablespoons	
Pepper	....	¼	¾ tablespoon	
Lemon juice	....	....	1 pint (8 lemons)	

Combine all ingredients and mix thoroughly.

NOTE.—1. Sweet pickle liquor may be used in place of lemon juice.

2. Hard-cooked egg may be omitted.

HOT MEAT SANDWICH

Portion: Approx. 4 ounces meat, approx. 4 ounces gravy.

INGREDIENTS	100 PORTIONS			...........PORTIONS
	WEIGHTS		AMOUNTS (approx.)	
	Pounds	*Ounces*		
Meat, cooked, sliced	25	....		
Bread, slices	....	....	200	
Gravy (page 212)....................	....	....	3½ gallons	

Make sandwiches.
Heat gravy to boiling temperature.
Place sandwich on serving plate or tray.
Ladle hot gravy on sandwich before serving.

NOTE.—The Hot Meat Sandwich may be used as a main dish. Serve in addition, 1 or 2 hot vegetables, other than potatoes, or 1 hot vegetable and 1 salad.

CHICKEN SALAD FILLING

Portion: 1½ ounces (approx. 3 tablespoons).

INGREDIENTS	100 PORTIONS			...........PORTIONS
	WEIGHTS		AMOUNTS (approx.)	
	Pounds	*Ounces*		
Chicken, cooked, chopped	8	....	1½ gallons	
Salt	....	½	1 tablespoon	
Celery, chopped fine	1	....	1 quart	
Vinegar	....	....	½ cup	
Mayonnaise (page 237)...........	1	....	1 pint	

Mix together all ingredients. Blend thoroughly.

NOTE.—1. Prepare all the ingredients for making the sandwiches before removing the chicken from refrigerator. Chicken meat should not remain in warm room temperatures longer than necessary.

2. Place made sandwiches in refrigerator if they are to be held 1 or 2 hours before serving.

Variation

Chicken and Watercress Filling

Use 4 bunches watercress, chopped coarse, in place of 1 quart celery, chopped.

EGG SALAD FILLING

Portion: Approx. 2 ounces.

INGREDIENTS	100 PORTIONS			............PORTIONS
	WEIGHTS		AMOUNTS (approx.)	
	Pounds	*Ounces*		
Eggs, hard-cooked, chopped fine.	8	....	80	
Celery, chopped fine	3	....	¾ gallon	
Mayonnaise (page 237)............	3	....	1½ quarts	
Salt	....	1	2 tablespoons	
Celery salt	....	1	2 tablespoons	
Pepper	....	½	1¾ tablespoons	
Onions, chopped fine	....	2	6 tablespoons	

Combine all ingredients and mix thoroughly.

NOTE.—Egg salad fillings are highly perishable and should not be made until just before sandwiches are to be used. If necessary to hold fillings or sandwiches 1 to 2 hours before using them, hold in refrigerator and not in a warm room.

Variation

Egg Salad with Bacon

Use 6 pounds (2¼ quarts) chopped, cooked bacon in place of celery.

HAM SALAD FILLING

Portion: Approx. 2 ounces.

INGREDIENTS	100 PORTIONS			............PORTIONS
	WEIGHTS		AMOUNTS (approx.)	
	Pounds	*Ounces*		
Ham, cooked, chopped fine.....	6	....	1 gallon	
Celery, chopped fine	3	....	¾ gallon	
Horse-radish	....	2	¼ cup	
Mustard, dry	....	1	¼ cup	
Mayonnaise (page 237)............	4	....	½ gallon	

Combine all ingredients and mix thoroughly.

NOTE.—1. 1½ quarts chopped sweet pickles may be used for half the celery.

2. Any cooked meat may be used.

3. Hold the ham in refrigerator until all the other ingredients are prepared. Ham is highly perishable and should not remain in warm room temperature longer than necessary.

4. Place filling in refrigerator immediately after making, if necessary to hold it 1 to 2 hours before making or serving the sandwiches.

SALMON SALAD FILLING

Portion: Approx. 2½ ounces.

INGREDIENTS	100 PORTIONS			............PORTIONS
	WEIGHTS		AMOUNTS (approx.)	
	Pounds	Ounces		
Salmon, flaked	8	....	8 No. 1 tall (16-oz.) cans (1 gallon).	....
Celery, chopped fine	3		¾ gallon	....
Onions, chopped fine	....	8	1½ cups	....
Pickles, sweet, chopped fine	....	8	1½ cups	....
Mayonnaise (page 237)..............	4	....	½ gallon	....
Salt	....	1	2 tablespoons	....

Combine all ingredients and mix thoroughly.
NOTE.—If the filling must be held 1 to 2 hours before using, place it in refrigerator immediately after it is made.

VEGETABLE SALAD FILLING

Portion: Approx. 2 ounces.

INGREDIENTS	100 PORTIONS			............PORTIONS
	WEIGHTS		AMOUNTS (approx.)	
	Pounds	Ounces		
Cabbage, shredded	2	....	½ gallon	....
Carrots, shredded	1	8	1½ quarts	....
Peppers, green, chopped fine.	....	12	1½ pints	....
Celery, chopped fine.....................	1	4	4½ cups	....
Mayonnaise (page 237)..............	2	....	1 quart	....
Salt	....	¾	1½ tablespoons	....

Combine all ingredients and mix well. Chill thoroughly before using.

NOTE.—½ pound (1½ cups) seedless raisins may be used in place of ½ pound cabbage.

BAKED BEAN FILLING

Portion: Approx. 2 ounces.

INGREDIENTS	100 PORTIONS			............PORTIONS
	WEIGHTS		AMOUNTS (approx.)	
	Pounds	Ounces		
Beans, baked	12	....	2 gallons	
Milk, evaporated	1	13	2 No. 1 tall (14½-oz.) cans (1½ pints).	

Mash beans.

Stir in milk and mix thoroughly.

NOTE.—This filling may be used hot or cold.

Variation

Baked Beans with Bologna

To 9 pounds (5½ quarts) baked beans add 3 pounds bologna, chopped fine. Mix together. Stir in milk and mix thoroughly.

LETTUCE AND TOMATO SANDWICH

INGREDIENTS	100 PORTIONS			............PORTIONS
	WEIGHTS		AMOUNTS (approx.)	
	Pounds	Ounces		
Lettuce	4	....	7 medium heads	
Mayonnaise (page 237).........	4	....	½ gallon	
Tomatoes, sliced	15	....	60	

Wash and separate lettuce heads into leaves.
Spread bread with mayonnaise.
Place tomato slices and lettuce on one slice of bread.
Cover with second slice of bread.

Variation

Lettuce, Tomato and Bacon Sandwich

Use 2 slices cooked bacon to each sandwich.

BOLOGNA AND CHEESE FILLING

Portion: Approx. 2 ounces.

INGREDIENTS	100 PORTIONS			............PORTIONS
	WEIGHTS		AMOUNTS (approx.)	
	Pounds	Ounces		
Bologna, ground	4	....	....	
Cheese, American cheddar, ground.	4	....	3½ quarts	
Milk, evaporated	2	12	3 No. 1 tall (14½-oz.) cans (1¼ quarts).	
Pickles, sweet, chopped fine ...	1	....	1½ pints	
Mustard, dry	....	½	2¼ tablespoons	
Pepper	....	....	½ teaspoon	
Salt	....	½	1 tablespoon	

Combine all ingredients and mix thoroughly.

LIVER AND EGG FILLING

Portion: Approx. 2 ounces.

INGREDIENTS	100 PORTIONS			............PORTIONS
	WEIGHTS		AMOUNTS (approx.)	
	Pounds	Ounces		
Liver, cooked, chopped fine.....	8	....	1 gallon	
Eggs, hard-cooked, chopped fine.	2	....	20	
Mayonnaise (page 237)	4	....	½ gallon	
Onions, minced	....	5	1 cup	
Salt	....	1	2 tablespoons	
Pepper	....	....	2 teaspoons	

Combine all ingredients. Stir together until well mixed.

NOTE.—1 quart catsup may be used in place of 1 quart mayonnaise.

Soups

Soups serve as one of the best carriers for additional highly nutritive foods such as milk, meat, and vegetables.

Soups range in variety from clear broth to the heavier types which include the cream and bean soups and chowders. If the meal tends to be of a hearty nature, it should be preceded by one of the lighter soups such as the clear broths and their variations. A light meal can be made more attractive and satisfying with the addition of a cream soup or chowder.

The meat stock, which forms the basis for many soups, is an important item when foods in quantity are being prepared. It can be used as a base for sauces and gravies. It is advisable to keep fresh stock on hand at all times.

Bouillon cubes, powdered bouillon, or bouillon type products can be used in place of, or as part of the meat stock. They are convenient to handle and can be used to advantage when bones are not available for making stock.

Dehydrated soup mixtures, now available, are highly nutritious and tasty. Directions for preparing them should be carefully followed.

The addition of fresh or canned vegetables to a soup prepared from a dehydrated soup base, and the use of meat stock for reconstituting these soups, enhance the flavor and contribute to the nutritional value of the soup.

Liquid from canned vegetables, or water in which vegetables have been cooked, should be used in place of part of the water specified in the recipe.

SOUP-MAKING GUIDE

Soup Base	Thickeners	Seasonings	Garnishes	Accompaniments
Brown Stock:	Barley	Allspice	*Cream Soups:*	Carrot strips, raw
Beef	Bread crumbs	Basil	Bacon, crisp, small pieces	Celery
Lamb	Corn meal	Bay leaves		Crackers
White Stock:	Corn Starch	Celery	Chives, chopped	Croutons
Veal	Flour	Celery Salt	Cream, whipped	Nuts
Chicken	Macaroni	Chives	Frankfurters, sliced thin	Olives
Fish Stock	Noodles	Cloves	Peppers, chopped	Radishes
Tomato Stock	Rice	Curry	Pimiento, chopped	Sandwiches
Vegetable Stock	Spaghetti	Mace		Toast, Melba sticks
Cream Sauce	Tapioca	Sweet Marjoram	*Stock Soups:*	
Milk		Nutmeg	Carrot strips	
		Onion, raw	Cheese, grated	
		Onion salt	Chives, chopped	
		Parsley	Croutons	
		Pepper	Egg custard cubes	
		Peppercorns	Lemon slices	
		Salt	Okra slices	
		Thyme	Rice cereal, crisp (freshly buttered)	

MEAT STOCK (BEEF OR VEAL)

Yield: Approx. 6 gallons.

INGREDIENTS	100 PORTIONS		............PORTIONS
	WEIGHTS	AMOUNTS (approx.)	
	Pounds	Ounces		
Bones, beef or veal	22	....	....	
Brisket, shank meat, boneless.	10	....	....	
Water, cold	....	....	8 gallons	
Onions, chopped	1	....	1½ pints	
Celery, chopped	1	....	1 quart	
Carrots, chopped	1	8	4½ cups	
Salt	....	4	½ cup	
Pepper	....	....	1 teaspoon	
Bay leaves	....	....	5	

Saw bones crosswise or lengthwise and remove the marrow. Brown the bones in oven.

Cut meat into 2-inch cubes. Brown in marrow fat.

Add bones, meat and remaining ingredients to water. Let simmer 5 to 6 hours. Strain and cool. When cool, place in refrigerator.

NOTE.—1. Use stock as base for soups and sauces.

2. Before using, carefully remove layer of hardened fat which helps seal the top.

3. Make Meat Stock without bones, if not available. Use only 10 pounds meat as specified.

MEAT STOCK
(Using powdered bouillon)

Yield: 6 gallons.

Portion: 1 cup (Approx. 8 ounces).

INGREDIENTS	100 PORTIONS		PORTIONS
	WEIGHTS	AMOUNTS (approx.)	
	Pounds	Ounces		
Bouillon, powdered		12	1½ pints	
Water, boiling			6 gallons	

Stir powdered bouillon into boiling water until completely dissolved. Heat to boiling temperature.

NOTE.—1. Serve plain or use as basic stock for other soups.

2. The flavor and palatability of soups made from dehydrated soup mixes is greatly improved when used with powdered bouillon.

3. Any bouillon type product may be used to make stock.

CHICKEN STOCK

Yield: Approx. 6 gallons.   Portion: 1 cup (approx. 8 ounces).

| INGREDIENTS | 100 PORTIONS | | | ....PORTIONS |
| | WEIGHTS | | AMOUNTS (approx.) | |
	Pounds	Ounces		
Fowl (chicken) fully drawn...	30	....		
Water	....	....	7½ gallons	
Carrots, chopped	....	10	1 pint	
Onions, diced	....	4	¾ cup	
Celery, cubed	....	4	1 cup	
Pepper	....	....	¾ teaspoon	
Salt	....	3	6 tablespoons	

Scrub chicken, including the feet, thoroughly. Disjoint or leave whole.

Add water. Heat slowly to boiling temperature.

Add carrots, onions, celery, pepper, and salt. Let simmer 2 to 3 hours. Strain and cool.

Hold, uncovered, in refrigerator until needed.

NOTE.—Before using, carefully remove layer of hardened fat which helps seal the top.

CONSOMME

Yield: Approx. 6 gallons.   Portion: 1 cup (approx. 8 ounces).

INGREDIENTS	100 PORTIONS			............PORTIONS
	WEIGHTS		AMOUNTS (approx.)	
	Pounds	*Ounces*		
Beef, shin	12	....	....	
Butter or other fat	1	....	1 pint	
Veal bones	12	....	....	
Salt	....	4	½ cup	
Water, cold	....	....	8 gallons	
Turnips, diced	1	....	1½ pints	
Celery, diced	2	....	½ gallon	
Onions, diced	1	8	4½ cups	
Summer savory, dried	....	½	2 tablespoons	
Cloves	....	½	2 tablespoons	
Thyme	....	½	2 tablespoons	
Cinnamon	....	½	2 tablespoons	
Eggs, whole	....	8	5 (1 cup)	
Water, cold	....	....	1 pint	

Cut meat into 1-inch cubes. Fry in ½ the fat, until lightly browned.

Add meat, bones and salt to water. Heat to boiling temperature. Let simmer about 45 minutes to 1 hour.

Fry together turnips, celery and onions in remaining fat. Add vegetables, savory, cloves, thyme and cinnamon to stock. Let simmer 3 hours.

Cool and skim off top layer of fat. Strain.

Add eggs to 1 pint water and beat. Stir into soup. Heat and let simmer about 20 minutes. Strain if desired.

NOTE.—1. Celery tops when available add extra flavor to soup.

2. Make Meat Stock without bones, if not available. Use only 12 pounds meat as specified.

HAM STOCK

Yield: Approx. 6 gallons.

INGREDIENTS	100 PORTIONS			..........PORTIONS
	WEIGHTS		AMOUNTS (approx.)	
	Pounds	*Ounces*		
Ham bones	25	....	....	
Onions, chopped	1	....	1½ pints	
Celery, chopped	1	....	1 quart	
Carrots, chopped	1	8	4½ cups	
Salt	....	4	½ cup	
Pepper	....	....	¾ teaspoon	
Bay leaves	....	....	5	
Water, cold	....	....	8 gallons	

Brown the bones in oven.

Add bones, onions, celery, carrots, salt, pepper and bay leaves to water.

Heat to boiling temperature. Let simmer 6 hours. Strain and cool.

Hold, uncovered, in refrigerator until needed.

NOTE.—1. Use stock as base for soups, gravies and sauces. Fat from the stock may be used for cooking.

2. Before using, carefully remove layer of hardened fat which helps seal the top.

SCOTCH BROTH

Yield: Approx. 6 gallons.　　　　　　　　Portion: 1 cup (approx. 8 ounces).

INGREDIENTS	100 PORTIONS			..........PORTIONS
	WEIGHTS		AMOUNTS (approx.)	
	Pounds	*Ounces*		
Lamb bones and meat	18	....	....	
Water	....	....	7½ gallons	
Salt	....	3	6 tablespoons	
Pepper	....	....	1 teaspoon	
Barley, pearl	1	8	1½ pints	
Carrots, shredded	3	....	1 gallon	
Turnips, shredded	3	....	1 gallon	
Onions, sliced	....	12	1½ pints	
Celery, diced	2	8	2½ quarts	

Wipe bones with damp cloth. Cover with water. Heat slowly to boiling temperature. Let simmer 2 hours. Skim. Remove meat and bones.

Add all other ingredients to stock. Let simmer 1 hour.

Cut meat from bones and chop. Add to soup.

NOTE.—1. The addition of 1½ teaspoons of curry powder makes a pleasing variation.

2. ¾ cup chopped parsley may also be added. Parsley should be added just before serving.

TOMATO STOCK OR BROTH

Yield. Approx. 6 gallons.

Portion: 1 cup (approx. 8 ounces).

INGREDIENTS	100 PORTIONS			----------PORTIONS
	WEIGHTS		AMOUNTS (approx.)	
	Pounds	*Ounces*		
Beef Stock (page 251) or water.	----	----	4½ gallons	
Celery, chopped	2	----	½ gallon	
Onions, chopped	2	----	1½ quarts	
Tomatoes	19	2	3 No. 10 cans (2½ gallons).	
Salt	----	6	¾ cup	
Pepper	----	¼	1 tablespoon	
Sugar	----	8	½ pint	
Butter or other fat, melted	2	----	1 quart	
Flour	----	12	1½ pints	

Heat stock or water to boiling temperature.

Add celery, onions, tomatoes, salt, pepper and sugar. Let simmer 20 minutes or until vegetables are tender.

Blend together fat and flour. Stir into hot mixture and cook until thickened. Strain.

BEEF BROTH WITH BARLEY, NOODLES, SPAGHETTI, OR RICE

Yield. Approx. 6 gallons.   Portion: 1 cup (approx. 8 ounces).

| INGREDIENTS | 100 PORTIONS | | | ....PORTIONS |
| | WEIGHTS | | AMOUNTS (approx.) | |
	Pounds	Ounces		
Celery, diced	1	....	1 quart	
Onions, chopped	1	....	1½ pints	
Barley, noodles, spaghetti, or rice uncooked.	1	8		
Beef Stock (page 251)............	....	....	6 gallons	

Add celery, onions and barley to stock. Heat to boiling temperature.

Let simmer 20 to 30 minutes or until celery is tender.

CREOLE SOUP

Yield: Approx. 6 gallons.   Portion: 1 cup (approx. 8 ounces).

| INGREDIENTS | 100 PORTIONS | | | ....PORTIONS |
| | WEIGHTS | | AMOUNTS (approx.) | |
	Pounds	Ounces		
Beef Stock (page 251), well seasoned.	....	....	5 gallons	
Onions, chopped	1	8	4½ cups	
Peppers, green, chopped	....	6	1½ cups	
Tomatoes	12	12	2 No. 10 cans (6½ quarts).	
Salt	....	2	¼ cup	
Pepper	....	....	1 teaspoon	
Spaghetti, broken into small pieces.	1	8		

Heat stock to boiling temperature. Add onions, green peppers, tomatoes, salt and pepper. Reheat.

Add spaghetti. Let simmer 1 hour. Stir occasionally to prevent spaghetti from sticking to bottom.

CHICKEN GUMBO

Yield: Approx. 6 gallons.   Portion: 1 cup (approx. 8 ounces).

INGREDIENTS	100 PORTIONS			..........PORTIONS
	WEIGHTS		AMOUNTS (approx.)	
	Pounds	Ounces		
Onions, chopped	1	8	4½ cups	
Carrots, chopped	2	....	1½ quarts	
Butter or chicken fat	....	4	½ cup	
Chicken Stock (page 252)........	....	....	5½ gallons	
Rice, uncooked, washed...........	1	4	1¼ pints	
Tomatoes	6	6	1 No. 10 can (3¼ quarts).	
Okra	6	3	1 No. 10 can (3¼ quarts).	
Salt	....	2	¼ cup	
Pepper	....	¼	¾ tablespoon	

Fry onions and carrots in fat until lightly browned.

Heat stock to boiling temperature.

Add onions, carrots, rice, tomatoes, okra, salt, and pepper to stock.

Let simmer 1½ hours.

CHICKEN SOUP WITH NOODLES OR RICE

Yield: Approx. 6 gallons.   Portion: 1 cup (approx. 8 ounces).

INGREDIENTS	100 PORTIONS			..........PORTIONS
	WEIGHTS		AMOUNTS (approx.)	
	Pounds	Ounces		
Chicken Stock (page 252), well seasoned.	....	....	6½ to 7 gallons	
Noodles, fine .... OR	....	10	1½ quarts	
Rice, uncooked, washed..........	1	8	1½ pints	

Heat strained chicken stock to boiling temperature. Add noodles or rice. Let simmer 1 hour.

Stir frequently to prevent noodles or rice from sticking to bottom.

MULLIGATAWNY SOUP

Yield: Approx. 6 gallons.   Portion: 1 cup (approx. 8 ounces).

INGREDIENTS	100 PORTIONS			............PORTIONS
	WEIGHTS		AMOUNTS (approx)	
	Pounds	*Ounces*		
Onions, chopped	....	12	2¼ cups	
Carrots, diced	1	....	1½ pints	
Celery, diced	1	....	1 quart	
Peppers, green, chopped	1	4	1¼ quarts	
Apples, sliced	1	8	1½ quarts	
Butter or other fat	1	....	1 pint	
Flour	....	12	1½ pints	
Chicken Stock (page 252)	....	....	5¾ gallons	
Tomatoes	6	6	1 No. 10 can (3¼ quarts).	
Curry powder	....	1	1½ tablespoons	
Cloves, ground	....	....	1 teaspoon	
Salt	....	1	2 tablespoons	
Pepper	....	....	2 teaspoons	

Fry together onions, carrots, celery, peppers and apples until lightly browned. Remove from fat.

Blend together fat and flour. Stir into chicken stock.

Add fried vegetables, apples, tomatoes and seasonings.

Heat and let simmer 1 hour.

VEGETABLE SOUP

Yield: Approx. 6 gallons.   Portion: 1 cup (approx. 8 ounces).

| INGREDIENTS | 100 PORTIONS | | ....PORTIONS |
| | WEIGHTS | AMOUNTS (approx.) | |
	Pounds / Ounces		
Carrots, chopped	2 / 8	½ gallon	
Celery, chopped	1 / 8	1½ quarts	
Onions, chopped	1 /	1½ pints	
Cabbage, chopped	1 / 4	1¼ quarts	
Tomatoes	12 / 12	2 No. 10 cans (6½ quarts).	
Beef Stock (page 251)	.... /	5 gallons	
Salt	.... / 4	½ cup	
Pepper	.... /	1 teaspoon	
Potatoes, cooked, cubed	3 /	½ gallon	
Peas	6 / 10	1 No. 10 can (3¼ quarts).	

Add carrots, celery, onions, cabbage and tomatoes to stock.

Heat to boiling temperature. Let simmer about 30 minutes or until carrots are tender.

Before serving, add salt, pepper, potatoes and peas. Reheat.

NOTE.—Parsley may be used as garnish, if desired.

TOMATO, BARLEY, MACARONI, NOODLE, OR RICE SOUP

Yield: Approx. 6 gallons.   Portion: 1 cup (approx. 8 ounces).

| INGREDIENTS | 100 PORTIONS | | ....PORTIONS |
| | WEIGHTS | AMOUNTS (approx.) | |
	Pounds / Ounces		
Tomato Stock (page 255)	.... /	6 gallons	
Barley, macaroni, noodles or rice, uncooked.	1 / 8		

Heat stock to boiling temperature.
Stir in barley, macaroni, noodles or rice.

Heat to boiling temperature. Let simmer about 20 to 30 minutes or until cereal is tender.

KNICKERBOCKER BEAN SOUP

Yield: Approx. 6 gallons.

Portion: 1 cup (approx. 8 ounces).

INGREDIENTS	100 PORTIONS			............Portions
	WEIGHTS		AMOUNTS (approx.)	
	Pounds	*Ounces*		
Beans, white, dried	7	....	1 gallon	
Water, cold	....	....	To cover	
Water, boiling	....	....	4 gallons	
Salt pork, cubed	....	8	½ pint	
Carrots, chopped	....	4	¾ cup	
Onions, chopped	....	12	2½ cups	
Meat Stock (page 251)	....	....	2¾ gallons	
Potatoes, diced	5	8	3½ quarts	
Bacon, diced	....	8	½ pint	
Tomatoes	6	6	1 No. 10 can (3¼ quarts).	
Salt	....	2	¼ cup	
Pepper	....	¼	¾ tablespoon	

Pick over, wash and soak beans 2 to 3 hours. Do not drain.

Combine with boiling water, salt pork, carrots and half the onions. Heat to boiling temperature. Cook about 3 hours or until beans are tender.

Add stock and potatoes. Cook about 30 minutes or until potatoes are tender.

Fry together bacon and remaining onions about 3 minutes, or until lightly browned.

Add tomatoes, salt and pepper.

Combine all ingredients. Reheat.

BEAN SOUP
(Using dehydrated bean soup and powdered bouillon)

Yield: Approx. 6 gallons.

Portion: 1 cup (approx. 8 ounces).

INGREDIENTS	100 PORTIONS			...........Portions
	WEIGHTS		AMOUNTS (approx.)	
	Pounds	*Ounces*		
Bouillon, powdered	---	12	1½ pints	
Water, boiling	---		6 gallons	
Bean soup, dehydrated	6		1 gallon	

Stir powdered bouillon into boiling water until completely dissolved.

Add bean soup, gradually, to stock, stirring constantly.

Heat to boiling temperature.

Variation

Pea Soup

Use 6 pounds (1 gallon) dehydrated pea soup in place of dehydrated bean soup.

NOTE.—Any bouillon type product may be used to make stock.

BEAN SOUP

Yield: Approx. 6 gallons.

Portion: 1 cup (approx. 8 ounces).

| INGREDIENTS | 100 PORTIONS | | ...PORTIONS |
| | WEIGHTS | AMOUNTS (approx.) | |
	Pounds	Ounces		
Beans, white, dried	5	8	3¼ quarts	
Water, cold	....	....	To cover	
Ham Stock (page 254)	....	....	5 gallons	
Onions, chopped	1	....	1½ pints	
Ham bones	....	....	8	
Cloves, whole	....	....	1 teaspoon	
Flour	....	8	1 pint	
Water, cold	....	....	1 quart	
Pepper	....	....	2 teaspoons	
Salt, if needed	....	4	½ cup	

Pick over, wash and soak beans, in water to cover, 2 to 3 hours.

Add ham stock, onions, bones and cloves. Heat to boiling temperature. Let simmer 2 to 3 hours. Remove bones.

Blend together flour and water to a smooth paste. Stir into soup. Add pepper, and salt if needed. Reheat to boiling temperature.

NOTE.—1. Ham bones may be omitted.

2. Flour may be omitted. If omitted, the soup must be stirred while serving, as beans will settle to bottom of the container upon standing.

Variation

Bean Soup with Tomatoes

Follow recipe for Bean Soup and add 1 No. 10 can (3¼ quarts) tomatoes to ham stock before simmering.

LENTIL SOUP

Yield: Approx. 6 gallons.   Portion: 1 cup (approx. 8 ounces).

INGREDIENTS	100 PORTIONS			......Portions
	WEIGHTS		AMOUNTS (approx.)	
	Pounds	*Ounces*		
Lentils	8	8	1¼ gallons	
Water, cold	....	....	To cover	
Ham Stock (page 254)	....	....	6 gallons	
Onions, diced	1	8	4½ cups	
Celery, cubed	1	8	1½ quarts	
Carrots, diced	1	8	4½ cups	
Sugar	....	¾	1½ tablespoons	
Salt	....	2	¼ cup	
Pepper	....	....	1½ teaspoons	
Mustard	....	....	1½ teaspoons	
Nutmeg, ground	....	....	1½ teaspoons	
Worcestershire sauce	....	....	1½ teaspoons	
Fat, melted	....	10	1¼ cups	
Flour	....	12	1½ pints	

Pick over and wash lentils. Cover with cold water. Soak 6 to 8 hours. Drain.

Add ham stock, onions, celery, carrots, sugar, salt, pepper, mustard and nutmeg. Heat to boiling temperature.

Let simmer 2 hours or until lentils are very soft. Press through sieve. Add Worcestershire sauce.

Blend together fat and flour to a smooth paste. Stir into lentil puree.

Let simmer about 20 minutes, stirring frequently.

YELLOW SPLIT PEA SOUP

Yield: Approx. 6 gallons.

Portion: 1 cup (approx. 8 ounces).

INGREDIENTS	100 PORTIONS			............PORTIONS
	WEIGHTS		AMOUNTS (approx.)	
	Pounds	*Ounces*		
Peas, yellow split	5	8	¾ gallon	
Ham Stock (page 254)	----	----	6 gallons	
Onions, chopped	6	---	4½ quarts	
Ham bones	....	---	8	
Salt, if needed	....	4	½ cup	
Pepper	....	....	2 teaspoons	
Cloves, whole	....	....	1 teaspoon	
Flour	....	8	1 pint	
Water, cold	....	....	1 quart	

Pick over, wash and soak peas 3 to 4 hours in ham stock. Do *not* drain.

Add onions, ham bones, salt, if needed, pepper and cloves. Heat to boiling temperature. Let simmer about 2 hours or until peas are tender.

Remove bones.

Blend together flour and water to a smooth paste. Stir into soup. Heat to boiling temperature.

FRENCH ONION SOUP

Yield: Approx. 6 gallons.   Portion: 1 cup (approx. 8 ounces).

INGREDIENTS	100 PORTIONS			............PORTIONS
	WEIGHTS		AMOUNTS (approx.)	
	Pounds	Ounces		
Meat Stock (page 251)	....	....	6 gallons	
Onions, thinly sliced	20	....		
Fat	2	....	1 quart	
Flour	....	8	1¾ cups	
Worcestershire sauce	....	....	½ cup	
Salt	....	4	½ cup	
Pepper, black	....	....	2 teaspoons	
Toast slices, rye or white.......	....	....	100	
Cheese, grated	....	....	2½ cups	

Heat stock to boiling temperature.

Fry onions in fat until lightly browned. Stir in flour. Add to stock. Add Worcestershire sauce, salt and pepper. Simmer 10 minutes.

Place one slice of toast in each soup bowl. Sprinkle with cheese. Fill with hot soup.

ONION SOUP
(Using dehydrated onions)

Yield: Approx. 6 gallons.   Portion: 1 cup (approx. 8 ounces).

INGREDIENTS	100 PORTIONS			............PORTIONS
	WEIGHTS		AMOUNTS (approx.)	
	Pounds	Ounces		
Onions, dehydrated	1	2	1¾ quarts	
Water (for onions).................	8	....	1 gallon	
Fat	2	....	1 quart	
Flour	2	....	1⅔ quarts	
Bouillon cubes	....	....	70	
Water, hot (for stock).............	....	....	5 gallons	
Salt	....	3	6 tablespoons	

Stir onions into water and let soak 60 minutes. Cover.

Heat to boiling temperature. Let simmer 15 to 20 minutes or until tender. Drain and reserve liquid.

Heat fat to frying temperature. Add reconstituted onions and cook until onions are lightly browned. Stir frequently.

Add flour gradually to fried onions and stir until flour is well distributed.

Dissolve bouillon cubes in water. Add reserved liquid.

Add part of hot stock to thin out the onion-flour paste. Combine thinned paste with remainder of the stock.

Add salt and let simmer 60 minutes.

CHICKEN RICE SOUP

Yield: Approx. 6 gallons.

Portion: 1 cup (approx. 8 ounces).

INGREDIENTS	100 PORTIONS			............PORTIONS
	WEIGHTS		AMOUNTS (approx.)	
	Pounds	Ounces		
Onions, chopped	2	12	½ gallon	
Celery, diced	2	....	½ gallon	
Rice, uncooked, washed	1	8	1½ pints	
Chicken Stock (page 252)	....	....	7 gallons	
Chicken fat, melted	1	8	1½ pints	
Flour	....	12	1½ pints	
Salt	....	4	½ cup	
Pepper	....	¼	¾ tablespoon	
Chicken, cooked, diced	2	8	½ gallon	

Add onions, celery and rice to stock.

Heat to boiling temperature. Let simmer 20 to 30 minutes or until rice is cooked.

Blend together fat and flour. Stir into soup.

Add salt, pepper and chicken. Cook 15 minutes or until thickened.

CREAM OF CHICKEN SOUP

Yield: Approx. 6 gallons.   Portion: 1 cup (approx. 8 ounces).

| INGREDIENTS | 100 PORTIONS | | | ....PORTIONS |
| | WEIGHTS | | AMOUNTS (approx.) | |
	Pounds	Ounces		
Chicken Stock (page 252), well seasoned.	....	....	3 gallons	
Chicken fat or butter, melted.	....	12	¾ pint	
Flour	....	12	1½ pints	
Milk, liquid, hot.	....	....	3 gallons	

Heat chicken stock to boiling temperature.
Blend together fat and flour. Stir into stock.
Let simmer 20 minutes, stirring frequently.
Add milk 10 minutes before serving.

NOTE.—4½ ounces (¾ pint) of finely chopped parsley or chives may be added just before serving.

VEGETABLE CREAM SOUPS
(Basic Recipe for Cream Soups)

Yield: Approx. 6 gallons.   Portion: 1 cup (approx. 8 ounces).

| INGREDIENTS | 100 PORTIONS | | | ....PORTIONS |
| | WEIGHTS | | AMOUNTS (approx.) | |
	Pounds	Ounces		
Milk, liquid	....	....	4 gallons	
Butter or other fat	1	8	1½ pints	
Onions, chopped	....	4	¾ cup	
Flour	....	12	1½ pints	
Salt	....	2	¼ cup	
Pepper	....	....	1 teaspoon	
Vegetables, cooked	....	....	2 gallons	

Heat milk to boiling temperature. Do *not* boil.

Melt fat, preferably part butter. Add onions. Cook about 10 minutes or until clear and tender.

Blend flour with fat. Stir into milk. Add onions.

Continue cooking about 20 minutes, stirring frequently until slightly thickened.

Add salt, pepper and vegetables, diced or pureed. Reheat before serving.

NOTE.—One or several kinds of vegetables may be used.

CREAM OF ASPARAGUS SOUP

Yield: Approx. 6 gallons.

Portion: 1 cup (approx. 8 ounces).

INGREDIENTS	100 PORTIONS			............PORTIONS
	WEIGHTS		AMOUNTS (approx.)	
	Pounds	*Ounces*		
Asparagus cuts, canned............	26	6	4 No. 10 cans (3¼ gallons).	
Beef Stock (page 251) or water.	....	....	1½ gallons	
Onions, chopped	....	8	1½ cups	
Butter or other fat............	1	...	1 pint	
Flour	1	...	1 quart	
Salt	....	2	¼ cup	
Pepper	....	....	½ teaspoon	
Nutmeg	....	....	½ teaspoon	
Milk, liquid, hot............	....	....	1¼ gallons	

Combine asparagus, including liquid from can, and stock or water. Heat to boiling temperature. Press through sieve, if desired.

Cook onions in fat until tender. Stir in flour, salt, pepper and nutmeg.

Add to hot milk, stirring until thoroughly mixed. Let simmer until thickened.

Combine asparagus and milk mixture just before serving.

CREAM OF CELERY SOUP

Yield: Approx. 6 gallons. Portion: 1 cup (approx. 8 ounces).

| INGREDIENTS | 100 PORTIONS | | ....PORTIONS |
| | WEIGHTS | AMOUNTS (approx.) | |
	Pounds	Ounces		
Celery, finely diced....................	12	....	3 gallons	
Beef Stock (page 251) or water, boiling.	....	....	1½ gallons	
Milk, liquid, hot....................	....	....	4 gallons	
Onions, chopped	....	12	2¼ cups	
Fat	1	8	1½ pints	
Flour	1	....	1 quart	
Salt	....	3	6 tablespoons	
Pepper	....	....	¾ teaspoon	

Cook celery in boiling stock or water about 35 minutes or until tender. Add milk.

Fry onions in fat until clear and stir in the flour. Stir into celery mixture.

Add salt and pepper. Let simmer 20 minutes.

CREAM OF CORN SOUP

Yield: Approx. 6 gallons. Portion: 1 cup (approx. 8 ounces).

| INGREDIENTS | 100 PORTIONS | | ....PORTIONS |
| | WEIGHTS | AMOUNTS (approx.) | |
	Pounds	Ounces		
Water	....	....	1 gallon	
Corn, cream style....................	12	8	10 No. 2 cans (1½ gallons).	
Celery, chopped	....	12	1½ pints	
Onions, chopped	2	....	1½ quarts	
Butter or other fat, melted....	1	....	1 pint	
Flour	....	8	1 pint	
Salt	....	4	½ cup	
Pepper	....	....	1 teaspoon	
Milk, liquid, hot....................	....	....	3½ gallons	

Heat water to boiling temperature. Add corn, celery and onions. Let simmer about 20 minutes.

Blend together fat and flour. Stir into boiling mixture and cook until slightly thickened, stirring frequently. Add pepper.

Add salt and stir the milk into soup mixture just before serving.

CREAM OF CARROT, PEA, AND CELERY SOUP

Yield: Approx. 6 gallons.

Portion: 1 cup (approx. 8 ounces).

INGREDIENTS	100 PORTIONS		............PORTIONS
	WEIGHTS	AMOUNTS (approx.)	
	Pounds	Ounces		
Celery, leaves and stalks, chopped.	10	....	2½ gallons	
Carrots, diced	3	....	2¼ quarts	
Onions, chopped..................	1	....	1½ pints	
Water, boiling	....	....	1 gallon	
Peas	6	10	1 No. 10 can (3¼ quarts).	
Butter or other fat, melted...	2	....	1 quart	
Flour	....	12	1½ pints	
Salt	....	4	½ cup	
Pepper	....	....	1 teaspoon	
Milk, liquid, hot..................	....	....	3½ gallons	

Add celery, carrots and onions to boiling water. Cook about 30 minutes or until tender. Add peas.

Blend together fat and flour. Stir into soup mixture and cook until slightly thickened, stirring frequently.

Add salt and pepper. Stir in the milk just before serving.

CREAM OF GREEN PEA SOUP

Yield: Approx. 6 gallons.   Portion: 1 cup (approx. 8 ounces).

| INGREDIENTS | 100 PORTIONS | | | ......Portions |
| | WEIGHTS | | AMOUNTS (approx.) | |
	Pounds	*Ounces*		
Beef Stock (page 251) or water.	....	....	2 gallons	
Peas, fresh, E.P., or frozen	16	....	2½ gallons	
Milk, liquid	....	....	2½ gallons	
Onions, chopped	....	10	1 pint	
Butter or other fat	1	....	1 pint	
Flour	1	....	1 quart	
Salt	....	2½	5 tablespoons	
Pepper	....	....	½ teaspoon	

Heat stock or water to boiling temperature. Add peas. Cook 15 to 20 minutes or until tender.

Press through sieve. Add milk to pureed peas. Let simmer 10 minutes.

Fry onions in fat until lightly browned. Stir in flour. Add to peas and milk. Stir well.

Add salt and pepper. Cook until slightly thickened.

NOTE.—3 No. 10 cans (2½ gallons) of peas, with liquid, may be used in place of 2½ gallons fresh or frozen peas.

CREAM OF POTATO SOUP WITH BACON

Yield: Approx. 6 gallons.   Portion: 1 cup (approx. 8 ounces).

| INGREDIENTS | 100 PORTIONS | | | ......Portions |
| | WEIGHTS | | AMOUNTS (approx.) | |
	Pounds	*Ounces*		
Potatoes, diced	20	....	3 gallons	
Water	....	....	3 gallons	
Bacon, diced small	1	8	1½ pints	
Onions, chopped	1	....	1½ pints	
Flour	....	6	1½ cups	
Celery salt	....	2	¼ cup	
Pepper	....	....	1 teaspoon	
Salt	....	4	½ cup	
Milk, liquid, hot	....	....	3 gallons	

Cook potatoes in water about 20 to 30 minutes or until tender. Drain and reserve cooking water.

Press potatoes through sieve and add to cooking water.

Fry bacon until crisp. Remove from fat.

Fry onions in bacon fat about 3 minutes until lightly browned. Add flour and blend.

Stir into potato puree. Cook until thickened, stirring occasionally.

Add bacon, celery salt and pepper to soup mixture.

Add salt and stir the milk into soup mixture just before serving.

CREAM OF GREEN SPLIT PEA SOUP

Yield: Approx. 6 gallons.   Portion: 1 cup (approx. 8 ounces).

INGREDIENTS	100 PORTIONS			..........PORTIONS
	WEIGHTS		AMOUNTS (approx.)	
	Pounds	*Ounces*		
Peas, green split	6	....	3¼ quarts	
Water	....	....	1½ gallons	
Celery leaves	....	1	¼ cup	
Onions, chopped	....	8	1½ cups	
Butter or other fat, melted	....	8	½ pint	
Flour	....	4	½ pint	
Salt	....	3	6 tablespoons	
Pepper	....	....	2 teaspoons	
Milk, liquid, hot	....	....	5½ gallons	

Sort and wash peas thoroughly. Soak in cold water 6 to 8 hours. Do *not* drain.

Add celery leaves and onions. Heat to boiling temperature. Cook about 1 hour or until peas are tender.

Press celery, onions and peas through sieve.

Return to water in which they were cooked.

Blend together fat and flour. Stir into pureed mixture and cook until slightly thickened, stirring frequently.

Add salt and pepper. Stir in the milk just before serving.

CREAM OF TOMATO SOUP

Yield: Approx. 6 gallons.　　　　　　　　　Portion: 1 cup (approx. 8 ounces).

INGREDIENTS	100 PORTIONS			............PORTIONS
	WEIGHTS		AMOUNTS (approx.)	
	Pounds	*Ounces*		
Tomatoes	25	8	4 No. 10 cans (3¼ gallons).	
Celery tops	....	8	1 pint	
Onions, chopped	....	8	¾ pint	
Mixed spices	....	....	2 teaspoons	
Salt	....	4	½ cup	
Sugar	....	8	1 cup	
Flour	....	8	1 pint	
Water, cold	....	....	1 quart	
Butter or other fat	....	8	½ pint	
Soda	....	1	2 tablespoons	
Milk, liquid, hot	....	....	3 gallons	

Combine tomatoes, celery tops, onions, mixed spices, salt and sugar.

Heat to boiling temperature. Let simmer 10 minutes. Strain.

Blend flour and water to a smooth paste. Stir into strained mixture and let simmer until slightly thickened.

Add butter and soda and stir well.

Add hot milk, stirring constantly. Heat to simmering temperature. Do not boil. Serve immediately.

CORN CHOWDER

Yield: Approx. 6 gallons.   Portion: 1 cup (approx. 8 ounces).

INGREDIENTS	100 PORTIONS		............PORTIONS
	WEIGHTS	AMOUNTS (approx.)	
	Pounds	*Ounces*		
Water	....	....	½ gallon	....
Onions, chopped	1	....	1½ pints	....
Peppers, green, chopped..........	....	8	1 pint	....
Corn, cream style.....................	18	12	15 No. 2 cans (2½ gallons).	....
Milk, liquid	....	....	3½ gallons	....
Salt	....	4	½ cup	....
Pepper	....	....	1 teaspoon	....

Heat water to boiling temperature. Add onions and peppers. Cook about 30 minutes or until tender.

Combine corn, milk, salt and pepper. Heat thoroughly. Add to onions, green peppers and water. Let simmer 40 minutes.

NOTE.—Chopped parsley or 18 hard-cooked eggs, sliced may be used as garnish.

CORN AND TOMATO CHOWDER

Yield: Approx. 6 gallons.   Portion: 1 cup (approx. 8 ounces).

INGREDIENTS	100 PORTIONS		............PORTIONS
	WEIGHTS	AMOUNTS (approx.)	
	Pounds	*Ounces*		
Milk, liquid	....	....	2 gallons	....
Sugar	....	1½	3 tablespoons	....
Pepper	....	....	1 teaspoon	....
Corn, cream style.....................	18	12	15 No. 2 cans (2½ gallons).	....
Onions, diced	....	12	1 pint	....
Tomatoes	19	2	3 No. 10 cans (9¾ quarts).	....
Salt	....	4	½ cup	....

Combine milk, sugar, pepper, corn and onions. Heat to boiling temperature. Let simmer 45 minutes.

Heat tomatoes to boiling temperature. Add salt. Combine with corn mixture just before serving.

CLAM CHOWDER—BOSTON STYLE

Yield: Approx. 6 gallons.   Portion: 1 cup (approx. 8 ounces).

INGREDIENTS	100 PORTIONS		......PORTIONS
	WEIGHTS	AMOUNTS (approx.)	
	Pounds	Ounces		
Celery, diced	2	8	2½ quarts	
Onions, chopped	2	8	½ gallon	
Potatoes, cubed	3	8	½ gallon	
Salt	....	2	¼ cùp	
Water, boiling	....	....	1½ gallons	
Clams, cooked and chopped.....	8	....	2 gallons	
Clam liquor, strained...............	....	....	¾ gallon	
Milk, liquid	....	....	2½ gallons	
Salt	....	1½	3 tablespoons	
Pepper	....	....	1 teaspoon	
Fat, melted	1	....	1 pint	
Flour	1	....	1 quart	

Combine celery, onions and potatoes. Add salt and vegetables to water. Cook about 20 minutes or until tender.

Add clams, clam liquor, milk, salt and pepper. Heat slowly to boiling temperature.

Blend fat and flour to a smooth paste. Stir into hot soup.

Cook about 15 minutes or until soup is smooth and slightly thickened.

MANHATTAN CLAM CHOWDER

Yield: Approx. 6 gallons.   Portion: 1 cup (approx. 8 ounces).

INGREDIENTS	100 PORTIONS			..........PORTIONS
	WEIGHTS		AMOUNTS (approx.)	
	Pounds	Ounces		
Fish, fresh (cod or haddock)	3	....		
Water, cold	....	....	3 gallons	
Bacon trimmings or salt pork, cubed.	....	12		
Onions, sliced	....	12	1 pint	
Celery, diced	....	12	1½ pints	
Potatoes, cubed	5	....	¾ gallon	
Tomatoes	12	12	2 No. 10 cans (1½ gallons).	
Clams (large) chopped and liquor.	....	....	60 (½ gallon)	
Worcestershire sauce	....	4	½ cup	
Paprika	....	....	1 teaspoon	
Pepper	....	½	1¾ tablespoons	
Parsley, chopped	....	3	½ pint	
Thyme	....	....	1 teaspoon	

Clean fish. Place fish in water. Heat to boiling temperature and let simmer 15 minutes.

Remove and flake. Return flaked fish to stock.

Fry bacon or salt pork until crisp. Add onions. Fry until lightly browned.

Add pork, onions, celery, potatoes, fish and stock. Let simmer 15 minutes.

Add tomatoes, clams, liquor and seasonings. Reheat.

NOTE.—1. Stir the chowder, while serving, to prevent clams and vegetables from settling to bottom.

2. Settling may also be prevented by blending together 6 ounces (¾ cup) butter or bacon fat and 5 ounces (½ pint) flour and stirring it into soup mixture with the clams.

3. 1 No. 10 can (¾ gallon) tomato juice may be used in place of 1 No. 10 can tomatoes.

FISH CHOWDER

Yield: Approx. 6 gallons.   Portion: 1 cup (approx. 8 ounces).

INGREDIENTS	100 PORTIONS			............PORTIONS
	WEIGHTS		AMOUNTS (approx.)	
	Pounds	Ounces		
Salt pork, diced....................	1	8	1 quart	
Onions, sliced	2	....	½ gallon	
Potatoes, sliced or diced........	6	8	1 gallon	
Water, boiling	....	....	2¼ gallons	
Haddock, boned and skinned.	15	....	....	
Salt	....	4	½ cup	
Pepper	....	....	1½ teaspoons	
Milk, liquid	....	....	2 gallons	

Fry salt pork until crisp. Remove fried pork from the fat. Drain.

Fry onions in pork fat until lightly browned. Add onions and potatoes to water. Heat to boiling temperature. Cook 10 minutes.

Add fish and continue cooking until fish can be easily separated into large pieces.

Stir in salt, pepper and milk. Let simmer 15 minutes.

Add crisp pork cubes just before serving.

NOTE.—Any other non-fatty fish similar to haddock such as cod, hake and pollock may be used.

OYSTER STEW

Yield: Approx. 6 gallons.   Portion: 1 cup (approx. 8 ounces).

INGREDIENTS	100 PORTIONS			............PORTIONS
	WEIGHTS		AMOUNTS (approx.)	
	Pounds	Ounces		
Oysters, with liquor....................	....	....	1¼ gallons	
Butter, melted	1	4	2¼ cups	
Salt	...	4	½ cup	
Pepper	....	....	¾ teaspoon	
Worcestershire sauce	....	....	2 teaspoons	
Milk, liquid	....	....	4¾ gallons	

Heat oysters in oyster liquor and melted butter until edges curl. Add salt, pepper and Worcestershire sauce.

Heat milk to boiling temperature. Do *not* boil.

Add milk to oysters about 10 minutes before serving.

OYSTER BISQUE

Yield: Approx. 6 gallons.

Portion: 1 cup (approx. 8 ounces).

INGREDIENTS	100 PORTIONS			............PORTIONS
	WEIGHTS		AMOUNTS (approx.)	
	Pounds	Ounces		
Onions, chopped	....	4	¾ cup	
Celery, chopped	1	8	1½ quarts	
Water	....	....	½ gallon	
Oysters, with liquor............	....	....	1 gallon	
Butter, melted	2	8	1¼ quarts	
Flour	1	4	1¼ quarts	
Pepper	....	¼	¾ tablespoon	
Salt	....	3	6 tablespoons	
Milk, liquid	....	....	5 gallons	

Cook onions and celery in water about 20 minutes or until tender.

Heat oysters, in oyster liquor, until edges begin to curl. Remove oysters and chop fine.

Blend together butter and flour, using part of oyster liquor for making paste. Stir into oyster liquor until slightly thickened.

Add onions, celery, pepper and oysters.

Heat milk to boiling temperature. Do *not* boil.

Add salt to oyster mixture and combine with milk. Serve immediately.

CROUTONS

Cut day-old bread in ½-inch thick slices. Cut into ½-inch strips, then into cubes.

Arrange layer of cubes on bottom of bun pan.

Bake in slow oven (300°F.) until golden brown. Turn occasionally to brown evenly.

NOTE—Serve as a garnish for soups or ingredient in stewed tomatoes.

Vegetables

Vegetables enhance a meal in many ways. They insure variety and interest, add color and flavor and increase the nutritive value of the meal. It is important that they be included daily in the Navy menu.

Their contribution to a meal, however, is greatly affected by the manner of handling and cooking.

Vegetables are purchased by the Navy in the following forms: canned, dehydrated, quick-frozen and fresh.

CANNED VEGETABLES

Canned vegetables have been cooked in the container at the cannery and need only to be reheated to boiling temperature just before serving. This relatively short period of preparation should be given careful consideration when planning the meals in order to avoid overcooking the vegetables. Overcooking not only reduces the food value but detracts from the appearance and flavor.

Retain the liquid from canned vegetables for use in soups, sauces and gravies.

DEHYDRATED VEGETABLES

Most dehydrated vegetables need to be refreshened or reconstituted by soaking in cold water before cooking. The water in which they have been soaked should be used for cooking in order to retain the soluble vitamins.

Reconstituted vegetables should be cooked in as little water as possible until just tender, in the same manner as fresh vegetables.

In the process of dehydration some of the delicate flavors and odors characteristic of the fresh vegetable may have been reduced or lost. Therefore, it may be necessary to use additional seasonings.

Individual recipes with full directions for reconstituting and cooking the dehydrated vegetables now issued for Navy use are included in this section. These directions should be carefully followed. See page 19 for more information on dehydrated foods.

QUICK-FROZEN VEGETABLES

Quick-frozen vegetables have the appearance and flavor of fresh vegetables. These vegetables are ready for cooking as they have been thoroughly cleaned and trimmed.

Quick-frozen vegetables take less time to prepare than fresh vegetables.

Follow carefully the directions for defrosting and cooking, given in a Table in this section (page 284) or as specified on the individual container, and see page 22 for additional information on quick-frozen foods.

FRESH VEGETABLES

Preparation for Cooking

Select Vegetables Uniform in Size: This allows all the vegetables to be cooked to the same degree of doneness in the same length of time.

Peel Vegetables Carefully in Order to Prevent Waste: Much of the nutritive value of the vegetable lies close to the peel.

Wash Thoroughly: Use a vegetable brush to clean celery, carrots, beets and potatoes.

Soak asparagus, broccoli, cauliflower, brussels sprouts and French artichokes in salted, cold water (1 tablespoon per 1 quart) about 30 to 60 minutes to eliminate worms and insects.

Wash spinach, kale, beet tops and similar greens in cold water several times to remove dirt and sand particles. Lift the greens from the water rather than "run the water off" the greens.

Keep in Cool Place until Time to Cook: Vegetables should be kept in a cool storage room until ready to prepare for cooking.

If vegetables are wilted they can be crisped and freshened by placing them in ice cold water or between layers of crushed ice. When freshened they should be covered with a clean damp cloth and placed in a cool storage room until ready to use.

Long Soaking and Warm Temperatures Cause Loss of Vitamins: Valuable vitamins and minerals are lost when vegetables are soaked too long or when allowed to remain in warm temperatures for several hours. Therefore, the length of time intervening between preparation and cooking should be short.

Cooking: Cook a small amount at one time. Reduce cooking time to a minimum. Overcooked vegetables are not as attractive, palatable or nutritious as those cooked for the proper length of time.

Use as little water as possible. Follow recipe directions for each individual recipe. Have water salted and boiling when adding vegetables.

Cook Vegetable with the Peel on When Possible: This is particularly desirable for potatoes.

Serve the Vegetable as Soon as it is Done: Long standing on a steam table causes loss of flavor and vitamins.

Retain Vegetable Cooking Water: Use cooking water in soups, sauces and gravies in place of all or part of water.

Add melted butter or sauce to vegetables just before serving.

Conserve Texture, Flavor and Appearance: Use vegetables which are in good condition.

Cook a small amount at one time.

Cook until just tender.

Serve immediately after cooking.

Taste before serving and add salt or extra seasoning if necessary. Avoid over-seasoning.

Consult and follow directions given in time-tables and recipes if perfect results are to be obtained.

The *Fresh Vegetable Guide* (page 280) indicates the amounts of the common fresh vegetables required for 100 portions.

The percentage-waste figures for each vegetable are average based on vegetables in good condition. If vegetables have become wilted due to long transportation, poor handling and storage, the waste is greater.

Weights of vegetables and types of pack will vary with the season of the year, the quality of the vegetables, and the section of the country from which they are shipped. All vegetables should *always be purchased by the pound.*

Weights of portions are for cooked vegetables. Weights of portions of baked vegetables served whole, such as potatoes, will depend upon the size and uniformity of the individual units.

FRESH VEGETABLE GUIDE

Percentage Waste, Portion, Yield and Weight (approx.)

VEGETABLE	CONTAINER	NET WEIGHT AS PURCHASED (A.P.)	WEIGHT EDIBLE PORTION (E.P.)	WASTE IN PREPARATION	WEIGHT 1 PORTION (E.P.)	EDIBLE PORTIONS PER LB. (E.P.)	EDIBLE PORTIONS PER LB. (A.P.)	NO. LBS. PER 100 PORTIONS AS PURCHASED (A.P.)
		Pounds	Pounds	Percent	Ounces			
Asparagus	crate	24	18	25	4½	3½	2.5	38
Beans, green or wax	hamper	32	28.8	10	3½	4½	4	25
Beans, lima	hamper	45	18	60	3½–4	4–4½	...	60
Beets	basket or sack	50	37.5	25	3½	4½	3	33
Broccoli	crate	45	21.15	53	3	4½–5	2	45
Brussels sprouts	drum	30	23.1	23	3½	4–4½	3	30
Cabbage, new	crate	75	56.25	25	Leaf, 3½	4½	3	29
Cabbage, old	crate or sack	50	35	30	Wedge, 3½	4½	3	31
Carrots	crate or sack	50	37	26	3½	4½	3	30
Cauliflower	crate	40	18	55	3½	4½	2	50
Celery	crate	72–92	45.36–57.96	37	3½	4½	3	34
Corn	crate or sack (100 ears)	55	33	40	5–6	...	2	50
Eggplant	crate	50	34	32	3	5	3.5	28
Lettuce	crate	60	41.40	31	2½	6	...	20
Onions, dry	sack	50	47	6	4	4	3.5	28
Parsnips	basket or sack	45	35	22	3½–4	4½	3	30
Peas	hamper	30	13.5	55	4	4	1.5	60
Peppers, green	crate	40	28.80	23	2½	6	...	20
Potatoes, white	sack or crate	100	84	16	5–6	3	2	44
Potatoes, sweet	crate	50	43	14	4–4½	4	3	30
Rutabagas	sack	50	38	25	4–5	4	3	33
Spinach	basket	18	14.76	18	4–4½	4	3	32
Squash, summer	crate or hamper	40	35.20	12	3½–4	4½	4	26
Squash, winter	crate or sack	...	...	34	Mashed,3½	4½	3	33
Swiss chard	basket	20	17	14	4	4	3	30
Tomatoes	lug	30	29	2	Grilled, 4–5	4	3	30
Turnips	basket or crate	50	43.5	13	4	4	3	30

WEIGHTS AND YIELDS OF CANNED VEGETABLES

PRODUCT—STYLE	SIZE OF CAN	NET WEIGHT PER CAN	WEIGHT OF PORTION OUNCES	AVERAGE NO. PORTIONS PER CAN	APPROX. NO. CANS FOR 100 PORTIONS
Asparagus, spears or stalks	No. 2	1 lb. 3 oz.	3½–4	6	16
	No. 2½ sq.	1 lb. 12 oz.	3½–4	9	11
	No. 10	6 lbs. 10 oz.	3½–4	36	3
Beans, snap green and wax	No. 2	1 lb. 3 oz.	4	4	25
	No. 2½	1 lb. 12 oz.	4	7	14
	No. 10	6 lbs. 5 oz.	4	25	4
Beets	No. 2	1 lb. 4 oz.	4	5	20
	No. 2½	1 lb. 12 oz.	4	7	14
	No. 10	6 lbs. 8 oz.	4	26	4
Carrots	No. 2	1 lb. 4 oz.	4	5	20
	No. 10	6 lbs. 8 oz.	3½–4	26	4
Corn	No. 2	1 lb. 4 oz.	4	5	20
	No. 10	6 lbs. 10 oz.	3–3½	23	4
Hominy	No. 2½	1 lb. 13 oz.	4	7	14
	No. 10	6 lbs. 9 oz.	4	26	4
Peas, early or sweet	No. 2	1 lb. 4 oz.	4	5	20
	No. 10	6 lbs. 9 oz.	4	26	4
Sauerkraut	No. 2½	1 lb. 11 oz.	4–5	5	20
	No. 10	6 lbs. 3 oz.	4–5	20	5
Spinach	No. 2½	1 lb. 11 oz.	4–5	5	20
	No. 10	6 lbs. 2 oz.	4	24	4
Squash	No. 2½	1 lb. 13 oz.	4	7	14
	No. 10	6 lbs. 10 oz.	4	26	4
Tomatoes	No. 2	1 lb. 3 oz.	4–5	5	20
	No. 2½	1 lb. 12 oz.	4	6	16
	No. 10	6 lbs. 6 oz.	4	25	4
Tomato juice	No. 2	1 pt. 2 fl. oz.	....	3	33
	No. 10	3 qts.	....	18	5½
Tomato puree, heavy	No. 2		4	5	20
	No. 10	6 lbs. 9 oz.	4	26	4

TIME-TABLE FOR COOKING FRESH VEGETABLES

VEGETABLE	IN BOILING WATER		IN STEAMER	IN OVEN
	MINUTES (ACTUAL BOILING)	AMOUNT (BOILING WATER)	MINUTES	MINUTES
Asparagus (bunched stalks)		Covered		....
Tips	5–10	(except tips)	12–15	....
Stalks	15–25	Covered	20–25	....
Beans, green	25–35	Covered	25–35	....
Beans, lima	20–30	Covered	20–25	....
Beet greens, young	6–12	Only that which clings to leaves.	....	....
Beets, new	35–60	Covered	40–60	60–90
Beets, old	60–120	Covered	60–150	90–120
Broccoli	15–25	Covered	20–25	....
Brussels sprouts	12–20	Covered	15–25	....
Cabbage, green (shredded)	10–12	¼ the volume of cabbage.	8–15	....
Cabbage, wedges	10–15	¼ the volume of cabbage.	15–20	....
Carrots, new	20–30	Covered	15–20	30–45
Carrots, old	25–40	Covered	30–40	45–60
Cauliflower (broken up)	10–20	Covered	15–18	20–30
Celery	10–20	Covered	10–15	....
Corn	8–15	Covered	12–15	....
Kale	20–30	Only that which clings to leaves.	30	....
Onions, whole	20–25	Covered	18–20	40–50
Parsnips	25–35	Covered	30–40	....
Peas	15–30	Covered	15–25	....
Potatoes, sweet	20–35	Covered	25–40	35–60
Potatoes, white	25–45	Covered	25–35	60–120
Rutabagas, cubed	30–40	Covered	35–45	....
Spinach	6–12	Only that which clings to leaves.	6–10	....
Squash, Hubbard	35–45	Covered	20–30	45–90
Squash, summer	20–25	Small amount	15–20	30–40
Swiss chard	15–25	Only that which clings to leaves.	15–20	....
Tomatoes	15–20	None	15–20	20–30
Turnips, white, cubed	25–30	Covered	20–25	....

VEGETABLE SUBSTITUTION CHART
Groups Classified According to Nutritive Values

CLASS OF FOODS	SUGGESTIONS FOR COOKING AND SERVING

Group I—Potatoes:

Potatoes, Irish .... Au Gratin, Boiled (with or without skins), Baked, Cakes, Creamed, Fried, French Fried, Hashed Browned, Lyonnaise, Mashed. O'Brien, Parsley, Roast Brown, Salad, Scalloped

Potatoes, sweet .... Baked, Boiled, Candied, Mashed, Scalloped

Group II—Legumes, Dried:

Beans, kidney .... Baked, Boiled, Salad
Beans, lima .... Baked, Boiled, Creamed, Soup, with Bacon, Ham
Beans, Navy .... Baked, Boiled, Soup
Peas, black-eye .... Baked, Boiled

Group III—Grain Products:

Hominy, grits .... Baked, Boiled, Creamed
Hominy, lye .... Boiled, Creamed
Macaroni .... Baked, Boiled, Salads, Scalloped; with Cheese, Tomatoes, Meat
Noodles .... Baked, Boiled, Scalloped; with Cheese, Tomatoes, Meat
Rice, white .... Baked, Boiled, Curried, Fried, Spanish
Spaghetti .... Baked, Boiled, Italian; with Cheese, Tomatoes, Meat

Group IV—Leafy, Green and Yellow Vegetables:

Asparagus .... Baked, Buttered, Creamed, Salad, Soup
Beans, string .... Boiled, Buttered, Lyonnaise, Salad, Spanish
Beet Greens .... Boiled, Buttered
Broccoli .... Au Gratin, Boiled, Buttered, Creamed, Salads, Soup
Brussels Sprouts .... Boiled, Buttered, Creamed
Cabbage, green .... Boiled, Buttered, Creamed, Fried. Slaw
Carrots .... Baked, Boiled, Buttered, Candied, Creamed, Fried, Raw, Soup
Chard .... Boiled, Buttered, Creamed
Collards .... Boiled, Buttered, Creamed
Kale .... Boiled, Buttered, Creamed
Lettuce .... Salads, Wilted
Lima Beans, green .... Baked, Buttered, Creamed, Succotash
Mustard Greens .... Boiled, Buttered, Creamed
Peas, green .... Boiled, Buttered, Creamed, Salads, Soup
Peppers, green .... Baked, Salads, Sauces, Stuffed
Spinach .... Boiled, Buttered, Creamed, Salads, Soup
Squash .... Baked, Mashed
Turnip Greens .... Boiled, Buttered, Creamed
Tomatoes, canned or fresh .... Baked, Salads, Sliced, Scalloped, Soup, Stewed, Stuffed

Group V—Other Vegetables:

Beets .... Boiled, Buttered, Harvard, Salads
Cauliflower .... Boiled, Buttered, Creamed, Salads
Celery .... Braised, Buttered, Creamed, Salads, Soups
Corn .... Cob, Creamed, Buttered, Fritters, Pudding, Relish, Scalloped, Soup
Cucumbers .... Garnish, Salads
Eggplant .... Baked, Fried, Scalloped, Spanish
Onions .... Baked, Creamed, Fried, Glazed. Savory, Salads, Sliced, Soups, Stewed
Parsnips .... Baked, Buttered, Fried
Radishes .... Garnish, Salads
Turnips, roots .... Baked, Boiled, Creamed, Diced, Fried, Mashed
Sauerkraut .... Baked, Boiled, Fried

The substitution of one vegetable for another within one group does not seriously affect the nutritional value of the menu.

Nutritionally, the foods in Groups I and II may be satisfactorily substituted for the foods in Group III but not vice versa.

Group IV foods may be substituted for Group V foods but not vice versa.

Groups I and II are generally nutritionally superior to Group III, and Group IV superior to V.

DIRECTIONS FOR COOKING QUICK-FROZEN VEGETABLES
(100 Portions)

VEGETABLE	POUNDS	BOILING SALTED WATER GALLONS	COOKING TIME Minutes (approx.)	PORTION Ounces (approx.)
Asparagus cuts	20	2	6 to 9	3½ to 4
Asparagus spears	20	2	6 to 9	4 to 5 stalks
Broccoli	17½	To cover	5 to 7	3 to 3½
Brussels sprouts	20	To cover	3 to 5	3½ to 4
Cauliflower	17½	To cover	3 to 5	3 to 3½
Corn	20	1	5 to 6	3½ to 4
Beans, green	20	2	8 to 13	3½ to 4
Beans, lima	20	2	10 to 13	3½ to 4
Peas	20	2	4 to 6	3½ to 4
Spinach	17½	2	4 to 6	3½ to 4
Beans, wax	20	2	8 to 13	3½ to 4

Break solid block of frozen vegetables, when not loose or individually frozen, into 4 to 5 pieces before removing from the carton, to hasten defrosting in the cooking water.

Remove from the carton. Drop into boiling water. Reheat to boiling temperature.

Count cooking time only from the time the water returns to boiling temperature after the addition of vegetable.

Stir occasionally and separate the vegetable while thawing in the water.

Cook vegetable the required length of time as specified on Time-Table or until tender. Drain thoroughly.

Season with butter, salt and pepper. *Serve immediately.*

NOTE.—1. For storage in excess of 2 weeks, store frozen vegetables at 10° F. or lower. When held for 2 days to 2 weeks, vegetables may be stored at 15° F. to 20° F. Store at 30° F. for period overnight or not to exceed 2 days. Frozen vegetables will keep as long as solidly frozen. If thawed, the vegetables must be used promptly. They cannot be refrozen.

2. The actual cooking time will vary as it depends upon the type of cooking vessel, the product and the length of time the vegetable must be held after cooking.

3. Avoid overcooking vegetables as this injures the appearance and flavor and reduces the food value. Long standing, after cooking, also affects the appearance, flavor, and food value.

4. Save water from drained vegetable for soups, gravies, or sauces.

BUTTERED FRESH ASPARAGUS

INGREDIENTS	100 PORTIONS			............PORTIONS
	WEIGHTS		AMOUNTS (approx.)	
	Pounds	*Ounces*		
Asparagus, A.P.	38	----	....	
Salt	----	2	¼ cup	
Water..	----	----	To cover	
Butter, melted	1	----	1 pint	

Cut off tough part of asparagus stalks. Reserve for soups.

Wash asparagus thoroughly. Soak in cold water about 20 minutes. Drain.

Add salt to water. Heat to boiling temperature.

Cut asparagus into 1½-inch lengths. Keep tips and stalks separate.

Cook stalks in boiling water about 15 minutes. Add tips.

Cook about 5 minutes or until tender. Drain. Add melted butter.

NOTE.—1. 3 No. 10 cans (2½ gallons) of spears or stalks, or 3 No. 10 cans of cuts may be used in place of 38 pounds fresh asparagus.

2. Stalks may be left whole and cooked in long baking pans or tied in bunches and placed upright in a deep kettle with water not quite covering tips.

Variation

Asparagus Hollandaise

Serve asparagus on buttered toast with Mock Hollandaise Sauce (page 214) or Cheese Sauce (page 210).

BUTTERED GREEN BEANS

INGREDIENTS	100 PORTIONS			............PORTIONS
	WEIGHTS		AMOUNTS (approx.)	
	Pounds	*Ounces*		
Salt	----	3	6 tablespoons	
Water, boiling	----	----	To cover	
Beans, green, A.P.	25	----	....	
Butter, melted	1	----	1 pint	

Add salt to water. Heat to boiling temperature.

Wash beans thoroughly. Break off stem ends. Cut or break into desired lengths.

Cook in boiling water about 30 minutes or until tender. Drain. Add butter.

NOTE.—4 No. 10 cans (3¼ gallons) green beans may be used in place of 25 pounds fresh beans.

Variations

Creamed Green Beans

Combine cooked green beans with 1½ gallons Medium Cream Sauce (page 208).

Green Beans, Southern Style

Cook fresh green beans with 2 pounds salt pork, bacon rind or ham hocks. Season to taste.

Serve with salt pork, ham from ham hocks or with Cornbread (page 370).

NEW YORK BAKED BEANS

Portion: 5 to 6 ounces (approx. ¾ cup).

Ingredients	100 Portions			............Portions
	Weights		Amounts (approx.)	
	Pounds	Ounces		
Beans, white, dried	12	----	1¾ gallons	
Water, cold	----	----	To cover	
Water, boiling	----	----	3 to 4 gallons.....................	
Onions, peeled, quartered......	----	12	1½ pints	
Molasses	1	6	1 pint	
Sugar, brown	1	----	1½ pints	
Mustard, dry	----	----	1 tablespoon	
Paprika	----	----	2 teaspoons	
Salt	----	5	10 tablespoons	
Catsup	3	8	½ No. 10 can (1¾ quarts).	
Vinegar	----	----	¼ cup	
Salt pork, sliced.....................	4	----	....	

Pick over and wash beans thoroughly. Soak in cold water about 6 hours.

Do not drain. Add boiling water to cover.

Add onions. Heat to boiling temperature. Let simmer about 1 hour until beans are tender but not mushy.

Add molasses, sugar, mustard, paprika, salt, catsup and vinegar.

Arrange alternate layers of pork and beans in greased baking pan, bottom layer of pork and top layer of beans.

Bake in slow oven (300° F.) 4 to 5 hours, adding liquid as needed.

BOSTON BAKED BEANS

Portion: 5 to 6 ounces (approx. ¾ cup).

| INGREDIENTS | 100 PORTIONS | | | ....PORTIONS |
	WEIGHTS		AMOUNTS (approx.)	
	Pounds	*Ounces*		
Beans, white, dried	12	....	1¾ gallons	
Water, cold	....	....	To cover	
Water, boiling	....	....	3 to 4 gallons	
Salt	....	5	10 tablespoons	
Mustard, dry	....	1	4½ tablespoons	
Salt pork, bacon, or ham fat, cubed.	4	....		
Molasses	2	12	1 quart	

Pick over and wash beans thoroughly. Soak in cold water about 6 hours.

Do not drain. Add boiling water to cover. Simmer about 1 hour until beans are tender, but not mushy. Drain off excess liquid. Reserve.

Add salt, mustard, salt pork and molasses. Place in baking pans.

Bake in slow oven (300° F.) 4 to 5 hours, adding liquid from the boiled beans as needed.

SAVORY GREEN BEANS

Portion: 4 to 4½ ounces (approx. ⅔ cup).

| INGREDIENTS | 100 PORTIONS | | | ....PORTIONS |
	WEIGHTS		AMOUNTS (approx.)	
	Pounds	*Ounces*		
Beans, green	21	4	4 No. 10 cans (3¼ gallons).	
Onions, chopped	2	....	1½ quarts	
Bacon fat	....	12	¾ pint	
Sugar	....	4	½ cup	
Cloves	....	¼	1 tablespoon	
Salt	....	2	¼ cup	
Pepper	....	....	1 teaspoon	
Tomatoes	6	6	1 No. 10 can (3¼ quarts).	

Heat beans to boiling temperature. Drain. Fry onions in bacon fat until lightly browned. Add sugar, cloves, salt, pepper and tomatoes.

Heat to boiling temperature.

Combine beans and tomato mixture just before serving.

BOILED WHITE, KIDNEY, OR LIMA BEANS, I

Portion: 5 ounces (approx. ⅔ cup).

INGREDIENTS	100 PORTIONS			............PORTIONS
	WEIGHTS		AMOUNTS (approx.)	
	Pounds	Ounces		
Beans, white, kidney or lima, dried.	10	....	1½ gallons	
Water, cold	....	....	To cover	
Water, boiling	....	....	2 gallons	
Bacon or salt pork, diced........	1	4	2½ cups	
Onions, chopped	1	4	1 quart	
Tomatoes	6	6	1 No. 10 can (3½ quarts).	
Sugar	....	2	¼ cup	
Mustard, dry	....	....	1 tablespoon	
Salt	....	3½	7 tablespoons	
Pepper	....	....	1 teaspoon	

Pick over and wash beans thoroughly. Soak in cold water about 6 hours.

Do not drain. Add boiling water to cover. Heat to boiling temperature.

Let simmer about 1 hour until tender but not mushy.

Fry together bacon and onions until lightly browned. Add tomatoes, sugar, mustard, salt and pepper.

Combine tomato mixture with beans. Cook 20 to 30 minutes.

NOTE—1 pint corn sirup may be used in place of sugar.

BOILED WHITE, KIDNEY, OR LIMA BEANS, II

Portion: 5 ounces (approx. 2/3 cup).

INGREDIENTS	100 PORTIONS			............PORTIONS
	WEIGHTS		AMOUNTS (approx.)	
	Pounds	*Ounces*		
Beans, white...................	12	....	1¾ gallons	
Water, cold	....	....	To cover	
Meat Stock (page 251) or water, hot.	....	....	3 gallons	
Salt pork or bacon, cubed.......	2	....		
Salt	....	3½	7 tablespoons	
Pepper	....	....	2 teaspoons	

Pick over and wash beans thoroughly. Soak in cold water about 6 hours. Do not drain.

Add hot meat stock or water to cover. Add salt pork. Heat to boiling temperature.

Let simmer about 30 minutes or until beans are partially tender.

Add salt and pepper. Continue cooking until beans are tender but not mushy.

NOTE.—Ham bones may be used in place of salt pork.

KIDNEY BEANS AND CORN

Portion: 4 to 5 ounces (approx. 2/3 cup).

INGREDIENTS	100 PORTIONS			............PORTIONS
	WEIGHTS		AMOUNTS (approx.)	
	Pounds	*Ounces*		
Corn, whole kernel, drained....	19	14	3 No. 10 cans (2½ gallons).	
Bacon	....	8		
Beans, kidney, cooked.............	6	....	1 gallon	
Chili sauce	....	8	½ pint	
Salt	....	3	6 tablespoons	
Pepper	....	....	1 teaspoon	

Heat corn to boiling temperature. Drain. Fry bacon until crisp. Chop medium fine.

Combine corn, bacon, kidney beans, chili sauce, salt and pepper.

Heat to boiling temperature.

NOTE.—2½ gallons cooked fresh corn cut from cob, may be used in place of canned corn.

LIMA BEANS, CREOLE

Portion: 4 to 5 ounces (approx. ⅔ cup).

INGREDIENTS	100 PORTIONS			............PORTIONS
	WEIGHTS		AMOUNTS (approx.)	
	Pounds	*Ounces*		
Beans, lima, dried......................	10	....	1½ gallons	....
Water, cold	....	....	To cover	....
Water, boiling	....	....	2 gallons	....
Onions, quartered	...	8	¾ pint	....
Bacon, diced	2	....	1 quart	....
Tomatoes	6	6	1 No. 10 can................... (3¼ quarts).	....
Chili sauce	1	....	1 pint	....
Salt	....	3½	7 tablespoons	....
Sugar	....	4	½ cup	....
Pepper	....	....	1 teaspoon	....
Meat Stock (page 251)	....	....	½ gallon	....

Pick over and wash beans thoroughly. Soak in cold water about 6 hours.

Do not drain. Add boiling water to cover. Add onions.

Heat to boiling temperature. Let simmer about 1 hour until beans are tender but not mushy.

Fry bacon. Add bacon, tomatoes, chili sauce, salt, sugar and pepper to stock.

Heat to boiling temperature.

Combine all ingredients and pour into greased baking pans.

Bake in moderate oven (350°F.) ½ to 1 hour.

SPANISH BEANS

Portion: 4 to 5 ounces (approx. ⅔ cup).

INGREDIENTS	100 PORTIONS			............PORTIONS
	WEIGHTS		AMOUNTS (approx.)	
	Pounds	Ounces		
Beans, kidney, dried............	10	....	1½ gallons	
Water, cold	....	....	To cover	
Water, boiling	....	....	2 gallons	
Onions, chopped	1	8	1½ quarts	
Peppers, green, chopped........	1	....	1 quart	
Paprika	....	....	1½ teaspoons	
Pepper	....	....	1 teaspoon	
Salt	....	3	6 tablespoons	
Tomato puree	6	9	1 No. 10 can (3¼ quarts).	
Meat Stock (page 251)	....	....	1½ pints	
Salt pork, diced........	1	8		

Pick over and wash beans thoroughly. Soak in cold water about 6 hours.

Do not drain. Add boiling water to cover.

Let simmer about 1 hour until tender, but not mushy.

Combine all ingredients and pour into greased baking pans.

Bake in moderate oven (350°F.) 1½ to 2 hours.

BUTTERED BEETS

Portion: 4 to 4½ ounces (approx. ⅔ cup).

INGREDIENTS	100 PORTIONS			............PORTIONS
	WEIGHTS		AMOUNTS (approx.)	
	Pounds	*Ounces*		
Beets, A.P.	33	....	....	
Water	....	....	To cover	
Butter, melted	1	....	1 pint	
Salt	...	2	¼ cup	
Sugar	....	2	¼ cup	
Pepper	....	....	1½ teaspoons	

Wash beets thoroughly. Trim stems 2 to 3 inches above beets. Retain roots.

Heat water to boiling temperature. Cook beets in boiling water 35 to 60 minutes or until tender. Drain.

Cover beets with cold water. Peel. Dice or slice.

Add butter, salt, sugar and pepper. Reheat.

NOTE.—4 No. 10 cans (3¼ gallons) of beets may be used in place of 33 pounds of fresh beets.

Variation

Buttered Beets and Greens

Cook 20 pounds young beet greens 6 to 12 minutes. Drain.

Combine with 4 No. 10 cans (3¼ gallons) beets, quartered or diced.

Add 1 pound (1 pint) butter, 2 ounces (¼ cup) salt and 1½ teaspoons pepper. Reheat.

BUTTERED BEETS
(Using dehydrated beets)

Portion: Approx. 3 ounces (½ to ⅔ cup).

INGREDIENTS	100 PORTIONS			............PORTIONS
	WEIGHTS		AMOUNTS (approx.)	
	Pounds	*Ounces*		
Beets, dehydrated	3	8	1 gallon	
Water	....	....	3 gallons	
Salt	....	2	¼ cup	
Pepper	....	½	1¾ tablespoons	
Butter, melted	1	....	1 pint	

Soak beets in water 60 minutes. Cover. Heat, slowly, to boiling temperature.

Let simmer 30 minutes or until tender. Drain. Add salt, pepper and butter.

NOTE.—1. Prolonged soaking may cause souring or spoilage.

2. 1 pound dehydrated beets is approximately equivalent to 12 pounds beets, A.P., or

to 8 pounds canned beets plus liquid in which they are packed.

3. Sliced, cubed, or Julienne style dehydrated beets may be used.

4. Dehydrated beets are preferable when prepared as Harvard Beets or Sweet Sour Beets.

Variation

Sweet Sour Beets

Soak beets and cook as for Buttered Beets. Drain.

Combine 1 quart vinegar, 1 pound (1 pint) sugar, 3 ounces (6 tablespoons) salt and 1 ounce (3½ tablespoons) pepper.

Heat to boiling temperature. Add to beets. Reheat.

HARVARD BEETS

Portion: 4 to 4½ ounces (approx. ⅔ cup).

INGREDIENTS	100 PORTIONS		..........PORTIONS
	WEIGHTS	AMOUNTS (approx.)	
	Pounds | *Ounces*		
Beets, A.P.	33 |	....	
Water	.... |	To cover	
Cloves	.... | ⅓		
Bay leaves	.... |	2	
Water	.... |	½ gallon	
Sugar	.... | 12	¾ pint	
Cornstarch	.... | 5	½ pint	
Salt	.... | 1½	3 tablespoons	
Pepper	.... |	1 teaspoon	
Butter, melted	.... | 8	½ pint	
Vinegar	.... |	¾ pint	

Wash beets thoroughly. Trim stems 2 to 3 inches above beets. Retain roots.

Heat water to boiling temperature. Add beets. Cook about 35 to 60 minutes or until beets are tender. Drain.

Cover beets with cold water. Peel. Dice or slice.

Add cloves and bay leaves to ½ gallon water. Heat to boiling temperature. Cook 1 minute. Remove cloves and bay leaves.

Mix together sugar, cornstarch, salt and pepper. Stir into hot water. Cook until thickened, stirring constantly.

Stir butter and vinegar into sauce. Pour over beets. Reheat.

NOTE.—1. Leave stems and roots of beets on during cooking to prevent juices from cooking out.

2. 4 No. 10 cans (3¼ gallons) of beets may be used in place of 33 pounds of fresh beets. Use the liquor for heating beets and making sauce.

3. Cook fresh beets in steamer, if possible.

SPICED BEETS

Portion: 4 to 5 ounces (approx. ⅔ cup).

INGREDIENTS	100 PORTIONS			..........PORTIONS
	WEIGHTS		AMOUNTS (approx.)	
	Pounds	*Ounces*		
Beets, A. P.	33	....		
Water	....	....	To cover	
Cloves, whole	....	¼	1½ tablespoons	
Water	....	....	1 gallon	
Cinnamon, ground	....	....	2 teaspoons	
Salt	....	2	¼ cup	
Pepper	....	....	1 teaspoon	
Sugar, brown	2	....	1½ quarts	
Sugar	1	....	1 pint	
Vinegar	....	....	½ gallon	
Butter	1	....	1 pint	

Wash beets thoroughly. Trim stems 2 to 3 inches above beets. Retain roots.

Heat water to boiling temperature. Add beets. Cook about 35 to 60 minutes or until tender. Drain.

Cover beets with cold water. Peel. Dice or slice.

Add cloves to 1 gallon water. Heat to boiling temperature. Add cinnamon, salt, pepper, sugar and vinegar. Cook 10 minutes. Strain.

Pour juice over beets. Heat to boiling temperature. Add butter.

NOTE.—1. 4 No. 10 cans (3¼ gallons) beets may be used in place of 33 pounds fresh beets.

2. Reduce sugar if a more sour sauce is preferred.

Variations

Cold Pickled Beets

Prepare beets as for Spiced Beets. Omit butter. Cool. Slice or quarter.

Chill before serving.

Beet Relish

Chop fine, 15 pounds Spiced Beets.

Add 8 pounds (2 gallons) finely chopped raw cabbage.

Add 4 ounces (½ cup) grated fresh horse-radish.

Mix well. Serve cold.

NOTE.—If fresh horse-radish is not available, use prepared horse-radish and season to taste.

BUTTERED BROCCOLI

Portion: 3 to 4 ounces.

INGREDIENTS	100 PORTIONS			............PORTIONS
	WEIGHTS		AMOUNTS (approx.)	
	Pounds	Ounces		
Broccoli, A.P.	45	....	....	
Salt	....	2	¼ cup	
Water	....	....	To cover	
Butter, melted	1	8	1½ pints	

Remove discolored outer leaves of broccoli. Cut off tougher part of stems.

Soak broccoli in cold salted water (¼ cup salt to 1 gallon water) about 30 minutes. Drain.

Add salt to water. Heat to boiling temperature. Add broccoli. Cook about 20 minutes or until tender. Drain.

Add butter just before serving.

NOTE.—Broccoli may be served with Mock Hollandaise Sauce (page 214).

BUTTERED BRUSSELS SPROUTS

Portion: 3 to 4 ounces.

INGREDIENTS	100 PORTIONS			............PORTIONS
	WEIGHTS		AMOUNTS (approx.)	
	Pounds	Ounces		
Brussels sprouts, A.P.	30	....	....	
Salt	....	2	¼ cup	
Water, boiling	....	....	To cover	
Butter, melted	1	8	1½ pints	

Remove discolored or wilted outside leaves. Trim the stem end. Wash thoroughly.

Soak in salted cold water (¼ cup salt to 1 gallon water) 20 to 30 minutes. Drain.

Add salt to boiling water. Add brussels sprouts.

Cook uncovered 15 to 20 minutes or until tender. Drain.

Add butter just before serving.

BUTTERED CABBAGE

Portion: 4 to 5 ounces (approx. ⅔ cup).

INGREDIENTS	100 PORTIONS			.... PORTIONS
	WEIGHTS		AMOUNTS (approx.)	
	Pounds	Ounces		
Salt	....	2	¼ cup	
Water	....	....	....	
Cabbage, A.P.	31	....		
Butter, melted	1	....	1 pint	
Paprika	....	....	To garnish	

Add salt to water which measures approximately ¼ the volume of cabbage to be cooked. Heat to boiling temperature.

Trim and wash cabbage. Cut into wedges.

Cook, covered, in boiling water about 10 to 15 minutes or until tender. Drain.

Add butter. Garnish with paprika if desired.

NOTE.—1. Cook cabbage in small batches. Overcooking causes cabbage to lose its natural color and become unpalatable.

2. Cabbage may be shredded and cooked with ham bones or salt pork.

Variations

Creamed Cabbage

Combine cabbage with 1½ gallons Medium Cream Sauce (page 208).

Cabbage with Bacon

Fry 2 pounds diced bacon until crisp. Use bacon fat as part of fat in Medium Cream Sauce (page 208).

Add bacon to 1½ gallons of sauce. Combine with cabbage.

SIMMERED CABBAGE

(Using dehydrated cabbage)

Portion: Approx. 3½ ounces (approx. ⅔ cup).

INGREDIENTS	100 PORTIONS			..... PORTIONS
	WEIGHTS		AMOUNTS (approx.)	
	Pounds	Ounces		
Cabbage, dehydrated	2	12	2¾ gallons	
Water	....	....	3 gallons	
Salt	....	3	6 tablespoons	
Bacon, diced	2¼	....	1 quart	
Pepper	....	⅜	1⅓ tablespoons	

Soak cabbage in water 45 to 60 minutes. Cover.

Heat, slowly, to boiling temperature, about 40 minutes. Add salt. Simmer 10 to 15 minutes.

Drain ½ the liquid from cabbage and reserve for soups or stews.

Fry bacon until lightly browned.

Add bacon, bacon fat and pepper to cabbage. Reheat.

NOTE.—1. 1 pound dehydrated cabbage is equivalent to 16 pounds cabbage, A.P., or to 8½ pounds cooked, drained cabbage.

2. Reconstituted cabbage may be used as an ingredient for soups and stews.

3. Dehydrated cabbage must be held in an air-tight container at all times. Absorption of too much moisture will result in development of unsatisfactory flavor.

Variations

Sweet Sour Cabbage

Soak and cook cabbage as for Simmered Cabbage, omitting bacon. Drain.

Add 1½ pints vinegar and 6 ounces (¾ cup) sugar.

Mix well and reheat.

Creamed Cabbage

Soak and cook cabbage as for Simmered Cabbage, omitting bacon. Drain.

Combine with 1 gallon Medium Cream Sauce (page 208). Reheat.

Corned Beef and Cabbage

Soak and cook cabbage as for Simmered Cabbage, omitting bacon. Drain.

Add 6 pounds canned corned beef, broken into small pieces. Mix well. Reheat.

BUTTERED CARROTS

Portion: 4 to 5 ounces (approx. ⅔ cup).

INGREDIENTS	100 PORTIONS			........PORTIONS
	WEIGHTS		AMOUNTS (approx.)	
	Pounds	Ounces		
Salt	....	3	6 tablespoons	
Sugar	....	2	¼ cup	
Water	....	....	To cover	
Carrots, A.P.	30	....		
Pepper	....	....	1 teaspoon	
Butter, melted	1	....	1 pint	

Add salt and sugar to water. Heat to boiling temperature. Wash carrots. Peel, slice or dice.

Cook in boiling water about 25 minutes or until tender. Drain. Stir in pepper and butter.

NOTE.—4 No. 10 cans (3¼ gallons) carrots may be used in place of 30 pounds fresh carrots.

Variations

Carrots Bechamel

Combine 25 pounds carrots, cooked, with 2 gallons Bechamel Sauce (page 211).

Buttered Carrots and Peas

Combine 3 No. 10 cans (2½ gallons) peas, drained, with 16 pounds carrots, cooked and diced, 1 pound butter and 2 ounces salt. Heat.

French Fried Carrots

Clean and cut carrots in strips.

Cook carrots. Cool. Dip in egg wash. Cover with crumbs.

Fry in hot deep fat at 375°F. 5 to 7 minutes.

BUTTERED CARROTS
(Using dehydrated carrots)

Portion: Approx. 3 ounces (approx. ½ cup).

| INGREDIENTS | 100 PORTIONS | | | ....Portions |
	WEIGHTS		AMOUNTS (approx.)	
	Pounds	*Ounces*		
Carrots, diced, dehydrated....	3	8	1 gallon	
Water	....	....	2½ gallons	
Butter, melted	....	12	1½ cups	
Salt	....	2½	5 tablespoons	
Pepper	....	½	1¾ tablespoons	

Soak carrots in water 45 minutes. Cover.

Heat, slowly, to boiling temperature, about 45 minutes.

Let simmer 10 minutes or until tender.

Remove from heat. Add butter, salt and pepper. Stir until thoroughly mixed.

NOTE.—1. 1 pound dehydrated carrots is approximately equivalent to 12½ pounds fresh, unpeeled carrots or to 6 pounds drained, cooked carrots, or to 7½ pounds canned carrots with liquor.

2. Cook carrots with minimum amount of water.

Variation

Creamed Carrots

Soak and cook carrots as for Buttered Carrots.

Combine with 1 gallon Medium Cream Sauce (page 208). Reheat

BUTTERED CELERY

Portion: 4 to 5 ounces.

| INGREDIENTS | 100 PORTIONS | | | ....Portions |
	WEIGHTS		AMOUNTS (approx.)	
	Pounds	*Ounces*		
Celery, A.P.	34	....		
Salt	....	2	¼ cup	
Water	....	....	To cover	
Butter, melted	1	....	1 pint	

Remove leaves. Trim roots and separate stalks. Wash thoroughly.

Cut stalks into 1 to 2-inch pieces.

Add salt to water. Heat to boiling temperature. Add celery.

Cook 10 to 20 minutes or until tender. Drain.

Add butter just before serving.

NOTE.—1. Celery hearts may be reserved and used as a relish or in salad.

2. Reserve leaves to use in soups, stews or salads.

3. Use soft brush to clean outer stalks. Scrape off any discoloration with a knife.

★ 298

BUTTERED CAULIFLOWER

Portion: 4 to 5 ounces (approx. ⅔ cup).

| INGREDIENTS | 100 PORTIONS | | | ....PORTIONS |
	WEIGHTS		AMOUNTS (approx.)	
	Pounds	*Ounces*		
Cauliflower, A.P.	50	....	....	
Salt	....	2	¼ cup	
Water, boiling	....	....	To cover	
Butter, melted	2	....	1 quart	

Remove outer leaves and stalks of cauliflower. Leave whole or break into sections. Soak in salted water (¼ cup salt to 1 gallon water) about ½ hour. Drain.

Add salt to water. Heat to boiling temperature. Add cauliflower. Cook about 15 minutes or until tender. Drain.

Pour butter over cauliflower. Garnish with paprika if desired.

Variations

Cauliflower Au Gratin

Place cooked cauliflower in greased baking pans. Cover with 1½ gallons Cheese Sauce (page 210).

Sprinkle with buttered crumbs. Bake in moderate oven (350°F.) about 30 minutes.

Cauliflower Hollandaise

Serve cauliflower with 1½ gallons Mock Hollandaise Sauce (page 214).

Cauliflower with Buttered Crumbs

Mix together 2 pounds (2½ quarts) dry, fine bread crumbs and 2 pounds (1 quart) melted butter.

Toast in moderate oven (350°F.) until lightly browned. Sprinkle on cooked cauliflower.

BUTTERED CORN

Portion: 3 to 3½ ounces (approx. ½ cup).

| INGREDIENTS | 100 PORTIONS | | | ....PORTIONS |
	WEIGHTS		AMOUNTS (approx.)	
	Pounds	*Ounces*		
Corn, cream style.............	25	....	20 No. 2 cans (3¼ gallons).	
Butter, melted	1	....	1 pint	
Sugar	....	4	½ cup	
Salt	....	2	¼ cup	
Pepper	....	....	1 teaspoon	

Heat corn to boiling temperature. Stir in butter, sugar, salt, and pepper.

NOTE.—When whole kernel corn is used, drain before adding butter and seasonings.

CORN ON THE COB

Portion: 1 (approx. 7-ounce) ear.

INGREDIENTS	100 PORTIONS			............PORTIONS
	WEIGHTS		AMOUNTS (approx.)	
	Pounds	*Ounces*		
Corn, A.P.	50	....	100 ears....................	
Salt	...	1–1½	2 to 3 tablespoons per gallon of water.	
Water	....	....	To cover	

Husk corn. Add salt to water. Heat to boiling temperature.

Cook corn in rapidly boiling water about 8 to 15 minutes or until tender. Drain. Serve very hot.

NOTE.—Add a small quantity of sugar to boiling water if corn is not fresh or young. Fresh corn should be cooked as soon as possible after purchase.

CORN FRITTERS
(Cream-style corn)

Portion: 2 medium fritters.

INGREDIENTS	100 PORTIONS			............PORTIONS
	WEIGHTS		AMOUNTS (approx.)	
	Pounds	*Ounces*		
Flour	5	....	1¼ gallons	
Baking powder	...	2½	6 tablespoons	
Salt	...	2½	5 tablespoons	
Sugar	...	2	¼ cup	
Eggs, beaten	1	....	10 (1 pint)	
Shortening, melted	...	8	½ pint	
Corn, cream-style	10	....	8 No. 2 cans (1¼ gallons).	

Sift together flour, baking powder, salt and sugar.

Combine eggs, shortening and corn. Add to flour mixture. Stir until smooth.

Drop by spoonsful into hot deep fat at 375°F. and fry 3 to 5 minutes, turning fritters frequently to brown them evenly.

Drain on absorbent paper. Serve very hot.

NOTE.—1. Serve with sirup or jelly, if desired.

2. To be crisp, fritters should be fried continuously, in small batches, and served immediately. They should not stand on the steam table or in oven.

3. For convenience and uniformity a No. 20 or No. 24 ice cream scoop can be used to drop batter into hot fat.

CORN FRITTERS
(Whole kernel corn)

Portion: 2 medium fritters.

INGREDIENTS	100 PORTIONS			..........PORTIONS
	WEIGHTS		AMOUNTS (approx.)	
	Pounds	*Ounces*		
Flour	4	....	1 gallon	
Baking powder	....	2⅛	5½ tablespoons	
Salt	....	2	¼ cup	
Sugar	....	2	¼ cup	
Eggs, beaten	....	14	9 (1 pint).................	
Milk, liquid	....	....	1¾ quarts	
Shortening, melted	....	6	¾ cup	
Corn, whole kernel.............	13	4	2 No. 10 cans (6½ quarts).	

Sift flour, baking powder, salt and sugar together.

Combine eggs, milk and shortening. Add flour mixture and stir until smooth.

Drain corn. Add to flour mixture and mix well.

Drop by spoonsful into hot deep fat at 375°F. and fry 3 to 5 minutes, turning fritters frequently to brown evenly.

Drain on absorbent paper. Serve very hot.

NOTE.—1. Serve with sirup or jelly, if desired.

2. To be crisp, fritters should be fried continuously, in small batches, and served immediately. They should not stand on the steam table or in oven.

3. For convenience and uniformity a No. 20 or No. 24 ice cream scoop can be used to drop batter into hot fat.

Variations

Corn and Ham Fritters

Use 4½ pounds cooked, finely chopped ham in place of half the kernel corn.

Carrot Fritters

Use 6½ quarts of cooked diced carrots, or 2 No. 10 cans diced carrots in place of kernel corn.

CORN PUDDING

Portion: 4 to 5 ounces (approx. ⅔ cup).

INGREDIENTS	100 PORTIONS			..........PORTIONS
	WEIGHTS		AMOUNTS (approx.)	
	Pounds	*Ounces*		
Corn, cream-style	28	12	23 No. 2 cans (3¾ gallons).	
Sugar	....	4	½ cup	
Salt	....	2	¼ cup	
Milk, liquid	....	....	5¼ quarts	
Eggs, lightly beaten................	3	9	36 (1¾ quarts)........	
Bread, soft, broken	1	....	2¼ quarts	

Combine corn, sugar, salt and milk. Heat to boiling temperature.

Mix together eggs and bread. Stir into corn mixture.

Bake in greased baking pans in slow oven (300°F.) until set.

Pans may be placed in hot water to bake to reduce tendency to curdle.

Variation

Southern Corn Pudding

Add 3 pounds (¾ gallon) finely chopped green peppers to corn pudding before baking.

SAUTEED CORN

Portion: 3 to 4 ounces (approx. ⅔ cup).

INGREDIENTS	100 PORTIONS			..........PORTIONS
	WEIGHTS		AMOUNTS (approx.)	
	Pounds	*Ounces*		
Corn, whole kernel....................	26	8	4 No. 10 cans (3¼ gallons).	
Bacon, chopped	2	....	1 quart	
Pimientos, chopped	....	7	1 (7-ounce can) (1 cup)	
Peppers, green, chopped..........	1	8	1½ quarts	
Salt	....	2	¼ cup	
Pepper	....	....	2 teaspoons	

Drain corn. Fry bacon until lightly browned.

Add corn, pimiento, green pepper, salt and pepper. Fry about 5 minutes.

SPOONBREAD

Portion: 4 to 5 ounces (approx. ⅔ cup).

INGREDIENTS	100 PORTIONS			............PORTIONS
	WEIGHTS		AMOUNTS (approx.)	
	Pounds	*Ounces*		
Cornmeal, yellow	4	8	3½ quarts	
Salt	....	3½	7 tablespoons	
Sugar	....	3½	7 tablespoons	
Water, boiling	....	....	1¾ gallons	
Milk, liquid	....	....	2¼ gallons	
Eggs, well beaten	3	8	35 (3½ pints)	
Butter or other fat, melted	....	8	1 cup	
Baking powder	....	6¾	1 cup	

Combine cornmeal, salt and sugar. Stir into water.

Heat to boiling temperature. Cook 5 minutes, stirring constantly, until thickened.

Heat milk to boiling temperature.

Stir eggs and fat into milk. Add to cornmeal mixture, stirring constantly.

Stir in baking powder. Mix thoroughly.

Pour into greased baking pan.

Bake in moderate oven (350°F.) 45 minutes or until set.

NOTE.—Before baking, set pan of spoon bread into pan of hot water to insure smooth texture. Bake.

FRIED EGGPLANT

Portion: 3½ to 4 ounces (approx. 2 slices).

INGREDIENTS	100 PORTIONS			............PORTIONS
	WEIGHTS		AMOUNTS (approx.)	
	Pounds	*Ounces*		
Eggplant, A.P.	28	....		
Eggs	2	6	24 (1⅓ quarts)	
Water	....	....	¾ pint	
Salt	....	3	6 tablespoons	
Bread crumbs, fine	1	....	½ gallon	

Peel eggplant. Cut crosswise into ¼-inch slices.

Beat eggs slightly. Stir in water and 1½ ounces salt.

Mix remaining salt with crumbs.

Dip eggplant in egg mixture. Drain well. Dip in crumbs, coating thoroughly.

Fry in hot deep fat at 375°F. 5 to 7 minutes or until golden brown and tender.

Drain on absorbent paper. Serve immediately.

NOTE.—1. 1 quart of undiluted evaporated milk may be used in place of beaten eggs.

2. Fry eggplant as near to serving time as possible as eggplant loses its crispness upon standing. Do not let stand on steam table.

ESCALLOPED EGGPLANT WITH TOMATO

Portion: 4 to 4½ ounces (approx. ⅔ cup).

INGREDIENTS	100 PORTIONS			..........PORTIONS
	WEIGHTS		AMOUNTS (approx.)	
	Pounds	*Ounces*		
Salt	....	2	¼ cup	
Water	....	....	To cover	
Eggplant, A.P.	28	....		
Onions, chopped	4	....	¾ gallon	
Butter or other fat	1	....	1 pint	
Bread, chopped	1	....	½ gallon	
Tomatoes	12	12	2 No. 10 cans (6½ quarts).	
Sugar	....	2	¼ cup	
Salt	....	1	2 tablespoons	
Pepper	....	....	1 teaspoon	

Add ¼ cup salt to water. Heat to boiling temperature.

Peel eggplant. Cut into cubes. Cook in boiling water about 10 minutes or until tender.

Fry onions in fat until clear. Add bread and fry until lightly browned.

Combine tomatoes, sugar, salt, pepper, eggplant and onion mixture.

Place in baking pans. Bake in moderate oven (350°F.) 30 to 40 minutes.

BUTTERED GREENS

Portion: 4 to 5 ounces (approx. ⅔ cup).

| INGREDIENTS | 100 PORTIONS | | | ....PORTIONS |
	WEIGHTS		AMOUNTS (approx.)	
	Pounds	*Ounces*		
Greens, A.P.	32	....		
Salt	....	2	¼ cup	
Pepper	....	....	1 teaspoon	
Bacon fat or butter, melted	1	8	1½ pints	

Remove roots and tougher parts of stems from greens.

Wash greens thoroughly several times in cold water. Drain.

Place in cooking vessel in 15 to 20-pound lots. Sprinkle with salt. Cover vessel.

Cook required length of time for particular "green." See Note.

Drain. Add pepper and bacon fat or butter.

NOTE.—1. COOKING TIME FOR GREENS

Beet, young .... 6 to 12 minutes
Dandelion, young .... 6 to 12 minutes
Kale ....20 to 30 minutes
Spinach .... 6 to 12 minutes
Swiss chard ....15 to 25 minutes

2. Vegetable greens require, for cooking, only the amount of water clinging to the leaves after washing them. Cooking in this amount of water helps to retain valuable vitamins and minerals. Reserve liquid drained off cooked greens.

3. Greens may be cut before or after cooking but pieces should be left fairly large.

Variation

Southern Greens

Cook greens in small amount of liquid in which ham or salt pork has been cooked.

Add ¼ pint vinegar.

Garnish with ham or diced salt pork.

CREAMED HOMINY

Portion: 4 to 4½ ounces (approx. ⅔ cup).

| INGREDIENTS | 100 PORTIONS | | | ....PORTIONS |
	WEIGHTS		AMOUNTS (approx.)	
	Pounds	*Ounces*		
Hominy	26	4	4 No. 10 cans (3¼ gallons).	
Cream Sauce (page 208)	....	....	1½ gallons	

Heat hominy and drain. Stir into cream sauce and reheat.

NOTE.—1 (7-ounce) can (½ pint) finely chopped pimientos may be added to Cream Sauce for color and flavor, if desired.

FRIED (SAUTEED) HOMINY

Portion: 4 ounces (approx. ⅔ cup).

INGREDIENTS	100 PORTIONS			..........PORTIONS
	WEIGHTS		AMOUNTS (approx.)	
	Pounds	Ounces		
Hominy	26	4	4 No. 10 cans (3¼ gallons).	....
Peppers, green, chopped.........	1	8	1½ quarts	....
Pimientos, chopped	....	15	1 (15-ounce) can (1 pint).	....
Salt	....	5	10 tablespoons	....
Butter or bacon fat................	1	8	1½ pints	....

Drain hominy and combine with green peppers, pimientos, and salt.

Fry in fat until lightly browned.

NOTE.—Peppers and pimientos may be omitted. Garnish with crisp parsley sprigs for color.

HOMINY SPOONBREAD

Portion: 4 to 5 ounces (approx. ⅔ cup).

INGREDIENTS	100 PORTIONS			..........PORTIONS
	WEIGHTS		AMOUNTS (approx.)	
	Pounds	Ounces		
Milk, liquid	....	....	3¾ gallons	....
Hominy grits	5	....	3¾ quarts	....
Salt	....	8	1 cup	....
Baking powder	....	3¾	9 tablespoons	....
Egg yolks, well beaten.........	2	8	60 (1¼ quarts)...........	....
Butter or other fat, melted.....	2	12	2¾ pints	....
Egg whites, stiffly beaten......	3	5	60 (3⅓ pints)...........	....

Heat milk to boiling temperature.

Add hominy and salt to milk, stirring constantly. Cover.

Cook 20 minutes, stirring occasionally. Cool slightly.

Stir baking powder into egg yolks. Add fat.

Stir into hominy mixture. Fold in egg whites.

Pour into well greased baking pans.

Bake in moderate oven (350°F.) 30 to 40 minutes or until set.

NOTE.—Before baking set pan of spoonbread in pan of hot water and bake to insure smooth texture.

NOODLES WITH BUTTERED CRUMBS

Portion: 5 to 6 ounces (approx. 1 cup).

INGREDIENTS	100 PORTIONS			............PORTIONS
	WEIGHTS		AMOUNTS (approx.)	
	Pounds	*Ounces*		
Salt	....	4	½ cup	
Water	....	....	10 gallons	
Noodles	8	....		
Salt	....	1	2 tablespoons	
Pepper	....	....	2 teaspoons	
Bread crumbs, dry..........	1	8	½ gallon	
Butter, melted	2	....	1 quart	

Add ½ cup salt to water. Heat to boiling temperature.

Stir in noodles. Cook 20 minutes or until tender. Drain well.

Add 2 tablespoons salt and pepper to bread crumbs. Brown in butter.

Combine with noodles.

NOTE.—Serve with meat in place of potatoes.

Variation

Fried Noodles

Cook noodles in boiling salted water 20 minutes or until tender. Drain well. Dry noodles between clean towels.

Fry in hot deep fat at 390°F. 1 minute or until brown. Drain on absorbent paper. Sprinkle with salt. Serve very hot.

FRENCH FRIED ONIONS

Portion: 2½ to 3 ounces (approx. ⅔ cup).

INGREDIENTS	100 PORTIONS			............PORTIONS
	WEIGHTS		AMOUNTS (approx.)	
	Pounds	*Ounces*		
Onions, Spanish, A.P.........	28	....		
Milk, liquid	....	....	½ gallon	
Flour	1	8	1½ quarts	
Salt	....	2	¼ cup	
Pepper	....	....	1 teaspoon	

Peel onions. Cut into ¼-inch thick slices. Separate slices into rings.

Dip into milk. Drain well.

Mix flour, salt and pepper. Dredge onion rings in flour.

Fry in hot deep fat at 345°F. 5 to 6 minutes or until golden brown.

Drain well on absorbent paper.

NOTE.—Let onion rings stand in ice water 10 to 15 minutes to crisp before dipping into milk and flour.

BUTTERED ONIONS

Portion: 4 to 4½ ounces (approx. ⅔ cup).

INGREDIENTS	100 PORTIONS			..........PORTIONS
	WEIGHTS		AMOUNTS (approx.)	
	Pounds	*Ounces*		
Onions, A.P.	28	....	....	....
Salt	....	4	½ cup	....
Water	....	....	6 gallons	....
Butter, melted	1	8	1½ pints	....

Peel onions. Wash. Quarter or slice.

Add salt to water. Heat to boiling temperature. Add onions. Cook, uncovered, about 25 minutes or until tender. Drain.

Add butter.

NOTE.—Garnish with paprika or chopped parsley, if desired.

Variations

Creamed Onions

Combine cooked onions with 1½ gallons Medium Cream Sauce (page 208).

Buttered Sweet Onion Rings

Peel Spanish onions. Wash. Slice crosswise in ¼-inch thick slices. Separate into rings before cooking.

Cook as for Buttered Onions.

Onions Au Gratin

Place cooked, quartered onions in greased baking pans.

Cover with 1½ gallons Cheese Sauce (page 210). Sprinkle with buttered bread crumbs.

Bake in moderate oven (350° F.) 20 minutes.

FRIED ONIONS

Portion: 4 to 4½ ounces (approx. ⅔ cup).

INGREDIENTS	100 PORTIONS			..........PORTIONS
	WEIGHTS		AMOUNTS (approx.)	
	Pounds	*Ounces*		
Onions, A.P.	35	....	....	....
Beef drippings, or other fat, melted.	3	8	1¾ quarts	....
Salt	....	3	6 tablespoons	....

Peel onions and cut into ¼ inch thick slices.

Add onions to fat and sprinkle with salt.

Fry over direct heat or in hot oven (400°F.) until golden brown. Stir frequently to prevent sticking.

SMOTHERED ONIONS
(Using dehydrated onions)

Portion: Approx. 2½ ounces (⅓ to ½ cup).

| INGREDIENTS | 100 PORTIONS | | | ....PORTIONS |
	WEIGHTS		AMOUNTS (approx.)	
	Pounds	Ounces		
Onions, dehyrdated	3	....	2½ gallons	
Water	....	....	2½ gallons	
Fat	1½	....	1½ pints	
Salt	....	2½	5 tablespoons	

Stir onions into water. Let soak 20 minutes. Drain. Reserve onion water.

Heat fat to frying temperature. Add reconstituted onions.

Cook, stirring frequently, until slightly brown and tender. Stir in salt and onion water. Cover. Let simmer 30 to 45 minutes until excess water cooks off.

NOTE.—1. 1 pound dehydrated onions is approximately equivalent to 12½ pounds unpeeled fresh onions or to 6½ to 7 pounds reconstituted (cooked) onions.

2. Reconstitute onions properly to avoid toughness.

Variation

Creamed Onions

Soak and cook onions as for Smothered Onions.

Combine with 1 gallon Medium Cream Sauce (page 208). Reheat.

Serve hot on toast, if desired.

GLAZED ONIONS

Portion: 4 to 5 ounces (approx. ⅔ cup).

| INGREDIENTS | 100 PORTIONS | | | ....PORTIONS |
	WEIGHTS		AMOUNTS (approx.)	
	Pounds	Ounces		
Onions, small, A.P.	28	....	....	
Salt	....	1½	3 tablespoons	
Water	....	....	To cover	
Sugar, brown	3	....	2¼ quarts	
Butter or other fat.................	1	12	1¾ pints	
Water (for sirup).................	....	....	3¼ quarts	

Peel onions. Leave whole. Wash.

Add 1 tablespoon of salt to water. Heat to boiling temperature. Add onions. Cook, uncovered, about 15 minutes or until partially tender. Drain.

Arrange onions in baking pans.

Mix thoroughly sugar, remaining salt, butter and water to make thin sirup. Pour over onions.

Bake in moderate oven (350°F.) about 30 minutes. Baste frequently to insure good glaze and uniform tenderness.

NOTE.—Pierce through onion with fork or small bladed knife to prevent breaking or bursting while cooking.

Portion: 4 to 5 ounces (approx. ⅔ cup).

INGREDIENTS	100 PORTIONS			............PORTIONS
	WEIGHTS		AMOUNTS (approx.)	
	Pounds	*Ounces*		
Onions, A.P.	28	....		
Salt	....	2½	5 tablespoons	
Water	....	....	To cover	
Bay leaves	....	....	6 to 8	
Sugar	....	4	½ cup	
Celery salt	....	1	3 tablespoons	
Pepper	....	....	1½ teaspoons	
Cloves, whole	....	....	6 to 8	
Tomatoes	12	12	2 No. 10 cans (6½ quarts).	
Butter or other fat	....	12	¾ pint	
Flour	....	4	½ pint	

Peel onions. Wash and quarter.

Add 1 tablespoon of salt to water. Heat to boiling temperature. Add onions. Cook about 25 minutes or until tender. Drain.

Add bay leaves, sugar, celery salt, pepper, remaining salt and cloves to tomatoes. Heat to boiling temperature. Cook about 5 minutes.

Remove bay leaves and cloves.

Blend together fat and flour. Stir into tomato mixture.

Place onions in baking pans. Pour tomato mixture over onions.

Bake in moderate oven (350°F.) about 15 minutes.

BUTTERED PARSNIPS

Portion: 4 to 4½ ounces (approx. ⅔ cup).

INGREDIENTS	100 PORTIONS			..........PORTIONS
	WEIGHTS		AMOUNTS (approx.)	
	Pounds	Ounces		
Parsnips, A.P.	30	....		
Salt	....	3	6 tablespoons	
Water	....	....	6 gallons	
Butter, melted	1	....	1 pint	
Pepper	....	....	1 teaspoon	

Peel parsnips. Split and quarter.

Add salt to water. Heat to boiling temperature. Add parsnips.

Cook in boiling water about 30 minutes or until tender. Drain.

Add melted butter and pepper.

NOTE.—Chopped parsley can be sprinkled over parsnips before serving.

BUTTERED PEAS

Portion: 3½ to 4 ounces (approx. ⅔ cup).

INGREDIENTS	100 PORTIONS			..........PORTIONS
	WEIGHTS		AMOUNTS (approx.)	
	Pounds	Ounces		
Peas, A.P.	60	....		
Salt	....	1½	3 tablespoons	
Water	....	....	To cover	
Sugar	....	2	¼ cup	
Butter, melted	1	....	1 pint	

Shell peas. Add salt to water. Heat to boiling temperature.

Add peas and cook, uncovered, about 20 minutes or until tender.

Drain. Stir in sugar and butter.

NOTE.—4 No. 10 cans (3¼ gallons) of peas may be used in place of 60 pounds of fresh peas. Heat peas in part of liquor from cans.

BUTTERED PEAS AND CELERY

Portion: 4 to 5 ounces (approx. ⅔ cup).

INGREDIENTS	100 PORTIONS			..........PORTIONS
	WEIGHTS		AMOUNTS (approx.)	
	Pounds	*Ounces*		
Peas	26	4	4 No. 10 cans (3¼ gallons).	....
Water............................	....	....	To cover	
Celery, diced............	13	....	3¼ gallons............	
Butter, melted	1	....	1 pint	
Salt	....	1	2 tablespoons	

Heat peas. Drain and reserve liquid.

Combine water and liquid from peas. Heat to boiling temperature.

Add celery. Cook about 15 minutes or until tender. Drain.

Combine peas and celery. Stir in butter and salt. Reheat.

Variation

Creamed Peas and Celery

Combine peas and celery and mix with 1½ gallons Cream Sauce (page 208). Reheat.

Use liquid from peas and celery as basis for sauce.

BLACK-EYED PEAS

Portion: 5 ounces (approx. ⅔ cup).

INGREDIENTS	100 PORTIONS			............PORTIONS
	WEIGHTS		AMOUNTS (approx.)	
	Pounds	*Ounces*		
Peas, black-eyed, dried....	12	....	1¾ gallons	
Water, boiling	....	....	5 gallons	
Salt pork	4	....		
Salt	....	3½	7 tablespoons	
Pepper, cayenne	....	....	¼ teaspoon	

Pick over and wash peas thoroughly. Cover with 2½ gallons water.

Let stand about 1 hour. Do not drain.

Score pork. Add 2½ gallons water. Cook 1 hour. Drain.

Combine peas, salt pork, salt and cayenne pepper. Cook 1 hour.

NOTE.—To score salt pork, cut in ⅓-inch slices down to skin side. Serve cooked peas with slices of salt pork, if desired. Cut salt pork off rind for slices.

Variations

Black-Eyed Peas and Rice

Combine black-eyed peas with cooked rice. Season with butter or bacon.

Chopped onion or canned tomatoes may be added, if desired.

BAKED WHITE OR SWEETPOTATOES

Portion: 7 to 8 ounces (1 potato).

| INGREDIENTS | 100 PORTIONS | | | ....PORTIONS |
	WEIGHTS		AMOUNTS (approx.)	
	Pounds	*Ounces*		
Potatoes, A.P.	44	....	100 medium	

Select potatoes of even shape and size. Scrub well.

Bake on shallow baking pans in hot oven (400°F.) about 1 to 1½ hours or until done.

NOTE.—1. Prick with fork or cut skins to allow for escape of steam, as soon as potatoes are removed from oven.

2. New white potatoes may be baked.

BOILED POTATOES IN JACKETS

Portion: 5 to 5½ ounces.

| INGREDIENTS | 100 PORTIONS | | | ....PORTIONS |
	WEIGHTS		AMOUNTS (approx.)	
	Pounds	*Ounces*		
Salt.................................	.....	4	½ cup...................	
Water	....	....	To cover	
Potatoes, A.P.	44	.....	100	

Add salt to water. Heat to boiling temperature. Add potatoes.

Cook 30 to 40 minutes or until tender. Drain.

NOTE.—Whole potatoes, peeled, or in jackets should be cooked, preferably in a steamer. Place potatoes in steamer basket. Place baskets in steamer. Lock cabinet. Turn on steam and cook required length of time. See Time-Table (page 282).

Variations

Creamed Potatoes

Peel boiled potatoes. Cut into ¾-inch cubes. Combine with 1½ gallons Medium Cream Sauce (page 208). Heat.

NOTE.—Paprika or finely chopped pimientos may be added to cream sauce.

Potatoes Au Gratin

Cook potatoes. Peel and dice. Place in greased baking pans.

Cover with Cheese Sauce (page 210) seasoned with 1 tablespoon dry mustard.

Sprinkle with 1½ quarts buttered bread crumbs.

Bake in moderate oven (375°F.) 10 to 20 minutes.

PARSLEY BUTTERED POTATOES

Portion: 5 to 5½ ounces.

INGREDIENTS	100 PORTIONS			............Portions
	WEIGHTS		AMOUNTS (approx.)	
	Pounds	Ounces		
Salt	....	4	½ cup	
Water	....	....	To cover	
Potatoes, A.P.	44	....		
Butter, melted	1	4	1¼ pints	
Parsley, finely chopped.............	....	1	⅓ cup	

Add salt to water. Heat to boiling temperature.

Peel and wash potatoes. Cook, whole, 30 to 40 minutes or until tender. Drain.

Pour butter over potatoes. Sprinkle with crisp parsley.

NOTE.—1. ½ ounce (2 tablespoons) paprika may be used in place of finely chopped parsley.

2. New potatoes are best to prepare in this manner.

Variations

Browned Potatoes

Cook potatoes. Drain well.

Fry in hot deep fat at 375° F. to 400° F. about 4 minutes.

Drain on absorbent paper. Sprinkle with salt.

Serve immediately.

ESCALLOPED POTATOES

Portion: 5 to 5½ ounces (approx. ⅔ cup).

INGREDIENTS	100 PORTIONS			...........Portions
	WEIGHTS		AMOUNTS (approx.)	
	Pounds	Ounces		
Potatoes, A.P.	44	....		
Salt	....	2½	5 tablespoons	
Cream Sauce (page 209).............	....	....	2½ gallons	

Peel and wash potatoes. Slice thin and season with salt.

Arrange alternate layers of cream sauce and potatoes in greased baking pans. Bottom and top layers should be cream sauce.

Bake in slow oven (325°F.) about 1½ to 2 hours or until potatoes are tender.

NOTE.—1. Finely diced, cooked bacon or ham, green peppers, pimientos or chives may be added to the cream sauce.

2. Grated cheese or buttered crumbs may be sprinkled over the top 5 to 10 minutes before removing from oven.

FRANCONIA POTATOES

Portion: 5 to 5½ ounces (approx. ⅔ cup).

Ingredients	100 Portions			..........Portions
	Weights		Amounts (approx.)	
	Pounds	*Ounces*		
Salt	....	4	½ cup	
Water	....	....	To cover	
Potatoes, A.P.	44	....		
Butter, melted	1	4	1¼ pints	

Add salt to water. Heat to boiling temperature.

Peel and cut potatoes into wedges or halves.

Cook in boiling water about 15 minutes or until half done. Drain.

Place in greased baking pans. Brush with butter.

Bake in hot oven (400°F.) 15 to 20 minutes or until done.

NOTE.—New potatoes, scrubbed, may be cooked, whole and unpeeled, then cut in half lengthwise, brushed with butter and browned.

FRENCH FRIED POTATOES

Portion: 4 to 4½ ounces.

Ingredients	100 Portions			..........Portions
	Weights		Amounts (approx.)	
	Pounds	*Ounces*		
Potatoes, A.P.	44	....		
Salt	....	3	6 tablespoons	
Fat, for deep frying..................	....	....		

Peel and wash potatoes. Cut into long narrow strips about ½ inch thick.

Cover with cold or ice water. Let stand 1 to 1½ hours.

Drain. Dry well in a cloth.

Fry in hot deep fat at 375°F. about 4 to 6 minutes or until tender and browned.

Drain on absorbent paper. Sprinkle with salt. Serve immediately.

NOTE.—Potatoes may be partially fried ahead of time, about 3 to 4 minutes in deep fat at 350°F. Just before serving complete the frying in deep fat at 375°F.

By using this "double frying" method, French fried potatoes can be served hot and crisp. The frying should be a continuous process, especially for "self service."

HASHED BROWNED POTATOES

Portion: 5 to 5½ ounces (approx. ⅔ cup).

| INGREDIENTS | 100 PORTIONS | | | ....PORTIONS |
	WEIGHTS		AMOUNTS (approx.)	
	Pounds	*Ounces*		
Potatoes, cooked	35	....	5½ gallons	
Fat, melted	2	....	1 quart	
Salt	....	3	6 tablespoons	
Pepper	....	....	2 teaspoons	

Chop potatoes into small pieces. Place in deep baking or roasting pans.

Pour fat over potatoes. Sprinkle with salt and pepper.

Bake in hot oven (400°F.) 20 to 25 minutes, or until well browned.

Turn potatoes several times to insure even browning.

HASHED BROWNED POTATOES
(Using dehydrated potatoes)

Portion: Approx. 4½ ounces (approx. ⅔ cup).

| INGREDIENTS | 100 PORTIONS | | | ....PORTIONS |
	WEIGHTS		AMOUNTS (approx.)	
	Pounds	*Ounces*		
Potato cubes, dehydrated........	5	8	2 gallons	
Water	....	....	3¼ gallons	
Salt	....	3	6 tablespoons	
Fat	2	....	1 quart	

Soak potatoes in water 60 minutes. Cover.

Heat slowly to boiling temperature about 45 minutes.

Add salt. Let simmer 10 minutes. Drain thoroughly. Cool.

Heat fat to frying temperature. Add potatoes and mix lightly with fat.

Fry at low temperature, without turning, 10 to 15 minutes or until potatoes on bottom are evenly browned.

Turn and continue frying about 20 minutes. Turn occasionally.

NOTE.—1. 1 pound dehydrated potatoes is approximately equivalent to 6 pounds raw unpeeled potatoes or to 4½ pounds peeled potatoes.

2. Drain potatoes well. Soggy potatoes will not brown well.

Variation

Lyonnaise Potatoes

Prepare as for Hashed Browned Potatoes.

Reconstitute 12 ounces dehydrated onions in ¾ gallon water, 45 minutes.

Heat to boiling temperature. Let simmer about 15 minutes or until onions are tender. Drain. Stir into potatoes. Fry potatoes until lightly browned.

HOME-FRIED POTATOES

Portion: 4 to 5 ounces (approx. ⅔ cup).

INGREDIENTS	100 PORTIONS			.........PORTIONS
	WEIGHTS		AMOUNTS (approx.)	
	Pounds	*Ounces*		
Potatoes, A.P.	44	....	....	....
Meat drippings or other fat....	2	....	1 quart	....
Salt	....	3	6 tablespoons	....
Pepper	....	....	1½ teaspoons	....

Peel potatoes. Rinse. Slice.

Heat fat to frying temperature. Add potatoes. Sprinkle with salt and pepper. Mix well.

Cook over direct heat or in hot oven (450°F.) 20 to 30 minutes until tender and well browned.

Turn potatoes occasionally to insure even cooking.

Variation

Cottage Fried Potatoes

Cook potatoes in jackets. Cool. Peel and slice in ¼-inch slices. Cook as for Home-Fried Potatoes.

LYONNAISE POTATOES

Portion: 4 to 5 ounces (approx. ⅔ cup).

INGREDIENTS	100 PORTIONS			PORTIONS
	WEIGHTS		AMOUNTS (approx.)	
	Pounds	*Ounces*		
Potatoes, cooked	35	....	5½ gallons	
Onions, minced	1	....	1½ pints	
Butter or other fat	2	....	1 quart	
Salt	....	3	6 tablespoons	
Pepper	....	....	1½ teaspoons	

Cut potatoes into ¼-inch slices. Fry onions in fat, about 3 minutes or until clear.

Combine onions, potatoes, salt and pepper. Place in greased baking pans. Cook in hot oven (400°F.) or on top of range until lightly browned.

NOTE.—¾ pint finely chopped parsley may be added to the potatoes with the onions.

MASHED POTATOES

Portion: 5 to 5½ ounces (approx. ⅔ cup).

INGREDIENTS	100 PORTIONS			..........PORTIONS
	WEIGHTS		AMOUNTS (approx.)	
	Pounds	*Ounces*		
Potatoes, A.P.	44	....		
Water	....	....	4 gallons	
Milk, liquid, hot......	....	....	5¼ quarts	
Salt	....	4	½ cup	
Butter, melted	1	....	1 pint	

Peel potatoes. Heat water to boiling temperature. Add potatoes and cook about 30 to 40 minutes or until tender. Drain.

Place in mixer and beat at low speed until potatoes are broken up.

Change to high speed and beat about 2 or 3 minutes until no lumps remain.

Add milk, salt and butter to potatoes.

Beat at low speed until mixture is blended. Beat at high speed about 2 minutes.

NOTE.—1. Serve potatoes as soon as mashed. If potatoes have to be held for any length of time, cover with a damp cloth or brown paper.

Keep warm in slow oven (250°F.).

2. 2 pounds (½ gallon) finely chopped parsley may be added with the salt, milk and butter, if desired.

Variation

Mashed Potatoes and Rutabagas

Combine 21 pounds (2½ gallons) hot, mashed white potatoes with 14 pounds (1½ gallons) hot, mashed rutabagas. Mix until well blended. Serve hot.

MASHED POTATOES
(Using dehydrated, shredded potatoes)

Portion: Approx. 4½ ounces (approx. ⅔ cup).

INGREDIENTS	100 PORTIONS			..........PORTIONS
	WEIGHTS		AMOUNTS (approx.)	
	Pounds	*Ounces*		
Water......	....	8	2 gallons	
Potato shreds, dehydrated, precooked.	5	....	2 gallons......	
Salt	....	3	6 tablespoons	
Milk, liquid, hot	....	....	¾ gallon	
Butter, melted	1	....	1 pint	

Heat water to vigorous boil. Pour over potatoes. Cover.

Let stand in warm place 15 minutes or over low heat 10 minutes.

Add salt. Stir vigorously 15 to 20 minutes or until smooth.

Add milk and butter. Whip until light. Serve immediately.

MASHED POTATOES

(Using dehydrated, Julienne style potatoes)

Portion: Approx. 4½ ounces (approx. ⅔ cup).

INGREDIENTS	100 PORTIONS			............PORTIONS
	WEIGHTS		AMOUNTS (approx.)	
	Pounds	*Ounces*		
Potatoes, dehydrated	5	8	2 gallons	
Water	....	....	3¼ gallons	
Milk, liquid, hot.................	....	....	¾ gallon	
Salt	....	3	6 tablespoons	
Butter	1	....	1 pint	

Soak potatoes in water 60 minutes. Cover.

Heat, slowly, to boiling temperature. Let simmer until tender. Drain thoroughly.

Mash potatoes until smooth as possible. Stir in, slowly, milk, salt and butter.

Beat thoroughly. Serve immediately.

NOTE.—1. If cubed style dehydrated potatoes are used, soak 60 minutes.

2. If powdered milk is used, reserve liquid from drained potatoes to reconstitute milk powder.

O'BRIEN POTATOES

Portion: 5 to 5½ ounces (approx. ⅔ cup).

INGREDIENTS	100 PORTIONS			............PORTIONS
	WEIGHTS		AMOUNTS (approx.)	
	Pounds	*Ounces*		
Potatoes, A.P.	44	....	....	
Salt	....	3	6 tablespoons	
Peppers, green, chopped fine..	1	....	1 quart	
Pimientos, chopped fine...........	1	6	1½ pints	
Butter or bacon fat................	....	8	½ pint	

Wash, peel and cut potatoes into ¾-inch cubes.

Cover with cold water. Let stand 1 to 1½ hours. Drain. Dry in a cloth.

Fry in hot deep fat at 350°F. about 4 minutes, or until evenly browned.

Drain on absorbent paper. Sprinkle with salt.

Fry pimientos and green peppers in fat about 3 minutes.

Combine potatoes, pimientos and green peppers, just before serving.

NOTE.—Instead of frying in deep fat, cubed potatoes, chopped green peppers and pimientos may be cooked and browned in moderate oven (350°F.).

Place potatoes, peppers and pimientos in baking pans in a small amount of bacon fat or beef drippings. Turn frequently to insure even cooking and browning. Bake about 30 minutes. Sprinkle with salt.

POTATOES AU GRATIN
(Using dehydrated potatoes)

Portion: Approx. 4½ ounces (approx. ⅔ cup).

INGREDIENTS	100 PORTIONS			..........PORTIONS
	WEIGHTS		AMOUNTS (approx.)	
	Pounds	*Ounces*		
Potatoes, dehydrated	5	8	2 gallons	
Water	....	....	3¼ gallons	
Milk, liquid	....	....	1 gallon	
Salt	....	6	¾ cup	
Pepper	....	½	1¾ tablespoons	
Cheese, American cheddar, sliced.	2	....		
Bread crumbs, dry.................	....	8	1 pint	
Butter	1	....	1 pint	

Soak potatoes in water 60 minutes. Cover. Heat, slowly, to boiling temperature. Let simmer about 1 hour or until tender. Drain.

Place potatoes in baking pans. Add milk, salt and pepper. Stir well.

Arrange cheese over potatoes. Sprinkle with crumbs. Dot with butter.

Bake in moderate oven (350°F.) about 30 minutes or until a brown crust has formed.

POTATO PUFF

Portion: 4 to 5 ounces.

INGREDIENTS	100 PORTIONS			..........PORTIONS
	WEIGHTS		AMOUNTS (approx.)	
	Pounds	*Ounces*		
Milk, liquid	....	....	3⅔ cups	
Potatoes, mashed, hot	32	....	5 gallons	
Egg yolks, beaten...................	....	10	15 (1¼ cups)................	
Butter, melted	1	....	1 pint	
Salt	....	4	½ cup	

Heat milk to boiling temperature.

Combine potatoes, milk, egg yolks, ½ pint butter and salt. Beat thoroughly in mixer.

Place in greased baking pans. Brush with remaining melted butter.

Bake in moderate oven (375°F.) until lightly browned.

NOTE.—1. Chopped chives, pimientos or green peppers may be added to potatoes before baking, if desired.

2. Grated cheese or paprika may be sprinkled over top of potatoes before browning.

★ 320

BAKED SWEETPOTATOES
(Using dehydrated sweet potatoes)

Portion: Approx. 4 ounces (approx. ½ cup).

INGREDIENTS	100 PORTIONS			............PORTIONS
	WEIGHTS		AMOUNTS (approx.)	
	Pounds	*Ounces*		
Potatoes, sweet, sliced, de-hydrated.	6	....	2 gallons	
Water	....	....	3 gallons	
Salt	....	1	2 tablespoons	
Butter, melted	1	12	1¾ pints	

Soak sweet potatoes 45 to 60 minutes. Cover. Heat, slowly, to boiling temperature. Let simmer 35 to 45 minutes or until tender and moist.

Add salt and butter. Stir vigorously to mash. Place in greased baking pan.

Bake in moderate oven (350°F.) 20 minutes.

NOTE.—1. 1 pound dehydrated sweet potatoes is approximately equivalent to 3⅓ pounds fresh, unpeeled sweet potatoes or to 2¾ to 3 pounds reconstituted sweet potatoes.

2. Avoid dryness when cooking sweet potatoes. Reconstitute to maximum moisture content to obtain moist, finished product.

Variation

Baked Sweet Potatoes with Raisins

Reconstitute sweet potatoes as for Baked Sweet Potatoes.

Drain well. Stir in 2 pounds (1½ quarts) raisins.

Place in greased baking pans. Sprinkle with 4 pounds (½ gallon) sugar. Dot with butter.

Bake in moderate oven (350°F.) 30 minutes.

NOTE.—1. 3 pounds (¾ gallon) nuts, chopped coarse, may be used in place of raisins.

2. Dot potatoes with marshmallows, if desired.

MASHED SWEETPOTATOES

Portion: 4 to 5 ounces (approx. ½ cup).

INGREDIENTS	100 PORTIONS			............PORTIONS
	WEIGHTS		AMOUNTS (approx.)	
	Pounds	*Ounces*		
Potatoes, sweet, A.P.............	30	....		
Milk, liquid, hot....................	....	....	½ gallon	
Salt	....	2	¼ cup	
Butter	1	....	1 pint	
Sugar (may be omitted).........	....	6	¾ cup	

Cook unpeeled sweet potatoes at boiling temperature 30 to 40 minutes or until soft. Drain and peel.

Mash thoroughly in mixer.

Add milk, salt, butter and sugar to potatoes. Beat thoroughly.

MASHED SWEETPOTATOES
(Using dehydrated sweet potatoes)

Portion: Approx. 4 ounces (approx. ½ cup).

INGREDIENTS	100 PORTIONS			..........PORTIONS
	WEIGHTS		AMOUNTS (approx.)	
	Pounds	*Ounces*		
Potatoes, sweet, sliced, dehydrated.	6	8	2 gallons	
Water	....	....	3 gallons	
Salt	....	1	2 tablespoons	
Butter, melted	2	....	1 quart	

Soak sweet potatoes 60 minutes. Cover. Heat, slowly, to boiling temperature.

Let simmer 35 to 45 minutes or until tender and moist. Drain off surplus water.

Add salt and butter. Mash and beat vigorously until smooth.

SWEETPOTATOES BAKED WITH APPLES

Portion: 4 to 5 ounces (approx. ⅔ cup).

INGREDIENTS	100 PORTIONS			..........PORTIONS
	WEIGHTS		AMOUNTS (approx.)	
	Pounds	*Ounces*		
Salt	....	3	6 tablespoons	
Water	....	....	To cover	
Potatoes, sweet, A.P.	30	....		
Sugar, brown	3	....	2¼ quarts	
Apples, tart, A.P.	10	....		
Butter	1	....	1 pint	

Add 2 tablespoons salt to water. Heat to boiling temperature. Add potatoes.

Cook 15 to 20 minutes or until half done. Drain. Peel and cut into ½-inch thick slices.

Arrange layer of overlapping slices in greased baking pans.

Sprinkle with remaining salt and 1 quart brown sugar.

Core unpeeled apples and slice. Place layer of apples on top of sweet potatoes. Arrange remaining sweet potatoes and apples in alternate layers.

Sprinkle remaining sugar on top layer. Dot with butter.

Bake in moderate oven (350°F.) 30 to 40 minutes or until apples are tender.

Variation

Sweet Potatoes Baked with Pineapple

Slices or pieces of pineapple may be used in place of apples. Reduce sugar to 1 pound 8 ounces (1¼ quarts).

GLAZED SWEETPOTATOES

Portion: 4 to 5 ounces.

INGREDIENTS	100 PORTIONS			........PORTIONS
	WEIGHTS		AMOUNTS (approx.)	
	Pounds	Ounces		
Salt	....	3	6 tablespoons	
Water	....	....	To cover	
Potatoes, sweet, A.P.	30	....		
Sugar, brown	3	....	2¼ quarts	
Water, hot	....	....	½ gallon	
Butter, melted	....	10	1¼ cups	

Add 2 tablespoons salt to water. Heat to boiling temperature.

Cook unpeeled sweet potatoes in water about 40 minutes or until soft. Drain. Partially cool.

Peel and cut into ½-inch thick slices. Arrange in greased baking pans.

Make a sirup of sugar, hot water, butter and remaining salt. Pour over potatoes.

Bake in moderate oven (350°F.) about 30 minutes.

Variation

Browned Sweet Potatoes

In place of sirup, sprinkle potatoes with the sugar and salt.

Add bacon fat or melted butter.

Brown in moderate oven (350°F.) about 20 to 30 minutes.

CANDIED SWEETPOTATOES
(Using dehydrated sweet potatoes)

Portion: Approx. 4 ounces (approx. ½ cup).

INGREDIENTS	100 PORTIONS			........PORTIONS
	WEIGHTS		AMOUNTS (approx.)	
	Pounds	Ounces		
Potatoes, sweet, sliced, dehydrated.	6	8	2 gallons	
Water	....	....	3 gallons	
Sugar	5	....	2½ quarts	
Salt	....	1	2 tablespoons	
Butter	1	....	1 pint	

Soak potatoes in water 45 to 60 minutes. Cover. Heat to boiling temperature.

Let simmer 30 to 45 minutes or until tender. Drain. Leave slices whole. Reserve liquid. Combine sugar, salt and liquid from potatoes.

Heat to boiling temperature. Cook 5 minutes.

Place sweet potatoes in greased baking pans. Pour sirup over potatoes. Dot with butter.

Bake in moderate oven (350°F.) about 30 minutes.

323 ★

SPANISH RICE

Portion: 5 to 6 ounces (approx. ⅔ cup).

INGREDIENTS	100 PORTIONS			............Portions
	WEIGHTS		AMOUNTS (approx.)	
	Pounds	*Ounces*		
Rice, uncooked	5	8	2¾ quarts	
Beef drippings or bacon fat....	2	....	1 pint	
Bacon, diced	....	8	½ pint	
Onions, diced	2	....	1½ quarts	
Peppers, green, diced........	2	....	½ gallon	
Tomatoes	12	12	2 No. 10 cans (6½ quarts).	
Chili powder	....	½	2¼ tablespoons	
Salt	....	4	½ cup	
Sugar	....	3	6 tablespoons	
Pepper	....	....	1 teaspoon	
Meat Stock (page 251)........	....	....	2 to 2½ gallons........	

Wash rice thoroughly. Drain well.

Brown the rice in drippings or bacon fat until golden brown.

Fry together bacon, onions and green peppers. Add tomatoes, chili powder, salt, sugar and pepper. Cook 10 minutes.

Pour mixture over rice. Add part of stock.

Cook about 20 minutes or until rice is tender, adding more stock as mixture thickens.

Bake in slow oven (325°F.) about 15 minutes.

SAUERKRAUT

Portion: 4 to 5 ounces (approx. ⅔ cup).

INGREDIENTS	100 PORTIONS			............Portions
	WEIGHTS		AMOUNTS (approx.)	
	Pounds	*Ounces*		
Sauerkraut	31	....	5 No. 10 cans (4 gallons).	
Bacon fat, melted........	1	....	1 pint	

Heat sauerkraut in liquid from cans and add bacon fat.

NOTE.—Diced bologna or sliced frankfurters may be added to sauerkraut.

SUCCOTASH

Portion: 4 to 5 ounces (approx. ⅔ cup).

| INGREDIENTS | 100 PORTIONS | | | ....PORTIONS |
	WEIGHTS		AMOUNTS (approx.)	
	Pounds	*Ounces*		
Beans, lima, dried.....................	4	8	¾ gallon	
Water, cold	....	....	To cover	
Water, boiling	....	....	1 gallon	
Corn, whole kernel....................	19	14	3 No. 10 cans (9¾ quarts).	
Sugar	....	2	¼ cup	
Salt	....	2½	5 tablespoons	
Onion juice	....	2	¼ cup	
Paprika	....	....	½ teaspoon	
Butter	1	....	1 pint	

Pick over and wash lima beans thoroughly. Soak in cold water about 6 hours.

Do not drain. Add boiling water to cover.

Let simmer about 1 hour until tender, but not mushy. Drain.

Combine corn and beans. Add sugar, salt, onion juice, paprika and butter. Reheat.

NOTE.—1. 10 pounds fresh lima beans may be used in place of dried beans.

2. Chopped, sweet red or green peppers add flavor and color. If chopped pepper is used, omit paprika.

BAKED ACORN SQUASH

Portion: ½ squash.

| INGREDIENTS | 100 PORTIONS | | | ....PORTIONS |
	WEIGHTS		AMOUNTS (approx.)	
	Pounds	*Ounces*		
Squash, acorn, medium-sized, A.P.	40	....	50	
Salt	....	4	½ cup	
Butter or bacon fat, melted....	1	....	1 pint	
Sugar, brown	1	....	1½ pints	

Wash and prepare squash. Cut in half.

Remove fibers and seeds. Arrange uncooked halves open side up, in baking pans. Add enough water to cover bottom of pans.

Sprinkle with salt. Bake in moderate oven (350° F.) about 25 minutes or until half done.

Brush halves with butter. Sprinkle with sugar. Bake about 25 minutes or until tender.

BAKED HUBBARD SQUASH

Portion: Approx. 4½ ounces.

INGREDIENTS	100 PORTIONS			.............Portions
	WEIGHTS		AMOUNTS (approx.)	
	Pounds	*Ounces*		
Squash, Hubbard, A.P............	33	....	....	....
Water, boiling	....	....	To cover	....
Butter, melted	1	....	1 pint	....
Salt	....	3	6 tablespoons	....
Pepper	....	....	1 teaspoon	....

Cook squash in boiling water about 10 minutes to soften skin. Drain.

Cut in half, remove seeds and peel. Cut into 4½-ounce pieces.

Arrange in greased baking pans. Brush with butter.

Sprinkle with salt and pepper.

Bake in moderate oven (350°F.) about 1 hour or until tender.

Variation

Mashed Hubbard Squash

Cook squash in boiling water or in steamer about 10 minutes to soften skin. Drain.

Cut in half. Remove seeds. Peel.

Cook in small amount of boiling water or steam until soft. Mash in mixer.

Add salt, pepper and butter.

NOTE.—If mixture is quite moist, place in greased pans, brush with butter and bake in moderate oven (350°F.) ½ to 1 hour.

BUTTERED SUMMER SQUASH

Portion: 4 ounces (approx. ⅔ cup).

INGREDIENTS	100 PORTIONS			.........Portions
	WEIGHTS		AMOUNTS (approx.)	
	Pounds	*Ounces*		
Squash, summer, A. P..........	26	....	....	....
Water, boiling	....	....	To cover bottom of pan	....
Onions, chopped	1	....	1½ pints	....
Butter or other fat............	1	....	1 pint	....
Sugar	....	2	¼ cup	....
Salt	....	3	6 tablespoons	....
Pepper	....	....	1 teaspoon	....
Paprika	....	....	To garnish	....

Wash, trim and peel squash. Slice or dice.

Cook in small amount of water about 20 minutes or until tender.

Fry onions until lightly browned. Add to squash.

Add sugar, salt and pepper. Garnish with paprika.

NOTE.—Squash can be peeled in potato peeling machine. Very young tender squash need not be peeled.

ESCALLOPED TOMATOES

Portion: 4 to 5 ounces (approx. ⅔ cup).

INGREDIENTS	100 PORTIONS			............PORTIONS
	WEIGHTS		AMOUNTS (approx.)	
	Pounds	Ounces		
Tomatoes	25	8	4 No. 10 cans (3¼ gallons).	
Sugar	....	8	1 cup	
Salt	....	2	¼ cup	
Pepper	....	....	1 teaspoon	
Onions, minced	....	4	¾ cup	
Bread, broken or cubed..........	5	....	2½ gallons	
Butter or other fat, melted......	1	....	1 pint	

Heat tomatoes with sugar, salt, pepper and onions.

Combine bread cubes and fat. Brown lightly in moderate oven (375°F.).

Arrange alternate layers of bread and tomatoes in greased baking pans. Bottom and top layers should be bread.

Bake in moderate oven (375°F.) 30 to 45 minutes.

NOTE.—Cooked celery, corn, cauliflower or onions may be used in place of part of tomatoes.

GRILLED TOMATOES

Portion: 2 halves.

INGREDIENTS	100 PORTIONS			............PORTIONS
	WEIGHTS		AMOUNTS (approx.)	
	Pounds	Ounces		
Tomatoes, A.P.	30	....	100	
French Dressing (page 239)	1	14	1 quart	

Wash tomatoes. Remove stem end. Do not peel.

Cut in halves, crosswise. Arrange, cut side up, in greased baking pans. Brush with French dressing.

Broil or bake in moderate oven (375°F.) 10 to 15 minutes, or until well heated through, but not soft.

BAKED STUFFED TOMATOES

Portion: 1 tomato.

INGREDIENTS	100 PORTIONS		AMOUNTS (approx.)	...........PORTIONS
	WEIGHTS		AMOUNTS (approx.)	
	Pounds	*Ounces*		
Tomatoes, A.P.	30	....	100	
FILLING				
Peppers, green, chopped............	1	....	1 quart	
Onions, chopped	....	8	¾ pint	
Bacon or ham, chopped............	2	....	1½ pints	
Butter or other fat............	1	....	1 pint	
Bread, chopped	3	....	1½ gallons	
Salt	....	1½	3 tablespoons	
Pepper	....	....	1 teaspoon	
Tomato pulp	....	....	½ gallon	

Wash tomatoes. Remove stem end and scoop out centers. Reserve pulp.

Fry green peppers and onions with bacon or ham in fat.

Combine with bread, salt, pepper and tomato pulp. Fill tomatoes with mixture.

Bake in moderate oven (350°F.) about 30 minutes or until tomatoes are tender but not soft.

STEWED TOMATOES

Portion: 4 ounces (approx. ⅔ cup).

INGREDIENTS	100 PORTIONS		AMOUNTS (approx.)	...........PORTIONS
	WEIGHTS		AMOUNTS (approx.)	
	Pounds	*Ounces*		
Onion, chopped	....	4	¾ cup	
Sugar	1	....	1 pint	
Salt	....	4	½ cup	
Fat	....	8	1 cup	
Bread, cubed	1	10	1 gallon	
Tomatoes	25	8	4 No. 10 cans (3¼ gallons).	

★ 328

Add onion, sugar, salt, fat and bread to tomatoes.

Heat and let simmer 20 to 30 minutes.

NOTE.—1. Onion may be omitted.

2. Toasted buttered bread cubes add flavor and body to tomatoes. Add to tomatoes just before serving.

Variations

Stewed Tomatoes and Celery

Heat 3 No. 10 cans (2½ gallons) tomatoes to boiling temperature. Add 10 pounds cooked celery, 2 ounces (¼ cup) salt, and 1 teaspoon pepper. Reheat.

Stewed Tomatoes and Corn

Combine 3 No. 10 cans (2½ gallons) tomatoes with 2 No. 10 cans (6½ quarts) whole kernel corn, drained.

Add 4 ounces (½ cup) salt. Heat to boiling temperature.

Stewed Tomatoes and Hominy

Combine 3 No. 10 cans (2½ gallons) tomatoes with 2 No. 10 cans (6½ quarts) hominy, drained. Add 4 ounces (½ cup) salt. Heat to boiling temperature.

Stewed Tomatoes and Onions

Heat 3 No. 10 cans (2½ gallons) tomatoes to boiling temperature. Add 5 pounds (1 gallon) cooked onions, quartered or sliced. Add 4 ounces (½ cup) salt. Reheat.

BUTTERED RUTABAGAS
(Swedish turnips)

Portion: 4 ounces (approx. ⅔ cup).

INGREDIENTS	100 PORTIONS			............PORTIONS
	WEIGHTS		AMOUNTS (approx.)	
	Pounds	*Ounces*		
Rutabagas, A.P.	33	....		
Salt	....	3	6 tablespoons	
Water	....	....	To cover	
Pepper, white	....	....	1 teaspoon	
Sugar	....	4	½ cup	
Butter, melted	....	12	¾ pint	

Wash and peel rutabagas. Cut into small cubes.

Add salt to water. Heat to boiling temperature. Add rutabagas.

Cook about 30 minutes or until tender. Drain. Sprinkle with pepper and sugar. Add butter.

NOTE.—30 pounds A.P. white turnips may be used in place of 33 pounds rutabagas.

Variations

Creamed White Turnips

Place cooked, drained turnip cubes in serving pans.

Sprinkle with sugar and pepper.

Pour ½ gallon hot Medium Cream Sauce (page 208) over turnips.

Garnish with chopped parsley or chives, if desired.

Mashed Rutabagas or Turnips

Cook rutabagas or turnips in boiling salted water until tender. Drain.

Mash in mixer, using heavy whip.

Add pepper, sugar, butter and 1½ cups liquid milk. Mix thoroughly.

TURNIPS (RUTABAGAS) WITH BACON
(Using dehydrated turnips)

Portion: Approx. 3 ounces (½ to ⅔ cup).

INGREDIENTS	100 PORTIONS			............PORTIONS
	WEIGHTS		AMOUNTS (approx.)	
	Pounds	*Ounces*		
Turnips, dehydrated	3	8	1¼ gallons	
Water	....	....	2½ gallons	
Salt	....	3	6 tablespoons	
Pepper	....	....	1⅓ tablespoons	
Bacon, diced	2	4	1 quart	

Soak turnips in water 45 to 60 minutes. Cover. Heat, slowly, to boiling temperature, about 35 minutes.

Let simmer about 10 minutes or until turnips are tender.

Remove from heat. Drain. Add salt and pepper.

Fry bacon until lightly browned. Add to turnips. Mix well.

NOTE.—Turnips may be reconstituted, then placed in baking pans with strips of bacon placed on top. Sprinkle with ¼ pound (½ cup) sugar. Bake in moderate oven (350° F.) about 20 minutes, turning bacon to brown evenly on both sides.

BAKED TURNIPS AND POTATOES
(Using dehydrated turnips and potatoes)

Portion: Approx. 3½ ounces (approx. ½ cup).

INGREDIENTS	100 PORTIONS			............PORTIONS
	WEIGHTS		AMOUNTS (approx.)	
	Pounds	*Ounces*		
Turnips, dehydrated	1	8	2½ quarts	
Water (for turnips)...............	....	....	1¼ gallons	
Potatoes, dehydrated	4	....	1½ gallons	
Water (for potatoes).............	....	....	2¼ gallons	
Salt	....	6	¾ cup	
Pepper	....	1	3½ tablespoons	
Bacon, sliced	3	....		

Soak turnips in water 45 to 60 minutes. Cover. Heat to boiling temperature.

Let simmer 25 to 30 minutes. Drain. Reserve liquid for soups.

Soak potatoes in water 40 minutes. Heat to boiling temperature.

Let simmer 25 to 30 minutes. Drain. Reserve liquid for soups.

Combine turnips and potatoes. Stir in salt and pepper.

Place in greased baking pans. Place bacon slices over top.

Bake in moderate oven (350°F.) about 20 minutes, turning bacon to brown evenly on both sides.

CURRIED MIXED VEGETABLES

Portion: 4 to 5 ounces (approx. ⅔ cup).

INGREDIENTS	100 PORTIONS			.... PORTIONS
	WEIGHTS		AMOUNTS (approx.)	
	Pou ds	Ounces		
Peas	6	9	1 No. 10 can (3¼ quarts).	
Beans, green	6	5	1 No. 10 can (3¼ quarts).	
Mushrooms	....	....	3 No. 1 cans	
Corn	6	10	1 No. 10 can (3¼ quarts).	
Carrots, diced, cooked	5	....	3¾ quarts	
Celery, diced, cooked	4	....	1 gallon	
Onions, chopped	5	8	1 gallon	
Butter or other fat	....	4	½ cup	
Cream Sauce (page 208)	....	....	2 gallons	
Curry powder	....	½	2 teaspoons	

Drain peas, beans and mushrooms. Reserve liquor for sauce.

Combine peas, beans, mushrooms, corn, carrots, and celery. Heat to boiling temperature.

Fry mushrooms and onions in fat.

Use mushroom liquor and part of vegetable liquor to make Cream Sauce.

Combine ingredients, except curry, with cream sauce.

Add curry powder just before serving.

NOTE.—1. 2½ pounds (1½ quarts) of cooked lima beans may be used in place of green beans.

2. Mushrooms may be omitted if desired.

VEGETABLE PIE

Portion: 6 ounces (approx. ¾ cup).

Ingredients	100 Portions			............Portions
	Weights		Amounts (approx.)	
	Pounds	*Ounces*		
Tomatoes	6	6	1 No. 10 can (3¼ quarts).	
Meat Stock (page 251)	....	....	1¼ gallons	
Salt	....	4	½ cup	
Sugar	....	2	¼ cup	
Onions, chopped	1	....	1½ pints	
Beef drippings	3	....	1½ quarts	
Flour	1	....	1 quart	
Carrots, cooked, diced	6	....	4½ quarts	
Potatoes, cooked, diced	9	....	5½ quarts	
Celery, cooked, diced	5	....	1¼ gallons	
Peas	6	9	1 No. 10 can (3¼ quarts).	
Biscuits (page 361)	....	....	100	

Combine tomatoes and stock. Add salt and sugar. Heat to boiling temperature.

Fry onions in drippings until lightly browned. Add flour and blend.

Stir onion-flour mixture into tomatoes. Add carrots, potatoes, celery and peas.

Fill greased baking pans with mixture. Place in oven and heat. When hot, place biscuits on top.

Bake in hot oven (425°F.) 15 minutes or until biscuits are done.

Baking

Information and Formulas

The bakery formulas have been developed and tested by Navy personnel for use by Navy bakers.

Bake shop equipment, Navy food issues, principles of nutrition and the latest developments in the bakery field have been taken into consideration in the selection of these formulas.

The introductory material in the various chapters of the bakery section and the notes accompanying the formulas contain pertinent and valuable information. These should be carefully read before the formulas are used.

INGREDIENTS

Flour

Functions of Flour in Baking: In addition to the food value of flour in baked goods, flour is important in forming structure to support other ingredients.

Types of Flour:
1. Hard Wheat Flour
2. Soft Wheat Flour

Hard wheat flour is characterized by its relatively high protein content. Soft wheat flour contains relatively lower amounts of protein. Both hard wheat and soft wheat flours are further classified into:

Plain flour
Enriched flour

Plain flour is flour milled in the regular way. Enriched flour has been enriched by the addition of:

Thiamine (Vitamin B_1)
Niacin or Niacin Amide
Iron
Riboflavin (Vitamin G) is added in some cases

Hard Wheat Flour: Hard wheat flour is used chiefly for making bread, rolls, Danish pastry and coffee cakes. It may be used for all general baking purposes provided suitable formulas, properly balanced for hard wheat flour are used.

Soft Wheat Flour: Soft wheat flour is used in production of cakes, cookies, pies and doughnuts. It is unsuitable for bread, rolls and other baked goods of that type because of insufficient protein to form dough structure.

Navy Issue Flour: Navy issue flour is enriched hard wheat flour. Formulas in the bakery section have been developed and tested with Navy issue flour.

Milk

Functions of Milk in Baking: Milk is used in bakery products to

Contribute to color of crust in such products as bread, rolls, doughnuts and cakes

Add moisture
Add richness
Add food value

Types of Milk: Milk in any of the following forms may be used in baking:

1. Liquid skim milk
2. Liquid whole milk
3. Powdered skim milk
4. Powdered whole milk
5. Evaporated milk
6. Sour milk
7. Buttermilk

Milk in any of the forms listed above, except sour and buttermilk, can be used interchangeably provided powdered or evaporated milk are properly reconstituted to give equivalents in milk solids content to milk specified in the formula. Directions for reconstituting powdered and evaporated milk are given on page (21).

When *sour milk or buttermilk* is used, the acidity of the milk is balanced with soda. Normally, ¼ ounce (1½ teaspoons) of soda per quart of sour milk or buttermilk will neutralize the acidity. Carbon dioxide gas is liberated in this process. Therefore, when sour milk or buttermilk are used with soda in a formula, their leavening effect must be taken into consideration, and the baking powder or other leavening ingredients in the formula reduced.

One quart of buttermilk or sour milk with ¼ ounce soda has the leavening power of approximately ½ ounce baking powder.

Handling Milk Products: Reconstituted evaporated or powdered milk is perishable and will spoil when held in warm temperatures, 70° F. or above. Place milk in refrigerator until ready to use.

Fresh liquid milk is perishable and should not stand in warm temperatures. It should be used immediately after removal from refrigerator.

Eggs

Functions of Eggs: Eggs are used in bakery products to

    Add color
    Add moisture
    Add richness
    Act as leavening agent (for sponge cake, angel food cake, and cream puffs)
    Add food value (protein and fat)

Types of Eggs: Eggs fresh, frozen, or powdered can be used in the formulas in this book. The following types may be available:

1. Fresh shell eggs
2. Fresh egg yolks
3. Fresh egg whites
4. Frozen whole eggs
5. Frozen egg yolks
6. Frozen egg whites
7. Powdered whole eggs
8. Powdered egg yolks
9. Powdered egg whites

Powdered eggs must be reconstituted with cold water before using. For directions see page 20. Each formula in this section requiring eggs gives exact instructions on using powdered eggs in place of fresh or frozen eggs.

Handling Egg Products: Fresh eggs, reconstituted powdered eggs, or frozen eggs are perishable when held at normal temperatures for any length of time. Eggs should be used within 3 or 4 hours after they have been held at temperatures of 70° F. to 80° F.

Shortening

Functions of Shortening: Shortening is used in bakery products to

    Produce tenderness
    Improve eating and keeping qualities
    Help produce better grain and texture
    Add richness
    Add food value

In yeast-raised bakery products such as bread, rolls and sweet doughs, shortening has the added function of lubricating the gluten in the flour developed during mixing, making it soft and pliable.

Shortening also helps emulsify and carry the moisture in yeast doughs, cake batters and icing.

Types of Shortening: Shortenings are edible fats and oils of animal or vegetable origin.

Oils: Shortenings which are fluid at ordinary temperatures are called oils.

Fats: Those which are solid are called fats. Fats which are plastic at ordinary temperatures are used in the preparation of bakery products. Oils are occasionally used in bread but are most generally used in the manufacture of mayonnaise, salad dressings and to some extent for frying purposes.

Shortenings may be classified as follows:

1. Lard
2. Pure vegetable shortening
3. Mixed animal and vegetable shortening

Any type of shortening may be used in these formulas. Type No. 2 is standard Navy issue shortening. Formulas in the bakery section were developed and tested with Type No. 2.

Sugar

Functions of Sugar: Granulated, powdered and brown sugar are standard Navy issue ingredients. Their functions are to

    Improve flavor
    Act as a shortener or tenderizer
    Contribute to the development of grain and texture
    Add richness
    Furnish food value in form of carbohydrates
    Improve keeping quality when added in form of sirup

Types of Sugar: Sugar is supplied in the form of

1. Granulated sugar
2. Confectioners' sugar
3. Brown sugar
4. Sugar sirups (malt, molasses, honey, corn sirup, invert sirup)

Sugar Sirups: Sugar sirups may or may not be available. Their functions are the same as for other sugar. In addition, corn sirup and invert sirup improve the keeping quality of products in which they are used. For example, the addition of corn sirup or honey to cookie dough helps produce cookies which retain their moisture and keep soft and fresh for a long period. Keeping qualities are not important from the Navy point of view because most foods produced in the galley are consumed within a few hours after preparation.

Sugar sirups are necessary in some specific types of products. For example, ginger bread contains only molasses as the sweetening and flavoring ingredient. Similarly, pecan pie is a special product made with only corn sirup, which gives the finished pie its characteristic eating quality. These, however, are isolated cases, and it is possible to make almost all bakery products without using sugar sirups.

When available and deemed necessary to use them, sirups can be used in amounts up to about 10% of sugar weight specified in the formula.

Baking Powder

Baking powder is a leavening agent produced by the mixture of an acid-reacting ingredient with an alkali-reacting one. These baking acids are tartrate, phosphates, and sodium aluminum sulphate, used alone, or in combination.

By the action of moisture and heat they liberate carbon dioxide gas which causes doughs and batters to "rise." All types of baking powders release not less than 12 per cent available carbon dioxide.

Types of Baking Powder: Package labels indicate the composition of the baking powder. The commonly used types are:

1. Tartrate base baking powder
2. Phosphate base baking powder
3. Sodium aluminum sulphate and phosphate combination base baking powder

4. Sodium acid pyrophosphate base baking powder

There is a difference in the rate of reactions of the different types of baking powder.

Type No. 1. Tartrate base baking powder starts releasing carbon dioxide gas as soon as it comes in contact with moisture. Baked goods made with tartrate base baking powders should be baked almost immediately after making up.

Type No. 2. Phosphate base baking powders are somewhat slower acting than Type No. 1 but more rapid than Types No. 3 and No. 4.

Type No. 3. Aluminum base baking powders are slower acting. They depend upon heat as well as upon moisture for releasing their full amount of carbon dioxide.

Type No. 4. Sodium acid pyrophosphate is a type baking powder, particularly manufactured for use in large quantity baking. It is a slow acting baking powder and releases carbon dioxide gas primarily in the presence of heat.

Formulas in this section have been developed and tested with Type No. 3 combination baking powder.

Yeast

Functions of Yeast: Yeast is used in bakery products to

Make a light porous dough
Condition the dough batch

Types of Yeast: The following types of yeast are used by the Navy:

1. Compressed yeast
2. Active dry yeast
3. Dry yeast in cake form

Compressed Yeast: Compressed yeast is supplied in 1-pound units approximately the size of 1-pound print of butter and in ½-ounce cakes.

Compressed yeast will keep its full baking strength about 2 weeks when held at a temperature of not higher than 40° F. If compressed yeast is to be kept longer than 2 weeks, it must be fresh and in excellent condition and frozen at 20° F. or lower until used. Before using, slowly thaw yeast by holding in refrigerator at a temperature of about 40° F.

The amount used in yeast-raised goods varies from about 1% (1 pound of yeast per 100 pounds of flour) in lean bread doughs to as much as 11% (11 pounds per 100 pounds of flour) in rich coffee cake and Danish pastry doughs. Richer doughs require more yeast to properly leaven or raise the dough. Normally, bread requires about 2% (2 pounds per 100 pounds of flour).

Add compressed yeast to dough by breaking it into small pieces and mixing or dissolving it thoroughly in part of the water used in doughs. Incorporate the yeast solution along with other ingredients. Yeast solutions should not be brought in contact with relatively high strength salt solutions.

Active Dry Yeast. Active dry yeast is usually supplied in small pellets or spheres. It may also be supplied in flakes or short rod-like pieces.

Active dry yeast is yeast in which the moisture content has been reduced to not more than 8%. In the drying process some of the yeast cells are killed and the balance are made inactive. The net result is an inactive yeast, with approximately double the amount of live but inactive dry yeast cells, as are present in compressed yeast.

Dried yeast functions in yeast-raised doughs exactly as compressed yeast. Half as much as the specified amount of compressed yeast is used. For example, a bread formula calling for 2 pounds of compressed yeast requires 1 pound of active dry yeast.

How to "Reactivate": It is necessary to "reactivate" the yeast before adding it to the dough mix. This is accomplished as follows:

Dissolve required quantity of yeast in lukewarm water (70° F. to 80° F.).

Add small amount of sugar to furnish food for yeast cells.

Allow mixture to stand at temperatures of 70° F. to 75° F. for 45 to 60 minutes. This step is usually termed "pre-treatment" of yeast.

Quantities of sugar and water used in pre-treatment are subtracted from the dough formula. Usual quantities for "pre-treatment" are as follows:

Yeast—5 parts, by weight
Sugar—1 part, by weight
Water—35 parts, by weight

Example: Bread formula calls for 2 pounds compressed yeast.

Active dry yeast—1 pound
Sugar—3 ounces
Water, warm—7 pounds (3½ quarts)

Dissolve ingredients in warm water and allow to remain in warm place, 70° F. to 75° F., for 45 to 60 minutes. Occasional stirring aids reactivation. Add to the dough mix in the same manner as compressed yeast. Deduct the 3 ounces sugar and 7 pounds (3½ quarts) water from quantities specified in formula.

Storage: Long periods of storage, or more particularly, high temperature storage, kills the inactive yeast cells in dried yeast as the following table shows.

Storage Temperature:	Results
98° F. for 6 weeks	Marked loss in leavening power.
86° F. for 10 weeks	Marked loss in leavening power.
70° F. for 6 months	Slight, but not materially significant, loss in leavening power.
40° F. to 50° F. (refrigerator) for 1 year	No appreciable loss in leavening power.

Active dry yeast can be frozen without ill effect, providing it is thawed slowly at a temperature of 40° F. to 50° F.

Use the following procedure to handle dried yeast which has been injured by adverse storage conditions:

Increase "pre-treatment" time from 1 hour to 2 hours, or longer. This longer period allows the dormant cells to grow and "bud" or to create new active cells.

"Fermenting time" and/or "proof time" of the finished dough may be lengthened so that required rise is obtained.

Adjustments in the procedure can best be determined by actual practice and depend on the condition of the yeast.

It is not desirable to increase the quantity of dried yeast in order to compensate for loss in leavening power. Dried yeast contains, in relatively small quantities, enzymes which affect the protein in the flour. If the quantities of these enzymes are too high, a sticky dough with lessened structure-building properties is obtained. When yeast shows decreased leavening power, do not increase the yeast quantities.

To extend the quantities of yeast on hand, the weight of yeast used can be decreased somewhat, and the pre-treating period lengthened. This permits new yeast cells to grow, which increases the fermenting power of the yeast.

Dry Yeast Mixed with Cereals: Dry yeast (cake form) with cereals is a mixture of yeast and cereals pressed into cakes weighing about 2 ounces each. Half as much as the specified amount of compressed yeast is used. Quantities and dough mixing are similar. However, from 12 to 20 hours are required to produce good bread. Fermentation times are considerably lengthened.

Keeping Qualities: Dry yeast with cereals has very good keeping qualities. It maintains satisfactory baking qualities for approximately 1 year when held at temperatures between 65° F. and 70° F.

Activating: The "activation" or "pre-treatment" period described for granular dried yeast may also be applied to dry cake yeast to speed up yeast activity. A pre-treatment of from 1 to 2 hours in dilute sugar solution is helpful.

EMERGENCY SPONGE METHOD

Use when the supply of granular dehydrated yeast (active dry yeast) is limited or has lost its strength due to improper storage.

This method of bread making can be used for any size dough batch on a continuous production basis.

Ingredients	100-Pound Flour Basis	42-Pound Flour Basis
SPONGE		
Flour	50 lbs.	21 lbs.
Water	26 lbs.	11 lbs.
Active dry yeast	2½ oz.	1 oz.
Sugar	8 oz.	3 oz.
Salt	4 oz.	1½ oz.
DOUGH		
Flour	50 lbs.	21 lbs.
Milk, liquid (variable)	3⅞ gals.	1⅝ gals.
Sugar	2 lbs. 8 oz.	1 lb.
Salt	1 lb. 12 oz.	10 oz.
Shortening	2 lbs.	13 oz.

Sponge.—Mix and allow to ferment for 12 hours at 82°F. to 84°F.

Dough.—Mix fermented sponge with dough ingredients at a temperature of 84°F.

Allow to rise 1 hour.

Scale, pan, and proof for approximately 1 hour or to desired height.

Bake in usual manner.

Pan Grease

Pan grease, while not actually an ingredient, is a prerequisite for good baking and is therefore included in this section.

The proper use of pan grease will eliminate waste through a reduction in cripples and breakage. Grease suitable for various kinds of bakery products are listed in the following tables.

Over-greased pans may produce poor volume in cakes, cookies with excessive spread and bread with greasy crust. Use only enough pan grease to cover suface of baking pan.

Table I.—PAN GREASE FOR CAKES

Ingredients	No. 1	No. 2
	For Hand Greasing (Using brush)	For Mechanical Greasing (Using machine)
Flour	10 pounds	10 pounds.
Shortening	20 pounds	10 pounds.
Salad oil		10 pounds.
METHOD	Whip very light	Melt shortening. Mix with oil and flour. Use warm.

Table II.—PAN GREASE FOR BREAD AND ROLLS

Ingredients	No. 1	No. 2	No. 3
	For Hand Greasing (Using cloth)	For Spray Greasing	For Mechanical Greasing (Using brush)
Shortening	6 pounds	5 pounds	6 pounds.
Hot water	2 pounds (1 quart)	2 pounds (1 quart)	
Salad oil		1 pound	6 pounds.
METHOD	Whip together	Whip together shortening and hot water. Add salad oil.	Melt together.

Table III.—PAN GREASE FOR COOKIES, COFFEE CAKES, ETC.

NOTE.—Use pan grease No. 1, Table I, for these types of bakery products.

Baking Terms

Bench Tolerance: The property of dough to ferment at a rate slow enough to prevent over-fermentation while dough is being made up into units on the bench.

Blending: Combining or thorough mixing of ingredients in making a food product.

Bun Press: A mechanical press which takes a large piece of dough and cuts it into 36 pieces suitable for making up into buns, rolls or similar products. Usually a 36-ounce piece of dough is used, which yields 36 pieces each weighing 1 ounce.

Creaming: Mixing until smooth, sugar, shortening and other ingredients to incorporate air so that resultant mixture is thoroughly blended and increases appreciably in volume.

Cripple: A misshapen, burnt or otherwise undesirable product.

Crusting: Formation of dough crust on surface of doughs due to evaporation of water from the surface.

Docking: Punching a number of impressions in a dough with a smooth round stick about the size of a pencil or with fingers. Docking is done so that doughs expand uniformly during baking.

Emulsification: The process of blending together fat and water or water solutions of ingredients to produce a stable mixture which will not separate on standing.

Fat Absorption: Fat which is absorbed in food products as they are fried in deep fat.

Fermentation, Primary: Time given to dough between mixing and punching, during which yeast grows, generating carbon dioxide gas which causes dough to expand.

Flaky Pie Crust: Pie crust made by leaving lumps of shortening in the dough which, as the dough is rolled out, form layers of fat to give a flaky effect to finished crust.

Floured Bench: Sprinkling flour on bench surface to prevent dough from sticking.

Function: Reason for the use of ingredients or procedures in baking.

Fondant: A mixture of sugar, water and corn sirup which is cooked to 240° F., grained or crystallized and beaten smooth. Fondant is used for icings and in making candy.

Gluten: The essential constituent of flour, which is primarily responsible for producing elasticity in dough. The elasticity enables the dough to retain the fermentation gases.

Graining: After boiling a sugar solution to the desired temperature the solution will crystallize upon cooling. If cooling is slow, large crystals will form. Rapid cooling produces small crystals as will rapid mixing during cooling. Small fine crystals are desired in making fondant and this is accomplished by cooling and mixing. This process is termed "graining".

Leavening:	The raising or lightening of a batter or dough by the use of baking powder (chemical ingredients) or yeast.
Make-Up:	The process of forming a dough or batter into specified units. For example, forming a yeast dough into cinnamon rolls, or cutting cookies from a cookie dough.
Mealy Pie Crust:	Pie crust made by thoroughly blending together flour and shortening so that a short tender crust is obtained.
Molding:	Forming bread or sweet yeast doughs into loaves or units of desired size and shape.
"Old" Doughs:	Yeast dough which has become over-fermented due to long fermentation. This produces finished yeast goods dark in color, sour in flavor, low in volume, coarse in grain and rough in texture.
Plasticity:	The consistency or "feel" of a shortening.
Proof Time:	The secondary fermentation period given to dough between make-up and baking, for the purpose of permitting further yeast growth. This in turn causes the dough to rise, giving a light finished product.
Punching Doughs:	The process of knocking out of yeast dough the gas formed during the primary fermentation period.
Quick Breads:	Biscuits, muffins, and bread-like products in which baking powder is used for leavening.
Rounding Up:	Forming bread or sweet yeast doughs into round balls of the desired size for later molding into the finished units.
Scaling:	Weighing of ingredients, doughs or batters into units of desired amount.
Stabilizers:	Commercial preparations sold for use in meringue, pie fillings and marshmallows. If used, follow package directions.
Starch Water:	A mixture of cornstarch and water made by boiling together 1 or 2 tablespoons of cornstarch with 1 quart of water. This is used for brushing on bread to give a shine to the crust.
Trough:	Pan or container for holding dough.
Usage:	Method of using baked goods.
Washing Down:	In boiling a sugar solution, crystals form on the sides of the container. A brush dipped in water can be used to wash these crystals back into the boiling sugar solution. This helps to produce a uniform sirup.
Water Absorption:	Water required to produce a bread dough of desired consistency. Flours vary in ability to absorb water. This depends on age of flour, moisture content, wheat from which it is milled, storage conditions and milling process. Navy issue flour normally absorbs water from 60 to 65 per cent of its weight.
Weak Egg Whites:	Egg whites which are old or do not have sufficient structural forming solids for beating.
"Young" Doughs:	Yeast dough which is under-fermented. This produces finished yeast goods which are light in color, tight in texture and low in volume (heavy).

Formulas — Baking
Yeast Breads

Production Pointers
Mixing

Three purposes of dough mixing are:

To bring about an intimate and uniform mixture of the ingredients to form a smooth dough.

To make possible the complete wetting of the flour and to develop the dough mechanically so that it becomes pliable and extensible.

To distribute the yeast cells throughout the dough.

Two standard methods of dough mixing are:

1. *The Straight-Dough Method:* In this method all the ingredients are mixed in one operation. The ordinary sequence is as follows:

Dissolve yeast in part of the water at 78° F. to 80° F.

Pour remaining water into mixer. Add salt, sugar, and milk.

Dissolve these ingredients by a few turns of the mixer arms.

Stir in yeast solution, OR

Add flour and yeast solution.

Mix dough about 1 minute. Add shortening and mix to completion.

2. *The Sponge-Dough Method:* This is a two-stage mixing process. Ordinary sequence is as follows:

Mix together 55% to 70% of the flour, 55% to 65% of the water and all of the yeast to form the "sponge."

After the sponge has risen for the desired length of time, put it back into the mixer and mix together with remaining flour, water, malt, sugar, salt, milk and shortening.

Formulas in the bakery section of the Navy Cook Book are based on the straight-dough method.

Fermentation

Place mixed dough in a trough which has been lightly greased. The sides of the dough should be pulled over so that the top is smooth. If standard troughs are used, straight doughs require 2 feet of trough length for each 100 pounds of flour used. Sponge doughs require 2 feet for each 50 pounds of flour used.

Dough temperatures: It is important that doughs should be set from 77° F. to 80° F. whenever possible. Low temperatures slow up yeast action. High temperatures make the dough difficult to handle. They may also cause the development of undesirable bacteria, such as rope, wild yeasts, and excessive acidity which tends to weaken the gluten, resulting in a coarse-grained loaf of poor flavor. Doughs set from 77° F. to 80° F. will produce bread having better flavor and keeping quality and whiter crumb color than bread made from warmer doughs.

Punching or turning and folding: A straight dough is allowed to rise until light, until it will just recede when the fingers are pushed down about 4 inches and quickly withdrawn. The dough is then "punched," or turned and folded.

A straight dough made with 2 per cent yeast will be ready for the "punch" in about 2 to 2½ hours. Dough is allowed to loosen up for about 20 minutes before making up.

The final maturity and, consequently, the quality of the bread, depends largely on the time the dough is punched. It is important that the time be gauged carefully.

Dividing and scaling: Divide dough either by hand on the bench, or by machine.

In hand dividing, each piece of dough should be scaled. In machine operation, only an occasional scaling is necessary as the dough pieces come from the divider. Under normal conditions, in making white pan bread a pound loaf *will be produced from 18 to 18½ ounces of dough.*

Rounding: Each piece is rounded or balled up so as to seal the cuts made in dividing.

Intermediate proof: The rounded pieces of dough are allowed to rest for 10 to 15 minutes. They should be covered and kept free from drafts so as to prevent drying out and crusting.

Molding: After the intermediate proof, mold the pieces into loaves, using as little dusting flour as possible.

Panning: Pans should be lightly greased. Only enough grease should be used to prevent loaves from sticking to the pan. Excess grease is not only wasteful but it causes the loaf to fry in the oven instead of baking properly.

Place each piece of dough so that the molding seam faces the bottom of the pan. The dough loaves should be long enough to reach the ends of the pan.

Bread pans should always be kept clean. Wipe clean with a dry cloth after each baking. At frequent intervals, wash the pans in a *dilute solution* of washing soda or tri-sodium phosphate using 2 ounces per gallon of water.

Pan proofing: Time, temperature and humidity: Since the molding process compresses each piece of dough, thereby expelling a large amount of the gas, it is necessary for the dough loaves to rise to the proper degree of lightness before baking. This is known as "proofing."

It is important to control proofing time, temperature and humidity. An underproofed dough will produce bread of small volume which will be soggy and heavy. Overproofing weakens the structure of the dough, and if excessive, may cause the loaf to drop. The resulting bread will be irregular in shape, small in volume and coarse in grain and texture.

The proofing cabinet or room is usually well insulated so as to maintain a uniform temperature of 95°F. to 98°F. and a relative humidity of 80% to 85%. At this temperature, yeast action is vigorous and the relatively high humidity prevents the dough loaves from crusting over. The loaves are allowed to proof from 30 to 60 minutes until they are double in size.

If pan racks are available, the upper shelves of the cabinet should be loaded first. If, however, the temperature and humidity of the proof box are not uniform and the upper part of the box is warmer than the bottom, the racks should be loaded from bottom to top.

Baking

Temperature and time: Oven temperatures range between 375°F. to 450°F., depending on type and size of loaf. Flash heat, a temporary excessive oven temperature at the start of the baking process, is to be avoided for it will cause a crust to form on the dough loaves before the inside is properly baked.

Spacing pans in oven: To insure uniform baking, the pans must be properly spaced. The exact space which will permit thorough baking of the center loaves in a set of pans depends on the type and size of pan as well as on the type of oven. 1-pound pans should be spaced about ¾ inch apart at the top.

Loading and unloading: Extreme care should be taken to avoid jarring the pans as they are removed from the proof box and loaded into the oven. In loading an oven, it is advisable to load one half first, working from the rear to the front, then the other half. In unloading, the half which was loaded first should be emptied first.

Loss of weight: Loss in weight during baking is due mainly to evaporation of moisture from the dough loaves and varies with the type of dough, size of loaf and general oven conditions. It must be determined by experience in order to set the necessary scaling weight.

Cooling: Cool bread gradually to avoid cracking of the crust.

Controlling Rope

Rope is a bread infection which may appear in 6 to 24 hours after baking. Rope can be detected in the bread by an odor resembling ripe cantaloupe. As rope develops yellow or brown spots, having soft sticky centers, form in the crumb. The spots increase in size until in about 48 hours the crumb of the loaf is changed into a strong smelling, brownish, soft, sticky mass which can be pulled into strings or rope.

Cause: Rope is caused by bacteria which are found on the surfaces of grains, potatoes and other vegetables and in the soil. Moist, warm conditions favor the development of rope.

Remedy: Keep bake shop in a clean, sanitary condition.

Sterilize equipment with live steam or boiling vinegar.

Keep doughs cool, not over 80°F.

Add vinegar to each dough in the proportion of 1 quart of vinegar to each 100 pounds of flour. This is an absolute preventative.

Cool bread as rapidly as possible after baking.

WHITE BREAD
(Average formula)

Yield: Approx. 160 (1-pound) loaves.   Portion: Approx. 4 ounces.

| INGREDIENTS | BASIS 100 POUNDS FLOUR | | MIXING METHOD | ....PORTIONS |
	WEIGHTS	AMOUNTS (approx.)		
	Pounds / *Ounces*			
Yeast, compressed.	2 /	....	Dissolve yeast in part of water. Add remaining water, sugar, salt and milk powder. Mix.	....
Water (variable).	65 /	8 gallons		....
Sugar	4 /	½ gallon		....
Salt	2 / 8	1¼ quarts	Ingredients, except yeast, need not be thoroughly dissolved.	....
Milk, skim, powdered.	6 /	5¼ quarts		....
Flour	100 /	25 gallons	Add flour and mix well.	....
Shortening	5 /	2½ quarts	Add and mix well, about 10 minutes.	....

Fermentation: Bring dough from mixer at a temperature of 78°F. to 80°F. Let dough rise about 2 hours.

Punch: Take to bench and let rest 20 minutes.

Make-up: Make up into loaves of desired size and pan.

Proof: Proof until double in size, at 95°F. and high humidity, if possible.

Baking: Bake at 450°F. for 35 to 45 minutes.

NOTE.—1. 8 gallons fresh liquid milk or reconstituted evaporated milk may be used in place of the water and powdered milk. See page 21.

2. 1 pound active dry yeast may be used in place of 2 pounds compressed yeast.

3. 1 pound malt may be used in place of 1 pound sugar.

4. For richer loaf with better keeping qualities, increase the sugar and shortening by about 30 to 40 percent.

Variation

"No Time Dough":

This requires short fermentation.

Increase compressed yeast to 3 pounds. For active dry yeast use 1 pound 8 ounces.

Bring dough from mixer at 88°F. to 90°F. This can be done by using warm water in the dough. *No other formula changes are necessary.*

Make-up: Let dough rest 15 minutes. Make up. Proof and bake as for regular dough.

WHITE BREAD
(Average formula)

Yield: Approx. 24 (1-pound) loaves.   Portion: Approx. 4 ounces.

INGREDIENTS	100 PORTIONS			MIXING METHOD	...........PORTIONS
	WEIGHTS		AMOUNTS (approx.)		
	Pounds	*Ounces*			
Yeast, compressed.	....	4¾	....	Dissolve yeast in part of water. Add remaining water, sugar, salt and milk powder. Mix.	....
Water (variable).	9	12	1¼ gallons		....
Sugar	....	9½	1¼ cups		....
Salt	....	6	¾ cup	Ingredients, except yeast, need not be thoroughly dissolved.	....
Milk, skim, powdered.	....	14	1½ pints		....
Flour	15	....	3¾ gallons	Add flour and mix well.	....
Shortening	....	12	1½ cups	Add and mix well, about 10 minutes.	....

Fermentation: Bring dough from mixer at a temperature of 78°F. to 80°F. Let dough rise about 2 hours.

Punch: Take to bench and let rest 20 minutes.

Make-up: Make up into loaves of desired size and pan.

Proof: Proof until double in size, at 95°F. and high humidity, if possible.

Baking: Bake at 450°F. for 35 to 45 minutes.

NOTE.—1. 1¼ gallons fresh liquid milk or reconstituted evaporated milk may be used in place of the water and powdered milk. See page 21.

2. 2 ounces malt may be used in place of 2 ounces sugar.

3. 2½ ounces active dry yeast may be used in place of 4¾ ounces compressed yeast.

4. For richer loaf with better keeping qualities increase the sugar and shortening by about 30 to 40 percent.

Variation

"No Time Dough":

This requires short fermentation.

Increase compressed yeast to 7 ounces. For active dry yeast use 3½ ounces.

Bring dough from mixer at 88°F. to 90°F. This can be done by using warm water in the dough. *No other formula changes are necessary.*

Make-up: Let dough rest 15 minutes. Make up. Proof and bake as for regular dough.

FIELD BREAD
(Straight dough method)

Yield: Approx. 35 (4-pound) loaves.   Portion: Approx. 4 ounces.

Ingredients	BASIS 100 POUNDS FLOUR			Mixing Method	Portions
	Weights		Amounts (approx.)		
	Pounds	Ounces			
Yeast, compressed.	....	12	....		....
Water (variable).	55	....	6⅞ gallons	Dissolve the yeast in part of water.	....
Salt	2	....	1 quart		....
Sugar	3	....	1½ quarts	Mix all ingredients to a very stiff dough.	....
Flour	100	....	25 gallons		....
Shortening	....	8	1 cup		....

Fermentation: Bring dough from mixing bowl at 78°F. to 80°F. Let rise about 4 hours.

Punch: Give second rise for 1 to 1½ hours. Punch again. Take to bench. Let dough stand about 20 minutes.

Make-up: Scale dough into 4½-pound pieces. Round up and flatten out into circular loaves about 10 inches in diameter and 1½ inches thick. Place 3 loaves on greased bun pan.

Proof: Proof for 15 minutes. Dock dough in 3 places by inserting thumb into dough to a depth of about 1 inch.

Baking: Bake at 450°F. for 1½ to 1¾ hours.

NOTE.—1. 6 ounces active dry yeast may be used in place of 12 ounces compressed yeast.

2. This bread is a circular loaf about 11 inches in diameter, 4 to 5 inches thick, with a thick, hard crust. The crust, if unbroken, lessens the possibility of mold development, permits rough handling and stacking in transportation without injury. It will keep the bread fresh and edible for a period of 2 to 3 weeks.

FIELD BREAD
(Straight dough method)

Yield: Approx. 5 (4-pound) loaves.   Portion: Approx. 4 ounces.

Ingredients	100 PORTIONS			Mixing Method	Portions
	Weights		Amounts (approx.)		
	Pounds	Ounces			
Yeast, compressed.	....	1¾	....		....
Water (variable).	8	4	4⅛ quarts	Dissolve the yeast in part of water.	....
Salt	....	4¾	½ cup		....
Sugar	....	8	1 cup	Mix all ingredients to a very stiff dough.	....
Flour	15	....	3¾ gallons		....
Shortening	....	1¼	2 tablespoons		....

345★

Fermentation: Bring dough from mixer at 78° F. to 80° F. Let rise about 4 hours.

Punch: Give second rise for 1 to 1½ hours. Punch again. Take to bench. Let dough stand about 20 minutes.

Make-up: Scale dough into 4½-pound pieces. Round up and flatten out into circular loaves about 10 inches in diameter and 1½ inches thick. Place 3 loaves on a greased bun pan.

Proof: Proof for 15 minutes. Dock the dough in 3 places by inserting thumb into dough to a depth of about 1 inch.

Baking: Bake at 450°F. for 1½ to 1¾ hours.

NOTE.—1. 1 ounce active dry yeast may be used in place of 1¾ ounces compressed yeast.

2. This bread is a circular loaf about 11 inches in diameter, 4 to 5 inches thick, with a thick, hard crust. The crust, if unbroken, lessens the possibility of mold development, permits rough handling and stacking in transportation without injury. It will keep the bread fresh and edible for a period of 2 to 3 weeks.

RYE BREAD

Yield: Approx. 145 (1-pound) loaves.   Portion: Approx. 4 ounces.

INGREDIENTS	BASIS 100 POUNDS FLOUR			MIXING METHOD	..........PORTIONS
	WEIGHTS		AMOUNTS (approx.)		
	Pounds	*Ounces*			
Yeast, compressed.	3	....	....	Dissolve yeast in part of water. Add remaining water, sugar and salt. Mix.	....
Water (variable).	58	....	7¼ gallons		....
Caraway seed (optional).	....	3½	½ cup		....
Sugar	2	8	1¼ quarts	Ingredients, except yeast, need not be thoroughly dissolved.	....
Salt	2	....	1 quart		....
Flour, white ...	80	....	20 gallons	Add flour and mix well.	....
Flour, dark or medium rye.	20	....	5 gallons		....
Shortening	2	8	1¼ quarts..........	Add and mix about 10 minutes.	....

Fermentation: Bring dough from mixer at a temperature of 77° F. Let dough rise about 1½ hours.

Punch: Take to bench and let rest 20 minutes.

Make-up: Make up into loaves of desired size. Place about 6 inches apart on bun pans sprinkled with corn meal.

Proof: Proof until double in size, at 95°F. and high humidity if possible. Make 3 or 4 cuts across the top of loaf with a sharp knife. Wash with Starch Water (page 340).

Baking: Bake at 425° F. for 25 to 35 minutes.

NOTE.—1. 1½ pounds active dry yeast may be used in place of 3 pounds compressed yeast.

2. 2½ pounds malt may be used in place of 2½ pounds sugar.

RYE BREAD

Yield: Approx. 22 (1-pound) loaves.   Portion: Approx. 4 ounces.

| INGREDIENTS | 100 PORTIONS | | | MIXING METHOD | ....PORTIONS |
| | WEIGHTS | | AMOUNTS (approx.) | | |
	Pounds	Ounces			
Yeast, compressed.	....	7¼	....	Dissolve yeast in part of water. Add remaining water, sugar and salt. Mix.	....
Water, cool (variable).	8	12	1⅛ gallons		....
Caraway seed (optional).	....	½	1½ teaspoons....		....
Sugar	....	6	¾ cup	Ingredients, except yeast, need not be thoroughly dissolved.	....
Salt	....	4¾	½ cup		....
Flour, white	12	....	3 gallons	Add flour and mix well.	....
Flour, dark or medium rye.	3	....	¾ gallon		....
Shortening	....	6	¾ cup	Add and mix for about 10 minutes.	....

Fermentation: Bring dough from mixer at a temperature of 77° F. Let dough rise about 1½ hours.

Punch: Take to bench and let rest 20 minutes.

Make-up: Make up into loaves of desired size. Place about 6 inches apart on bun pans sprinkled with corn meal.

Proof: Proof until double in size, at 95°F.

and high humidity if possible. Make 3 or 4 cuts across the top of loaf with a sharp knife. Wash with Starch Water (page 340).

Baking: Bake at 425° F. for 35 to 45 minutes.

NOTE.—1. 3½ ounces active dry yeast may be used in place of 7¼ ounces compressed yeast.

2. 6 ounces malt may be used in place of 6 ounces sugar.

50 PER CENT WHOLE WHEAT BREAD

Yield: Approx. 153 (1-pound) loaves.　　　　　　　　Portion: Approx. 4 ounces.

| INGREDIENTS | BASIS 100 POUNDS FLOUR | | MIXING METHOD | ....PORTIONS |
	WEIGHTS	AMOUNTS (approx.)		
	Pounds | *Ounces*			
Yeast, compressed.	3 |	....	Dissolve yeast in part of water. Add remaining water, sugar, salt and powdered milk. Mix.	....
Water (variable).	62 |	7¾ gallons		....
Sugar	4 |	½ gallon		....
Salt	2 |	1 quart	Ingredients, except yeast, need not be thoroughly dissolved.	....
Milk, skim, powdered.	3 |	2½ quarts		....
Flour, whole wheat.	50 |	12½ gallons	Add flour and mix well.	....
Flour, white	50 |	12½ gallons		....
Shortening	3 |	1½ quarts	Add and mix well, about 10 minutes.	....

Fermentation: Bring dough from mixer at 78° F. to 80° F. Let rise about 2 hours.

Punch: Take to bench and let rest 30 minutes.

Make-up: Make up into loaves of desired size and pan.

Proof: Proof until dough increases in size by 50% to 75%. Do not let dough double in size. Proof at 95° F. and high humidity, if possible.

Baking: Bake at 425° F. about 35 minutes.

NOTE.—1. 1 pound 8 ounces active dry yeast may be used in place of 3 pounds compressed yeast.

2. 2 pounds malt may be used in place of 2 pounds sugar.

3. 7¾ gallons fresh liquid milk or reconstituted evaporated milk may be used in place of the water and powdered milk. See page 21.

50 PER CENT WHOLE WHEAT BREAD

Yield: Approx. 23 (1-pound) loaves.   Portion: Approx. 4 ounces.

| INGREDIENTS | 100 PORTIONS | | MIXING METHOD | ....PORTIONS |
	WEIGHTS	AMOUNTS (approx.)		
	Pounds	*Ounces*			
Yeast, compressed.	....	7	....	Dissolve yeast in part of water. Add remaining water, sugar, salt and powdered milk. Mix.	....
Water (variable).	9	4	1⅛ gallons		....
Sugar	....	9½	1¼ cups		....
Salt	....	4¾	½ cup	Ingredients, except yeast, need not be thoroughly dissolved.	....
Milk, skim, powdered.	....	7¼	1½ cups		....
Flour, whole wheat.	7	8	7½ quarts	Add flour and mix well.	....
Flour, white	7	8	7½ quarts		....
Shortening	....	7¼	⅞ cup	Add and mix well, about 10 minutes.	....

Fermentation: Bring dough from mixer at 78° F. to 80° F. Let dough rise about 2 hours.

Punch: Take to bench and let rest 30 minutes.

Make-up: Make up into loaves of desired size and pan.

Proof: Proof until dough increases in size by 50% to 75%. Do not let dough double in size. Proof at 95° F. and high humidity, if possible.

Baking: Bake at 425° F. about 35 minutes.

NOTE.—1. 3½ ounces active dry yeast may be used in place of 7 ounces compressed yeast.

2. 4½ ounces malt may be used in place of 4½ ounces sugar.

3. 1⅛ gallons fresh liquid milk or reconstituted evaporated milk may be used in place of the water and powdered milk. See page 21.

PLAIN SOFT ROLLS

Yield: Approx. 250 dozen (3,000 rolls).   Portion: 2 rolls.

| INGREDIENTS | BASIS 100 POUNDS FLOUR | | | MIXING METHOD | ....PORTIONS |
| | WEIGHTS | | AMOUNTS (approx.) | | |
	Pounds	Ounces			
Yeast, compressed.	2	....	....	Dissolve yeast in part of water. Add remaining water, sugar, salt and powdered milk. Mix.	....
Water (variable).	62	....	7¾ gallons		....
Sugar	8	....	1 gallon		....
Salt	2	....	1 quart	Ingredients, except yeast, need not be thoroughly dissolved.	....
Milk, skim, powdered.	5	....	4½ quarts		....
Flour, white	100	....	25 gallons	Add flour and mix well.	
Shortening	8	....	1 gallon	Add and mix well, about 10 minutes.	....

Fermentation: Bring dough from mixer at 78°F. to 80°F. Let dough rise about 2 hours.

Punch: Take to bench and let rest 20 minutes.

Make-up: Scale into 36-ounce pieces. Take to bun press. Flatten out in press pan. Cut into 36 pieces.

Proof: Proof until rolls are about double in size, at 95° F. and high humidity, if possible.

Baking: Bake at 425° F. about 25 minutes.

NOTE—1. 1 pound active dry yeast may be used in place of 2 pounds compressed yeast.

2. 7¾ gallons fresh liquid milk or reconstituted evaporated milk may be used in place of the water and powdered milk. See page 21.

3. If bun press is not available, pinch off 1-ounce pieces of dough and round up.

4. Rolls may be made up into a number of styles such as finger rolls, parker house rolls and buns.

PLAIN SOFT ROLLS

Yield: Approx. 18 dozen.   Portion: 2 rolls.

Ingredients	100 Portions		Mixing Method	...........Portions
	Weights	Amounts (approx.)		
	Pounds | *Ounces*			
Yeast, compressed.	.... | 2¼	....	Dissolve yeast in part of water. Add remaining water, sugar, salt and powdered milk. Mix.	....
Water (variable).	4 | 8	2¼ quarts		....
Sugar	.... | 9¼	1¼ cups		....
Salt	.... | 2¼	¼ cup	Ingredients, except yeast, need not be thoroughly dissolved.	....
Milk, skim, powdered.	.... | 5¾	1¼ cups		....
Flour	7 | 4	7¼ quarts	Add flour and mix well.	....
Shortening	.... | 9¼	1¼ cups	Add and mix well, about 10 minutes.	....

Fermentation: Bring dough from mixer at 78° F. to 80° F. Let dough rise about 2 hours.

Punch: Take to bench and let rest 20 minutes.

Make-up: Scale into 36-ounce pieces. Take to bun press. Flatten out in press pan. Cut into 36 pieces.

Proof: Proof until rolls are about double in size, at 95° F. and high humidity, if possible.

Baking: Bake at 425° F. about 25 minutes.

NOTE—1. 1⅛ ounces active dry yeast may be used in place of 2¼ ounces compressed yeast.

2. 2¼ quarts fresh liquid milk or reconstituted evaporated milk may be used in place of the water and powdered milk. See page 21.

3. If bun press is not available, pinch off 1-ounce pieces of dough and round up.

4. Rolls may be made into a number of styles such as finger rolls, parker house rolls and buns.

Sweet Yeast Dough

Production Pointers

Basic Types:

1. Ordinary sweet yeast dough.
2. "Rolled In" or Danish dough.

The basic difference between the two types is in the handling after mixing.

Ordinary sweet yeast dough is mixed, given fermentation time, made up, proofed, baked and finished.

Danish dough is mixed, shortening or butter is rolled in, and then handled the same as ordinary sweet yeast dough.

The basic sweet yeast dough formula given on page 353 is suitable for mixing up into either regular sweet yeast goods or into Danish pastry.

Danish pastry is made by rolling in from 2 ounces to 5 ounces shortening or butter to 1 pound of dough. The higher the amount of "rolled in" fat used, the richer the finished Danish pastry.

Mixing: The purposes of the mixing operation are:

To blend thoroughly all ingredients
To develop sufficient structure-forming gluten

These two objectives can be accomplished by adding ingredients to the mixing bowl either singly or in groups.

An easier way is to mix sweet doughs by the

351★

simplified mixing method outlined on page 353. In this method all the ingredients are added to the mixing bowl and mixed until a smooth uniform dough is obtained.

This saves time and aids in more uniform production of sweet yeast goods. Sweet doughs can be mixed by this method in as short a time as 3 minutes.

Fermentation: Sweet doughs, because of their richness, have wider fermentation tolerance than bread doughs. The dough temperatures do not have to be carefully controlled. Doughs may be taken from the mixer at temperatures ranging from 78° F. to 85° F. Primary fermentation from 1½ to 2 hours is necessary. Higher dough temperatures require a shorter time.

Sweet doughs have good bench tolerance. They do not become overfermented if made up within 1 hour after primary fermentation. Secondary fermentation, or pan proofing, requires about 1 hour.

Sweet doughs produce best finished products when handled on the "young" side. "Old" (overfermented) doughs produce baked goods poor in flavor and appearance.

Refrigeration: Sweet yeast doughs lend themselves readily to refrigeration. If refrigeration facilities are available, it is possible to make up the Basic Sweet Dough (page 353) many hours before baking time.

The following table shows 2 general methods of handling refrigerated doughs.

HANDLING REFRIGERATED SWEET YEAST DOUGHS

Method I	Method II
Mix the dough.	Mix the dough.
Bring dough from mixer at normal temperature, 78° F. to 85° F.	Bring dough from mixer at normal temperature, 78° F. to 85° F.
Give dough from ½ to ¾ normal fermentation time.	Give dough from ½ to ¾ normal fermentation time.
Punch and flatten 8 to 10-pound pieces of dough on bun pans. Cover with greased paper. Refrigerate at 32° F. to 40° F.	Make up into various units. Place individual pieces on bun pans. Cover with greased paper.
Bring each 8 to 10-pound piece to room temperature.	Refrigerate at 32° F. to 40° F.
Make up into various units.	Bring individual pieces on each pan to room temperature.
Proof in normal way.	Proof in normal way.
Bake in normal way.	Bake in normal way.

Avoid "Old" Doughs When Handling Refrigerated Sweet Yeast Doughs: Maintain refrigerator temperature under 40° F.

Open refrigerator no more than necessary.

Scale dough pieces to weigh less than 10 pounds. Larger pieces ferment too much before the cold temperature of the refrigerator penetrates to the center of the dough to prevent yeast activity.

Doughs cannot be successfully refrigerated for more than 72 hours.

BASIC SWEET DOUGH

Yield: Approx. 223 pounds.   Portion: Approx. 5½ ounces.

Ingredients	Basis 100 Pounds Flour		Mixing Method	Portions
	Weights	Amounts (approx.)		
	Pounds	Ounces			

Ingredients	Pounds	Ounces	Amounts (approx.)	Mixing Method	Portions
Sugar	18	....	2¼ gallons		
Salt	1	12	3½ cups		
Malt	1	12	2½ cups	Place all dry ingredients and shortening in mixing bowl.	
Shortening	20	....	2½ gallons		
Eggs, whole	20	....	200 (10 quarts)		
Flavoring	....	1½	3 tablespoons	Dissolve yeast in part of milk. Add with eggs and remaining milk.	
Yeast	6	12			
Milk, liquid (variable).	55	....	6¾ gallons	Mix to a smooth dough, about 2 to 5 minutes.	
Flour	100	....	25 gallons		
Mace	....	2	½ cup		

Fermentation: Bring dough from mixer at 78° F. to 85° F. Allow about 2 hours for fermentation.

Punch: Take to bench and let rest about 20 minutes.

Make-up: Make up into units of desired size and shapes (pages 354, 355, 356.)

Proof: Proof until pieces are about double in size.

Baking: Bake large units at about 375° F. and small units at temperatures up to 425° F.

NOTE.—1. 1 pound 12 ounces sugar may be used in place of 1 pound 12 ounces malt.

2. 5 pounds powdered eggs and 15 pounds water may be used in place of 20 pounds eggs.

3. 3 pounds 6 ounces active dry yeast may be used in place of 6 pounds 12 ounces compressed yeast.

4. Increase shortening and eggs to 26¾ pounds each to make a richer dough. Part butter may be used as shortening.

5. 2 ounces nutmeg may be used in place of 2 ounces mace.

BASIC SWEET DOUGH

Yield: Approx. 33½ pounds.

Portion: Approx. 5½ ounces.

INGREDIENTS	100 PORTIONS			MIXING METHOD	...........PORTIONS
	WEIGHTS		AMOUNTS (approx.)		
	Pounds	Ounces			
Sugar	2	12	1⅜ quarts		....
Salt	....	4	½ cup		....
Malt	....	4	½ cup	Place all dry ingredients and shortening in mixing bowl.	....
Shortening	3	....	1½ quarts		....
Eggs, whole	3	....	30 (1½ quarts)		....
Flavoring	....	¼	½ tablespoon ...	Dissolve yeast in part of milk. Add with eggs and remaining milk.	....
Yeast	1	....	....		....
Milk, liquid (variable).	8	4	1 gallon	Mix to a smooth dough, about 2 to 5 minutes.	....
Flour	15	....	3¾ gallons		....
Mace	....	¼	1 tablespoon		....

Fermentation: Bring dough from mixer at 78° F. to 85° F. Allow about 2 hours for fermentation.

Punch: Take to bench and let rest 20 minutes.

Make-up: Make up into units of desired size and shapes (pages 354, 355, 356).

Proof: Proof until pieces are about double in size.

Baking: Bake large units at about 375° F. and small units at temperatures up to 425° F.

NOTE.—1. 4 ounces sugar may be used in place of 4 ounces malt.

2. 12 ounces powdered eggs and 2 pounds 4 ounces water may be used in place of the 3 pounds eggs.

3. 8 ounces active dry yeast may be used in place of 1 pound compressed yeast.

4. Increase shortening and eggs to 4 pounds each to make a richer dough.

5. ¼ ounce nutmeg may be used in place of ¼ ounce mace.

Variations

Cinnamon Buns

Make-up: Roll out a strip of fermented Basic Sweet Dough ⅛ inch to ¼ inch thick, about 15 inches wide and as long as desired.

Brush with melted butter and sprinkle liberally with cinnamon, sugar and raisins.

Brush bottom edge of dough with egg wash (page 357). Roll like a Jelly Roll (page 390). Seal edge.

Cut off pieces approximately 1 inch long. Place cut-side down on greased sheet pans.

Proof: Proof until about double in size.

Baking: Bake at 400° F. to 425° F. for 15 to 20 minutes.

Finishing: Ice, while warm with Vanilla Water Icing (page 357).

Butterfly Buns

Make-up: Make up like cinnamon buns. Cut off pieces approximately 1 inch long. Press a round dowel or small pie pin firmly down the center of each roll at right angles to the 1-inch direction.

Press or flatten out the folds of each end. Place on lightly greased pans.

Proof: Proof until approximately double in size.

Baking: Bake at 400° F. to 425° F. for 15 to 20 minutes.

Finishing: Ice, while warm, with Vanilla Water Icing (page 357) or wash with Shine (page 358).

Raisin Buns

Make-up: Just before sweet dough is ready to be removed from the mixer, add 4 ounces soaked seedless raisins per 1 pound of dough.

Give dough usual fermentation period. Scale into 1½-ounce pieces. Round up. Place close together on greased sheet pans.

Proof: Proof until approximately double in size.

Baking: Bake at 400° F. to 425° F. for 15 to 20 minutes.

Finishing: Ice, while warm, with Vanilla Water Icing (page 357).

Flat-Top Coffee Cake

Make-up: Roll out a 5-pound piece of fermented Basic Sweet Dough. Place on bun pan or make individual 10-ounce coffee cakes in 8-inch round layer cake tins.

Roll lightly toward sides of pan until the whole pan is covered. Dock dough. Wash with water. Spread with Butter Topping (page 356) or Streusel Topping (page 357).

Proof: Proof until approximately double in size.

Baking: Bake at 375° F. to 400° F. for 20 to 25 minutes.

Finishing: Sprinkle with powdered sugar, if desired. Do not use icing.

Doughnuts

Make-up: Roll out dough ¼ inch thick and cut doughnuts. Various shapes may be used. Place on floured cloths.

Proof: Proof until approximately double in size.

Frying: Fry in hot deep fat at 365° F. to 375° F. for 1¾ to 2½ minutes.

Finishing: Dust with powdered sugar which has been sifted with a little cinnamon or serve plain.

Pershings

Make-up: Make up like Cinnamon Buns but *do not brush with butter or other fat.* Cut off thin slices (about ½ inch thick) to insure thorough frying and place on cloth.

Proof: Proof until approximately double in size.

Frying: Fry in hot deep fat at 365° F. to 375° F. for 1¾ to 2½ minutes.

Finishing: Place a dot of jelly in the center of each Pershing. Ice with Vanilla Water Icing (page 357).

Long Johns

Make-up: Roll out dough to a thickness of about ¼ inch. Cut dough into rectangular pieces about ½ inch x 4 inches. Place on floured cloths.

Proof: Proof until about double in size.

Frying: Fry in hot deep fat at 365° F. to 375° F. for 1¾ to 2½ minutes.

Finishing: Sugar or ice with Vanilla Water Icing (page 357).

Twists

Make-up: Roll out dough to a thickness of about ¼ inch and cut into strips about ½ inch x 8 inches. Fold each strip in the middle and twist. Place on floured cloths.

Proof: Proof until approximately double in size.

Frying: Fry in deep fat at 370° F. to 380° F. for 1¾ to 2½ minutes.

Finishing: Sugar or ice with Vanilla Water Icing (page 357).

Jelly Doughnuts

Make-up: Roll dough to a thickness of about ¼ inch. Cut round or diamond-shaped pieces of dough weighing 1½ ounces. Place on floured cloths.

Proof: Proof until about double in size.

Frying: Fry in hot deep fat at 370° F. to 380° F. for 1¾ to 2½ minutes.

Finishing: Fill with jelly, using a cream-filling machine; or split, spread with jelly and replace top.

Danish Pastry

Make-up: Scale Basic Sweet Dough into pieces convenient for rolling (about 4 or 5 pounds). Roll dough into rectangular shape about ¼ inch thick.

Start at one edge and cover completely ⅔ of dough with small pieces of butter or shortening. Use from 2 to 5 ounces of fat per pound of dough.

Fold the ⅓ portion of dough which is not covered by shortening over an equal portion of the buttered dough.

Fold the remaining ⅓ of the buttered dough over the top to make 3 layers of dough each separated by a layer of butter or shortening.

Roll dough out to a thickness of about ¼ inch. This constitutes the first roll.

Give two more rolls, folding the dough in exactly the same way. Do not roll in any more butter or shortening.

Let dough rest for about 45 minutes. Make up into any desired units.

Danish Twist

Make-up: Cut off a 1½-ounce strip of rolled dough. Divide into 3 pieces of equal weight.

Twist ends of each piece in opposite directions. Let rest on bench for a short time.

Twist each piece again. Braid the 3 together. Place on greased pans. Brush with egg wash. Sprinkle with sliced nuts, if desired.

Proof: Proof until not quite double in size, about ¾ of normal proof.

Baking: Bake at 375° F. to 400° F. for 15 to 20 minutes.

Finishing: Ice, while warm, with Vanilla Water Icing (page 357).

Danish Butter-Horns or Snail Buns

Make-up: Roll 4 or 5-pound piece of rolled-in dough to a thickness of about ¼ inch and width of about 12 inches.

Cut into strips ½ inch wide. Twist ends of strips in opposite directions. Coil up entire strip. Place on greased sheet pans. Coil each end toward center for butter horns.

Proof: Proof until approximately double in size.

Baking: Bake at 375° F. to 400° F. for 15 to 20 minutes.

Finishing: Brush with Shine (page 358), or ice with Vanilla Water Icing (page 357), or dust with powdered sugar.

Toppings for Sweet Yeast Dough Products

BUTTER TOPPING

Yield: Approx. 7 pounds.   Portion: 1 to 2 ounces per 10-ounce coffee cake.

INGREDIENTS	100 PORTIONS			MIXING METHOD	..........PORTIONS
	WEIGHTS		AMOUNTS (approx.)		
	Pounds	Ounces			
Sugar, confectioners.	4	....	3½ quarts		....
Butter	2	....	1 quart		....
Egg yolks	1	....	24 (1 pint)	Mix ingredients together thoroughly.	....
Flavoring	....	½	1 tablespoon		....
Water	....	....	To make a paste		....

Usage: Spread on coffee cake before proofing dough.

NOTE.—Equal parts of powdered egg yolk and water may be used in place of egg yolks.

STREUSEL TOPPING

Yield: Approx. 6 pounds.   Portion: Approx. 1 to 2 ounces per 10-ounce coffee cake.

INGREDIENTS	100 PORTIONS		MIXING METHOD	...........PORTIONS
	WEIGHTS	AMOUNTS (approx.)		
	Pounds	Ounces			
Butter	1	....	1 pint		
Sugar	4	....	½ gallon	Mix ingredients together to a crumblike consistency.	
Cinnamon	....	1	¼ cup		
Flour	1	....	1 quart		

Usage: Sprinkle on coffee cakes before proofing.

VANILLA WATER ICING

Yield: Approx. 2 pounds.   Portion: Approx. ½ ounce per 10-ounce coffee cake.

INGREDIENTS	100 PORTIONS		MIXING METHOD	...........PORTIONS
	WEIGHTS	AMOUNTS (approx.)		
	Pounds	Ounces			
Sugar, confec- tioners'.	1	8	1¼ quarts		
Sirup, corn	....	4	⅜ cup	Combine all ingredients and beat thoroughly.	
Water, hot	....	4	½ cup		
Vanilla	....	⅛	¼ tablespoon		

Usage: Brush on sweet yeast dough products as they come from oven.

NOTE. —4 ounces sugar may be used in place of corn sirup.

EGG WASH

Mix equal parts of whole egg and liquid milk or mix 1 part by weight of powdered egg to 7 parts by weight of liquid milk.

Brush on sweet yeast dough products before putting into oven.

357★

SHINE

Yield: Approx. 30 ounces.   Portion: ½ ounce per 10-ounce coffee cake.

Ingredients	100 Portions		Mixing Method	...........Portions
	Weights	Amounts (approx.)		
	Pounds / Ounces			
Gelatin, unflavored.	.... / ¼	1 tablespoon	Soak gelatin in cold water. 5 minutes. Heat sugar, sirup and water to a boil. Add soaked gelatin and stir until dissolved. Use hot.	....
Water, cold	.... / 2	¼ cup		....
Sugar	.... / 10	1¼ cups		....
Sirup, corn	.... / 10	1 cup		....
Sirup drained from canned fruits or ground peach or apricot pulp.	.... / 8	1 cup		....

Usage: Brush on coffee cakes as they come from oven.

NOTE.—10 ounces sugar may be used in place of 10 ounces corn sirup.

Fillings For Sweet Yeast Dough Products

FRUIT FILLING

Yield: Approx. 5 pounds.   Portion: 1 to 2 ounces per 10-ounce coffee cake.

Ingredients	100 Portions		Mixing Method	...........Portions
	Weights	Amounts (approx.)		
	Pounds / Ounces			
Cake crumbs	2 /	1½ quarts	Mix ingredients together thoroughly.	....
Raisins	1 /	1½ pints		....
Nuts, chopped ..	.... / 8	1 pint		....
Fruits, chopped ..	.... / 8	1 pint		....
Cinnamon	.... / 1	¼ cup		....
Milk, liquid (variable).	1 /	1 pint	Add and mix to proper consistency.	....

Usage: Spread on dough as it is being made up into units of desired shapes and sizes.

APPLESAUCE PECAN FILLING

Yield: Approx. 5½ pounds.   Portion: 1 to 2 ounces per 10-ounce coffee cake.

INGREDIENTS	100 PORTIONS		MIXING METHOD	..........PORTIONS
	WEIGHTS	AMOUNTS (approx.)		
	Pounds	Ounces			
Pecans, chopped	1	8	1½ quarts		....
Cake crumbs	2	....	1½ quarts	Mix together to a smooth spreading paste.	....
Sugar, brown ..	1	....	3 cups		....
Applesauce	1	....	1 pint		....

Usage: Spread on dough as it is being made up into units of desired shapes and sizes.

BUTTER CREAM FILLING

Yield: Approx. 6 pounds.   Portion: 1 to 2 ounces per 10-ounce coffee cake.

INGREDIENTS	100 PORTIONS		MIXING METHOD	..........PORTIONS
	WEIGHTS	AMOUNTS (approx.)		
	Pounds	Ounces			
Sugar, confectioners'.	3	....	2½ quarts		....
Shortening	....	12	1½ cups	Cream ingredients together thoroughly.	....
Butter	....	4	½ cup		....
Eggs, whole	....	12	8 (¾ pint)	Add and cream in.	....
Flour	1	4	1¼ quarts	Add and mix in.	....

Usage: Spread on dough as it is being made up into units of desired shapes and sizes.

NOTE.—3 ounces powdered eggs and 9 ounces (1 cup) water may be used in place of 12 ounces eggs.

NUT FILLING

Yield: Approx. 7½ pounds.   Portion: 1 to 2 ounces per 10-ounce coffee cake.

INGREDIENTS	100 PORTIONS		MIXING METHOD	..........PORTIONS
	WEIGHTS	AMOUNTS (approx.)		
	Pounds | *Ounces*			
Nuts, finely chopped	1 |	1½ pints		....
Sugar	2 |	1 quart		....
Cinnamon	.... | ½	2 tablespoons ...	Mix together to a smooth spreading paste.	....
Eggs, whole	.... | 6	4 (¾ cup)		....
Cake crumbs	3 |	2¼ quarts		....
Milk, liquid (variable).	1 |	1 pint		....

Usage: Spread on dough as it is being made up into units of desired shapes and sizes.

NOTE.—1½ ounces powdered eggs and 4½ ounces (½ cup) water may be used in place of 6 ounces eggs.

Quick Breads and Griddle Products

Production Pointers

The term "quick breads" covers all types of breads and griddle products in which baking powder is used as the leavening ingredient.

Mixing: Mix batters just enough to properly combine ingredients for making tender, fluffy textured, finished products.

The simplified mixing procedure outlined for the formulas in this chapter is easy to follow and aids in producing uniform breads and griddle products.

Avoid over-mixing of these batters as they are all soft due to high liquid content. Over-mixing develops the elasticity of the flour gluten; this has a toughening effect.

Make-up and Scaling: Quick breads are most conveniently made up by spreading the batter on a thoroughly greased bun pan. Use from 4 to 5 pounds of batter per pan to give finished breads of proper volume for serving.

Baking: Bake small units, such as muffins and biscuits at temperatures ranging from 400° F. to 425° F. Bake larger units, such as quick breads scaled in bun pans, at approximately 375° F.

BAKING POWDER BISCUITS AND SHORT CAKE

Yield: Approx. 29¼ pounds.

Portion: 2 biscuits.

INGREDIENTS	100 PORTIONS		AMOUNTS (approx.)	MIXING METHOD	PORTIONS
	Pounds	*Ounces*			
Flour	14	....	3½ gallons	Sift ingredients together.	....
Baking powder	....	9	1½ cups		....
Salt	....	2½	5 tablespoons ...		....
Shortening	3	8	1¾ quarts	Cut in shortening and mix to a fine crumb.	....
Milk, liquid (variable).	11	....	1⅜ gallons	Add and mix to a soft dough.	....

Make-up: Roll dough ½ inch thick. Cut with 2-inch floured biscuit cutter. Place side by side on ungreased baking sheets.

Baking: Bake at 425° F. for 12 to 15 minutes.

Serving: Serve hot.

Variations

Shortcake (Large)

Make-up: Roll biscuit dough ¼ inch thick. Fit ½ of dough into greased bun pans. Brush with melted butter. Place remaining ½ on top.

Baking: Bake at 425° F. for 15 to 20 minutes.

Serving: Cut into 2-inch squares. Split hot shortcakes. Pile sliced fruit or crushed sweetened fruit between halves and over top.

Shortcake (Individual)

Make-up: Roll dough ¼ inch thick. Cut with 2-inch floured cutter. Place half of biscuits on ungreased baking sheets. Brush with melted butter. Place remaining biscuits on top.

Baking: Bake at 425° F. for 12 to 15 minutes.

Serving: Split hot shortcakes. Pile crushed sweetened fruit between halves and over tops.

COFFEE CAKE

Yield: Approx. 15¾ pounds.

Portion: 2 pieces, 2 x 3 inches.

INGREDIENTS	100 PORTIONS		AMOUNTS (approx.)	MIXING METHOD	PORTIONS
	Pounds	*Ounces*			
Shortening	1	....	1 pint	Cream shortening and sugar.	....
Sugar	2	8	1¼ quarts		....
Eggs, whole	1	4	12 (1¼ pints)	Add eggs. Beat well.	....
Flour	5	....	1¼ gallons	Sift flour with baking powder, salt and nutmeg. Add alternately with the milk.	....
Baking powder	....	4	10 tablespoons		....
Salt	....	1½	3 tablespoons ...		....
Nutmeg	....	½	2 tablespoons ...		....
Milk, liquid (variable).	5	12	2⅞ quarts		....

Make-up: Pour into greased baking pans, scaling about 4 pounds per bun pan. Sprinkle with Streusel Topping (page 357).

Baking: Bake at 375° F. to 400° F. for 20 to 30 minutes.

NOTE.—4¾ ounces powdered eggs and 15¼ ounces (1¾ cups) water may be used in place of 1 pound 4 ounces eggs.

QUICK CINNAMON BUNS

Yield: Approx. 24½ pounds.   Portion: 2 buns.

INGREDIENTS	100 PORTIONS		MIXING METHOD	..........PORTIONS
	WEIGHTS	AMOUNTS (approx.)		
	Pounds / *Ounces*			
Baking Powder Biscuit Dough (page 361).	14 /	....		....
Sugar	1 / 8	1½ pints	Mix ingredients together thoroughly.	....
Salt	.... / ½	1 tablespoon ...		....
Cinnamon	.... / ½	2 tablespoons		....
Shortening	1 / 12	3½ cups		....
Sugar	3 /	1½ quarts	Mix thoroughly together.	....
Water	1 / 8	1½ pints		....
Shortening, melted.	.... / 10	1¼ cups		....
Raisins, seedless	2 /	1½ quarts		....

Make-up: Roll biscuit dough into rectangular pieces about 12 inches wide and ¼ inch thick. Spread on sugar, salt, cinnamon and shortening.

Sprinkle with raisins. Roll as for jelly roll. Cut into 1-inch slices.

Spread shortening, water and sugar mixture in bottom of sheet pans. Place rolls cut-side down on pan.

Baking: Bake at 375° F. for 25 to 30 minutes. Remove rolls from pans at once.

Serving: Serve warm.

NOTE.—3 pounds (4¼ cups) corn sirup may be used in place of 3 pounds sugar.

Variation

Quick Pecan Rolls

Use coarsely chopped nuts in place of raisins.

APPLE CRISP

Yield: Approx. 38¼ pounds.

Portion: 4 ounces (approx. 2-inch square).

INGREDIENTS	100 PORTIONS			MIXING METHOD	........PORTIONS
	WEIGHTS		AMOUNTS (approx.)		
	Pounds	Ounces			
Apples, sliced	20	---	5 gallons	Place in greased baking pans	
Water	---	---	2½ quarts	Pour over apples	
Sugar	8	---	1 gallon		
Flour	3	---	¾ gallon	Mix together until crumbly	
Cinnamon	---	1	¼ cup		
Shortening	2	4	1⅛ quarts		

Make-up: Sprinkle flour mixture over apples.
Baking: Bake in moderate oven (375° F.) 15 minutes or until apples are tender.

NOTE.—Serve with Whipped Evaporated Milk Topping (page 75), Custard Sauce (page 72), or Vanilla Sauce (page 76).

APPLE CRISP

(Using dehydrated apple nuggets)

Portion: 4 ounces (approx. 2-inch square).

INGREDIENTS	100 PORTIONS			MIXING METHOD	........PORTIONS
	WEIGHTS		AMOUNTS (approx.)		
	Pounds	Ounces			
Apple nuggets, dehydrated.	3	---	1 gallon	Soak nuggets in water 60 minutes. Spread in greased baking pans.	
Water	---	---	7½ quarts		
Nutmeg	---	¾	3 tablespoons	Mix together. Sprinkle over apples.	
Sugar	2	---	1 quart		
Sugar, brown	6	---	4½ quarts		
Flour	3	---	¾ gallon	Mix together until crumbly	
Shortening	2	---	1 quart		

Make-up: Sprinkle flour mixture over apples.
Baking: Bake in moderate oven (350° F.) 1½ hours until well browned.

Serving: Serve while hot.

APPLE DUMPLINGS

Yield: 100 dumplings.   Portion: 1 dumpling.

INGREDIENTS	100 PORTIONS		MIXING METHOD	........PORTIONS
	WEIGHTS	AMOUNTS (approx.)		
	Pounds / Ounces			
Flour	10 / ---	2½ gallons	Sift together	
Salt	--- / 3	6 tablespoons		
Baking powder	--- / 6	1 cup		
Shortening	3 / ---	1½ quarts	Cut in. Mix to a fine crumb	
Milk, liquid (variable).	5 / 12	2⅞ quarts	Add. Mix to a consistency of pie dough.	
Apples, pared, cored, sliced, or halved.	20 / ---	5 gallons		
Sugar	5 / 8	2¾ quarts	Mix together	
Cinnamon	--- / 6	1½ cups		
Sugar	4 / ---	½ gallon		
Water, boiling	6 / ---	¾ gallon		

Make-up: Roll dough on floured surface to ¼ inch thickness. Cut into 5-inch squares. Place apples in center of each square.

Sprinkle each with 1 ounce sugar-cinnamon mixture. Fold opposite corners of dough over apples. Pinch edges together firmly.

Place on greased bun pans. Sprinkle with 4 pounds sugar. Add water.

Baking: Bake in hot oven (400° F.) about 40 minutes.

NOTE.—1. Fresh, frozen, or canned apples may be used.

2. Nutmeg may be used in place of cinnamon.

APPLE PANDOWDY

Yield: Approx. 39 pounds.

Portion: 3- or 4-inch cut or ⅙ (10-inch) pie.

INGREDIENTS	100 PORTIONS			MIXING METHOD	PORTIONS
	WEIGHTS		AMOUNTS (approx.)		
	Pounds	*Ounces*			
Flour	4	10	4⅔ quarts	Sift together.	
Salt	---	1	2 tablespoons		
Sugar	---	6	¾ cup		
Baking powder	---	3½	½ cup		
Shortening	---	14	1¾ cups	Cut in.	
Milk, liquid (variable).	3	12	1¾ quarts	Add. Mix to biscuit dough consistency.	
Apples, peeled, cored, sliced.	24	---	6 gallons		
Sugar	5	---	3¾ quarts	Mix together.	
Cinnamon	---	2	½ cup		
Nutmeg	---	2	½ cup		

Make-up: Roll dough on floured surface to ¼ inch thickness. Line 3 bun pans or 17 (10-inch) pie tins with dough.

Place layer of apples on dough. Sprinkle with sugar mixture. Cover with another layer of dough.

Baking: Bake in hot oven (400° F.) about 35 minutes.

NOTE.—1. Serve with Hard Sauce (page 73) or Lemon Sauce (page 73).

2. Fresh, frozen or canned apples may be used.

APPLE TORTE

Yield: Approx. 17½ pounds.   Portion: 2 pieces, 2 x 3 inches.

Ingredients	100 Portions		Mixing Method	..........Portions
	Weights	Amounts (approx.)		
	Pounds / Ounces			
Flour	5 / 8	5¼ quarts	Sift flour, baking powder, sugar and salt.	
Baking powder	.... / 2½	6½ tablespoons		
Sugar	3 /	1½ quarts		
Salt	.... / 2	¼ cup		
Lemon rind, grated.	.... / 1	¼ cup	Add lemon rind and 1½ quarts apples to flour mixture.	
Apples, sliced	2 /	½ gallon		
Eggs, whole	.... / 12	8 (½ cup)	Combine eggs and milk; add flour mixture and blend.	
Milk, liquid	3 / 8	1¾ quarts		
Shortening, melted.	1 / 4	2½ cups	Add shortening.	
Sugar	.... / 12	1½ cups	Blend sugar and cinnamon.	
Cinnamon	.... / ⅛	1½ teaspoons		
Butter, melted	.... / 6	¾ cup		

Make-up: Spread in bun pans. Brush with melted butter. Sprinkle with sugar-cinnamon mixture. Garnish with remaining apple slices.
Baking: Bake at 375° F. for 20 to 25 minutes.

NOTE.—3 ounces powdered eggs and 9 ounces (1⅛ cups) water may be used in place of 12 ounces eggs.

Yield: Approx. 26¼ pounds.

Portion: 1 roll.

INGREDIENTS	100 PORTIONS			MIXING METHOD	........PORTIONS
	WEIGHTS		AMOUNTS (approx.)		
	Pounds	Ounces			
Flour...............	4	10	4⅔ quarts..........	} Sift together.	------
Salt...............	---	1	2 tablespoons....		------
Sugar...............	---	6	¾ cup............		------
Baking powder....	---	3½	½ cup............		------
Shortening.........	---	14	1¾ cups..........	Cut in	------
Milk, liquid (variable).	3	12	1⅞ quarts........	Add. Mix to biscuit dough consistency.	------
Cherries, red, sour	13	6	2 No. 10 cans (6½ quarts).	Drain and pit. Reserve juice for sauce.	------
Sugar...............	3	--	1½ quarts......	} Mix together.	------
Cinnamon....	--	¼	1 tablespoon......		------

Make-up: Roll dough on floured surface to thickness of ¼ inch.   Spread cherries over dough. Sprinkle with sugar mixture.

Roll as for jelly roll.   Place on greased bun pans in strips about 22 inches long.

Baking: Bake in moderate oven (375° F.) about 30 minutes.

Serving: Cut roll into 1½- to 2-inch thick slices. Serve with Cherry Sauce (page 73), Hard Sauce (page 73), or Lemon Sauce (page 73).

NOTE.—Roll can be cut into 2-inch slices, placed cut side down in greased muffin tins, and baked.

Variations

Berry Roll

Use berries, fresh or canned, in place of cherries.

Cherry Cobbler

Mix drained, pitted cherries with sugar and cinnamon.   Place in greased baking pans.   Cover with biscuit dough.

Bake in moderate oven (375° F.) about 30 minutes.

PLAIN CORN PONE OR DODGERS

Yield: Approx. 26½ pounds.   Portion: 2 pones.

INGREDIENTS	100 PORTIONS		MIXING METHOD	............PORTIONS
	WEIGHTS	AMOUNTS (approx.)		
	Pounds	Ounces			
Corn meal	12	....	2¼ gallons	Mix ingredients together thoroughly.	
Salt	....	4	½ cup		
Shortening	1	2	2¼ cups		
Water, boiling....	13	....	6½ quarts	Stir in rapidly. Cool...........	

Make-up: Drop by spoonful scaling about 2 ounces each and placing about 2 inches apart onto greased pans. Flatten to ½ inch thickness.

Baking: Bake at 425° F. for 30 minutes.

NOTE.—Batter may be dropped out of bag and tube onto pan for baking.

BRAN PAN BREAD

Yield: Approx. 18 pounds.   Portion: 2 pieces, 2 x 3 inches.

INGREDIENTS	100 PORTIONS		MIXING METHOD	............PORTIONS
	WEIGHTS	AMOUNTS (approx.)		
	Pounds	Ounces			
Shortening	1	....	1 pint	Blend together shortening and sugar.	
Sugar	1	....	1 pint		
Eggs, whole	1	10	16 (1⅝ pints)..	Add eggs and beat well...........	
Bran, prepared	2	....	1 gallon	Soak bran in milk and add.	
Milk, liquid (variable).	8	....	1 gallon		
Flour	4	....	1 gallon	Sift flour, salt and baking powder. Add to first mixture. Stir only until all flour is dampened.	
Salt	....	2½	5 tablespoons ...		
Baking powder	....	6	1 cup		

Make-up: Pour into greased baking pans, scaling about 4½ pounds per bun pan.

Baking: Bake at 375° F. for 35 minutes.

Serving: Serve hot.

NOTE.—6½ ounces powdered eggs and 1 pound 3½ ounces (2½ cups) water may be used in place of the 1 pound 10 ounces eggs.

★ 368

RAISIN BROWN BREAD

Yield: Approx. 35½ pounds.

Portion: 2 slices ⅜-inch thick.

INGREDIENTS	100 PORTIONS			MIXING METHOD	--------PORTIONS
	WEIGHTS		AMOUNTS (approx.)		
	Pounds	*Ounces*			
Flour, graham....	2	4	2¼ quarts.........	Blend together thoroughly.	
Flour, rye.........	2	4	2¼ quarts.........		
Cornmeal.........	3	...	2¼ quarts.........		
Baking, soda.....	...	2½	5 tablespoons.....		
Salt...............	...	2½	5 tablespoons.....		
Sugar, brown	3		1½ quarts.........		
Sugar.............	3		1½ quarts.........	Carmelize by heating in pan over direct heat until melted and browned. Stir constantly to avoid burning.	
Milk, liquid	18	...	2¼ gallons........	Stir into carmelized sugar. Add to dry ingredients. Mix to form a smooth batter.	
Vinegar..........	1	...	1 pint............	Add.............	
Raisins...........	3	...	2¼ quarts.........	Stir into batter......	

Make-up: Fill greased molds about ⅔ full. Cover.

Baking: Place in steamer. Steam about 3 hours.

NOTE.—1. If bread molds are not available, thoroughly cleaned empty No. 2 or No. 2½ cans with the top cut off may be used.

2. Bread may be baked if steamer is not available. Cover molds. Place in suitable pan containing ½ inch water. Bake in moderate oven (375° F.) 1½ hours.

CORN BREAD

Yield: Approx. 24¾ pounds.   Portion: 2 pieces, 2 x 3 inches.

| INGREDIENTS | 100 PORTIONS | | MIXING METHOD | ....PORTIONS |
| | WEIGHTS | AMOUNTS (approx.) | | |
	Pounds	Ounces			
Flour	5	....	1¼ gallons		....
Shortening	2	4	1⅛ quarts		....
Baking powder	....	9	1½ cups	Blend ingredients together thoroughly.	....
Sugar	2	....	1 quart		....
Salt	....	1	2 tablespoons ...		....
Corn meal	4	12	3½ quarts		....
Eggs, whole	1	4	12 (1¼ pints).	Mix eggs and milk. Add and mix to a smooth batter.	....
Milk, liquid (variable).	9	....	1⅛ gallons		....

Make-up: Spread in greased bun pans, scaling about 6 pounds per bun pan.

Baking: Bake at 425° F. for 25 to 30 minutes.

NOTE.—4¾ ounces powdered eggs and 15¼ ounces (1¾ cups) water may be used in place of the 1 pound 4 ounces eggs.

DUMPLINGS

Yield: Approx. 13 pounds.   Portion: 2 dumplings.

| INGREDIENTS | 100 PORTIONS | | MIXING METHOD | ....PORTIONS |
| | WEIGHTS | AMOUNTS (approx.) | | |
	Pounds	Ounces			
Flour	6	....	1½ gallons		....
Baking powder	....	4½	¾ cup		....
Salt	....	2¼	4½ tablespoons	Blend together thoroughly.	....
Shortening	....	4	½ cup		....
Milk, liquid (variable).	6	4	3⅛ quarts	Add and mix to soft dough....	....

Make-up: Scale in 1 ounce dumplings. Drop on boiling stew or on lightly greased steamer tray. Cover tightly.

Cook 10 minutes or until dumplings are done.

Variation

Tomato Dumpling

Use 6¼ pounds (¾ gallon) tomato juice in place of 6¼ pounds (3⅛ quarts) milk.

★ 370

GINGERBREAD

Yield: Approx. 24½ pounds.   Portion: 2 pieces, 2 x 3 inches.

INGREDIENTS	100 PORTIONS		MIXING METHOD	............PORTIONS
	WEIGHTS	AMOUNTS (approx.)		
	Pounds / Ounces			
Flour	7 / 8	7½ quarts	Mix together thoroughly.	
Baking powder	.... / 1	2½ tablespoons		
Soda	.... / 2	¼ cup		
Salt	.... / 1	2 tablespoons ...		
Ginger	.... / 2	10 tablespoons .		
Cinnamon	.... / 1	¼ cup		
Sugar	2 /	1 quart		
Shortening	1 / 12	3½ cups	Mix in.	
Eggs, whole	.... / 12	8 (¾ pint)	Stir together. Add and mix smooth.	
Molasses	8 /	¾ gallon		
Water	4 /	½ gallon		

Make-up: Scale about 6 to 7 pounds in greased and floured bun pan.

Baking: Bake at 375° F. for 35 to 45 minutes.

NOTE.—3 ounces powdered eggs and 9 ounces (1⅛ cups) water may be used in place of the 12 ounces eggs.

MEAT PIE CRUST

Yield: Approx. 13 pounds.

INGREDIENTS	100 PORTIONS		MIXING METHOD	............PORTIONS
	WEIGHTS	AMOUNTS (approx.)		
	Pounds / Ounces			
Flour	6 / 12	1⅝ gallons	Sift together dry ingredients.	
Baking powder	.... / 4½	¾ cup		
Salt	.... / 1	2 tablespoons...		
Shortening	3 / 8	1¾ quarts	Work in shortening until mixture is as fine as corn meal.	
Milk, liquid (variable).	2 / 8	1¼ quarts	Add milk all at once. Mix thoroughly.	

Make-up: Roll dough to a thickness of ¼ inch. Place on meat pie to completely cover top of pie. Cut slits to allow steam to escape.

Baking: Bake at 450° F. for 20 minutes.

371★

QUICK BUCKWHEAT GRIDDLE CAKES

Yield: Approx. 49¼ pounds.   Portion: 4 griddle cakes.

Ingredients	100 Portions		Mixing Method	............Portions
	Weights	Amounts (approx.)		
	Pounds / *Ounces*			
Flour, buckwheat.	11 / 4	2¾ gallons	Sift together flours, baking powder and salt. Combine with shortening.	....
Flour	5 / 12	1¼ gallons		....
Baking powder	.... / 12	1 pint		....
Salt	.... / 3¼	6½ tablespoons		....
Shortening	1 / 12	3½ cups		....
Eggs, whole, well beaten.	2 /	20 (1 quart)	Combine eggs and milk. Add to flour mixture. Stir only until smooth.	....
Milk, liquid (variable).	27 / 8	3⅓ gallons		....

Baking: Bake on hot griddle. Bake on one side until firm around edge and full of bubbles. Turn and finish baking.

NOTE.—8 ounces powdered eggs and 1 pound 8 ounces (1½ pints) water may be used in place of 2 pounds eggs.

WHEAT GRIDDLE CAKES

Yield: Approx. 44½ pounds.   Portion: 4 griddle cakes.

Ingredients	100 Portions		Mixing Method	............Portions
	Weights	Amounts (approx.)		
	Pounds / *Ounces*			
Flour	15 /	3¾ gallons	Sift together flour, baking powder, salt and sugar. Mix with shortening.	....
Baking powder	.... / 12	1 pint		....
Salt	.... / 3	6 tablespoons ...		....
Sugar	1 / 8	1½ pints		....
Shortening	1 / 12	3½ cups		....
Eggs, whole, well beaten.	1 / 4	12 (1¼ pints) .	Combine eggs and milk. Add to flour mixture. Stir only until smooth.	....
Milk, liquid (variable).	24 /	3 gallons		....

Baking: Bake on hot griddle. Bake on one side until firm around edge and full of bubbles. Turn and finish baking.

NOTE.—4¾ ounces powdered eggs and 15¼ ounces (1¾ cups) water may be used in place of 1 pound 4 ounces eggs.

WHOLE WHEAT GRIDDLE CAKES

Yield: Approx. 44¾ pounds.   Portion: 4 griddle cakes.

INGREDIENTS	100 PORTIONS		MIXING METHOD	............PORTIONS
	WEIGHTS	AMOUNTS (approx.)		
	Pounds | Ounces			
Flour	8 |	2 gallons	Sift together flour, baking powder, salt, and sugar. Mix with whole wheat flour and shortening.	....
Baking powder	.... | 12	1 pint		....
Salt	.... | 1¼	2½ tablespoons		....
Sugar	.... | 8	1 cup		....
Flour, whole wheat.	8 |	2 gallons		....
Shortening	1 | 12	3½ cups		....
Eggs, whole, well beaten.	1 | 10	16 (1⅝ pints)..	Combine eggs and milk. Add to flour mixture. Stir only until smooth.	....
Milk, liquid (variable).	24 |	3 gallons		....

Baking: Bake on hot griddle. Bake on one side until firm around edge and full of bubbles. Turn and finish baking.

NOTE.—8 ounces powdered eggs and 1 pound 8 ounces (1½ pints) water may be used in place of 2 pounds eggs.

CORN GRIDDLE CAKES

Yield: Approx. 38½ pounds.   Portion: 4 griddle cakes.

INGREDIENTS	100 PORTIONS		MIXING METHOD	............PORTIONS
	WEIGHTS	AMOUNTS (approx.)		
	Pounds | Ounces			
Flour	6 | 12	6¾ quarts	Sift together flour, baking powder, salt and sugar. Mix with corn meal and shortening.	....
Baking powder	.... | 9	¾ pint		....
Salt	.... | 2½	5 tablespoons		....
Sugar	1 | 12	3½ cups		....
Corn meal	6 | 12	1¼ gallons		....
Shortening	1 | 12	3½ cups		....
Eggs, whole, well beaten.	2 | 12	27 (2¾ pints).	Combine eggs and milk. Add to flour. Stir only until smooth.	....
Milk, liquid (variable).	18 |	2¼ gallons		....

373★

Baking: Bake on hot griddle. Bake on one side until firm around edge and full of bubbles. Turn and finish baking.

NOTE.—12 ounces powdered eggs and 2 pounds (1 quart) water may be used in place of 2 pounds 12 ounces eggs.

MUFFINS

Yield: Approx. 23¼ pounds.

Portion: 2 muffins.

INGREDIENTS	100 PORTIONS			MIXING METHOD	............PORTIONS
	WEIGHTS		AMOUNTS (approx.)		
	Pounds	*Ounces*			
Flour	9	....	2¼ gallons	Sift together flour, baking powder, sugar and salt. Mix with shortening.	
Baking powder	....	9	1½ cups		
Sugar	3	12	2½ quarts		
Salt	---	1½	3 tablespoons		
Shortening	2	12	5½ cups		
Eggs, whole, well beaten.	1	12	18 (1¾ pints)	Combine eggs, milk, and vanilla. Add to flour mixture. Mix to a soft batter.	
Milk, liquid (variable).	7	12	3⅞ quarts		
Vanilla	---	1	2 tablespoons		

Make-up: Fill greased muffin tins ⅔ full.

Baking: Bake at 400° F. for 25 to 30 minutes.

NOTE.—7 ounces powdered eggs and 1 pound 5 ounces (2½ cups) water may be used in place of 1 pound 12 ounces eggs.

Variations

Apricot Muffins

Add 1 pound (1½ pints) finely cut, dried apricots to batter.

Date Muffins

Add 1¼ pounds (1½ pints) finely cut dates to batter.

Nut Muffins

Add 12 ounces (1½ pints) chopped nuts to batter.

Raisin Muffins

Add 1 pound (1½ pints) raisins to batter.

MOLASSES BRAN MUFFINS

Yield: Approx. 28¾ pounds.

Portion: 2 muffins.

INGREDIENTS	100 PORTIONS			MIXING METHOD	...........PORTIONS
	WEIGHTS		AMOUNTS (approx.)		
	Pounds	*Ounces*			
Bran, prepared	4	....	2 gallons	Soak bran in molasses and milk 15 minutes.	
Molasses	5	12	½ gallon		
Milk, liquid (variable).	13	....	6½ quarts		
Eggs, whole	1	10	16 (1⅝ pints)..	Stir in beaten eggs. Mix well.	
Flour	4	...	1 gallon	Sift together flour, salt, and soda. Add to bran mixture. Stir only until all flour is dampened. Stir in shortening.	
Salt	....	1½	3 tablespoons		
Soda	....	2¼	5 tablespoons		
Shortening, melted.	....	12	1½ cups		

Make-up: Fill greased muffin pans about ⅔ full.

Baking: Bake at 425° F. for 25 minutes.

NOTE.—1. 6½ ounces powdered eggs and 19½ ounces (2½ cups) water may be used in place of 1 pound 10 ounces eggs.

2. 4 pounds 10 ounces (¾ gallon) brown sugar and 1 pound 4 ounces (2½ cups) water may be used in place of 5 pounds 12 ounces molasses.

CREAM PUFFS AND ECLAIRS

Yield: Approx. 10 pounds.   Portion: 1 cream puff or eclair.

INGREDIENTS	100 PORTIONS		MIXING METHOD	..........PORTIONS
	WEIGHTS	AMOUNTS (approx.)		
	Pounds	Ounces			
Shortening........	1	8	1½ pints............	Combine. Heat to a vigorous boil.	....
Water.............	3	...	1½ quarts.........		....
Flour...........	2	4	2⅛ quarts........	Combine. Stir in steadily boiling water and shortening mixture.	....
Salt.............	...	1	2 tablespoons.....		....
Eggs, whole.......	3	4	32 (1½ quarts)...		....

Make-up: Cook flour mixture, stirring constantly, until mixture leaves sides of cooking vessel in smooth, compact mass.

Cool mixture to about 160° F. Add eggs, 1 or 2 at a time, beating after each addition until thoroughly blended.

Drop 1½ ounces batter, approximately the size of a walnut, from pastry bag onto lightly greased baking sheets.

Baking: Bake in hot oven (400° F.) 20 to 30 minutes or until light brown.

Serving: Cool. Fill with Chocolate Cream (page 416), Butterscotch Cream (page 416), or Vanilla Cream (page 415)

NOTE.—1. 13 ounces powdered eggs and 1½ quarts water may be used in place of 3 pounds 4 ounces eggs.

2. Mixture may be shaped with machine depositor or by dropping with No. 20 ice cream scoop.

PLUM PUDDING

Yield: Approx. 28½ pounds.

Portion: Approx. 4 ounces.

INGREDIENTS	100 PORTIONS			MIXING METHOD	............PORTIONS
	WEIGHTS		AMOUNTS (approx.)		
	Pounds	Ounces			
Flour................	2	...	½ gallon............		
Baking powder.	..	2	5 tablespoons.....		
Soda..............	...	¾	4 teaspoons........	Sift together.	
Cinnamon.......	...	1	¼ cup........		
Nutmeg..........	...	¼	1 tablespoon......		
Sugar, brown.....	3	...	2¼ quarts........		
Bread crumbs....	2	8	¾ gallon..........		
Apples, chopped.	1	..	1 quart...........		
Mixed fruits, glazed.	1	8	4½ cups	Add to flour mixture.	
Milk, liquid.......	4	...	½ gallon..........		
Eggs, whole.	1	8	15 (1½ pints).....	Mix thoroughly.	
Molasses..........	2	12	1 quart..........		
Raisins, seedless.	1	8	4½ cups..........		
Nuts, chopped...	1	8	1½ quarts........		

Make-up: Fill greased pudding molds ⅔ full. Cover securely.

Baking: Place in steamer. Steam 1 to 1½ hours. Remove from steamer. Allow to cool in molds.

Serving: Cut in ¾-inch slices. Serve with Hard Sauce (page 73).

NOTE.—1. Filled pudding molds may be placed in water bath on range and boiled slowly 1 to 1½ hours.

2. Mincemeat or canned fruits, drained, or dried fruits, cooked and thoroughly drained, may be used as mixed fruit.

Cakes

Production Pointers

Cakes Requiring Chemical Leavening Ingredients to Produce Proper Lightness: The function of the mixing process is to properly blend ingredients and to build up a cellular structure which will expand during baking and produce cakes with desired volume, grain and texture.

Much work and experimentation has been done to develop cake mixing methods which accomplish this with a minimum of time and effort. The result is the "simplified cake mixing method" specified in the following formulas for layer cakes.

1. *Simplified Cake Mixing Method*: This method essentially consists of blending all dry ingredients with eggs and part of milk to produce a smooth batter and then gradually incorporating remaining milk. First speed of a 3-speed machine, or second-speed of a 4-speed mixing machine are usually used in putting batters together.

Mixing time required, using this simplified method, is about 7 minutes.

The temperature of all ingredients should be about 75° F.

Cold shortening may give a lumpy batter because it will not blend uniformly with other ingredients.

Cold milk or eggs produce a stiff batter which results in cakes that have poor volume or split during baking.

Warm batters produce cakes with poor volume and a grain in which tunnels and large holes are formed during baking.

For best results, cake batters should be mixed at temperatures between 60° F. and 85° F. A temperature of 75° F. gives best results.

Cool The Ingredients

In warm locations where outside temperatures may be 100° F. or more, it is possible when refrigeration is available, to cool ingredients to desired temperature.

Milk and eggs can be refrigerated so that when added to other ingredients, the resultant batter is at proper temperature. Dried milk, reconstituted double strength and diluted with equal parts of cracked ice, or evaporated milk diluted with cracked ice, can be added to the cake ingredients to produce batters of proper temperature. As ice melts, the warm ingredients cool down to desired mixing temperature.

Cakes Requiring Incorporation of Air for Proper Lightness: Pound cakes, in general, are mixed in the same way as layer cakes except that higher mixing speeds are used. This is necessary in order to incorporate more air into the batter.

Pound cakes may contain little or no baking powder and their lightness depends upon the amount of air incorporated during mixing. Second speed on a 3-speed machine, or third speed on a 4-speed mixing machine are used in making pound cake.

Pound cake batters which are too cold or too warm will not incorporate air in the desired amounts. It is practically impossible to produce good pound cake if batter temperature is above 85° F. or less than 60° F.

Cakes Dependent upon the Development of Egg Structure for Proper Volume:

Sponge Cakes

Sponge cakes may contain little or no baking powder and depend upon the development of egg structure for their lightness. Eggs and sugar can be whipped to their maximum lightness at a temperature of approximately 120° F. It is difficult to make good sponge cake with cold ingredients.

The foam structure which has been built up by whipping or beating sugar and eggs must be carefully incorporated with the remaining ingredients. Two methods are usually employed:

1. Build the egg structure first and add other ingredients; OR
2. Blend other ingredients and fold in the sugar and egg structure.

Either method gives satisfactory results.

2. *Hand Mixing*: Cake batters up to 25 pounds in weight can be put together by blending the ingredients by hand. The same general method outlined in the formulas should be followed. Blend ingredients sufficiently to produce a smooth, light batter.

Batters mixed by hand require a longer mixing time than do batters mixed by machine.

SCALING AND BAKING CAKE

Type	Scaling Weight		Pan Size	Baking Temperature	Baking Time
	Pounds	Ounces	Inches		Minutes (approx.)
Layer		12 to 14	8	375°F.	22
Layer		9 to 11	7	375°F.	21
Layer		6 to 8	6	375°F.	20
Layer	6 to 7		Sheet pan 18x25	375°F.	22
Cup	1 (per doz.)		1½	375°F. to 400°F.	15
Loaf		12 to 14	7½x3½x2¼	375°F. to 400°F.	30
Ring		12 to 14	6 (Ring pan)	375°F. to 400°F.	25
Pound	3		6x11	300°F. to 330°F.	110
Pound	1		7½x3½x2¼	350°F.	50
Sponge		8	8	375°F.	15
Sponge		7	7	375°F.	14
Sponge		4 to 6	6	375°F.	13
Sheet	3		18x25	375°F.	20
Jelly Roll	2		18x25	375°F.	18
Angel Food		8	6 (Ring pan)	325°F.	30

Batch sizes.—The batter yields of the cake formulas range from 12 pounds for Angel Food Cake to 50 pounds for Fruit Cake.

BASIC YELLOW CAKE

Yield: Approx. 18¼ pounds.   Portion: Approx. 3 ounces.

INGREDIENTS	100 PORTIONS			MIXING METHOD	......PORTIONS
	WEIGHTS		AMOUNTS (approx.)		
	Pounds	Ounces			
Flour	5	....	1¼ gallons	Blend together 3 to 5 minutes, using low speed on a 3-speed machine, or second speed on a 4-speed machine.	....
Shortening	2	4	1⅛ quarts		....
Sugar	5	....	2½ quarts		....
Salt	....	3	6 tablespoons		....
Baking powder	....	3¾	10 tablespoons ..		....
Milk, liquid	1	8	1½ pints		....
Eggs, whole	2	4	22 (1⅛ quarts)..		....
Milk, liquid	2	4	1⅛ quarts	Add and blend 2 to 3 minutes, using low speed on a 3-speed machine or second on a 4-speed machine.	....
Vanilla	....	1	2 tablespoons		....

Make-up: See page 379 for scaling weights.
Use for layer, loaf, ring, sheet and cup cakes.
Baking: Bake at 375° F. to 400° F.

NOTE.—10 ounces powdered eggs and 1 pound 10 ounces (3¼ cups) water may be used in place of 2 pounds 4 ounces eggs.

BASIC WHITE CAKE

Yield: Approx. 19 pounds.   Portion: Approx. 3 ounces.

INGREDIENTS	100 PORTIONS			MIXING METHOD	......PORTIONS
	WEIGHTS		AMOUNTS (approx.)		
	Pounds	Ounces			
Flour	5	....	1¼ gallons	Blend together 3 to 5 minutes, using low speed on a 3-speed machine, or second on a 4-speed machine.	....
Shortening	2	4	1⅛ quarts		....
Sugar	5	....	2½ quarts		....
Salt	....	3	6 tablespoons		....
Milk, liquid	1	....	1 pint		....
Baking powder..	....	3¾	10 tablespoons ..		....
Egg whites	3	....	1½ quarts		....
Milk, liquid	2	4	1⅛ quarts	Add and blend 2 to 3 minutes, using low speed on a 3-speed machine, or second on a 4-speed machine.	....
Vanilla	....	1	2 tablespoons		....

Make-up: See page 379 for scaling weights. Use for layer, loaf, ring, sheet and cup cakes.

Baking: Bake at 375° F. to 400° F.

NOTE.—5 ounces powdered egg white and 2 pounds 11 ounces (1⅜ quarts) water may be used in place of 3 pounds egg whites.

Variations

Boston Cream Pie

Make-up: Bake basic yellow or white cake in sheets. Cool. Spread sheets generously with Cream Filling (page 415) or Chocolate Cream Filling (page 416). Place a second sheet on top. Sprinkle with powdered sugar or ice with Marshmallow Icing (page 395). Cut and serve.

Chocolate Squares

Make-up: Bake basic yellow, white or chocolate cake in sheets. Ice finished cakes with Cocoa Cream Icing (page 392) or Chocolate Fudge Icing (page 392). Cut and serve.

Coconut Squares

Make-up: Bake basic yellow, white or chocolate cake in sheets. Ice with Marshmallow Icing (page 395). Sprinkle top with coconut. Cut and serve.

Pineapple Upside Down Cake

Make-up: Grease cake pans, extra heavy, using part butter if desired. Sprinkle bottom with brown sugar. Place drained sliced or crushed pineapple on bottom. Pour in yellow cake batter using 10 ounces for an 8-inch cake pan.

Baking: Bake at 375° F. Dump cakes from pans while warm.

NOTE.—Sliced peaches, halved apricots, sliced apples and other fruits may be used to make a variety of upside down cakes.

BANANA CAKE

Yield: Approx. 22¼ pounds.　　　　　　　　　　Portion: Approx. 3 ounces.

INGREDIENTS	100 PORTIONS		MIXING METHOD	..........PORTIONS
	WEIGHTS	AMOUNTS (approx.)		
	Pounds | *Ounces*			
Flour	4 | 8	4½ quarts	Blend together 3 to 5 minutes, using low speed on a 3-speed machine, or second speed on a 4-speed machine.	....
Shortening	1 | 12	3½ cups		....
Sugar	6 |	¾ gallon		....
Salt	.... | 3	6 tablespoons		....
Baking powder	.... | 4	10 tablespoons ...		....
Bananas, ripe	4 |	12 to 16 bananas		....
Eggs, whole	3 | 8	35 (1¾ quarts)		....
Milk, liquid	2 |	1 quart	Add and blend together 2 to 3 minutes, using low speed on a 3-speed machine or second speed on a 4-speed machine.	....
Vanilla	.... | 1	2 tablespoons		....

Make-up: See page 379 for scaling weights. Use for layer, loaf, sheet, ring and cup cakes.

Baking: Bake at 375° F. to 400° F.

NOTE.—1. 1 pound powdered eggs and 2 pounds 8 ounces (1¼ quarts) water may be used in place of 3 pounds 8 ounces eggs.

2. Bananas, because they discolor fairly rapidly, should not be peeled until just before placing in mixer. Fully ripe bananas, flecked with brown, do not discolor as quickly as those with all yellow peel or deep green tip. Fully ripe bananas also have a richer, sweeter flavor.

APPLESAUCE CAKE

Yield: Approx. 21¼ pounds.   Portion: Approx. 3 ounces.

Ingredients	100 Portions		Mixing Method	............Portions
	Weights	Amounts (approx.)		
	Pounds / Ounces			
Flour	5 /	1¼ gallons	Blend together 3 to 5 minutes, using low speed on a 3-speed machine, or second speed on a 4-speed machine.	
Shortening	2 / 4	4½ cups		
Sugar	4 / 8	2¼ quarts		
Soda	.... / 1	2 tablespoons		
Baking powder	.... / 2	5 tablespoons		
Cinnamon	.... / ½	2 tablespoons		
Cloves	.... / ½	2 tablespoons		
Salt	.... / 3	6 tablespoons		
Eggs, whole	1 / 4	13 (1¼ pints)		
Raisins	2 / 4	1¾ quarts		
Applesauce	3 /	1½ quarts		
Applesauce	2 / 8	1¼ quarts	Add and blend 2 to 3 minutes, using low speed on a 3-speed machine, or second speed on a 4-speed machine.	
Vanilla	.... / 1	2 tablespoons		

Make-up: See page 379 for scaling weights. Use for layer, loaf, sheet, ring and cup cakes.
Baking: Bake at 375° F. to 400° F.

NOTE.—6 ounces powdered eggs and 14 ounces (1¾ cups) water may be used in place of 1 pound 4 ounces eggs.

CARAMEL CAKE

Yield: Approx. 18¼ pounds.

Portion: Approx. 3 ounces.

INGREDIENTS	100 PORTIONS			MIXING METHOD	............PORTIONS
	WEIGHTS		AMOUNTS (approx.)		
	Pounds	Ounces			
Flour	5	....	1¼ gallons	Blend together 3 to 5 minutes, using low speed on a 3-speed machine, or second speed on a 4-speed machine.	....
Shortening	2	4	1⅛ quarts		....
Sugar, brown	5	....	3¾ quarts		....
Salt	....	3	6 tablespoons		....
Baking powder..	....	3¾	10 tablespoons ..		....
Milk, liquid	1	8	1½ pints.............		....
Eggs, whole	2	4	22 (1⅛ quarts)		....
Milk, liquid	2	4	1⅛ quarts	Add and blend 2 to 3 minutes, using low speed on a 3-speed machine or second speed on a 4-speed machine.	....
Maple flavor......	....	1	2 tablespoons		....

Make-up: See page 379 for scaling weights. Use for layer, loaf, sheet, ring and cup cakes.
Baking: Bake at 375° F. to 400 F.

NOTE.—10 ounces powdered eggs and 1 pound 10 ounces (3¼ cups) water may be used in place of 2 pounds 4 ounces eggs.

CRUMB CAKE

Yield: Approx. 21½ pounds.　　　　　　　　　　　　　　Portion: Approx. 3 ounces.

INGREDIENTS	100 PORTIONS			MIXING METHOD	..........PORTIONS
	WEIGHTS		AMOUNTS (approx.)		
	Pounds	*Ounces*			
Flour	5	....	1¼ gallons		
Shortening	2	4	1⅛ quarts		
Sugar	2	8	1¼ quarts		
Sugar, brown	2	8	1⅝ quarts	Blend together 3 to 5 minutes, using low speed on a 3-speed machine, or second speed on a 4-speed machine.	
Salt	....	3	6 tablespoons		
Baking powder..	....	3¾	10 tablespoons ..		
Milk, liquid	1	8	1½ pints.............		
Eggs, whole	2	4	22 (1⅛ quarts)		
Cake crumbs	3	....	2¼ quarts		
Milk, liquid	2	8	1¼ quarts	Add and blend 2 to 3 minutes, using low speed on a 3-speed machine or second speed on a 4-speed machine.	
Vanilla	....	1	2 tablespoons		

Make-up: See page 379 for scaling weights.
Use for layer, loaf, ring, sheet and cup cakes.
Baking: Bake at 375° F. to 400 F.

NOTE.—10 ounces powdered eggs and 1 pound 10 ounces (3¼ cups) water may be used in place of 2 pounds 4 ounces eggs.

DEVIL'S FOOD CAKE

Yield: Approx. 23½ pounds.   Portion: Approx. 3 ounces.

INGREDIENTS	100 PORTIONS			MIXING METHOD	..........PORTIONS
	WEIGHTS		AMOUNTS (approx.)		
	Pounds	*Ounces*			
Flour	5	....	1¼ gallons		....
Shortening	2	4	1⅛ quarts		....
Sugar	7	....	3½ quarts		....
Cocoa	1	4	1¼ quarts	Blend together 3 to 5 min-	....
Soda	....	2½	5 tablespoons	utes, using low speed on a 3-speed machine, or	....
Baking powder..	....	2½	6¼ tablespoons	second speed on a 4-speed machine.	....
Salt	....	3	6 tablespoons		....
Eggs, whole	3	....	30 (1½ quarts)		....
Milk, liquid	2	8	1¼ quarts............		....
Milk, liquid	3	....	1½ quarts	Add and blend 2 to 3 min-	....
Vanilla	....	1	2 tablespoons	utes, using low speed on a 3-speed machine, or sec- ond speed on a 4-speed machine.	....

Make-up: See page 379 for scaling weights. Use for layer, loaf, ring, sheet and cup cakes.
Baking: Bake at 375° F. to 400 F.

NOTE.—12 ounces powdered eggs and 1 pound 12 ounces (3½ cups) water may be used in place of 2 pounds 8 ounces eggs.

SPICE CAKE

Yield: Approx. 18¼ pounds.   Portion: Approx. 3 ounces.

INGREDIENTS	100 PORTIONS			MIXING METHOD	...........PORTIONS
	WEIGHTS		AMOUNTS (approx.)		
	Pounds	Ounces			
Flour	5	....	1¼ gallons		....
Shortening	2	4	1⅛ quarts		....
Sugar	2	8	1¼ quarts		....
Sugar, brown	2	8	1⅝ quarts	Blend together 3 to 5 minutes, using low speed on a 3-speed machine, or second speed on a 4-speed machine.	....
Salt	....	3	6 tablespoons		....
Baking powder..	....	3¾	10 tablespoons ..		....
Milk, liquid	1	8	1½ pints..............		....
Eggs, whole	2	4	22 (1⅛ quarts)		....
Spice mix	....	1¾	½ cup		....
Milk, liquid	2	4	1⅛ quarts	Add and blend 2 to 3 minutes, using low speed on a 3-speed machine or second speed on a 4-speed machine.	....
Vanilla	....	1	2 tablespoons		....

Make-up: See page 379 for scaling weights.

Use for layer, loaf, ring, sheet, and cup cakes.

Baking: Bake at 375° F. to 400° F.

NOTE—1. **Spice mix:** Blend together 1 ounce cinnamon with ¼ ounce mace, ⅛ ounce ginger, ¼ ounce nutmeg and ⅛ ounce allspice.

2. 10 ounces powdered eggs and 1 pound 10 ounces (3¼ cups) water may be used in place of 2 pounds 4 ounces eggs.

YELLOW POUND CAKE

Yield: Approx. 20¼ pounds.

Portion: Approx. 3 ounces.

INGREDIENTS	100 PORTIONS			MIXING METHOD	............PORTIONS
	WEIGHTS		AMOUNTS (approx.)		
	Pounds	Ounces			
Flour	5	....	1¼ gallons		....
Shortening	3	....	1½ quarts		....
Sugar	6	....	¾ gallon		....
Baking powder..	....	1	2½ tablespoons	Blend together thoroughly 3 to 5 minutes, using second speed on a 3-speed machine, or third speed on a 4-speed machine.	....
Salt	....	3	6 tablespoons		....
Nutmeg	....	½	2 tablespoons		....
Eggs, whole	3	....	30 (1½ quarts)		....
Milk, liquid	1	8	1½ pints		....
Milk, liquid	1	8	1½ pints	Add and blend together 5 to 8 minutes, using second speed on a 3-speed machine, or third speed on a 4-speed machine.	....
Vanilla	....	1	2 tablespoons		....

Make-up: See page 379 for scaling weights. for pound cake units.

Baking: Bake at 330° F. to 350° F.

NOTE.—14 ounces powdered eggs and 2 pounds 2 ounces (4¼ cups) water may be used in place of 3 pounds eggs.

WHITE POUND CAKE

Yield: Approx. 19½ pounds.

Portion: Approx. 3 ounces.

| INGREDIENTS | 100 PORTIONS | | MIXING METHOD | ....PORTIONS |
	WEIGHTS	AMOUNTS (approx.)		
	Pounds / *Ounces*			
Flour	5 /	1¼ gallons		....
Shortening	2 / 8	1¼ quarts		....
Sugar	5 /	2½ quarts	Blend together 5 to 7 minutes, using second speed on a 3-speed machine or third speed on a 4-speed machine.	....
Salt	.... / 3	6 tablespoons		....
Baking powder..	.... / 2	5 tablespoons		....
Egg whites	3 /	1½ quarts		....
Milk, liquid	1 / 8	1½ pints		....
Milk, liquid	2 /	1 quart	Add and blend 2 to 3 minutes, using second speed on a 3-speed machine or third speed on a 4-speed machine.	....
Vanilla	.... / 1	2 tablespoons		....

Make-up: See page 379 for scaling weights for pound cake units.

Baking: Bake at 330° F. to 350° F.

NOTE.—5 ounces powdered egg white and 2 pounds 11 ounces (1⅜ quarts) water may be used in place of 3 pounds egg whites.

Pound Cake Variations

Raisin Pound Cake

Make-up: Mix together 3 pounds (2¼ quarts) raisins with 8 ounces (1 pint) flour and blend into either the Yellow Pound Cake (page 387) or the White Pound Cake batters.

Scale about 20% heavier than ordinary Pound Cake to give cakes of comparable volume.

Baking: Bake at the same temperature as regular Pound Cake.

Nut Pound Cake

Make-up: Mix 2 pounds (1½ quarts) of chopped or shaved nuts into either the Yellow Pound Cake (page 387) or the White Pound Cake batters.

Scale about 10% heavier than ordinary Pound Cake to give cakes of comparable volume.

Baking: Bake at the same temperature as regular Pound Cake.

Light Fruit Cake

Make-up: Blend together 20 to 30 pounds of mixed fruits, nuts, and raisins. Incorporate in Yellow Pound Cake (page 387) batter.

Scale 50% heavier than Yellow Pound Cake to give cakes of comparable volume.

Baking: Bake at temperature about 30° F. lower than temperature for comparable Pound Cake units. Increase baking time about 75%.

Dark Fruit Cake

Make-up: Blend together 1 pound dark molasses and 20 to 30 pounds of mixed fruits, nuts and raisins. Incorporate in Yellow Pound Cake (page 387) batter.

Scale 50% heavier than Yellow Pound Cake to give cakes of comparable volume.

Baking: Bake at temperature about 30° F. lower than temperature for comparable Pound Cake units. Increase baking time about 75%.

NOTE.—12 ounces (1½ pints) cocoa or 12 ounces melted chocolate may be used in place of molasses to produce a Dark Fruit Cake.

WEDDING CAKES

Use White Pound Cake (page 388) or Light Fruit Cake (page 388) for making Wedding Cakes. Either cake is traditional for Wedding Cakes.

Make-up: Build up different size layer cakes into tiers to form a finished cake of the desired size and symmetry.

For a cake of good symmetry, use 2 (14-inch) layers for the first tier; 2 (10-inch) layers for the second tier; and 2 (6-inch) layers for the top or third tier.

Use scaling weights in Table III for making cakes suitable for building into Wedding Cakes.

Table III.—WHITE POUND CAKE AND LIGHT FRUIT CAKE

	WHITE POUND CAKE				LIGHT FRUIT CAKE			
PAN SIZE INCHES	SCALING WEIGHT (approx.)		BAKING TEMPERATURE (approx.)	BAKING TIME, Minutes (approx.)	SCALING WEIGHT (approx.)		BAKING TEMPERATURE (approx.)	BAKING TIME, Minutes (approx.)
	Pounds	*Ounces*			*Pounds*	*Ounces*		
6	....	8	360° F.	15	....	12	350° F.	25
7	....	11	360° F.	20	1	....	350° F.	40
8	1	....	360° F.	25	1	8	330° F.	60
9	1	8	350° F.	35	2	4	300° F.	80
10	2	....	350° F.	50	3	....	300° F.	90
14	5	....	330° F.	90	7	8	300° F.	130

ANGEL FOOD

Yield: Approx. 12½ pounds.

Portion: Approx. 2 ounces.

INGREDIENTS	100 PORTIONS			MIXING METHOD	........PORTIONS
	WEIGHTS		AMOUNTS (approx.)		
	Pounds	*Ounces*			
Sugar	2	8	1¼ quarts	Whip together to a light froth.	
Egg whites	5	....	2½ quarts		
Vanilla	....	½	1 tablespoon		
Sugar	2	8	1¼ quarts	Sift together 3 times. Fold by hand into egg white-sugar mixture.	
Flour	2	4	2¼ quarts		
Salt	....	1½	3 tablespoons		
Cream of tartar	....	1¼	3⅓ tablespoons		

Make-up: See page 379 for scaling weights for ring and loaf cakes.

Baking: Bake at 325° F. to 350° F.

NOTE.—8 ounces powdered egg white and 4 pounds 8 ounces (2¼ quarts) water may be used in place of 5 pounds egg whites.

SPONGE CAKE

Yield: Approx. 19½ pounds.   Portion: Approx. 3 ounces.

INGREDIENTS	100 PORTIONS		MIXING METHOD	..........PORTIONS
	WEIGHTS	AMOUNTS (approx.)		
	Pounds	*Ounces*			
Eggs, whole	6	....	60 (¾ gallon).....	Combine ingredients. Beat lightly.	....
Sugar	6	....	¾ gallon		....
Vanilla	....	1	2 tablespoons		....
Salt	....	2	¼ cup		....
Water, warm...... (110° F.).	2	....	1 quart	Mix in slowly	....
Flour	5	....	1¼ gallons	Sift together and fold in. Do not break down structure by over-mixing.	....
Baking powder..	....	3	½ cup		....

Make-up: See page 379 for scaling weights. Use for layer, loaf, sheet, ring and cup cakes.

Baking: Bake at 375° F. to 400° F.

Variations

Jelly Roll

Make-up: Scale 2 to 3 pounds batter into a 16x26-inch bun pan.

Baking: Bake at 375° F.

Finishing: Dump on sugared cloth or paper. Spread with jelly, jam or filling. Roll up. Cool. Remove cloth or paper. Slice and serve.

Cream Roll

Make-up: Make up and bake as for Jelly Roll.

Finishing: Allow cake to cool before spreading with Cream Icing (page 392) or Chocolate Cream Icing (page 393). Roll as for Jelly Roll.

NOTE.—1. 1¾ pounds powdered eggs and 4 pounds 4 ounces (2⅛ quarts) water may be used in place of 6 pounds eggs.

2. Eggs and sugar whip up best when warmed to 120° F.

Cake Icings

Types of Icings

1. Fudge type icing
2. Cream icing
3. Fondant cream icing
4. Marshmallow icing

Proper Use of Icings

Ice cakes carefully to give best appearance and flavor.

Have cakes cooled to room temperature before icing.

Use a liberal quantity of icing.

Use icings at proper temperature.

Storage: Store all icings, except marshmallow, in refrigerator when not in use. Cover the icing container with wax paper to prevent crusting. Icings stored under 60° F. will keep fully a week.

Marshmallow Icing: Make up marshmallow icing as needed because this icing toughens on standing. Leftover marshmallow may be added to a new batch of icing as it is being mixed.

Conservation of Sugar in Icings: A knowledge of the sugar content of icings, and information on the amount of icing required per cake, proves helpful in using sugar supplies judiciously.

Use the icing which will ice more cakes for each pound of sugar used.

A GUIDE FOR CONSERVING SUGAR IN ICINGS

	CREAM ICING	FUDGE OR FONDANT ICING	MARSHMALLOW ICING
Sugar Content	60% to 70%.......	60% to 65%..............	50% to 80%
Icing required for 1 (8-inch) 2-layer cake.	9 to 10 ounces....	14 to 16 ounces.............	6 to 7 ounces
Icing produced from 100 pounds sugar (average).	150 pounds	160 pounds	190 pounds
Sugar required for icing 100 (8-inch) 2-layer cakes.	40 pounds	60 pounds	20 pounds

WHITE CREAM ICING

Yield: Approx. 12 pounds. Portion: 8 to 9 ounces per 8-inch (2 layer) cake.

INGREDIENTS	100 PORTIONS		MIXING METHOD	..........PORTIONS
	WEIGHTS	AMOUNTS (approx.)		
	Pounds / Ounces			
Shortening	2 /	1 quart	Mix on slow speed about 5 minutes. Whip at medium speed 10 to 15 minutes to desired lightness.	
Salt	.... / 1	2 tablespoons		
Milk, liquid	1 / 4	2½ cups		
Vanilla	.... / 1	2 tablespoons		
Sugar, confectioners'.	8 /	1¾ gallons		

Apply icing at a temperature of 70°F. to 80°F.

Variations

Butter Cream Icing

Use 1 pound (1 pint) butter in place of 1 pound (1 pint) shortening.

Fruit, Nut, Jam, or Marmalade Cream Icing

Add any of the following ingredients:

For	To 10 pounds *White Cream Icing* Add
Nut Icing	1 pound (1 quart) chopped nuts
Raisin Icing	1 pound (1½ pints) ground raisins
Candied Fruit Icing	1 pound (1½ pints) chopped fruits
Jam or Marmalade Icing	1 pound (1 pint) jam or marmalade
Almond Icing	1 pound (1 pint) almond paste and almond flavor
Coconut Icing	1 pound (1¾ quarts) macaroon coconut
Fondant Icing	5 pounds (2½ quarts) fondant
Cocoa Icing	10 ounces (1¼ cups) cocoa, plus 4 ounces (½ cup) water
Peppermint Candy Icing	8 ounces (1½ cups) crushed peppermint candy
Lady Baltimore Filling	1 to 3 pounds (3 to 9 cups) chopped cherries, nuts and raisins
Fresh Fruit Icing	4 ounces (½ cup) ground citrus or other fresh fruit

CHOCOLATE FUDGE ICING

Yield: Approx. 20½ pounds.   Portion: Approx. 15 ounces per 8-inch (2 layer) cake.

INGREDIENTS	100 PORTIONS WEIGHTS Pounds	100 PORTIONS WEIGHTS Ounces	AMOUNTS (approx.)	MIXING METHOD	............PORTIONS
Sugar	3	....	1½ quarts	Combine. Boil to 244° F.	
Butter	1	....	1 pint		
Salt	....	1½	3 tablespoons		
Water	1	...	1 pint		
Cream of tartar	....	¼	2 teaspoons		
Sugar, confectioners'.	10	....	2¼ gallons	Cream together. Add above sirup quickly. Beat smooth.	
Shortening	2	8	1¼ quarts		
Milk, liquid	....	12	1½ cups		
Milk, liquid	....	12	1½ cups	Stir in and beat icing to desired consistency.	
Chocolate, bitter, melted.	1	8	24 squares		
Vanilla	....	2	¼ cup		

Apply icing at a temperature of about 80° F.

CHOCOLATE MALTED MILK CREAM ICING

Yield: Approx. 10 pounds.   Portion: Approx. 10 ounces per 8-inch (2 layer) cake.

INGREDIENTS	100 PORTIONS		MIXING METHOD	..........PORTIONS
	WEIGHTS	AMOUNTS (approx.)		
	Pounds	Ounces			
Shortening	1	4	1¼ pints	Cream together until light.	......
Salt	....	¾	1½ tablespoons		......
Malted milk	....	6	1 cup		......
Chocolate, melted.	1	8	24 squares	Add and stir in.	......
Milk liquid	1	8	1½ pints	Add and stir in.	......
Sugar, confectioners'.	5	....	4½ quarts	Stir in. Mix until smooth.	......

Apply icing at a temperature of 70° F. to 80° F.

MAPLE CREAM ICING

Yield: Approx. 11½ pounds.   Portion: Approx. 12 ounces per 8-inch (2 layer) cake.

INGREDIENTS	100 PORTIONS		MIXING METHOD	..........PORTIONS
	WEIGHTS	AMOUNTS (approx.)		
	Pounds	Ounces			
Sugar, light brown.	3	12	2¾ quarts	Heat to boiling temperature. Cool to temperature of 70° F. to 75° F.	......
Milk, liquid	1	12	3½ cups		......
Salt	....	¾	1½ tablespoons		......
Shortening	1	14	3¾ cups	Whip together. Add gradually above sirup. Continue beating about 5 minutes.	......
Maple flavor	....	¼	½ tablespoon....		......
Fondant	3	12	1½ quarts	Add and whip lightly about 10 minutes.	......

Apply icing at a temperature of 70° F. to 80° F.

FONDANT

INGREDIENTS	100 PORTIONS		MIXING METHOD	............Portions
	WEIGHTS	AMOUNTS (approx.)		
	Pounds	Ounces			

INGREDIENTS	Pounds	Ounces	AMOUNTS (approx.)	MIXING METHOD	............Portions
Sugar	10	....	1¼ gallons	Heat to temperature of 240° F. Wash sides of kettle carefully. Pour into mixing bowl. Cool in cold water bath to 150° F. Grain at high speed on machine.	
Sirup, corn	1	....	1½ cups		
Water	4	....	½ gallon		

NOTE: 1 pound (1 pint) sugar may be used in place of 1 pound corn sirup.

PINEAPPLE FONDANT ICING

Yield: Approx. 13¼ pounds.   Portion: Approx. 15 ounces per 8-inch (2 layer) cake.

INGREDIENTS	Pounds	Ounces	AMOUNTS (approx.)	MIXING METHOD	............Portions
Fondant	9	8	3¾ quarts	Mix slowly at 70°F. to 80°F. until smooth. Cream 2 minutes at medium speed.	
Shortening	2	8	1¼ quarts		
Salt	....	½	1 tablespoon		
Milk, liquid (variable).	....	8	1 cup	Add and mix until smooth. Cream at medium speed 3 minutes.	
Pineapple, crushed, drained.	....	12	1½ cups	Blend into icing. Cream 2 minutes at medium speed.	

Apply icing at a temperature of 70° F. to 80° F.

NOTE: Other fruits, drained, may be used in place of pineapple. Canned or stewed apricots, or strawberries make a delicious icing.

MARSHMALLOW ICING
(Egg white type)

Yield: Approx. 6 pounds.   Portion: Approx. 6 ounces per 8-inch (2 layer) cake.

Ingredients	100 PORTIONS			Mixing Method	Portions
	Weights		Amounts (approx.)		
	Pounds	Ounces			
Sugar	3	4	1⅝ quarts	Boil to 240° F. washing down the sides of the kettle carefully.	
Sirup, corn	....	12	1 cup		
Cream of tartar	....	¼	2 teaspoons		
Water	....	10	1¼ cups		
Egg whites	....	10	1¼ cups	Whip to a dry peak, using medium speed. Add the above sirup slowly and beat until fluffy, about 10 minutes.	
Sugar, confectioners'.	....	12	1¼ pints	Stir in and beat until smooth.	

Apply icing at a temperature of about 90° F.

NOTE.—1. 12 ounces (1½ cups) sugar may be used in place of 12 ounces corn sirup.

2. 1 ounce powdered egg white and 9 ounces (1⅛ cups) water may be used in place of 10 ounces (1¼ cups) egg whites.

MARSHMALLOW ICING
(Gelatin type)

Yield: Approx. 7¾ pounds.   Portion: Approx. 6 ounces per 8-inch (2 layer) cake.

Ingredients	100 PORTIONS			Mixing Method	Portions
	Weights		Amounts (approx.)		
	Pounds	Ounces			
Gelatin, unflavored.	....	1¼	5 tablespoons	Soak gelatin in cold water 10 minutes.	
Water, cold	....	6	¾ cup		
Water, boiling	1	8	¾ quart	Add gelatin mixture.	
Sugar, confectioners'.	5	10	1¼ gallons	Add gradually and beat until fluffy.	
Vanilla	....	2	¼ cup	Stir in.	

Apply icing at a temperature of about 90° F.

Cake Doughnuts

Production Pointers

Dough Handling: Mix doughnut doughs according to dough temperature. Cold doughs require more mixing than warm doughs. A dough temperature of about 75° F. is normal for most cake doughnut mixes.

Allow dough mixed for machine doughnuts to stand 15 to 20 minutes before it is put through the mechanical dropper. This practice permits dough to "open up" somewhat, and helps to prevent formation of objectionable tight center cores.

Allow doughnuts, made by rolling and cutting out dough, to rest on a wire screen 15 to 60 minutes before they are dropped into frying fat. This resting period, helps produce doughnuts with desired expansion, grain and texture.

Frying: To produce quality doughnuts economically, it is necessary to keep the frying fat in the best possible condition.

Deep frying subjects fat to strenuous treatment. Every precaution should be taken to keep frying fat up to standard at all times. The better the condition of frying fat, the better will be the taste and flavor of finished doughnuts. At the same time proper care of frying fat will prolong its frying life and result in more economical frying.

How to Keep Frying Fat in Best Possible Condition

1. Avoid heating frying fat to high temperatures (above 400°F.).
2. Regulate heating of frying fat to eliminate hot spots.
3. Strain out, regularly, burnt food particles which accumulate during frying.
4. Reduce temperature of frying fat to 250° F. during periods when no food is being fried.
5. Fry in the smallest quantity of fat that is practical and thus insure rapid turnover of fresh fat.
6. Clean frying kettles thoroughly after each 24-hour frying period. Rinse thoroughly so that no particle of cleaning product is left which may contaminate the frying pan.

DOUGHNUTS
(Hand cut)

Yield: Approx. 19½ pounds.

Portion: 2 Doughnuts.

Ingredients	100 Portions			Mixing Method	............Portions
	Weights		Amounts (approx.)		
	Pounds	Ounces			
Flour	9	7	2¼ gallons	Blend ingredients together thoroughly.	
Baking powder	....	7	1⅛ cups		
Salt	....	¾	1½ tablespoons		
Nutmeg	....	½	2 tablespoons		
Shortening	....	12	1½ cups		
Sugar	2	12	1⅜ quarts		
Milk, liquid (variable).	4	4	2⅛ quarts	Mix milk, eggs and flavoring together. Add and mix to a smooth dough, about 2 minutes.	
Eggs, whole	2	4	22 (1⅛ quarts)		
Vanilla	....	1½	3 tablespoons		

Make-up: Roll dough to a thickness of approximately ¼ inch. Cut out doughnuts with a 1½-inch to 2-inch floured cutter. Allow to rest for approximately 20 minutes.

Frying: Fry in hot deep fat at 380°F. to 390°F., about 1½ minutes.

NOTE.—1. For *Machine Doughnuts*, make a slightly softer dough by adding approximately 8 ounces (1 cup) more milk.

2. 9 ounces powdered eggs and 1 pound 11 ounces (3¼ cups) water may be used in place of 2 pounds 4 ounces whole eggs.

Variations

Coconut Jelly Doughnuts

Whip jelly until smooth. Spread on top of doughnuts. Sprinkle surface with shredded coconut.

Frosted Doughnuts

Spread tops with Butter Cream Frosting (page 391) in any desired flavor. Chopped nuts or coconut may be sprinkled over frosting.

Frosted Doughnut Pinwheels

Spread Butter Cream Frosting (page 391) around outer rim of doughnut. Roll, as a wheel, in shredded coconut or chopped nuts.

Lemon Doughnuts

Omit nutmeg and vanilla and add 1¼ ounces (5 tablespoons) grated lemon rind or ¾ ounce (1½ tablespoons) lemon extract.

Lemon Doughnut Dessert

Split doughnuts. Put a generous amount of Lemon Filling (page 419) between cut surfaces. Sprinkle with powdered sugar or spread with additional Lemon Filling and sprinkle with shredded coconut.

Orange Doughnuts

Omit nutmeg and vanilla. Add 1¾ ounces (7 tablespoons) grated orange rind or 1 ounce (2 tablespoons) orange extract.

Yeast Raised Doughnuts

See Sweet Yeast Goods Section (page 351).

DOUGHNUT ICING FORMULA
(Suitable for any cake doughnut)

INGREDIENTS	100 PORTIONS		MIXING METHOD	PORTIONS
	WEIGHTS	AMOUNTS (approx.)		
	Pounds / Ounces			
Water	.... / 6	¾ cup	Combine. Heat to boiling temperature.	
Sirup, corn	.... / 2	3 tablespoons		
Gelatin, unflavored.	.... / ⅛	1 teaspoon	Soak gelatin in water. Dissolve in above sirup.	
Water	.... / 2	¼ cup		
Sugar, confectioners'.	3 /	2½ quarts	Stir sirup slowly into the sugar. Beat until smooth. Heat to temperature of 90 F. to 100°F. for use.	

Usage: Dip doughnuts in icing as they come from frying kettle.

NOTE.—2 ounces (1¼ cup) granulated sugar may be used in place of 2 ounces (3 tablespoons) corn sirup.

DOUGHNUT SUGARING FORMULA
(Suitable for any cake doughnut)

| INGREDIENTS | 100 PORTIONS | | MIXING METHOD | ....PORTIONS |
	WEIGHTS	AMOUNTS (approx.)		
	Pounds | *Ounces*			
Sugar, confectioners'.	2 |	1¾ quarts	Cream together 10 to 15 minutes.	....
Shortening	.... | 2	¼ cup		....
Milk, skim, powdered.	.... | 2	½ cup	Add and mix several minutes. Run mix through very fine sieve.	....
Cornstarch	.... | 4	¾ cup		....

Usage: Sugar the doughnuts which have been cooled to room temperature about 70°F.

NOTE.—Amount of shortening in doughnut sugaring mix can be varied. By increasing shortening, a heavier type doughnut sugar is produced.

Pies

Production Pointers

Pie Crust: A good pie consists of a good filling and a good crust.

To make good pie crust, proper mixing and an adequate amount of shortening are necessary.

Causes For Tough Crust:

    Too little shortening
    Too much water
    Shortening and flour are not properly
        blended before water is added
    Pie dough is overmixed after water is added

Pie dough formulas on pages 399 and 400, can be used for making varied types of pie crust by varying mixing procedure.

Three Types Of Pie Crust:

1. Flaky type crust
2. Short mealy type crust
3. Short flaky type crust

Mixing Methods:

1. *Flaky Type Crust:* Mix all the shortening with all the flour to obtain an irregular mixture, so that small lumps of fat remain throughout the mixture.

Add cold water and incorporate. This dough requires more water than other type doughs, because less flour is coated with fat, hence more water is absorbed by flour.

2. *Short Mealy Type Crust:* Mix all the shortening thoroughly with ½ the flour. Add balance of flour and mix in to break up creamed mass. Add cold water. Mix just enough to properly incorporate water.

3. *Short Flaky Type Crust:* Mix ½ the shortening with all the flour until a thorough distribution of fat is obtained.

Add balance of shortening. Mix in lightly so that small lumps remain throughout dough.

Add cold water and mix just enough to properly incorporate.

Handling The Dough: When pie dough is made up into pies, there is a certain amount of dough trimmings left. Utilizing this dough, by making up into additional pies, is not too satisfactory since additional working of the dough may give a tough finished crust.

Dough trimmings are best utilized by blending them into a new batch of pie dough in amounts up to about 25 per cent of the weight of fresh dough. The trimming should be blended with flour and shortening.

Baking: Pies bake best when there is a good solid bottom heat in the oven.

Bake fruit pies, in general, at 425° F. to 450° F.

Bake custard, pumpkin and soft pies at about 400° F.

Bake pie shells for soft cream type pies at about 425° F.

Fillings

Fruit Fillings: Vary the amount of sugar in proportion to the tartness of the fruit in making fruit pies. The formulas in this book have a sugar content adjusted for fruits of average tartness.

A good fruit pie should "run" slightly when cut. Use a minimum amount of flour, cornstarch, tapioca or other thickeners.

Soft Fillings: Eggs, cornstarch, flour or tapioca are the thickening ingredients usually used for soft type pies. Eggs are best but are more expensive than other thickeners.

Economy and quality can be procured by using both cornstarch or another thickening ingredient of this type together with eggs, in soft fillings.

Separation In Baking: Separation during baking, resulting in a finished pie with a "honeycomb" filling, is often encountered in custard pie fillings. This may be due to baking at a too high temperature (above 400° F.) or using insufficient eggs or cornstarch in the filling.

Toppings: Soft pies are usually finished with an egg-white meringue. Occasionally the meringue becomes watery and tends to break down. This gives the pie an unappetizing appearance and disagreeable eating qualities.

To Eliminate Difficulties With Watery Meringue

Use ample amounts of egg whites. Use at least 1 pound of egg whites for each pound of sugar in meringue formula.

Brown the meringue at 400° F. A temperature much higher or much lower than 400° F. will cause the development of a watery meringue after the pie is baked.

Check the amount of stabilizer (cornstarch, tapioca, flour, etc.) in the meringue formula. Up to 4 ounces of stabilizer can be used for each 2 pounds of egg whites.

PIE PASTRY

Yield: 17 (10-inch) 2-crust pies.   Portion: 14 ounces per 2-crust pie.

INGREDIENTS	100 PORTIONS			MIXING METHOD	..........PORTIONS
	WEIGHTS		AMOUNTS (approx.)		
	Pounds	*Ounces*			
Flour	7	8	7½ quarts	Rub ingredients together to a fine crumb the size of a pea.	....
Shortening	4	8	2¼ quarts		....
Sugar	....	6	¾ cup	Dissolve sugar and salt in water. Add to flour and shortening. Mix just enough to form a dough. Roll to a thickness of ⅛ inch. Line pie tins.	....
Salt	....	4	½ cup		....
Water, cold (variable).	3	....	1½ quarts		....

PIE PASTRY

Yield: 17 (10-inch) 2-crust pies.   Portion: 14 ounces per 2-crust pies.

INGREDIENTS	100 PORTIONS		MIXING METHOD	............PORTIONS
	WEIGHTS	AMOUNTS (approx.)		
	Pounds	*Ounces*			
Flour	7	8	7½ quarts	Sift ingredients together.	....
Milk, skim, powdered.	....	4	1 cup		....
Baking powder.	....	2	5 tablespoons ..		....
Shortening	2	12	1⅜ quarts	Rub into flour until thoroughly mixed.	....
Shortening	2	12	1⅜ quarts	Add in small pieces to above mix.	....
Salt	....	4	½ cup	Dissolve salt in milk. Add. Mix lightly so as not to toughen the mix. Roll to a thickness of ⅛ inch. Line pie tins.	....
Milk, liquid (variable).	3	....	1½ quarts		....

PIE PASTRY

(Rolled pie crust)

Yield: 17 (10-inch) 2-crust pies.   Portion: 14 ounces per 2-crust pies.

INGREDIENTS	100 PORTIONS		MIXING METHOD	............PORTIONS
	WEIGHTS	AMOUNTS (approx.)		
	Pounds	*Ounces*			
Flour	7	8	7½ quarts	Mix ingredients together thoroughly.	....
Shortening	1	14	3¾ cups		....
Salt	....	4	½ cup		....
Shortening	3	4	3¼ pints	Mix in, leaving the shortening in small lumps throughout the mixture.	....
Water, cold (variable).	3	....	1½ quarts	Add water. Mix in lightly.	....

Make-up: Roll out dough to a thickness of approximately ¼ inch. Fold ⅓ of dough over ½ the remaining dough.

Fold final ⅓ of dough over on top to make third layer. Roll out to a thickness of ¼ inch.

Fold to give 3 layers again. Roll out to a thickness of approximately ½ inch.

Cut dough into 7 to 8-ounce pieces which, when rolled out thin, will be the approximate size crust for a 10-inch pie.

Place pieces on pans in refrigerator and use as needed.

APPLE PIE

INGREDIENTS	100 PORTIONS			MIXING METHOD	........PORTIONS
	WEIGHTS		AMOUNTS (approx.)		
	Pounds	Ounces			
Sugar	7	8	3¾ quarts	Sift ingredients together.	
Cinnamon	....	1	¼ cup		
Nutmeg	....	¼	1 tablespoon		
Flour or corn-starch.	....	4	1 cup		
Salt	....	¼	½ tablespoon		
Apples	24	....	4 No. 10 cans (3¼ gallons).		
Butter or shortening.	1	....	1 pint	Melt.	
Pie Pastry (page 399).	14	....		Roll to a thickness of ⅛ inch.	

Make-up: Line pie tins with pie dough. Add apples. Sprinkle each pie with 1 cup sugared spice mixture.

Add 2 tablespoons butter. Brush edges with cold water. Add top crust. Perforate.

Press edges firmly together. Brush top with milk.

Baking: Bake at 425°F. to 450°F. for 45 minutes.

NOTE.—1. Vary sugar with the tartness of the fruit to give the desired flavor to the pie.

2. 3¼ gallons of sliced or quartered fresh apples may be used in place of canned apples.

Variation

Apple Turnover:

Make-up: Cut pie pastry into 6 to 6½-inch circle. Place ½ cup sliced apples in center.

Sprinkle with sugared spice mixture and melted butter or shortening.

Fold dough over. Press edges together firmly. Brush with milk. Place on bun pan.

Baking: Bake at 425°F. to 450°F. for 30 to 35 minutes.

APPLE PIE

(Using dried apples)

Yield: 17 (10-inch) pies.   Portion: ⅙ pie.

INGREDIENTS	100 PORTIONS		MIXING METHOD	.... PORTIONS
	WEIGHTS	AMOUNTS (approx.)		
	Pounds	Ounces				

INGREDIENTS	Pounds	Ounces	AMOUNTS (approx.)	MIXING METHOD	.... PORTIONS
Apples, dried	10	..	4⅜ gallons	Combine. Soak 45 to 60 minutes.	....
Water, cool	— 27	...	3⅜ gallons	Heat to boiling temperature. Let simmer 20 minutes.	....
Sugar	6	...	¾ gallon	Stir into apple mixture. Let simmer 10 minutes, stirring occasionally.	....
Cinnamon	...	¾	3⅔ tablespoons		....
Pie Pastry (page 399).	14			Roll to a thickness of ⅛ inch. Line pie tins.	....

Make-up: Use approximately 2 pounds (1 quart) filling per pie. Fill. Brush edge of bottom crust with cold water.

Add top crust. Perforate. Press edges together firmly. Brush top with milk.

Baking: Bake at 425° F. to 450° F. about 45 minutes.

APPLE PIE

(Using dehydrated apple nuggets)

Yield: 17 (10-inch) pies.   Portion: ⅙ pie.

INGREDIENTS	Pounds	Ounces	AMOUNTS (approx.)	MIXING METHOD	.... PORTIONS
Apple nuggets	4	---	1¾ gallons	Combine. Soak 45 to 60 minutes. Heat to boiling temperature. Let simmer 20 minutes.	....
Water, cool	26	---	3¼ gallons		....
Sugar	5	....	2½ quarts	Stir into apple mixture. Let simmer 10 minutes, stirring occasionally.	....
Cinnamon	....	¾	3⅔ tablespoons		....
Pie Pastry (page 399).	14	....	....	Roll to a thickness of ⅛ inch. Line pie tins.	....

Make-up: Use approximately 2 pounds (1 quart) filling per pie. Fill. Brush edge of bottom crust with cold water.

Add top crust. Perforate. Press edges together firmly. Brush top with milk.

Baking: Bake at 425° F. to 450° F. about 45 minutes.

DEEP DISH APPLE PIE

Yield: 2 bun pans.   Portion: 1 piece, 2¼ x 2½ inches.

INGREDIENTS	100 PORTIONS			MIXING METHOD	............PORTIONS
	WEIGHTS		AMOUNTS (approx.)		
	Pounds	*Ounces*			
Sugar	7	8	3¾ quarts	⎫	
Cinnamon	....	1	¼ cup	⎪	
Nutmeg	....	¼	1 tablespoon	⎬ Sift ingredients together.	
Flour or corn-starch.	....	3	¾ cup	⎪	
Salt	....	¼	½ tablespoon	⎭	
Apples	24	....	4 No. 10 cans (3¼ gallons).		
Butter or shortening.	1	....	1 pint	Melt.	
Pie Pastry (page 399).	8	....	....	Roll to a thickness of ⅛ inch. Cut into strips 3 inches wide.	

Make-up: Spread apples evenly in greased baking pans. Sprinkle with sugar-spice mixture. Pour melted shortening over top.

Lay strips of pastry across pan so that the surface is entirely covered. Brush top with milk.

Baking: Bake at 425° F. to 450° F. for 1 hour or until apples are tender.

NOTE.—Vary sugar with the tartness of the fruit to give the desired flavor to finished pie.

DUTCH APPLE PIE

Yield: 17 (10-inch) pies; or 2 bun pans. Portion: ⅙ pie or 1 piece, 2½ x 2½ inches.

| INGREDIENTS | 100 PORTIONS | | MIXING METHOD | ....PORTIONS |
	WEIGHTS	AMOUNTS (approx.)		
	Pounds	*Ounces*			
Eggs, whole	1	10	16 (1½ pints) .	Beat until light...................	
Sugar	6	8	3¼ quarts	} Mix ingredients together thoroughly. Add lightly beaten eggs.	
Flour	3	8	3½ quarts		
Salt	....	¼	½ tablespoon		
Cinnamon	....	¼	1 tablespoon		
Nutmeg	....	⅛	½ tablespoon ...		
Butter or shortening.	1	....	1 pint	Melt. Add to egg mixture.	
Apples	18	....	3 No. 10 cans (2½ gallons).	Chop coarsely. Drain.	
Pie Pastry (page 399).	8	....	....	Roll to a thickness of ⅛ inch.	

Make-up: Line pie tins or bun pans with pie dough. Spread with chopped apples. Cover with sugar-egg mixture.

Baking: Bake at 400° F. for 45 minutes.

NOTE.—1. 2 pounds (1½ quarts) raisins may be added to the mixture.

2. Vary sugar with the tartness of the fruit to give desired flavor to finished pie.

APRICOT PIE

Yield: 17 (10-inch) pies. (Using dried apricots) Portion: ⅙ pie.

| INGREDIENTS | 100 PORTIONS | | MIXING METHOD | ....PORTIONS |
	WEIGHTS	AMOUNTS (approx.)		
	Pounds	*Ounces*			
Apricots, dried....	10	...	2½ gallons	} Combine. Soak 45 to 60 minutes. Heat to boiling temperature. Let simmer 20 minutes.	
Water, cool........	20	...	2½ gallons		
Sugar...............	10	...	1¼ gallons........	} Mix together. Stir into simmering apricots. Cook, stirring occasionally, until mixture thickens slightly. Cool and use.	
Cornstarch........		10	1 pint.............		
Pie Pastry (page 399).	14	...	....	Roll to a thickness of ⅛ inch. Line pie tins.	

Make-up: Use approximately 2 pounds (1 quart) filling per pie. Fill. Brush edge of bottom crust with cold water.

Add top crust. Perforate. Press edges together firmly. Brush top with milk.

Baking: Bake at 425° F. to 450° F. about 45 minutes.

★ 404

BERRY OR CHERRY PIE
(Fresh or canned)

Yield: 17 (10-inch) pies.   Portion: ⅙ pie.

| INGREDIENTS | 100 PORTIONS | | MIXING METHOD | ....PORTIONS |
	WEIGHTS	AMOUNTS (approx.)		
	Pounds / *Ounces*			
Berries or cherries.	25 / 12	4 No. 10 cans of pie cherries or berries (3¼ gallons)	Drain cherries or berries. Reserve juice.	....
Cornstarch	1 / 4	3¾ cups	Mix together cornstarch, water and fruit juice until smooth. Stir in sugar and salt. Cook until mixture is slightly thickened. Stir in fruit. Cool.	....
Water	2 / 8	1¼ quarts		....
Sugar	12 /	1½ gallons		....
Salt	.... / ¼	½ tablespoon		....
Pie Pastry (page 399).	14 /	....	Roll to a thickness of ⅛ inch. Line pie tins.	....

Make-up: Use 2 pounds 4 ounces (1 quart) of filling per pie. Brush edge of bottom crust with cold water.

Add top crust. Perforate. Press edges together firmly. Brush top with milk.

Baking: Bake at 425°F. to 450°F. for 45 minutes.

NOTE.—Vary sugar with the tartness of the fruit to give desired flavor to finished pie.

MOCK CHERRY PIE
(Using dehydrated apple nuggets and dehydrated cranberries)

Yield: 17 (10-inch) pies.   Portion: ⅙ pie.

| INGREDIENTS | 100 PORTIONS | | MIXING METHOD | ....PORTIONS |
	WEIGHTS	AMOUNTS (approx.)		
	Pounds / *Ounces*			
Apple nuggets.	3 /	4½ quarts	Combine, let soak 45 to 60 minutes. Heat to boiling temperature. Let simmer 20 minutes.	....
Cranberries, sliced, dehydrated.	1 / 12	3½ quarts		....
Water, cool	36 /	4½ gallons		....
Sugar	12 /	1½ gallons	Add to fruit mixture. Let simmer 10 minutes.	
Pie Pastry (page 399).	14 /	....	Roll to a thickness of ⅛ inch. Line pie tins.	

Make-up: Use approximately 2 pounds (1 quart) filling per pie. Fill. Brush edge of bottom crust with cold water.

Add top crust. Perforate. Press edges together firmly.

Baking: Bake at 425° F. to 450° F. about 45 minutes.

CRANBERRY AND ORANGE PIE

Yield: 17 (10-inch) pies.

Portion: ⅙ pie.

INGREDIENTS	100 PORTIONS			MIXING METHOD	..........PORTIONS
	WEIGHTS		AMOUNTS (approx.)		
	Pounds	*Ounces*			
Cranberries	19	....	4¾ gallons	Chop cranberries. Add orange juice, grated rind and sugar. Let stand 4 hours.	....
Orange juice ...	6	....	¾ gallon		....
Orange rind, grated.	....	1½	⅜ cup		....
Sugar	6	....	¾ gallon		....
Flour	....	12	1½ pints	Mix. Add to fruit mixture when ready to use.	....
Sugar	6	....	¾ gallon		....
Salt	....	¼	½ tablespoon		....
Butter or shortening, melted.	....	12	¾ pint		....
Pie Pastry (page 399).	14	....	....	Roll to a thickness of ⅛ inch. Line pie tins.	....

Make-up: Use approximately 2 pounds 2 ounces (1 quart) of filling per pie. Brush edge of bottom crust with cold water.

Add top crust. Perforate. Press edges together firmly. Brush top with milk.

Baking: Bake at 425° F. to 450° F. for 45 minutes.

NOTE.—1. 2 pounds (1½ quarts) raisins may be used in place of 1½ quarts cranberries.

2. Frozen or canned cranberries may be used. Canned cranberries should be thoroughly drained before using.

PEACH PIE
(Using dried peaches)

Yield: 17 (10-inch) pies.   Portion: ⅙ pie.

INGREDIENTS	100 PORTIONS			MIXING METHOD	........PORTIONS
	WEIGHTS		AMOUNTS (approx.)		
	Pounds	*Ounces*			
Peaches, dried	10	---	2½ gallons	Combine. Soak 45 to 60 minutes.	
Water, cool	20	---	2½ gallons	Heat to boiling temperature. Let simmer 20 minutes.	
Sugar	10	---	1¼ gallons	Mix together. Stir into simmering peaches. Cook, stirring occasionally, until mixture thickens slightly. Cool and use.	
Cornstarch	---	10	1 pint		
Pie Pastry (page 399).	14	---		Roll to a thickness of ⅛ inch. Line pie tins.	

Make-up: Use approximately 2 pounds (1 quart) filling per pie. Brush edge of bottom crust with cold water.

Add top crust. Perforate. Press edges together firmly. Brush top with milk.

Baking: Bake at 425° F. to 450° F. about 45 minutes.

PEAR PIE
(Using dried pears)

Yield: 17 (10-inch) pies.   Portion: ⅙ pie.

INGREDIENTS	100 PORTIONS			MIXING METHOD	........PORTIONS
	WEIGHTS		AMOUNTS (approx.)		
	Pounds	*Ounces*			
Pears, dried	12	12	3 gallons	Combine. Soak 45 to 60 minutes. Heat to boiling temperature. Let simmer 20 minutes.	
Water, cool	16	---	2 gallons		
Sugar	12	---	1½ gallons	Mix together. Stir into simmering pears. Cook, stirring occasionally, until mixture thickens slightly. Cool and use.	
Cornstarch	---	10	1 pint		
Pie Pastry (page 399).	14	---		Roll to a thickness of ⅛ inch. Line pie tins.	

Make-up: Use approximately 2 pounds (1 quart) filling per pie. Brush edge of bottom crust with cold water.

Add top crust. Perforate. Press edges together firmly. Brush top with milk.

Baking: Bake at 425° F. to 450° F. about 45 minutes.

MINCE PIE

Yield: 17 (10-inch) pies.   Portion: ⅙ pie.

INGREDIENTS	100 PORTIONS		MIXING METHOD	..........PORTIONS
	WEIGHTS	AMOUNTS (approx.)		
	Pounds	Ounces			
Mincemeat	22	8	3 No. 10 cans (2¼ gals.).	Mix ingredients together thoroughly.	....
Apples, chopped	12	....	2 No. 10 cans (1⅝ gals.).		....
Fruit juice or water.	2	8	1¼ quarts		....
Sugar	1	....	1 pint		....
Pie Pastry (page 399).	14	....	....	Roll to a thickness of ⅛ inch. Line pie tins.	....

Make-up: Use approximately 2 pounds (1 quart) filling per pie. Brush edge of bottom crust with cold water.

Add top crust. Perforate. Press edges together firmly. Brush top with milk.

Baking: Bake at 425°F. to 450°F. for 45 minutes.

NOTE.—1. A mixture of fruit juice may be used although pineapple, apricot, apple juice or cider add zest when used alone.

2. Allow filling to set in refrigerator over night, if possible. This procedure will give a better flavored pie.

PEACH OR APRICOT PIE

Yield: 17 (10-inch) pies.   Portion: ⅙ pie.

INGREDIENTS	100 PORTIONS		MIXING METHOD	..........PORTIONS
	WEIGHTS	AMOUNTS (approx.)		
	Pounds	Ounces			
Peaches or apricots.	25	12	4 No. 10 cans (3¼ gals.).	Drain juice from peaches or apricots.	....
Cornstarch	....	12	⅝ quart	Mix together cornstarch, water and fruit juice until smooth. Add sugar and salt. Cook until mixture thickens slightly. Stir in fruit. Cool.	....
Water	1	8	¾ quart		....
Sugar	10	....	1¼ gallons		....
Salt	....	¼	½ tablespoon		....
Pie Pastry (page 399).	14	....	....	Roll to a thickness of ⅛ inch. Line pie tins.	....

Make-up: Use approximately 2 pounds 4 ounces (1 quart) filling per pie. Brush edge of bottom crust with cold water.

Add top crust. Perforate. Press edges together firmly. Brush top with milk.

Baking: Bake at 425° F. to 450° F. for 45 minutes.

NOTE.—Vary sugar with the tartness of the fruit to give desired flavor to finished pie.

PINEAPPLE PIE

Yield: 17 (10-inch) pies.   Portion: ⅙ pie.

INGREDIENTS	100 PORTIONS			MIXING METHOD	..........PORTIONS
	WEIGHTS		AMOUNTS (approx.)		
	Pounds	*Ounces*			
Pineapple, grated or crushed.	26	....	4 No. 10 cans (3¼ gallons).	Drain juice from pineapple.	....
Cornstarch..........	1	2	⅞ quart	Mix together cornstarch, water and fruit juice until smooth. Add sugar and salt. Cook until mixture thickens slightly. Stir in fruit. Cool.	....
Water	2	4	1⅛ quarts		....
Sugar	8	....	1 gallon		
Salt	....	¼	½ tablespoon		
Pie Pastry (page 399).	14	....	....	Roll to a thickness of ⅛ inch. Line pie tins.	....

Make-up: Use approximately 2 pounds (1 quart) filling per pie. Brush edge of bottom crust with cold water.

Add top crust. Perforate. Press edges together firmly. Brush top with milk.

Baking: Bake at 425° F. to 450° F. for 45 minutes.

NOTE.—1. Filling may be put into baked pie shells and covered with Meringue (page 420). Brown at 400° F. for 3 to 5 minutes.

2. Vary sugar with the tartness of the fruit to give desired flavor to finished pie.

PRUNE AND APPLE PIE

Yield: 17 (10-inch) pies.   Portion: ⅙ pie.

| INGREDIENTS | 100 PORTIONS | | MIXING METHOD | ....PORTIONS |
	WEIGHTS	AMOUNTS (approx.)		
	Pounds / *Ounces*			
Prunes	18 /	4 No. 10 cans (3¼ gals.).	Drain prunes and reserve juice. Remove pits.	....
Sugar, brown	2 / 4	1½ quarts.........		....
Apples	13 / 8	2 No. 10 cans (1⅝ gals.).		....
Allspice	.... / ⅛	½ tablespoon		....
Cinnamon	.... / ¼	1 tablespoon		....
Salt	.... / ¼	½ tablespoon	Combine and mix with prunes.	....
Butter or shortening.	.... / 8	1 cup		....
Juice from canned prunes.	3 /	1½ pints		....
Lemon juice	.... / 3	⅜ cup (2 lemons).		....
Lemon rind	.... / ½	⅛ cup		....
Pie Pastry (page 399).	14 /	....	Roll to a thickness of ⅛ inch. Line pie tins.	....

Make-up: Use approximately 2 pounds (1 quart) filling per pie. Brush edge of bottom crust with cold water.

Add top crust. Perforate. Press edges together firmly. Brush top with milk.

Baking: Bake at 425° F. to 450° F. for 45 minutes.

NOTE.—1. Vary sugar with tartness of the fruit to give desired flavor to finished pie.

2. 18 pounds dried prunes, cooked, pitted, may be used in place of 4 No. 10 cans (3¼ gallons) prunes.

PRUNE AND APRICOT PIE

Yield: 17 (10-inch) pies.

Portion: ⅙ pie.

Ingredients	100 Portions		Mixing Method	Portions
	Weights	Amounts (approx.)		
	Pounds	*Ounces*			
Prunes, pitted	14	....	3 No. 10 cans (2½ gals.).	Place prunes in bowl. Beat to pulp. Slice apricots. Blend lightly with prunes. Add sugar. Stir until dissolved.	
Apricots	15	....	3 No. 10 cans (2½ gals.).		
Sugar	6	....	¾ gallon		
Pie shells, baked (page 399).	....	....	17		

Make-up: Use approximately 2 pounds (1 quart) filling per pie. Spread smoothly and cover with Meringue (page 420). Brown at 400°F. from 3 to 5 minutes.

Note.—Vary sugar with the tartness of the fruit to give desired flavor to finished pie.

PRUNE PIE
(Using dried prunes)

Yield: 17 (10-inch) pies.

Portion: ⅙ pie.

Ingredients	100 Portions		Mixing Method	Portions
	Weights	Amounts (approx.)		
	Pounds	*Ounces*			
Prunes, dried	10	---	2½ gallons	Combine. Soak 45 to 60 minutes.	
Water, cool	20	---	2½ gallons	Heat to boiling temperature. Let simmer 20 minutes.	
Sugar	10	---	1¼ gallons	Mix together. Stir into simmering prunes. Cook, stirring occasionally, until mixture thickens slightly. Cool and use.	
Cornstarch	---	10	1 pint		
Pie Pastry (page 399).	14	---		Roll to a thickness of ⅛ inch. Line pie tins.	

Make-up: Use approximately 2 pounds (1 quart) filling per pie. Fill. Brush edge of bottom crust with cold water.

Add top crust. Perforate. Press edges together firmly. Brush top with milk.

Baking: Bake at 425° F. to 450° F. about 45 minutes.

RHUBARB PIE
(Canned)

Yield: 17 (10-inch) pies.   Portion: ⅙ pie.

INGREDIENTS	100 PORTIONS			MIXING METHOD	..........PORTIONS
	WEIGHTS		AMOUNTS (approx.)		
	Pounds	*Ounces*			
Rhubarb	19	8	3 No. 10 cans (2½ gallons) .	Drain juice from canned rhubarb for at least ½ hour. Reserve juice.	....
Rhubarb juice.... and water.	7	8	3¾ quarts	Add water to the rhubarb juice to make 7½ pounds (3¾ quarts) of liquid. Heat liquid to boiling temperature.	....
Sugar	7	....	3½ quarts	Mix remaining ingredients. Add. Cook about 10 minutes, stirring constantly. Remove from heat and stir in rhubarb. Cool.	....
Cornstarch	....	9	1¾ cups		....
Salt	....	¼	½ tablespoon		....
Butter or shortening.	1	....	1 pint		....
Pie Pastry (page 399).	14	....	....	Roll to a thickness of ⅛ inch.	....

Make-up: Use approximately 2 pounds (1 quart) filling per pie. Brush edge of bottom crust with cold water.

Add top crust. Perforate. Press edges together firmly. Brush top with milk.

Baking: Bake at 425° F. to 450° F. for 45 minutes.

NOTE.—Vary sugar with tartness of fruit to give desired flavor to finished pie.

RAISIN AND APPLE PIE

Yield: 17 (10-inch) pies.

Portion: ⅙ pie.

| INGREDIENTS | 100 PORTIONS | | MIXING METHOD | ....PORTIONS |
	WEIGHTS	AMOUNTS (approx.)		
	Pounds | *Ounces*			
Raisins, seedless	8 | 12	1⅝ gallons	Wash raisins. Cook in water until tender, about 15 minutes. Drain. Reserve juice.	....
Water	14 |	1¾ gallons		....
Raisin juice and water.	10 |	1¼ gallons	Add water to raisin juice to make 10 pounds (1¼ gallons) of liquid. Heat to boiling temperature.	....
Sugar	6 |	¾ gallon		....
Cornstarch	.... | 9	1¾ cups		....
Water (to dissolve cornstarch).	.... | 14	1¾ cups	Mix together until smooth. Heat to boiling temperature. Cook about 10 minutes, stirring constantly. Remove from heat.	....
Lemon juice	.... | 4	½ cup (2 lemons).		....
Orange rind, grated.	.... | ¾	3 tablespoons		....
Salt	.... | ¼	½ tablespoon		....
Butter or shortening.	1 |	1 pint		....
Apples, chopped	8 |	2 gallons	Stir in raisins and chopped apples. Cool.	....
Pie Pastry (page 399).	14 |	....	Roll to a thickness of ⅛ inch. Line pie tins.	....

Make-up: Use approximately 2 pounds (1 quart) filling per pie. Brush edge of bottom crust with cold water.

Add top crust. Perforate. Press edges together firmly. Brush top with milk.

Baking: Bake at 425° F. to 450° F. for 45 minutes.

NOTE.—Vary sugar with the tartness of fruit to give desired flavor to finished pie.

RAISIN AND APPLE PIE

(Using dried apples and raisins)

Yield: 17 (10-inch) pies.

| INGREDIENTS | 100 PORTIONS | | MIXING METHOD | ....PORTIONS |
	WEIGHTS	AMOUNTS (approx.)		
	Pounds / *Ounces*			
Apples, dried.....	6 / 12	3 gallons............	Combine. Soak 45 to 60 minutes.	....
Raisins, dried....	3 / 4	1¼ quarts.........	Heat to boiling temperature. Let simmer 20 minutes.	....
Water, cool........	27 / ---	3⅜ gallons........		....
Sugar..............	6 / ---	¾ gallon............	Stir into apple mixture. Let simmer 10 minutes, stirring occasionally.	....
Cinnamon..........	--- / ¾	3⅔ tablespoons...		....
Pie Pastry (page 399).	14 / ---	....	Roll to a thickness of ⅛ inch. Line pie tins.	....

Make-up: Use approximately 2 pounds (1 quart) filling per pie. Fill. Brush edges of bottom crust with cold water.

Add top crust. Perforate. Press edges together firmly. Brush top with milk.

Baking: Bake at 425° F. to 450° F. about 45 minutes.

Yield: 17 (10-inch) pies.

Portion: ⅙ pie.

INGREDIENTS	100 PORTIONS			MIXING METHOD	............PORTIONS
	WEIGHTS		AMOUNTS (approx.)		
	Pounds	*Ounces*			
Milk, liquid	28	....	3½ gallons	Combine ingredients. Heat to boiling temperature.	
Sugar	7	....	3½ quarts		
Salt	....	1½	3 tablespoons		
Cornstarch	2	10	½ gallon	Mix together thoroughly. Stir slowly into boiling mixture. Cook 1 to 2 minutes.	
Milk, liquid	1	12	1¾ pints		
Eggs, whole	6	....	60 (¾ gallon)....		
Butter	1	....	1 pint	Remove filling from heat. Stir in butter and flavor.	
Vanilla	....	2	¼ cup		

Make-up: Pour about 2¼ pounds (1 quart) filling into baked pie shells. Cool and top with Meringue (page 420). Brown in 400° F. oven 2 to 3 minutes.

NOTE.—1½ pounds powdered eggs and 4½ pounds (2¼ quarts) water may be used in place of 6 pounds eggs.

Variations

Banana Cream Pie

Cover bottom of baked pie shell with sliced ripe bananas (about 12 ounces, 2 or 3 bananas, per pie). Add cooled filling.

Top with Meringue (page 420). Brown at 400° F. 2 to 3 minutes.

NOTE.—Slice bananas just before filling pie shells to prevent discoloration.

Black Bottom Cream Pie

Pour a layer of cool Chocolate Cream Filling (page 416) into each baked pie shell. Cover with an equal amount of Cream Filling.

Top with Meringue (page 420). Brown at 400° F. 2 to 3 minutes.

Finely shaved chocolate may be used as topping.

Coconut Cream Pie

Stir in 3 pounds (4½ quarts) shredded coconut. Pour filling into baked pie shell.

Top with Meringue (page 420). Sprinkle with coconut. Brown at 400° F. 2 to 3 minutes.

Peach Cream Pie

Place sliced peaches on bottom of baked pie shell. 1½ No. 10 cans (4¾ quarts) should be sufficient for 17 (10-inch) pies.

Cover with Cream Filling. Top with Meringue (page 420). Brown at 400° F. 2 to 3 minutes.

Strawberry Cream Pie

Cover bottom of baked pie shell with strawberries. Fresh, frozen or canned strawberries may be used. Cover with Cream Filling.

Top with Meringue (page 420). Brown at 400° F. 2 to 3 minutes.

BUTTERSCOTCH PIE

Yield: 17 (10-inch) pies.   Portion: ⅙ pie.

| INGREDIENTS | 100 PORTIONS | | MIXING METHOD | ....PORTIONS |
	WEIGHTS	AMOUNTS (approx.)		
	Pounds / *Ounces*			
Milk, liquid	28 /	3½ gallons	Mix together. Heat to boiling temperature.	....
Sugar, brown	7 /	4⅝ quarts		....
Salt	.... / 1½	3 tablespoons ...		....
Cornstarch	2 / 10	½ gallon	Mix together until smooth. Add slowly to boiling mixture. Cook 1 to 2 minutes.	....
Milk, liquid	1 / 12	1¾ pints		....
Eggs, whole	6 /	60 (¾ gallon)		....
Butter	1 /	1 pint	Remove filling from heat. Add butter and flavor.	....
Vanilla	.... / 2	¼ cup		....

Make-up: Pour about 2¼ pounds (1 quart) of filling into baked pie shells. Cool. Top with Meringue (page 420). Brown in 400° F. oven 2 to 3 minutes.

NOTE.—1½ pounds powdered eggs and 4½ pounds (2¼ quarts) water may be used in place of 6 pounds eggs.

Variation

Banana Butterscotch Pie

Cover bottom of baked pie shells with sliced ripe bananas (about 12 ounces, 2 or 3 bananas per pie). Add cooled filling. Top with meringue. Brown in 400° F. oven for 2 to 3 minutes.

CHOCOLATE CREAM PIE

Yield: 17 (10-inch) pies.   Portion: ⅙ pie.

| INGREDIENTS | 100 PORTIONS | | MIXING METHOD | ....PORTIONS |
	WEIGHTS	AMOUNTS (approx.)		
	Pounds / *Ounces*			
Milk, liquid........	15 / 12	2 gallons	Combine. Heat to boiling temperature.	....
Chocolate	2 / 4	36 squares		....
Sugar	7 / 8	2¾ quarts	Mix to a smooth paste. Stir into above mix. Cook until thick, stirring constantly.	....
Salt	.... / 1½	3 tablespoons ...		....
Flour	2 / 8	2½ quarts		....
Milk, liquid	6 / 12	3⅜ quarts		....
Eggs, whole	4 /	½ gallon		....
Butter	1 /	1 pint	Stir in and cool filling.	....
Vanilla	.... / 1	2 tablespoons ...		....

Make-up: Pour about 2¼ pounds (1 quart) filling into baked pie shells. Cool. Top with Meringue (page 420). Brown in 400° F. oven 2 to 3 minutes.

NOTE.—1 pound powdered eggs and 3 pounds (1½ quarts) water may be used in place of 4 pounds eggs.

PINEAPPLE CHIFFON PIE

Yield: 17 (10-inch) pies.

Portion: ⅙ pie.

INGREDIENTS	100 PORTIONS			MIXING METHOD	........PORTIONS
	WEIGHTS		AMOUNTS (approx.)		
	Pounds	Ounces			
Pineapple juice.	6	....	¾ gallon	Heat pineapple juice to boiling temperature. Mix dry ingredients. Stir into juice. Cook until slightly thickened. Stir in pineapple pulp.	....
Sugar	2	....	1 quart		
Salt	....	1½	3 tablespoons ...		....
Cornstarch	1	....	1½ pints		....
Pineapple, canned, crushed or sliced, drained.	8	....	2 No. 10 cans (6½ quarts).		....
Egg whites	2	....	36 (1 quart)	Beat together to a stiff meringue. Fold into the pineapple mixture.	....
Sugar	1	8	¾ quart		....
Lemon juice	....	4	½ cup (2 lemons)	Stir in.	....

Make-up: Pour 1 to 1½ pounds (1 quart) filling into baked pie shell. Chill and serve plain or top with whipped cream.

NOTE.—3¼ ounces powdered egg whites and 1 pound 12¾ ounces (1¾ pints) water may be used in place of 2 pounds egg whites.

CUSTARD PIE

Yield: 17 (10-inch) pies.   Portion: ⅙ pie.

INGREDIENTS	100 PORTIONS		MIXING METHOD	............PORTIONS
	WEIGHTS	AMOUNTS (approx.)		
	Pounds / *Ounces*			
Sugar	6 /	¾ gallon		
Cornstarch	.... / 1½	¼ cup	Blend ingredients together until smooth.	
Salt	.... / 1	2 tablespoons		
Eggs, whole	7 /	70 (3½ quarts)	Mix in thoroughly.	
Milk, liquid	24 /	3 gallons		
Butter, melted...	.... / 6	¾ cup	Stir into the total mixture. Blend thoroughly.	
Vanilla	.... / 2	¼ cup		
Nutmeg	.... / ¼	1 tablespoon		

Make-up: Pour about 2¼ pounds (1 quart) of filling into unbaked pie shell.

Baking: Bake at 400° F. about 45 minutes.

NOTE:—1 pound 12 ounces powdered eggs and 5 pounds 4 ounces (2⅝ quarts) water may be used in place of 7 pounds eggs.

Variations

Coconut Custard Pie

Place 3 pounds 4 ounces (1¼ gallons) shredded coconut into unbaked shells, using 3 ounces (1¼ cups) to each shell.

Fill with custard mixture. Bake at 400° F. 45 minutes.

Caramel Custard Pie

Replace sugar with 6 pounds (1 gallon) brown sugar.

PECAN PIE

Yield: 17 (10-inch) pies.   Portion: ⅙ pie.

INGREDIENTS	100 PORTIONS		MIXING METHOD	............PORTIONS
	WEIGHTS	AMOUNTS (approx.)		
	Pounds / *Ounces*			
Eggs, whole	9 /	90 (4½ quarts)		
Sugar	13 / 8	6¾ quarts		
Butter	.... / 12	1½ cups		
Salt	.... / 1½	3 tablespoons	Beat eggs slightly. Stir in all ingredients to make a smooth filling.	
Sirup, corn	11 / 4	1 gallon		
Vanilla	.... / 3	6 tablespoons		
Pecans	3 / 12	3¾ quarts		

★418

Make-up: Pour about 2¼ pounds (1 quart) filling into unbaked pie shells.

Baking: Bake at 400° F. for about 45 minutes.

NOTE.—2 pounds 4 ounces powdered eggs and 6 pounds 12 ounces (3⅝ quarts) water may be used in place of 9 pounds whole eggs.

LEMON MERINGUE PIE

Yield: 17 (10-inch) pies.

Portion: ⅙ pie.

INGREDIENTS	100 PORTIONS			MIXING METHOD	............PORTIONS
	WEIGHTS		AMOUNTS (approx.)		
	Pounds	*Ounces*			
Cornstarch	2	....	1½ quarts	Mix cornstarch with enough water to make smooth paste. Add rest of ingredients. Cook about 20 minutes. Remove from heat.	....
Water	15	....	2 gallons		....
Lemon juice	3	12	1⅞ quarts (30 lemons)		....
Lemon rind, grated.	....	6	1½ cups		....
Salt	....	2	¼ cup		....
Sugar	12	....	1½ gallons		....
Egg yolks	1	14	45 (1 quart)	Beat yolks. Slowly add to filling, stirring constantly. Cool.	....
Butter	1	8	1½ pints	Stir in.	....

Make-up: Pour about 2¼ pounds (1 quart) filling into baked pie shells. Cool. Top with Meringue (page 420). Brown in 400° F. oven for 2 to 3 minutes.

NOTE.—1. Equal parts of powdered eggs or egg yolk and water may be used in place of egg yolks.

2. 5 ounces lemon juice powder, synthetic, reconstituted with 3 pounds 12 ounces (1⅞ quarts) water may be used in place of 1⅞ quarts fresh lemon juice.

Variation

Orange Meringue Pie

Use 1½ pounds (1½ pints) lemon juice, 2¼ pounds (1⅛ quarts) orange juice, 2 ounces ground lemon rind and 4 ounces ground orange rind in place of lemon juice and lemon rind specified in formula for Lemon Meringue Pie.

PUMPKIN PIE

Yield: 17 (10-inch) pies.   Portion: ⅙ pie.

INGREDIENTS	100 PORTIONS			MIXING METHOD	..........PORTIONS
	WEIGHTS		AMOUNTS (approx.)		
	Pounds	*Ounces*			
Pumpkin	12	....	2 No. 10 cans (6½ quarts).		
Sugar	6	....	¾ gallon		
Milk, liquid	12	....	1½ gallons		
Flour	....	6	1½ cups	Combine pumpkin with dry ingredients. Stir in eggs and milk. Blend until smooth.	
Cinnamon	....	¾	3 tablespoons		
Nutmeg	....	¾	2½ tablespoons		
Ginger	....	½	2½ tablespoons		
Salt	....	½	1 tablespoon		
Eggs, whole	2	6	24 (2½ pints) ..		

Make-up: Pour about 2¼ pounds (1 quart) filling into unbaked pie shell.

Baking: Bake at 400° F. for about 45 minutes.

NOTE.—9½ ounces powdered eggs and 1 pound 12½ ounces (3½ cups) water may be used in place of 2 pounds 6 ounces eggs.

MERINGUE FOR PIES

Yield: 17 (10-inch) pies.   Portion: 6 ounces per pie.

INGREDIENTS	100 PORTIONS			MIXING METHOD	..........PORTIONS
	WEIGHTS		AMOUNTS (approx.)		
	Pounds	*Ounces*			
Egg whites	3	....	54 (1½ quarts)	Whip to a dry peak.	
Salt	....	¾	1½ tablespoons		
Sugar	3	....	1½ quarts	Add sugar slowly and continue whipping until light. Stir in vanilla.	
Vanilla	....	1	2 tablespoons ...		

NOTE:—5 ounces powdered egg whites and 3 pounds (1½ quarts) water may be used in place of 3 pounds egg whites.

420

Cookies

Production Pointers

Mixing

The character of the finished cookie depends upon proper mixing of the ingredients.

Cookie doughs should be put together by simply adding all ingredients to mixing bowl and mixing until properly blended. This can be accomplished under most conditions in 2 or 3 minutes, using medium speed on mixing machine.

Over-Mixing

Over-mixing produces a tight dough which will not "spread" properly during baking. The cookies tend to become tough, have tight grain and close texture.

Under-mixing produces a coarse dough which may cause cookies to spread excessively during baking. This may result in producing cookies with distorted shapes, too large in diameter, no volume, coarse grain and harsh texture.

Control of Spread

The spread, or lateral expansion of the cookie on the pan, should be carefully controlled in order to produce a finished cookie of excellent shape and texture.

Vary The Amount Of Sugar: The amount of sugar in the dough has an effect on spread. Increased sugar causes greater spread in cookies during baking. By varying the sugar it is possible to adjust the spread.

Vary The Amount Of Moisture: Spread is also influenced by the amount of moisture in the cookie dough. Slack doughs spread more during baking than do stiff doughs. Variations in moisture, therefore, should be used to control the spread of finished cookies.

Soda: Soda also affects spread of the cookie during baking. More soda produces a greater spread. Exact specifications for soda given in the formulas should be followed.

Baking

Proper baking at the correct temperatures for the correct length of time is most important in making good cookies.

If attention is not given to proper baking, a cookie poor in flavor, eating qualities and appearance may result even though a good formula has been used, quality ingredients employed and careful handling of dough followed. Use information in the following paragraphs as a guide in baking cookies.

Bake cookies on pans which are
1. Greased and floured for cookie doughs high in moisture
2. Greased for average rich doughs
3. Ungreased for doughs rich in shortening

Give careful attention to condition of pans before the cookies are dropped on them. This may eliminate sticking.

Cookies may stick when pans
Are not clean
Are dry
Are not conditioned properly. New pans should be lightly greased and baked in a hot oven (450° F.) about 4 hours before using.
Are not thoroughly greased
Are uneven on bottom. Heat from oven will not reach cookies evenly on battered, bent or scratched pans.

Temperatures

Most cookies are baked at temperatures between 375° F. and 400° F.

Cookies should be baked at constant heat. Flash heat should be avoided. Double panning is often essential in ovens where bottom heat is excessive and cannot be easily controlled.

It is a good practice always to under-bake cookies slightly since there is enough heat in cookie pans to complete baking process after removing from oven. Over-baking dries out cookies and impairs the normal good flavor and texture.

BROWNIES

Yield: Approx. 17 pounds.   Portion: 2 cookies.

INGREDIENTS	100 PORTIONS			MIXING METHOD	............Portions
	WEIGHTS		AMOUNTS (approx.)		
	Pounds	Ounces			
Sugar	5	....	2½ quarts		
Shortening	2	....	1 quart		
Butter	....	8	1 cup		
Cocoa	1	....	4½ cups		
Sirup, corn	1	8	2¼ cups	Scale all the ingredients except nuts in the mixing bowl. Mix at medium speed to a smooth dough.	
Salt	....	2	¼ cup		
Flour	3	....	¾ gallon		
Nuts	2	....	½ gallon		
Eggs, whole	1	8	15 (1½ pints).		
Vanilla	....	¼	½ tablespoon		
Water	....	8	1 cup		

Make-up: Spread about 8 pounds of batter in a greased bun pan. Sprinkle with chopped nuts.

Baking: Bake at 375° F. to 400° F. for 15 to 20 minutes.

Finishing: Cool. Cut into bars.

NOTE:—6 ounces powdered eggs and 18 ounces (2¼ cups) water may be used in place of 1 pound 8 ounces eggs.

BUTTER COOKIES

Yield: Approx. 9½ pounds.   Portion: 2 cookies.

INGREDIENTS	100 PORTIONS			MIXING METHOD	............Portions
	WEIGHTS		AMOUNTS (approx.)		
	Pounds	Ounces			
Flour	3	8	3½ quarts		
Salt	....	¾	1½ tablespoons..		
Shortening	2	4	4½ cups	Scale the ingredients into the mixing bowl. Mix at medium speed to a smooth dough.	
Sugar	2	....	1 quart		
Eggs	1	12	18 (1¾ pints) ..		
Vanilla	....	¾	1½ tablespoons.		

Make-up: Drop on greased baking sheet.

Baking: Bake at 375° F. for 8 to 10 minutes. Remove cookies while warm from pan.

NOTE.—1. To make fancy shapes, use star pastry tube for rosettes, star shapes and other varieties.

2. 7 ounces powdered eggs and 1 pound 5 ounces (2½ cups) water may be used in place of 1 pound 12 ounces eggs.

Variations

Chocolate Butter Cookies

Sift 10 ounces (2½ cups) cocoa with flour and salt.

Coconut Butter Cookies

Add 1 pound 8 ounces (2½ quarts) shredded coconut with flour. Flavor with lemon or almond extract. Shape as desired. Bake.

Coconut Chocolate Cookies

Add 1 pound 8 ounces (2½ quarts) shredded coconut to chocolate butter cookie mixture.

Ice Box Cookies

Roll dough into cylindrical shape, 1½ inches in diameter. Wrap in waxed paper and chill. Cut in thin slices. Bake.

Shortbread

Decrease eggs to 4 (6½ ounces). Roll dough into rectangular sheet ⅛ inch thick. Cut into 2-inch squares. Bake on greased baking sheets in moderate oven (350° F.) 10 to 12 minutes.

FRUIT BARS

Yield: Approx. 14½ pounds.   Portion: 2 cookies.

INGREDIENTS	100 PORTIONS		MIXING METHOD	....PORTIONS
	WEIGHTS	AMOUNTS (approx.)		
	Pounds | *Ounces*			
Flour	5 |	1¼ gallons		
Molasses	2 | 8	⅞ quart		
Sugar	2 | 8	1¼ quarts		
Salt	.... | 1¼	2½ tablespoons	Scale the ingredients into the mixing bowl. Mix at medium speed to a smooth dough.	
Cinnamon	.... | 1¼	5 tablespoons		
Ginger	.... | ⅝	2 tablespoons		
Soda	.... | 1¼	2½ tablespoons		
Eggs, whole	1 | 8	15 (1½ pints)		
Raisins	3 | 12	2¾ quarts		
Shortening	1 | 12	3½ cups		

Make-up: Mold 12-ounce pieces of dough into strips approximately 22 inches long, 2 inches wide and ¼ inch thick.

Place 3 strips on 18 x 25-inch bun pan. Wash with Egg Wash (page 357).

Baking: Bake at 375° F. to 400° F. for 15 to 20 minutes.

Finishing: Cool. Cut into bars about 2 inches in width.

NOTE.—1. 2 pounds brown sugar and 8 ounces water may be used in place of 2½ pounds molasses.

2. 6 ounces powdered eggs and 18 ounces (2¼ cups) water may be used in place of 1 pound 8 ounces eggs.

CRUMB COOKIES

Yield: Approx. 15 pounds.   Portion: 2 cookies.

INGREDIENTS	100 PORTIONS		MIXING METHOD	..........PORTIONS
	WEIGHTS	AMOUNTS (approx.)		
	Pounds	Ounces			
Flour	4	....	1 gallon		
Baking powder..	....	1½	¼ cup		
Soda	....	1	2 tablespoons ...		
Salt	....	1	2 tablespoons		
Ginger	....	½	2 tablespoons		
Cinnamon	....	1	¼ cup	Scale the ingredients into the mixing bowl. Mix at medium speed to a smooth dough.	
Cloves	....	¼	1 tablespoon		
Cake crumbs	1	8	¾ quart		
Shortening	1	8	1½ pints		
Eggs, whole	1	....	10 (1 pint)		
Sugar, brown	1	8	4½ cups		
Water	....	12	1½ cups		
Sugar	2	....	1 quart		

Make-up: Drop dough by teaspoonful on greased baking sheet.

Baking: Bake at 375° F. for 8 to 10 minutes. Remove cookies while warm from pan.

NOTE:—4 ounces powdered eggs and 12 ounces (1½ cups) water may be used in place of 1 pound eggs.

FUDGE COOKIES

| INGREDIENTS | 100 PORTIONS | | MIXING METHOD | ....PORTIONS |
	WEIGHTS	AMOUNTS (approx.)		
	Pounds / *Ounces*			
Flour	4 / 8	4¼ quarts		....
Baking powder..	.... / 2	5 tablespoons		....
Salt	.... / 1	2 tablespoons		....
Soda	.... / ¼	½ tablespoon		....
Cocoa	.... / 12	¾ quart	Scale the ingredients into the mixing bowl. Mix at medium speed to a smooth dough.	....
Shortening	2 / 4	4½ cups		....
Sugar	3 /	1½ quarts..........		....
Eggs, whole	.... / 12	8 (¾ pint)		....
Vanilla	.... / 1	2 tablespoons		....
Milk, liquid (variable).	3 /	1½ quarts..........		....

Make-up: Drop on greased baking sheets.

Baking: Bake at 375° F. for 10 to 12 minutes. Remove while warm from pans.

NOTE.—1. Reduce liquid milk to 2 pounds (1 quart) for rolled and cut cookies. Mix as for cookie dough. Roll dough to a thickness of ¼ inch. Cut out cookies. Pan and bake.

2. 3 ounces powdered eggs and 9 ounces (1⅛ cups) water may be used in place of the 12 ounces eggs.

GINGER COOKIES

| Ingredients | 100 Portions | | Mixing Method | ....Portions |
	Weights	Amounts (approx.)		
	Pounds / Ounces			
Sugar	3 /	1½ quarts		
Shortening	1 /	1 pint		
Ginger	.... / 1½	7 tablespoons		
Cinnamon	.... / ½	2 tablespoons	Scale the ingredients into the mixing bowl. Mix at medium speed to a smooth dough.	
Salt	.... / 1¼	2½ tablespoons		
Eggs, whole	.... / 12	8 (¾ pint)		
Soda	.... / 1½	3 tablespoons		
Molasses	2 / 12	1 quart		
Water (variable).	.... / 10	1¼ cups		
Flour	5 /	1¼ gallons		

Make-up: Roll to a thickness of ¼ inch. Cut with 2-inch floured cookie cutter. Place on well greased baking sheets.

Baking: Bake at 375° F. for 10 to 12 minutes. Remove cookies while warm from pan.

NOTE.—1. 3 ounces powdered eggs and 9 ounces (1⅛ cups) water may be used in place of 12 ounces eggs.

2. 2 pounds 4 ounces (1½ quarts) brown sugar and 8 ounces (1 cup) water may be used in place of 2 pounds 12 ounces (1 quart) molasses.

HERMITS
(Raisin and Nut Drop Cookies)

Yield: Approx. 15¾ pounds.   Portion: 2 cookies.

INGREDIENTS	100 PORTIONS		MIXING METHOD	............PORTIONS
	WEIGHTS	AMOUNTS (approx.)		
	Pounds	*Ounces*			
Flour	3	....	¾ gallon		....
Baking powder..	....	2½	6 tablespoons		....
Salt	....	1	2 tablespoons		....
Cinnamon	....	1	¼ cup		....
Shortening	2	....	1 quart	Scale the ingredients into the mixing bowl. Mix at medium speed to a smooth dough.	....
Sugar	2	....	1 quart		....
Eggs, whole	2	....	20 (1 quart)		....
Milk, liquid (variable).	2	....	1 quart		....
Raisins, seedless.	2	8	1¾ quarts		....
Nuts, coarsely chopped.	2	....	½ gallon		....

Make-up: Drop dough on greased baking sheets.

Baking: Bake at 375° F. for 10 to 12 minutes. Remove cookies while warm from pan.

NOTE.—8 ounces powdered eggs and 1 pound 8 ounces (1½ pints) water may be used in place of 2 pound eggs.

OATMEAL COOKIES

Yield: Approx. 14¼ pounds.   Portion: 2 cookies.

INGREDIENTS	100 PORTIONS		MIXING METHOD	............PORTIONS
	WEIGHTS	AMOUNTS (approx.)		
	Pounds	Ounces			
Flour	3	....	¾ gallon		....
Baking powder..	....	1¼	3 tablespoons......		....
Soda	....	½	1 tablespoon		....
Salt	....	1	2 tablespoons......		....
Cinnamon	....	¼	1 tablespoon		....
Nutmeg	....	¼	1 tablespoon	Scale the ingredients into the mixing bowl. Mix at medium speed to a smooth dough.	....
Cloves	....	⅛	1¼ teaspoons.....		....
Oatmeal	2	4	2⅛ quarts		....
Shortening	2	4	4½ cups		....
Sugar	2	12	1⅜ quarts		....
Molasses or sirup, corn.	....	12	1 cup		....
Eggs, whole	1	....	10 (1 pint)		....
Milk, liquid	2	....	1 quart		....

Make-up: Drop dough on greased baking sheets.

Baking: Bake at 375° F. for 10 to 12 minutes. Remove cookies while warm from pan.

NOTE.—1. 10 ounces (1¾ cups) brown sugar and 2 ounces (¼ cup) water may be used in place of 12 ounces molasses or sirup.

2. 4 ounces powdered eggs and 12 ounces (1½ cups) water may be used in place of 1 pound eggs.

SOFT MOLASSES COOKIES

Yield: Approx. 18¼ pounds.

INGREDIENTS	100 PORTIONS			MIXING METHOD	............PORTIONS
	WEIGHTS		AMOUNTS (approx.)		
	Pounds	*Ounces*			
Flour	6	....	1½ gallons		....
Baking powder..	....	½	1 tablespoon		....
Soda	....	¾	1½ tablespoons..		....
Salt	....	¾	1½ tablespoons..		....
Ginger	....	½	2½ tablespoons..	Scale the ingredients into the mixing bowl. Mix at medium speed to a smooth dough.	....
Cinnamon	....	½	2 tablespoons......		....
Shortening	2	4	4½ cups		....
Sugar	2	4	4½ cups		....
Eggs, whole	1	8	15 (1½ pints)		....
Molasses	3	4	2¼ pints		....
Milk, liquid	2	12	2¾ pints		....

Make-up: Drop dough on greased baking sheets.

Baking: Bake at 375° F. for 10 to 12 minutes. Remove cookies while warm from pan.

NOTE.—1. 6 ounces powdered eggs and 1 pound 2 ounces (2¼ cups) water may be used in place of 1 pound 8 ounces eggs.

2. 2½ pounds (6⅔ cups) brown sugar and 12 ounces (1½ cups) water may be used in place of 3 pounds 4 ounces (1¼ quarts) molasses.

SOFT SUGAR COOKIES

Yield: Approx. 18 pounds.   Portion: 2 cookies.

INGREDIENTS	100 PORTIONS		MIXING METHOD	...........PORTIONS
	WEIGHTS	AMOUNTS (approx.)		
	Pounds	Ounces			
Flour	6	....	1½ gallons		
Baking powder	....	2	5 tablespoons ...		
Salt	....	1	2 tablespoons ...		
Nutmeg	....	2	7 tablespoons ...	Scale the ingredients into the mixing bowl. Mix at medium speed to a smooth dough.	
Shortening	3	....	1½ quarts		
Sugar	4	8	2¼ quarts		
Eggs, whole	1	4	12 (1¼ pints) .		
Vanilla	....	1	2 tablespoons ...		
Milk, liquid	2	12	1⅜ quarts		

Make-up: Drop dough on greased baking sheets.

Baking: Bake at 375° F. for 8 to 10 minutes. Remove cookies while warm from pan.

NOTE.—5 ounces powdered eggs and 15 ounces (1⅞ cups) water may be used in place of 1 pound 4 ounces eggs.

RICH SUGAR COOKIES

Yield: Approx. 14¾ pounds.   Portion: 2 cookies.

INGREDIENTS	100 PORTIONS		MIXING METHOD	...........PORTIONS
	WEIGHTS	AMOUNTS (approx.)		
	Pounds	Ounces			
Sugar	4	....	½ gallon		
Shortening	3	....	1½ quarts		
Salt	....	1½	3 tablespoons ...		
Mace	....	¼	1 tablespoon	Scale the ingredients into the mixing bowl. Mix at medium speed to a smooth dough.	
Flour	5	8	5¼ quarts		
Baking powder.	....	3	½ cup		
Eggs, whole	1	....	10 (1 pint)		
Milk, liquid	1	....	1 pint		

Make-up: Roll dough out to thickness of approximately ¼ inch. Cut out cookies. Place on greased baking sheets.

Baking: Bake at 375° F. to 400° F. for about 10 minutes.

NOTE.—1. This cookie dough is excellent for making filled cookies. Place about ½ ounce jam, raisin filling, or other fruit filling in center of cookie after it has been cut out. Fold over dough. Crimp edges. Place on greased baking sheet. Bake at 375° F. for 10 minutes.

2. 4 ounces powdered eggs and 12 ounces (1½ cups) water may be used in place of 1 pound eggs.

CRISP SUGAR COOKIES

Yield: Approx. 14 pounds.

Portion: 2 cookies.

INGREDIENTS	100 PORTIONS			MIXING METHOD	..........PORTIONS
	WEIGHTS		AMOUNTS (approx.)		
	Pounds	*Ounces*			
Flour	6	....	1¼ gallons		
Baking powder	....	2	5 tablespoons ...		
Salt	....	1¼	2½ tablespoons		
Nutmeg	....	¼	1 tablespoon		
Shortening	1	8	1½ pints	Scale the ingredients into the mixing bowl. Mix at medium speed to a smooth dough.	
Sugar	3	8	1¾ quarts		
Eggs, whole	....	12	8 (¾ pint)........		
Vanilla	....	1½	3 tablespoons ...		
Milk, liquid	2	....	1 quart		

Make-up: Roll ¼ inch thick on slightly floured board. Cut with floured cookie cutter.

Place on greased baking sheets. Brush with egg white. Sprinkle with sugar.

Baking: Bake at 375° F. for 8 to 10 minutes. Remove cookies while warm from pan.

NOTE.—3 ounces powdered eggs and 9 ounces (1⅛ cups) water may be used in place of 12 ounces eggs.

Variation

Filled Cookies

Make-up: Roll dough ¼ inch thick. Cut with floured 4-inch cookie cutter or cut into 3½ to 4-inch squares.

Place 1 generous teaspoon jam or marmalade on cookies on one side of center.

Moisten edge. Fold over to make half-circles or triangles. Press edges together. Place on greased baking sheets.

Baking: Bake at 375° F. 10 to 12 minutes. Remove cookies while warm from pan.

Trouble Shooting

In the best regulated mess kitchens and galleys there are times when the finished product may fall short of the standard. Some of the common difficulties, encountered in the preparation of various types of food, are listed together with the possible causes and suggested remedies. The difficulty can be overcome by trying each of the suggested remedies until the cause is discovered.

CAKES

Possible Cause	Remedy
Fall in the Oven	
Too much baking powder	Reduce baking powder
Excessive sugar	Reduce sugar
Excessive liquid	Reduce liquid
Weak flour	Use stronger flour
Insufficient eggs	Increase eggs
Peak During Baking	
Too hot an oven	Reduce heat
Stiff batter	Increase liquid
Tight batter	Decrease mixing
Shrink After Baking	
Over-mixing	Decrease mixing
Excessive liquid	Decrease liquid

Possible Cause	Remedy
Over-greased pans	Use less pan grease
Over-baking	Reduce baking time
Lack Volume	
Over-mixing	Decrease mixing
Low baking temperature	Increase baking temperature
Insufficient baking powder	Increase baking powder
Too little shortening (pound cake)	Increase shortening
Poor Texture	
Insufficient mixing	Increase mixing
Lacks richness	Increase richness (sugar, shortening, milk, and eggs)
Cold ingredients	Warm ingredients to room temperature (75° F.)

ICINGS OR FROSTINGS

Cream Icings Separate	
Too much liquid	Reduce liquid
Fudge and Fondant Type Icings Separate	
Insufficient liquid	Add milk to produce desired consistency

Marshmallow Icings Break Down	
Insufficient egg white	Use more egg white
Insufficient gelatin	Use more gelatin
Insufficient sugar	Increase sugar content
Insufficient beating	Increase beating

PIES

Crust Shrinks After Baking	
Too much water	Decrease water
Over-mixing after water is added	Decrease mixing
Failure to properly mix flour with fat	Mix fat and flour more carefully
Tough Crust	
Too much water	Decrease water
Over-mixing after water is added	Decrease mixing
Failure to cut flour with fat	Mix fat and flour more carefully
Insufficient shortening	Increase shortening
Soggy Crust	
Under-baking	Increase baking time
Insufficient bottom heat	Increase bottom heat
Too sweet a filling	Decrease sugar in filling

Watery Meringue	
Weak egg whites	Use stronger egg whites
Old egg whites	Use fresh egg whites
Insufficient sugar	Increase sugar
Insufficient stabilizer	Increase stabilizer
Brown at too high temperature	Reduce temperature
Placing on hot filling	Cool filling before topping with meringue
Watery Custard Pies	
Insufficient eggs	Increase eggs
Insufficient cornstarch or other thickener	Increase cornstarch or other thickener
Over-baking	Reduce baking time
Baking at too hot temperature	Reduce baking temperature (to 400° F.)

COOKIES

Possible Cause	Remedy

Spread Too Much

Possible Cause	Remedy
Excessive amount of soda	Reduce the soda in the dough
Too much sugar in the mix	Reduce the amount of sugar in the dough
Insufficient mixing of the dough	Increase mixing time after flour is added
Dough too soft	Decrease the moisture in the mix

Dry Out Rapidly

Possible Cause	Remedy
Lack of enrichening ingredients in the formula	Increase sugar, shortening' or milk in the mix
Baking at too low temperature	Bake at higher temperature
Over-baking	Cut baking time
Lack of moisture-retaining materials in the dough	Replace part of the sugar with invert sugar, glucose, or honey

Are Not Tender

Possible Cause	Remedy
Lack of enrichening ingredients in the formula	Increase the amount of sugar and shortening in the mix
Over-mixing of the dough	Cut down on the mixing time after the flour is added

Possible Cause	Remedy
Use of too strong a flour	Cut down on the amount of bread flour in the formula

Ice Box Cookie Doughs Are Difficult to Slice

Possible Cause	Remedy
The doughs are not properly chilled	Increase the chilling time in the refrigerator
Fruit and nuts in the dough too coarse.	Use more finely chopped fruits and nuts in the doughs

Do Not Have the Proper Crack on the Surface

Possible Cause	Remedy
Too much mixing of the dough	Decrease the mixing
Improper proportion of leavening ingredients	Vary amounts of soda and baking powder in the mix
Cool oven	Bake at higher heat

Too Tender

Possible Cause	Remedy
Excess sugar	Reduce the amount
Excess shortening	Reduce the amount
Excess baking powder	Reduce the amount
Insufficient mixing	Increase the mixing time
Use of a weak flour	Use a stronger flour
Too few eggs	Increase egg content

DOUGHNUTS

Are Tough

Possible Cause	Remedy
Over-mixing	Reduce mixing
Insufficient richness in dough	Increase sugar, shortening, milk, and eggs

Absorb Too Much Fat During Frying

Possible Cause	Remedy
Low frying temperature	Increase frying temperature (375° F. to 390° F.)
Too rich a dough	Reduce richness
Excessive baking powder	Reduce baking powder
Excessive liquid	Reduce liquid
Break-down of frying fat	Keep fat in good condition
Stiff dough	Increase liquid

Retain Flavor of Frying Fat

Possible Cause	Remedy
Break-down of frying fat	Take proper care of frying fat

Crack During Frying

Possible Cause	Remedy
Stiff dough	Increase liquid
Too much baking powder	Decrease baking powder

Sweat When Sugared

Possible Cause	Remedy
Sugar applied before doughnuts are cooled	Cool doughnuts before they are sugared
Using improperly prepared doughnut sugar	Follow formula (page 398)

BREAD

Poor Flavor

Possible Cause	Remedy
"Old" dough	Reduce fermentation
Lack of richness	Increase sugar, milk, and shortening
Unclean pans	Clean pans
Warm doughs	Reduce dough temperature

Poor Volume

Possible Cause	Remedy
"Old" dough	Reduce fermentation
"Young" dough	Increase fermentation
Under-proofing	Increase proofing time
Insufficient mixing	Increase mixing time

Thick Crust

Possible Cause	Remedy
"Old" dough	Reduce fermentation
Over-baking	Reduce baking time

Possible Cause	Remedy
Crusting in proof box	Use steam in proof box or cover doughs

Coarse Grain

Possible Cause	Remedy
"Old" dough	Reduce fermentation
Slack dough	Decrease moisture
Over-proofing	Reduce proofing time
Insufficient mixing	Increase mixing time
Low baking temperature	Increase baking temperature

Holes in Bread

Possible Cause	Remedy
Insufficient richness	Increase sugar, milk, and shortening
Insufficient salt	Increase salt
Stiff doughs	Increase moisture
"Old" doughs	Reduce fermentation
Flashy oven	Eliminate flash heat

Index

INDEX (Continued)

INDEX (Continued)

Made in the USA
Monee, IL
06 June 2021